A WHO'S WHO OF YOUR ANCESTRAL SAINTS

A WHO'S WHO OF YOUR ANCESTRAL SAINTS

BY

ALAN J. KOMAN

GENEALOGICAL PUBLISHING COMPANY
BALTIMORE

Published by Genealogical Publishing Company
3600 Clipper Mill Rd., Suite 260
Baltimore, Maryland 21211-1953

Library of Congress Catalogue Card Number 2009939972
ISBN 978-0-8063-1824-0
Made in the United States of America

To Lana and Tim
sine qua non
and
To Marjorie Ruth Morgan,
who was very surprised by the people
that were waiting for her
in Paradise

For we are the children of saints, and look for that life which God will give to those that never change their faith from Him.

Tobias 2:18

O death, where is thy victory? O death, where is thy sting?

1 Cor. 15:55

Contents

Introduction

Standing before the throne of God are a large number of very unusual men and women. While they were on earth, some of them were patriarchs, prophets, and other figures from the Old Testament. Others lived during or after the time of Christ and were put to death for refusing to renounce their faith in Him. The rest led lives of such extraordinary fidelity to the Risen Christ that they became examples of "heroic virtue" and were rewarded with eternal life. They all stand so close to God that petitions for help which they receive from the faithful on earth are presented by them to God Himself.[1]

These men and women have been called many things by many people. The Catholic Church and some of the other Christian religions call them saints.[2] A very large number of people who are alive today can also call many of them father, mother, aunt, and uncle. Only the several generations between their time and ours separate them from the latest generation of their descendants.

Consider the ways in which the religions that acknowledge the existence and power of the saints have honored them.

- They are offered to the faithful as models, protectors, and intercessors.
- Their relics are put in precious vessels and publicly honored.
- Churches are dedicated to them.
- Images showing them surrounded by a glorious light are produced by artists and craftsmen, often in vast quantities.
- On their feast days, masses are celebrated in their honor. In the rites of all the masses that are ever said, there is a moment where everyone who is present asks for their help.
- Many parents name their children after them.
- Every day, more people than could ever be counted privately pray to them for strength and assistance, sometimes even for miracles.

In the midst of so much spiritual activity, the faithful are normally quite unaware that it is their own relatives that they are honoring or petitioning.

In order to start thinking about the saints as relatives, there are a couple of subjects that the living descendants of long-ago saints must become more familiar with. The story of how men and women who really lived have been recognized as saints from the earliest days of Christianity is one of them. Besides the Virgin Mary, John the Baptist, and the Apostles, the first men and women whom the Church honored with the title of "Sanctus" (the Latin word for "Holy") were the martyrs who died during the Roman

---

Full citations of the authorities referred to in these footnotes can be found in the "List of Abbreviated Sources" located at the back of this volume.

[1] Catechism, p. 645; Cunningham, p. 26; Woodward, p. 378.

[2] Catechism, p. 21.

persecutions.[3] Early Christians would gather at their graves and pray for their protection and help. Written versions of these prayers can still be found on the walls of Roman catacombs today. From the earliest days, a relic of a martyr was placed somewhere inside each new Christian altar while it was being built. In the Catholic Church, the custom of embedding a saint's relics under the spot on an altar where the priest consecrates the bread and wine survives down to the present day.[4]

After the persecutions finally ended, the persons recognized as holy by the Christians began to include people whose lives had not ended in martyrdom. Collectively, these new saints were called "confessors." A confessor in this sense was anyone whose life on earth rose to the level of the heroic in the opinion of the faithful who had known him (or her).[5] The more perfectly someone's response to the hardships confronting him exemplified the Christian virtues, the more convinced his survivors would be that their departed friend had entered eternal life and could be found there right next to God. What all the confessors had in common was that they possessed such "heroic virtue" that the faithful prayed to them spontaneously, not because anyone in the Church told them to but because they wanted to. Then and now, prayers for help were the most common kind of prayer.[6]

After the Roman Empire faded away in the West and Europe entered the Dark Ages, most of the Church's new saints were created by this form of popular recognition.[7] Outside of the areas where they had actually lived, these new saints might be and often were completely unknown. Lists of the names of the members of the kingdom of Heaven were therefore very different in the different parts of Europe.

The first form of oversight over this spontaneous process grew out of the frequent desire of the faithful, once they had recognized the holiness of one of their departed, to move their saint's earthly remains to a more splendid grave. This reburial of a saint in a more fitting place—often inside a church and perhaps next to or even under the altar, followed by a solemn mass—was called "translation and elevation."[8] Gradually, bishops began to require that written, convincing accounts of a decedent's life and holiness be presented to them before anyone's remains could be translated within their diocese.[9] Later, such petitions were required before any of the other honors customarily bestowed upon saints could be given to any departed member of their diocese.[10]

This method of recognizing saints—where proponents of a cause would rise up among the faithful and ask their bishop to acknowledge the holiness of someone on behalf of the Church—was followed everywhere in Europe for the rest of the first millennium and beyond.[11] On questions of recognition, no bishop was superior to any other. No complex systems of general or local rules for recognition have come down to us, because there were none.[12] In faraway Rome, neither the pope nor his cardinals or other servants ever became involved in any way.[13]

---

[3] Kemp, p. 7; Vauchez, p. 13; Woodward, p. 52.
[4] Kemp, p. 6; Woodward, p. 59.
[5] Vauchez, p. 15.
[6] Cunningham, pp. 22, 23, and 26; Vauchez, p. 13.
[7] Parish, p. 6; Weinstein and Bell, p. 142.
[8] Goodich, p. 21; Parish, p. 7.
[9] Goodich, p. 21; Woodward, p. 65.
[10] Cunningham, p. 37; Vauchez, p. 91.
[11] Cunningham, pp. 37 and 44; Kemp, p. 73.
[12] Cunningham, p. 36; Vauchez, p. 99.
[13] Langmuir, p. 29; Vauchez, pp. 27 and 88–89.

In reading the lives of the holy men and women who were recognized during this era, it would be a great mistake to conclude, because some of these persons are called "Saint" today and others are called "Blessed," that Christianity of the first millennium had a multilevel idea of sanctity and that some of the heroes of its faith had been found to be holier than others. In fact, the terms "Saint" and "Blessed" were used interchangeably.[14] The idea that there was or could be any form of limited vs. universal or first- vs. second-class sanctity was definitely not part of the Christianity of this era. All the "Saints" and the "Blesseds" were equal. They were all "Sanctus."[15]

The involvement of the papacy in the recognition of saints began around the end of the first millennium and was at first just an additional way that a saint could be recognized.[16] When it began, no one saw it as replacing the process of local recognition by bishops that had been followed throughout Europe for centuries. Ultimately of course the recognition of new saints became a decision for the pope alone. Bishops no longer officially recognized the holiness of any new member of the kingdom of Heaven unless Rome had done so first. This papal monopoly was itself not universally recognized in the Western Church until the Middle Ages were almost over.[17] Even then, no one thought that the earlier saints who had been recognized only by the bishops or the people had lost any of their status or required "re-canonization" by the pope.[18]

Only God knows how many saints there are. All the Catholic Church has ever claimed is the ability to recognize whether someone is a saint. Even then, one would search in vain for one big book or a series of books containing the names of all the saints that have ever been recognized by the Church.

In the modern world, all candidates for beatification and canonization are examined—often for a very long time—by the office in the Vatican known as the "Congregation for the Causes of Saints." To mark its 400th anniversary in 1988, it published the first edition of what has become an occasional volume called the *Index ac Status Causarum*. This book is entirely in Latin and is considered the definitive index of all the causes of saints presented to the Congregation since its creation. In the 1988 edition, one reads that in the Congregation's first 400 years and prior to the papacy of John Paul II, 285 saints were proclaimed, 565 persons were beatified, 1,385 persons were recognized as "Venerable," and 3,464 causes were still pending. John Paul II himself proclaimed 482 new saints, beatified 1,338 new blesseds, and radically reformed the standard operating procedures of the Congregation.[19]

All the totals of papal activity since 1588 should be compared with the numbers in reference works which attempt to catalog all the saints and beati from the earliest days of Christianity. One such work is the multivolume *Bibliotheca Sanctorum* published in the middle of the 20th century. It contains more than 10,000 names and does not claim to be complete.[20]

Of all the historic figures of the European Middle Ages, the following men and women have people in their family trees whom Christianity has recognized as holy.

---

[14] Goodich, p. 21; Vauchez, pp. 85 and 87; Woodward, p. 68.
[15] Vauchez, p. 95; Weinstein and Bell, p. 14.
[16] Goodich, p. 22; Kemp, p. 57; Langmuir, p. 27; Vauchez, p. 24.
[17] Goodich, pp. 22 and 26; Vauchez, pp. 30, 32, 91, and 94; Woodward, pp. 64–65.
[18] Cunningham, pp. 38 and 54; Holweck, p. v.
[19] "John Paul II: Beatification and Canonization Ceremonies," p. 5; "Making Saints," p. 2.
[20] Woodward, p. 51.

- Aethelred II "the Redeless," King of England
- St. Alfred the Great, King of Wessex and England
- St. Edgar "the Peaceful," King of England
- Edmund "Ironside," King of England
- Edmund I "the Magnificent," King of England
- Edward "the Elder," King of England
- Edward I, King of England
- Eleanor of Aquitaine, who married (1) Louis VII, King of France and married (2) Henry II, King of England
- Eleanor of Castile, who was the first wife of Edward I, King of England
- Bl. Eleanor of Provence, who married Henry III, King of England
- Henry II, King of England
- Isabel of Mar, who was the first wife of Robert I the Bruce, King of Scotland
- Isabella of France, who married Edward II, King of England
- John Stewart of Balveny, First Earl of Atholl
- Mathilda (also known as Eadgyth) of Scotland, who married Henry I, King of England
- Mathilde of Flanders, who married William I the Conqueror, King of England
- Matilda of Huntingdon, who married (1) Simon de St. Liz, Earl of Huntingdon and Northampton, and married (2) David I, King of Scotland
- Philippa of Hainault, who married Edward III, King of England
- Robert I the Bruce, King of Scotland
- Robert III Stewart, King of Scotland
- Saher de Quincy, First Earl of Winchester, Magna Charta Surety, and Crusader
- Stephen of Blois, King of England
- William de Plumpton, Knight and High Sheriff of Yorkshire, and
- William I the Conqueror, King of England

Genealogically, most of these men and women have both direct ancestors and aunts and uncles that have been recognized as holy. Close examination of modern scholarship yields 275 saints who are definitely in their ancestry.

There is something else which is notable about these twenty-four men and women from the Middle Ages. They have an unimaginably vast number of direct descendants among men and women who are alive today.[21] These descendants live in Europe and in all other parts of the world that were once European colonies. Many of their living descendants are Americans. To be sure, the chains of descent from ancient saints are longer today than they were for people in the Middle Ages. Yet the fact that living Americans are related to these holy men and women in the same way as Eleanor of Provence, Philippa of Hainault, or any of the others were is indisputable.

What is the purpose of this book? It is not an all-in-one genealogical bridge from the present day back to our ancestral saints. Such a journey must begin in other books. The first scholarly volume that attempted to genealogically connect large numbers of Amer-

[21] Olson, pp. 62–64; Roberts, p. 18; Salter, pp. 338–341; Stratton, pp. 15–17 and 19–20; Stuart, p. vii, Weis *AR* (1st ed.), p. 7.

icans to their ancestry in England at the time of Elizabeth I was *The Prescott Memorial* written by William Prescott and published in Boston in 1870. A large number of similar books about other early settlers of North America have been published since then, and any individual research must begin there.

My book contains brief biographies of these 275 saints in the ancestry of the twenty-four people named above and outlines the lineage that connects them to their two dozen progeny. The genealogical charts for each saint have been written in a way that makes them easy to read. In each generation, the person whose name is in boldface is the child of the man and woman in the preceding generation. The parents of the saint whose life has just been presented are always in the very first generation, and both of their names are in boldface.

My book basically doubles the reward that awaits the millions of people today who could link themselves to medieval Europe and to any of these 24 men and women specifically. To their ancestors among the princes of the earth, genealogical researchers can now add some ancestors among the princes of heaven.

Over time, our knowledge of medieval family relationships will slowly grow, and so will our known number of ancestral saints. The ultimate total of course is only known in the kingdom of Heaven and is unimaginably large. If this book helps anyone to prepare at any level for the moment when all will be revealed, it will have achieved its purpose.

Atlanta, Georgia
Anno Domini 2009

ALAN J. KOMAN

PART I

Twenty-Four Medieval Europeans and Their Two Hundred and Seventy-Five Ancestral Saints

1. Aethelred II "the Redeless," King of England

(b. ca. 968 – d. 23 April 1016)

Direct Ancestors (2)

St. Edgar "the Peaceful," King of England
(b. 943 – d. 8 July 975)

St. Elgiva, first wife of Edmund I
"the Magnificent," King of England

Aunts and Uncles (1)

St. Edith of Wilton
(b. 962 – d. 16 Sept 984)

2. St. Alfred "the Great," King of Wessex

(b. 849 – d. 26 Oct 899)

Direct Ancestors (6)

St. Aethelbert I, King of Kent
(b. ca. 552 – d. 24 Feb 616)

St. Bertha
(b. ca. 560 – d. ca. 602)

St. Ceolwald, a war leader in Wessex
(b. ca. 622 – d. 20 April 689)

St. Emma, daughter of King Clothaire II of Neustria
(who was b. 584 and d. 629)

St. Hereswitha
(b. shortly bef. 616 – d. 680/690)

St. Sexburga
(md. ca. 640 – d. 6 July 699)

Aunts and Uncles (17)

St. Alburga
(d. ca. 810)

St. Cuthburga
(d. 725)

St. Eanswitha
(d. ca. 640)

St. Edith of Polesworth
(d. 15 March 871)

St. Ercongota
(d. 660)

St. Erconwald, Bishop of London
(b. ca. 630 – d. ca. 690)

St. Ermenburga
(d. ca. 590)

St. Ermengytha
(d. ca. 580)

St. Ermenilda
(d. 703)
St. Ethelburga, Queen of Northumbria
(d. ca. 647)
St. Ethelburga, Princess of the East Angles
(d. ca. 664)
St. Etheldreda
(b. ca. 636 – d. 23 June 679)
St. Hilda of Whitby
(b. 614 – d. 17 Nov 680)
St. Ina, King of Wessex
(b. 660/664 – d. 728)
St. Quenburga
(d. ca. 735)
St. Sethryda
(d. ca. 660)
St. Withburga, Abbess of Dereham and
daughter of King Anna of East Anglia
(who ruled ca. 641–653)

3. St. Edgar "the Peaceful," King of England

(b. 943 – d. 8 July 975)

Aunts and Uncles (1)

St. Edburga of Winchester
(b. ca. 920 – d. 15 June 960)

4. Edmund "Ironside," King of England

(b. ca. 989 – d. 30 Nov 1016)

Aunts and Uncles (1)

St. Edward the Martyr, King of England
(b. 962 – d. 18 March 978)

5. Edmund I "the Magnificent," King of England

(b. ca. 920 – d. 26 May 946)

Aunts and Uncles (1)

St. Ethelgiva
(d. 896)

6. Edward "the Elder," King of England

(b. ca. 869 – d. 924)

Direct Ancestors (2)

St. Alfred the Great, King of Wessex
(b. ca. 849 – d. 26 Oct 899)

Saints of Edward "the Elder"

St. Ealhswith of Mercia
(b. ca. 852 – d. 903/905)

Aunts and Uncles (1)

St. Wistan
(d. 1 June 849)

7. Edward I, King of England

(b. 17 June 1239 – d. 8 July 1307)

Direct Ancestors (1)

Bl. Eleanor of Provence
(b. 1222 – d. 24 June 1291)

8. Eleanor of Aquitaine

(b. 1122 – d. 31 March 1204), who married (1) 25 July 1137 Louis VII, King of France, and (2) 18 May 1152 Henry II, King of England

Direct Ancestors (3)

St. Liévin, Bishop of Trier
(b. 660/665 – d. 722/724)

St. William of Gellone
(b. 755 – d. 28 May 812)

St. William X, Duke of Aquitaine
(b. 1099 – d. 9 April 1137)

9. Eleanor of Castile

(b. 1240 – d. 28 Nov 1290), the first wife of Edward I, King of England

Saints of Eleanor of Castile

Direct Ancestors (2)

St. Fernando III, King of Castile and Leon
(b. 24 June 1198 – d. 30 May 1252)

Bl. Ida of Boulogne
(b. ca. 1040 – d. 13 April 1113)

Aunts and Uncles (4)

Bl. Berengaria
(b. 1228 – d. 1288)

St. Hugh the Great, Abbot of Cluny
(b. 1024 – d. 29 April 1109)

Bl. Sancia
(b. ca. 1180 – d. 13 March 1229)

St. Trigidia, daughter of Count Sancho Garcia of Castile
(who was b. ca. 965 and d. 5 Feb 1017)

Saints of
Bl. Eleanor
of Provence

10. Bl. Eleanor of Provence
(b. ca. 1223 – d. 25 June 1291),
who married Henry III, King of England

Direct Ancestors (27)

St. Adelaide of Burgundy
(b. 931 – d. 16 Dec 999)

Bl. Adelaide of Susa
(b. ca. 1015 – d. 19 Dec 1091)

Bl. Agnes of Franconia
(b. ca. 1073 – d. 24 Sept 1143)

Bl. Agnes of Poitou
(b. 1024 – d. 14 Dec 1077)

St. Ashken
(md. 298/299)

St. Gregory "the Illuminator"
(b. 256 – d. 326)

St. Hmayeak Mamikonian
(b. 410 – d. 2 June 451)

Bl. Humbert III, Count of Savoy
(b. 14 Aug 1135 – d. 4 March 1188)

St. Ilduara Eriz
(d. 958)

St. Isaac I "the Great"
(b. ca. 350 – d. Sept 439/440)

St. Izyaslav I Yaroslavich, Grand Prince of Kiev
(b. 1024/1025 – d. 3 Oct 1078)

St. Leopold III, Margrave of Austria
(b. ca. 1075 – d. 15 Nov 1136)

St. Ludmilla, Duchess of Bohemia
(b. ca. 860 – d. 15 Sept 921)

St. Matilda of Ringelheim
(b. ca. 892 – d. 14 March 968)

Bl. Mathilde of Saxony
(b. 981 – d. 1025)

St. Nerses I "the Great"
(b. 333/337 – d. 369)

St. Olga, Princess of Izborsk
(md. 930/935 – d. 11 July 969)

St. Peter Orseolo I, Doge of Venice
(b. 928 – d. 10 Jan 987)

Raymond Berenger IV "the Saint," Count of Barcelona
(b. ca. 1113 – d. 6 Aug 1162)

St. Richenza of Pfalz-Lorraine
(b. ca. 1000 – d. 21 March 1063)

St. Theophano Skleros
(b. 956 – d. 15 Sept 991)

St. Tiridates "the Great," King of Armenia
(b. ca. 280 – d. 330)

St. Vardanes, Bishop of Armenia
(d. 342)

St. Vladimir I Sviatoslavich, Grand Prince of Kiev
(b. ca. 955 – d. 15 July 1015)

Bl. Widukind, Duke of Saxony
(d. ca. 804)

St. Yaroslav I Vladimirovich "the Wise," Grand Prince of Kiev
(b. 978 – d. 20 Feb 1054)

St. Yusik, Bishop of Armenia
(b. ca. 305 – d. ca. 348)

Aunts and Uncles (29)

St. Aristakes, Bishop of Armenia
(d. 333)

Bl. Ayrald
(d. ca. 1146)

St. Balderic, son of King Sigebert I of Austrasia
(who d. 575)

Bl. Boniface of Savoy, Archbishop of Canterbury
(b. ca. 1207 – d. 14 July 1270)

St. Boris the Passion-Bearer, Prince of Kiev
(b. 990/994 – d. 24 July 1014)

St. Bova, daughter of King Sigebert I of Austrasia
(who d. 575)

St. Bruno the Great, Archbishop of Cologne
(b. 925 – d. 11 Oct 965)

St. Florentia
(b. ca. 554 – d. 633)

St. Fulgentius, Bishop of Ecija
(b. late 500's – d. ca. 633)

St. Galswitha
(d. ca. 568)

St. Gleb the Passion-Bearer, Prince of Kiev
(b. 995/1000 – d. 5 Sept 1015)

St. Grigoris
(b. early 300's – d. 348)

Bl. Henry Zdik, Bishop of Olmuetz
(d. 25 June 1151)

St. Hermenegild
(b. early 560's – d. 13 April 585)

Saints of Bl. Eleanor of Provence

St. Isidore of Seville,
Doctor of the Church
(b. ca. 560 – d. 4 April 636)

St. Khosrowidukht
(d. ca. 340)

St. Leander, Archbishop of Seville
(b. ca. 535 – d. 13 March 600/601)

Bl. Mary, Princess of Bohemia
(d. 994)

Bl. Mathilde of Quedlinburg
(b. 955 – d. 7 Feb 999)

St. Octavian
(b. ca. 1060 – d. 6 Aug 1128)

St. Podius
(b. 930 – d. 1002)

St. Richardis
(b. 840 – d. ca. 895)

St. Rosendo
(b. 26 Nov 907 – d. 1 March 977)

St. Stephen I, King of Hungary
(b. 969 – d. 15 Aug 1038)

St. Sviatoslav II Yaroslavich, Grand Prince of Kiev
(b. 1027 – d. 27 Dec 1076)

St. Theobald, Archbishop of Vienne
(b. ca. 927 – d. 21 May 1001)

St. Vardan II, Prince of the Mamikonids
(d. 2 June 451)

St. Wenceslaus I, Duke of Bohemia
(b. ca. 903 – d. 28 Sept 929)

St. Yaropolk Izyaslavich,
Prince of Turov and Vladimir-in-Volynia
(d. 22 Nov 1087)

11. Henry II, King of England
(b. 5 March 1133 – d. 6 July 1189)

Direct Ancestors (11)

St. Adela, Princess of Austrasia
(d. 734/735)

St. Clodulf, Bishop of Metz
(b. 605 – d. 8 June 696)

St. Clothilde
(b. 470/475 – d. 3 June 545)

St. Dagobert II, King of Austrasia
(b. 652 – murdered 23 Dec 678)

Bl. Emma of Bavaria
(b. ca. 808 – d. 31 Jan 876)
Bl. Ermengarde of Orleans
(b. ca. 800 – d. 20 March 851)
St. Gertrude of Hamage
St. Guerin
(d. 677)
St. Ida of Herzfeld
(d. aft. 21 Nov 838)
St. Sigebert III, King of Austrasia
(b. 630 – d. 1 Feb 656)
St. Sigrada
(d. ca. 678)

Aunts and Uncles (11)

St. Edmund, King of the Scottish Lowlands
(b. ca. 1071 – d. aft. 1097)
Bl. Ermengard, Abbess of Buchan and Chiemsee
(b. 832 – d. 16 July 866)
Bl. Ermengarde of Anjou
(b. aft. 1068 – d. 1147)
St. Guntram I, King of Burgundy
(b. ca. 525 – d. 592)
Bl. Hathumoda
(b. ca. 839 – d. 28 Nov 874)
St. Irmina (d. 708), daughter of
St. Dagobert II, King of Austrasia
St. Leodegar of Autun
(b. ca. 616 – d. 2 Oct 678)
St. Theodehilda, daughter of King Clovis "the Great" of the Salic Franks
(who was b. 466 and d. 511)
St. Verona, daughter of King Louis II
of the East Franks
(who was b. 806 and d. 28 Aug 876)
Bl. Warin, Abbot of Corvie
(b. 20/21 Sept 856)
St. Zwentibold, King of Lorraine
(b. 870 – d. 13 Aug 900)

12. Isabel of Mar (md. ca. 1295 – d. bef. 1302),

the first wife of Robert I the Bruce,
King of Scotland

Direct Ancestors (9)

St. Arddun "Benasgell," daughter of St. Pabo "Post Prydyn"
(who was b. ca. 430 and d. ca. 510)

St. Brochwel "Ysgithrog," King of Powys
(b. ca. 502 – d. ca. 560)

St. Cadwalader, King of Gwynedd
(b. ca. 633 – d. ca. 682)

St. Ceneu
(b. ca. 400 – d. ca. 450)

St. Coel Hen, ruler of Northern Britain
(b. ca. 370 – d. ca. 420/430)

Saints of Isabel of Mar

St. Edith of Polesworth, daughter of
King Edward "the Elder" of England
(who was b. 875 and d. 924)

St. Meurig ap Tewdrig, King of Gwent and Glywysing
(b. mid 500's)

St. Pabo "Post Prydyn"
(b. ca. 430 – d. ca. 510)

St. Tewdrig ap Llywarch, King of Gwent
(liv. early-mid 500's)

Aunts and Uncles (5)

St. Cynfarch Gul, son of King Meirchion Gul of Rheged
(who was b. ca. 470 and d. ca. 535)

St. Dunawd "Fawr"
(d. ca. 535)

St. Owain
(d. ca. 1001)

St. Sawyl "Benisel," son of St. Pabo "Post Prydyn"
(who was b. ca. 430 and d. 510)

St. Tysilio, son of St. Brochwel Ysgithrog, King of Powys
(who was b. ca. 502 and d. ca. 560)

13. Isabella of France (b. 1292 – d. 27 Aug 1357), who married Edward II, King of England

Direct Ancestors (18)

Saints of Isabella of France

Bl. Blanche of Castile
(b. 4 March 1988 – d. 27 Nov 1252)

St. Boris I, Khan of the Bulgars
(d. 2 May 907)

Bl. Frederick of Arras
(b. aft. 962 – d. 6 Jan 1020)

St. Harold III "Bluetooth,"
King of Denmark
(b. ca. 910 – d. 1 Nov 985/986)

St. Ingigerd, Princess of Sweden
(b. ca. 1000 – d. 10 Feb 1050)

St. Irene Doukaina
(b. ca. 1066 – d. 19 Feb 1127)

St. Ladislas, King of Hungary
(b. 29 July 1040 – d. 27 July 1095)
St. Louis IX, King of France
(b. 25 April 1214 – d. 25 Aug 1270)
St. Mstislav I Vladimirovich "the Great,"
Grand Prince of Kiev
(b. 1076 – d. 14 April 1132)
St. Olaf II, King of Norway
(b. ca. 995 – d. 29 July 1030)
St. Olaf Bjornsson, King at Uppsala
(d. ca. 964)
St. Olaf III "Skotkonung" (the Tax King),
King of Sweden
(b. ca. 980 – d. 1021/1022)
St. Prisca
(b. ca. 1088 – d. 13 Aug 1134)
St. Reginlink
(d. 959)
St. Sigismund, King of Burgundy
(d. 523)
St. Vladimir Vsevolodovich Monomach,
Grand Prince of Kiev
(b. 1053 – d. 19 May 1125)
St. William VI, Lord of Montpellier
(b. ca. 1100 – d. 1162)
St. Wiltrudis
(d. ca. 986)

Aunts and Uncles (17)

Bl. Adalbero, Bishop of Liège
(d. 1 Jan 1128)
St. Alaricus
(d. 29 Sept 975)
St. Albert of Louvain, Bishop of Liège
(b. 1166 – d. 24 Nov 1192)
St. Anna of Kiev
(d. 1112/1116)
St. Benedict of Aniane
(b. ca. 750 – d. 11 Feb 821)
St. Conrad, Bishop of Constance
(b. ca. 905 – d. 26 Nov 975)
Bl. Conrad of Bavaria
(b. 1105 – d. 17 March 1154)
St. Gistald
(d. 523/524)
St. Gundebald
(d. 523/524)

Bl. Isabel
(b. March 1225 – d. 23 Feb 1270)

Bl. Margaret of Vau-le-Duc
(d. 4 June 1277)

Bl. Marie of Brabant
(b. ca. 1226 – d. 18 Jan 1256)

St. Rostislav I Mstislavich, Grand Prince of Kiev
(b. ca. 1110 – d. 14 March 1167)

Bl. Urban II, Pope
(b. 1035/1042 – d. 29 July 1099)

St. Vladimir II Yaroslavich, Prince of Novgorod
(b. 1020 – d. 1052)

St. Vsevolod Mstislavich,
Prince of Novgorod and Pskov
(b. 1092 – d. 11 Feb 1138)

St. Wulfhilda
(b. ca. 1117 – d. aft. 1180)

14. Sir John Stewart of Balveny, First Earl of Atholl

(b. ca. 1440 – d. 15 Sept 1512)

Direct Ancestors (1)

Bl. Ela, Countess of Salisbury
(b. 1187/1190 – d. 24 Aug 1261)

Aunts and Uncles (1)

St. Thomas, 2nd Earl of Lancaster
(b. ca. 1277 – d. 22 March 1322)

15. Mathilda (or Eadgyth) of Scotland

(b. 1079 – d. 1 May 1118),
who married Henry I, King of England

Direct Ancestors (6)

St. Brychan, ruler of Brecknock
(b. 480/490)

St. Constantine I, King of Scotland
(b. ca. 836 – d. 877)

St. Gabran mac Domangart, King of Dalriada
(b. ca. 500 – d. ca. 559)

St. Lleian, wife of St. Gabran mac Domangart, King of Dalriada
(who was b. ca. 500 and d. ca. 559)

St. Marchell, mother of St. Brychan
(who was b. 480/490)

St. Margaret of Scotland
(b. ca. 1046 – d. 16 Nov 1093)

Saints of Mathilda of Scotland

Aunts and Uncles (11)

St. Canoc, son of St. Brychan
(who was b. 480/490)

St. Cledwyn, son of St. Brychan
(who was b. 480/490)

St. Cynfran, son of St. Brychan
(who was b. 480/490)

St. Dwynwen, daughter of St. Brychan
(who was b. 480/490)

St. Ebba "the Elder"
(b. ca. 615 – d. 25 Aug 683)

St. Edward the Confessor, King of England
(b. 1004 – d. 5 Jan 1066)

St. Gladys, daughter of St. Brychan
(who was b. 480/490)

St. Leo IX, Pope
(b. 21 June 1002 – d. 19 April 1054)

St. Nefyn, daughter of St. Brychan
(who was b. 480/490)

St. Oswald, King of Northumbria
(b. 604/605 – d. 5 Aug 642)

St. Oswy, King of Northumbria
(b. ca. 611 – d. 15 Feb 670)

16. Mathilde of Flanders

(b. 1032 – d. 3 Nov 1083), who married William I the Conqueror, King of England

Saints of Mathilde of Flanders

Direct Ancestors (17)

St. Adela, Princess of France
(b. 1009 – d. 8 Jan 1079)

St. Arnulf, Bishop of Metz
(b. 13 Aug 582 – d. 16 Aug 640)

St. Bathildis
(b. ca. 630 – d. Jan 680)

St. Begga
(b. 613 – d. 17 Dec 694/695)

St. Bodegeisel II, Governor of Aquitaine
(d. 588)

Bl. Carloman, Mayor of the Palace in Austrasia
(b. 707 – d. 17 Aug 754)

Bl. Charlemagne, King of the Franks
and First Emperor of the West
(b. 2 April 747 – d. 28 Jan 814)

St. Germanus, Bishop of Auxerre
(b. ca. 378 – d. 31 July 448)

St. Gondolfus, Bishop of Tongres
(b. mid 500's – d. 16 July 604)

Bl. Hildegarde (b. ca. 754 – d. 30 April 783),
wife of Bl. Charlemagne

St. Irene, Empress of Byzantium
(b. 752 – d. 9 Aug 803)

Bl. Itta
(b. ca. 597 – d. 8 May 652)

St. Leo VI "the Philosopher,"
Emperor of Byzantium
(b. 1 Sept 866 – d. 12 May 912)

St. Oda
(b. ca. 567 – d. ca. 640)

Bl. Pepin of Landen,
Mayor of the Palace in Austrasia
(b. 580/585 – d. 640/646)

St. Theodora, Empress of Byzantium
(b. ca. 815 – d. aft. 24 Sept 867)

Bl. Theudelinde
(md. (2) Nov 590 – d. 22 Jan 628)

Saints of Mathilde of Flanders

Aunts and Uncles (15)

St. Adalard
(b. ca. 751 – d. 2 Jan 826)

St. Adeloga
(d. ca. 745)

St. Anthusa
(b. 757 – d. 809/811)

St. Attalia
(b. 687/690 – d. Dec 741)

St. Cunegund, Empress of the Holy Roman Empire
(b. ca. 978 – d. 3 March 1039/1040)

St. Eugenia
(d. 735)

St. Gertrude of Nivelles
(b. 626 – d. 17 March 659)

St. Gisela, Abbess of Chelles
(b. 757 – d. 30 July 810)

St. Gundelindis of Alsace
(d. ca. 750)

St. Modoald, Bishop of Trier
(d. 646/647)

St. Odilia
(b. ca. 660 – d. 13 Dec 720)

St. Remigius of Rouen
(d. ca. 772)

St. Severa, Abbess of St. Sevère
(d. ca. 600)
St. Stephen, Patriarch of Constantinople
(b. ca. 870 – d. 893)
St. Wala
(b. ca. 755 – d. 31 Aug 836)

17. Matilda of Huntingdon

(b. 1072 – d. 1130/1131), who married
(1) ca. 1090 Simon de St. Liz,
Earl of Huntingdon and Northampton, and
(2) in 1113 David I "the Saint," King of Scotland

Direct Ancestors (1)

St. Waltheof II, Earl of Huntingdon and Northampton
(b. 1045 – d. 31 May 1076)

18. Philippa of Hainault

(b. 24 June 1311 – d. 15 Aug 1369),
who married Edward III, King of England

Direct Ancestors (7)

Bl. Adelheid von Odenkirchen
(d. 5 July 1158)
Bl. Aleth of Montbard
(b. ca. 1070 – d. ca. 1105/1110)
St. David I, King of Scotland
(b. ca. 1084 – d. 24 May 1153)
Bl. Eberhard V
(b. ca. 1010 – d. 1076/1079)
Bl. Ermengarde of Zutphen
(b. ca. 1090 – d. bef. 1134)
Bl. Haziga of Diessen
(d. 1 Aug 1103)
Bl. Humbeline of Troyes
(b. 1092 – d. 21 Aug 1141)

Aunts and Uncles (21)

St. Adalbero, Bishop of Wuerzburg
(b. 1010 – d. 6 Oct 1090)
St. Bernard of Clairvaux,
Doctor of the Church
(b. 1091 – 20 Aug 1153)
St. Christina
(b. ca. 1055 – d. bef. 1102)
Bl. Constance, daughter of King Bela IV of Hungary
(who was b. 1026 and d. 3 May 1270)

St. Cunegund, Patron Saint of Poland and Lithuania
(b. ca. 1224 – d. 24 July 1292)
St. Elizabeth of Hungary
(b. 7 June 1207 – d. 19 Nov 1231)
St. Elizabeth Rose
(d. 13 Dec 1130)
Bl. Euphemia of Andechs
(d. 1180)
Bl. Gerard
(b. bef. 1090 – d. 13 June 1138)
Bl. Guy, son of Tescelin Sorrel
(who md. ca. 1085)
St. Hedwig of Silesia
(b. 1174 – d. 15 Oct 1243)
Bl. Jeanne of Flanders
(b. 1200 – d. 5 Dec 1244)
Bl. Jutta of Diessenberg
(b. ca. 1090 – d. 1136)
St. Louis, Bishop of Toulouse
(b. Feb 1274 – d. 19 Aug 1297)
Bl. Ludwig III, Count of Arnstein
(b. 1109 – d. 25 Oct 1185)
St. Margaret of Hungary
(b. 1242 – d. 18 Jan 1270)
St. Mechtildis of Diessen
(b. 1125 – d. 31 May 1160)
Bl. Nivard
(b. ca. 1100 – d. 1150)
St. Simon, Count of Crepy
(b. ca. 1047 – d. ca. 1081)
St. Ulric, Bishop of Augsburg
(b. 890 – d. 4 July 973)
Bl. Yolande of Hungary
(b. ca. 1235 – d. 6 March 1298)

Saints of Philippa of Nainault

19. Robert I the Bruce, King of Scotland
(b. 11 July 1274 – d. 7 June 1329)

Aunts and Uncles (4)

St. Abban
St. Aidan of Ferns
(b. ca. 558 – d. 626/632)
St. Feidhlimidh
(d. ca. 560)

St. Laurence O'Toole, Archbishop of Dublin
(b. ca. 1128 – d. 14 Nov 1180)

20. Robert III Stewart, King of Scotland

(b. 1337 – d. 4 April 1406)

Direct Ancestors (1)

St. Ragnald III, Earl of Orkney and Caithness
(b. ca. 1100 – d. 20 Aug 1158)

Aunts and Uncles (1)

St. Magnus of Orkney
(b. 1075 – d. 16 April 1115)

21. Saher de Quincy, First Earl of Winchester, Magna Charta Surety, and Crusader

(b. 1155 – d. 3 Nov 1219)

Aunts and Uncles (1)

St. Waltheof, Abbot of Melrose
(b. ca. 1100 – d. ca. 1160)

22. Stephen of Blois, King of England

(b. ca. 1095 – d. 25 Oct 1154)

Direct Ancestors (1)

St. Adela, Princess of England
(b. ca. 1062 – d. 8 March 1137)

23. Sir William de Plumpton, Knight and High Sheriff of Yorkshire

(md. (1) ca. 1330 and (2) ca. 1338 – d. 1362)

Aunts and Uncles (1)

St. William, Archbishop of York
(b. 1085/1090 – d. 8 June 1154)

24. William I the Conqueror, King of England

(b. 1027 – d. 9 Sept 1087)

Direct Ancestors (7)

St. Cunedda Wledig, founder of the Kingdom of Gwynedd
(b. ca. 400 – d. 460/470)

St. Geraint, King of Brittany

Saints of William I the Conqueror

St. Gwen, wife of St. Salamon I
"the Handsome," King of Brittany
(who was liv. in the 400's)

St. Judicael II, King of Brittany
(b. ca. 590 – d. 17 Dec 658)

St. Pompeja, wife of King Hoel I
"the Great" of Brittany
(who d. ca. 545)

St. Salamon I "the Handsome," King of Brittany
(liv. in the 400's)

St. William I "Longsword," Duke of Normandy
(b. ca. 900 – d. 17 Dec 942)

Aunts and Uncles (10)

St. Cado
(lived in the 400's)

St. Cybi
(b. ca. 490 – d. 8 Nov 554)

St. Cyngar
(b. ca. 470 – d. ca. 530)

St. Euriella, daughter of King Hoel III of Brittany
(who d. 612)

St. Jestin, son of St. Geraint, King of Brittany

St. Judoc
(b. ca. 600 – d. ca. 669)

St. Leonorius
(d. 560/570)

St. Non, mother of St. David of Wales
(who d. ca. 601)

St. Sève
(b. ca. 539)

St. Tugdual, Bishop of Tréguier
(b. 509 – d. 559/564)

PART II

Saints Who Are Direct Ancestors

Contents for Part II

Direct Ancestors

St. Adela, Princess of Austrasia

Adela was the daughter of St. Dagobert II, King of Austrasia, and his wife Matilda (or Mechtilde), said to be an Anglo-Saxon princess. A Dark Ages kingdom, Austrasia consisted of the eastern part of France, most of Germany, and Belgium, Luxemburg, and the Netherlands. Its capital was at Metz.

Adela married Alberic of Austrasia and had several children. After Alberic died, Adela founded a convent around 690 at Pfalzel near Trier. She then became a Benedictine nun, entered her convent, and became its first abbess. Her reputation for holiness was widespread. St. Boniface visited her there in 722, and a letter to her written by St. Elfleda has survived.

After several years of prayer and good works, Adela died in 734/735. Her relics are at the convent.

Her Line

Husband		Wife
St. Dagobert II, King of Austrasia (b. 652 – murdered 23 Dec 678)	+	**Mechtilde**
Alberic	+	**St. Adela**, Princess of Austrasia (d. 734/735)
Aubri I, Count of Blois	+	N.N.
Aubri II, Count of Blois	+	N.N.
Gainfroi, Count of Sens	+	**Theidlindis** (liv. 795)
Giselbert, Count in the Maasgau (md. 846 – d. ca. 885)	+	Ermengarde (or Irmgarde) of Lorraine and Burgundy (md. 846), daughter of Lothar I, King of Italy and Emperor of the West
Regnier I "Longhals," Duke of Lorraine and Count of Hainault (d. aft. 15 Oct 915 and bef. 19 Jan 916)	+	md. (1) Hersent, daughter of Charles II "the Bald," Emperor of the West
Giselbert, Duke of Lorraine and Count of Hainault (b. ca 890 – md. 929 – d. 2 Oct 934)	+	Gerberga of Saxony (b. 913/914 – md. (1) 929 – d. 5 May 984)
Ragnvald, Count of Roucy and Rheims (b. ca. 926 – md. 944/ 947 – d. 10 May 967)	+	**Alberade of Lorraine** (b. ca. 930 – md. 944/947 – d. 15 March 973)
Alberic (or Aubri) II, Count of Macon and Burgundy (liv. 952 – md. bef. 971 – d. 981/982)	+	**Ermentrude de Roucy** (b. 958 – md. (2) bef. 971 – d. 5 March 1005)
Geoffrey I "Ferreol," Count in the Gatinais and Chateau-Landon (liv. 990)	+	**Beatrice of Macon**

Geoffrey II "Ferreol," Count in the Gatinais and Chateau-Landon (b. ca. 1004 – md. 1035 – d. 1043/1046)	+	Ermengarde of Anjou (called Blanche) (b. ca. 1018 – md. (1) 1035 – d. 21 March 1076)
Fulk IV "Rechin," Count of Anjou (b. 1043 – md. (5) ca. 1090 – d. 14 April 1109)	+	Bertrade de Montfort (b. ca. 1060 – md. (1) ca. 1090 – d. 14 Feb 1117)
Fulk V "le Jeune," Count of Anjou, Crusader, and King of Jerusalem (b. 1092 – md. (1) ca. 1108 – d. 10 Nov 1143)	+	Erembourge, heiress of Maine (md. ca. 1108 – d. 1126)
Geoffrey V Plantagenet, Count of Anjou and Duke of Normandy (b. 24 Aug 1113 – md. 22 May 1127 – d. 7 Sept 1151)	+	Matilda, Princess of England and Empress of Germany (b. ca. Feb 1102 – md. (2) 22 May 1127 – d. 10 Sept 1167)
Henry II, King of England (b. 5 March 1133 – md. 18 May 1152 – d. 6 July 1189)	+	Eleanor of Aquitaine (b. 1122 – md. (2) 18 May 1152 – d. 31 March 1204)

Sources: *Baring-Gould*, Vol. 15, pp. 274–275; *Benedictine Monks*, p. 10; *Bunson*, p. 35; *Butler*, Vol. IV, pp. 605–606; *Delaney*, p. 26; *Delaney and Tobin*, p. 9; *Dunbar*, Vol. I, p. 3; *Englebert*, p. 487; *Holweck*, p. 15; *NCE*, p. 125; *Snodgrass*, p. 9; *Stuart*: line 303, nos. 45 through 39 + line 207, nos. 39 through 37 + line 92, nos. 35 through 32 + line 2, nos. 32 through 27; *WWH*, Vol. 1, p. 72

St. Adela,
Princess of France

Adela was born in 1009 and was the daughter of Robert II "the Pious," King of France, and his third wife Constance of Arles. In 1027 at the age of 18, Adela married her first husband, who was Richard III, Duke of Normandy. Richard died later that same year, and Adela remarried in 1028. Her second husband was Baldwin V de Lille, Count of Flanders.

During their long marriage, Baldwin and Adela founded several churches and a Benedictine convent in western Belgium in the village of Mesen (sometimes called Messines). They also rebuilt the monastery of Einham. After Baldwin's death in 1067, Adela became a nun, receiving her veil from the hand of Pope Alexander II. She then retired to her convent at Mesen. She died on 8 January 1079 and was buried in the crypt of the convent's church, which is called the Church of St. Nicholas.

Adela had no children with Richard and five with Baldwin. Her daughter Mathilde would marry William the Conqueror.

Her Line

Husband		Wife
Robert II "the Pious," King of France (b. 27 March 972 – md. (3) 998 – d. 20 July 1031)	+	**Constance of Arles** (b. 986 – md. 998 – d. 25 July 1032)
Baldwin V de Lille, Count of Flanders (b. ca. 1013 – md. 1028 – d. 1 Sept 1067)	+	**St. Adela**, Princess of France (b. 1009 – md. (2) 1028 – d. 8 Jan 1079)
William I the Conqueror, Duke of Normandy and King of England (b. 1027/1028 – md. 1053 – d. 9 Sept 1087)	+	**Mathilde of Flanders** (b. 1032 – md. 1053 – d. 3 Nov 1083)

Sources: *Benedictine Monks*, p. 10; *Bunson*, p. 35; *Dunbar*, Vol. I, pp. 3–5; *Holweck*, p. 16; *Stuart*: line 140, nos. 33 through 31; *Weis, AR*: line 128, nos. 21 and 22 + line 162, nos. 22 and 23

St. Adela, Princess of England

Adela was born around 1062 and was the youngest daughter of William the Conqueror and his wife Mathilde of Flanders. She was very well educated, spoke several languages, and was deeply religious. Around 1080/1081, she married Stephen III, Count of Blois, who was one of the richest men in Europe and a king in all but name. They had eleven children.

Adela's formidable political abilities first showed themselves in 1095 when Stephen became one of the leaders of the First Crusade and left for the Holy Land. He was Count of Blois, Champagne, Brie, and Chartres and controlled hundreds of estates in France. He was away four years, and Adela was such an effective ruler of his domains in his absence that she became known as "the heroine of the First Crusade."

From 1099 when Stephen returned until he departed again on the Crusade of 1101, Adela continued to support several scholars and poets that she had invited to her court and that significantly contributed to the spiritual and cultural life of her era.

From 1101, Adela was once again ruling Stephen's domains. After May 1102 when he was killed at the battle of Ramleh, she became regent for their eldest son Thibaud and was the most important woman in Europe until he came of age in 1109. She generously endowed abbeys and churches. Several letters on ecclesiastical matters written to her by Hildebert, bishop of Le Mans, have survived.

Around 1122, Adela became a nun, entered the Cluniac priory of Marigney-sur-Loire, and died there on 8 March 1137. She was buried in Caen in the abbey of the Holy Trinity next to her mother and her sister Cecilia.

Adela's brothers William and Henry both became kings of England, as William II and Henry I. So did her son Stephen.

Her Line

Husband		Wife
William I the Conqueror, Duke of Normandy and King of England (b. 1027/1028 – md. 1053 – d. 9 Sept 1087)	+	**Mathilde of Flanders** (b. 1032 – md. 1053 – d. 3 Nov 1083)
Stephen III (Étienne Henri), Count of Blois, Champagne, Brie, and Chartres, a leader of the First Crusade (b. 1046 – md. 1080/1081 – slain 19 or 27 May 1102 at the battle of Ramleh in the Holy Land)	+	**St. Adela, Princess of Eng land** (b. ca. 1062 – md. 1080/ 1081 – d. 8 March 1137)
Stephen of Blois, King of England (b. ca. 1095 – md. ca. 1120 – d. 25 Oct 1154)	+	Mathilda of Boulogne (b. ca. 1105 – md. ca. 1120 – d. 3 July 1151)

Sources: *Benedictine Monks*, p. 10; *HBC*, p. 35; *Parbury*, p. 79; *Stuart*: line 81, nos. 31 and 30 + line 299, nos. 31 and 30; *Weir*, pp. 44 and 51; *Weis, AR*, line 169, nos. 23 through 25; *WWH*, Vol. 1, pp. 72–73

St. Adelaide of Burgundy

Adelaide was born in 931 and was the daughter of Rudolph II, King of Burgundy, and his wife Bertha of Swabia.

Adelaide's two marriages were the stuff of high drama. Betrothed at two, Adelaide married Lothair II, King of Italy, fourteen years later in 947. After three years of marriage, Lothair was poisoned on 22 November 950 by Berengar, a rival for the Italian crown. When Adelaide then refused to marry Berengar's son Adalbert, Berengar threw her into prison and treated her brutally. After four months in captivity, Adelaide managed to escape and make her way north to the castle of Canossa. From there she sent a plea for help to emperor Otto I of the Holy Roman Empire. Otto then led an army from Germany down to Italy, met Berengar in battle, defeated him, was crowned King of Italy, and then freed Adelaide and took her back to Germany. On 25 December 951, Otto married Adelaide.

The marriage of Otto and Adelaide was a very happy one. They had four children and were very close. She was interested in affairs of state, and Otto often asked her for advice. After Otto defeated the Magyars at the battle of Lechfeld in 955, he became known as the deliverer of western Christendom, and Adelaide became the most prominent woman in Europe. Loved by Otto's people, she was a very popular queen.

Besides helping Otto, Adelaide also assisted Christianity. She founded and restored convents and monasteries. She also worked for the conversion of the Slavic peoples, who were still pagans at the time.

When Otto I died on 7 May 973, their son Otto II was eighteen years old and able to rule in his own right. Adelaide began to devote more of her energy to the church. She continued to give money to religious foundations, personally distributed food and clothing to the poor, and became interested in the monastic reform efforts centered at Cluny. She was so generous that Otto II at one point accused her of squandering the imperial treasury. Adelaide left the court, and two years would pass before Otto II reconciled with his mother and she returned to the palace.

The reconciliation was very timely, for when Otto II died on 7 December 983, his son and heir Otto III was just three years old. Adelaide became co-regent of the empire along with Otto III's mother Theophano. After conflict with Theophano, Adelaide once again left the court. Following Theophano's death in 991, she returned and ruled alone until Otto III came of age in 995.

Having finally retired from political responsibilities, Adelaide now devoted herself entirely to religious causes. She continued to personally minister to the poor. She also made pilgrimages to several religious sites in France, Germany, and Italy.

Shortly before her death, Adelaide retired to the convent of Saints Peter and Paul which she had founded at Selz in Alsace. She died there on 16 December 999. Her grave is at the convent, but several of her relics are in Hanover.

Her Line

Husband		Wife
Rudolph II, King of Burgundy and Italy (md. 922 – d. 11 July 937)	+	**Bertha of Swabia** (md. (1) 922 – d. 2 Jan 966)

Otto I "the Great," King of Germany and Italy, Emperor of the West (b. 23 Nov 912 – md. (2) 25 Dec 951 – d. 7 May 973)	+	**St. Adelaide of Burgundy** (b. 932 – md. (2) 25 Dec 951 – d. 16 Dec 999)
Otto II, King of Italy and Emperor of the West (b. 955 – md. (2) 14 April 972 – d. 7 Dec 983)	+	St. Theophano Skleros (b. 956 – md. 14 April 972 – d. 15 Sept. 991)
Ezzo, Count Palatine of Lorraine, Lord of Duisburg and Kaiserwerth (b. ca. 955 – md. 991 – d. 21 May 1034)	+	**Bl. Matilda of Saxony** (b. 981 – md. 991 – d. 4 Nov 1025)
Mieszko II, King of Poland (b. ca. 990 – md. 1013 – d. 10 May 1034)	+	**St. Richenza of Pfalz-Lorraine** (b. ca. 1000 – md. (1) 1013 – d. 21 March 1063)
Casimir "the Great," King of Poland (b. 25 July 1016 – md. 1041/1042 – d. 19 March 1058)	+	Dobronega Maria of Kiev (b. aft. 1012 – md. 1041/1042 – d. 1087), daughter of St. Vladimir I Sviatoslavich "the Great"
Ladislas I (or Wladislaw I Hermann), King of Poland (b. ca. 1040 – md. ca. 1080 – d. 4 June 1102)	+	Judith of Bohemia (b. ca. 1058 – md. ca. 1080 – d. 25 Dec 1086)
Boleslas III, King of Poland (b. 20 Aug 1086 – md. (1) 1103 – d. 28 Oct 1138)	+	Zbyslava of Kiev (md. 1103 – d. 1110/1111)
Ladislas (or Wladislaw) II, King of Poland (b. 1105 – md. (1) ca. 1126 – (d. 30 May 1159)	+	Agnes of Austria (md. ca. 1126), daughter of St. Leopold III, Margrave of Austria
Alfonso VII "el Emperador," King of Castile, Leon, Galicia, Toledo, Zaragoza, and the Asturias (b. 1 March 1105 – md. (2) July 1152 – d. 21 Aug 1157)	+	**Richilde (or Richenza) of Poland** (b. 1130/1140 – md. July 1152 – d. 1166)
Alfonso II, King of Aragon (b. March 1157 – md. (2) 18 Jan 1174 – d. 25 Apr 1196)	+	**Sancha** (b. 21 Sept 1154 – md. 18 Jan 1174 – d. 9 Nov 1208)
Alfonso, Count of Provence (b. 1180 – md. 1193 – d. Feb 1209)	+	Gersinde of Sabran, heiress of Forcalquier (md. 1193 – d. aft. 1222)
Raymond Berenger V, Count of Provence and Forcalquier (b. 1198 – md. Dec 1220 – d. 19 Aug 1245)	+	Beatrice of Savoy (b. 1198 – md. Dec 1220 – d. Dec 1266)
Henry III, King of England (b. 1 Oct 1207 – md. 14 Jan 1236 – d. 16 Nov 1272)	+	**Bl. Eleanor of Provence** (b. ca. 1223 – md. 14 Jan 1236 – d. 25 June 1291)

Sources: *Baring-Gould*, Vol. 15, pp. 161–167; *BBKL*, Vol. 1, col. 35; *Benedictine Monks*, p. 10; *Bentley*, p. 241; *Bunson*, pp. 35–36; *Butler*, Vol. IV, pp. 572–573; *CE*, Vol. I, pp. 140–141; *Chervin*, pp. 52–53; *Cruz*, pp. 3–6; *Delaney*, p. 27; *Delaney and Tobin*, pp. 9–10; *Dunbar*, Vol. I, pp. 5–9; *Englebert*, pp. 476–477; *Giorgi*, pp. 736–737; *Guiley*, pp. 2–3; *Holboeck*, pp. 126–130; *Holweck*, p. 16; *Klaniczay*, pp. 197 and 432; *Snodgrass*, pp. 9–10; *Stuart*: line 323 + line 237, nos. 37 through 34 + line 378, nos. 34

through 29 + line 94, nos. 29 and 28 + line 54, nos. 28 through 25; *Tucker:* Vol. I, pp. 146, 337–338, and 295 + Vol. II, p. 701; *Weis, AR*: line 147, nos. 19 through 27 + line 116 + line 111, nos. 27 through 30; *Wells*, pp. 110, 270, 83, 474, 141, 24, and 482; *WWH*, Vol. 1, pp. 74–77

Bl. Adelaide of Susa

Adelaide was born around 1015 and was the daughter of Odalrico Manfredo II, Margrave of Turin and Susa, and his wife Bertha of Este. Odalrico died while Adelaide was still a young, unmarried woman, and she inherited most of his vast domains in northern Italy.

Adelaide was a beautiful woman with the soul of a lion. She had learned martial arts as a girl and bore her own arms and armor. She had masculine courage and energy and knew how to rule her inheritance. More than once she waged war on rebels in her own territories, burning Asti, Lodi, and other towns that had risen against her.

Adelaide had three husbands. The first was Hermann, Duke of Swabia, whom she married in January 1037 and who died of plague in 1038. Her second was Henry of Montferrat, whom she married in 1041 and who died in 1045. Her third husband was Otto of Savoy, whom she married in 1046 and who died about twelve years later. It was through her children with Otto that Adelaide became one of the founders of the house of Savoy.

Adelaide's involvement in politics did not stop at her own borders. In the struggle between the German emperors and the papacy, she strongly supported the imperial side. In the quarrel between her son-in-law Emperor Henry IV and Pope Gregory VII, her advice to Henry saved his crown for him. When Henry went to Canossa to seek forgiveness from the Pope, Adelaide went with him.

In her old age, Adelaide brooded over her three marriages. No one today knows what was troubling her. She did decide to seek God's forgiveness by doing works of charity, and she began to give generously to religious institutions. She died on 19 December 1091.

Her Line

Husband		Wife
Odalrico Manfredo II, Margrave of Turin and Susa (md. bef. 1014 – d. 23 Dec 1035)	+	**Bertha of Este** (md. bef. 1014 – d. 29 Dec 1037)
Odo (or Otto) I, Count of Maurienne (md. ca. 1036 – d. 19 Jan 1057/1058)	+	**Bl. Adelaide of Susa** (b. ca. 1015 – md. (3) ca. 1036 – d. 19 Dec 1091)
Amadeus (or Amadeo) II, Count of Savoy and Margrave of Susa (b. ca. 1046 – md. 1065/1070 – d. 26 Jan 1080)	+	Johanna of Geneva (md. 1065/1070 – d. ca. 1095)
Humbert (or Umberto) II, Count of Maurienne and Savoy and Marquis of Turin (b. ca. 1070 – md. (1) 1090 – d. 14 Oct 1103)	+	Gisela of Burgundy (b. ca. 1070 – md. 1090 – d. aft. 1133)
Amadeus (or Amadeo) III, Count of Savoy, Marquis of Maurienne, and Crusader (b. 1080/ 1092 – md. 1133/1134 – d. 30 March 1148 on the 2nd Crusade)	+	Matilda d'Albon (md. 1133/1134 – d. aft. Jan 1145)

Bl. Humbert (or Umberto) III, Count of Savoy and Marquis of Italy (b. 4 Aug 1136 – md. (4) 1175 – d. 4 March 1189)	+	Beatrice of Macon (b. ca. 1160 – md. 1175 – d. 8 April 1230)
Thomas I, Count of Savoy (b. 20 May 1178 – md. 1196 – d. 1 March 1233)	+	Margaret of Geneva (b. ca. 1180 – md. 1196 – d. 13 April 1236)
Raymond Berenger V, Count of Provence and Forcalquier (b. 1198 – md. Dec 1220 – d. 19 Aug 1245)	+	**Beatrice of Savoy** (b. 1198 – md. Dec 1220 – d. Dec 1266)
Henry III, King of England (b. 1 Oct 1207 – md. 14 Jan 1236 – d. 16 Nov 1272)	+	**Bl. Eleanor of Provence** (b. ca. 1223 – md. 14 Jan 1236 – d. 25 June 1291)

Sources: *Dunbar*, Vol. I, pp. 10-12; *Stuart*: line 315, no. 34 + line 93, nos. 33 through 26 + line 54, nos. 26 and 25; *Tucker*, Vol. II, pp. 806, 750–751, and 701; *Weis, AR*: line 133, nos. 26 and 27 + line 111, nos. 29 and 30; *Wells*, pp. 567, 511–512, and 482

Bl. Adelheid von Odenkirchen

Adelheid's parents and birth date are unknown. She married Ludwig II, Count in the Einrichgau. Several years after Ludwig's death, Adelheid founded a convent in 1139 near Koblenz and became its abbess. After nineteen years of prayer and service to God, she died on 5 July 1158.

Her Line

Husband		Wife
N.N.	+	**N.N.**
Ludwig II, Count of Arnstein and in the Einrichgau (b. ca. 1094 – d. aft. 1117)	+	**Bl. Adelheid (or Udalheid) von Odenkirchen** (d. 5 July 1158)
Henry I, Count of Guelders and Zutphen (b. 1117 – md. 1135 – d. 1182)	+	**Agnes von Arnstein** (md. 1135 – d. 1179)
Otto I, Count of Friesland, Guelders, Holland, Sealand, and Zutphen, Crusader (md. bef. 1188 – d. betw. 30 April and 24 Sept 1207)	+	Richardis von Wittelsbach (md. bef. 1188 – d. 7 Dec 1231)
William I, Count of Holland (France) and East Friesland, Crusader (b. ca. 1174 – md. 1198 – d. 2 July 1222)	+	**Adelaide of Guelders** (b. ca. 1186 – md. 1198 – d. 4 Feb 1218)
Florenz IV, Count of Holland and Sealand (b. 24 June 1210 – d. 19 July 1234)	+	Matilda of Brabant (d. 21 Dec 1267)
Jean I d'Avesnes, Count of Hainault, Holland and Flanders (b. 1 May 1218 – md. 9 Oct 1246 – d. 24 Dec 1257)	+	**Adelaide of Holland** (b. ca. 1225 – md. 9 Oct 1246 – d. 1284)
Jean II d'Avesnes, Count of Hainault and Holland (b. 1247 – md. 1270 – d. 22 Aug 1304)	+	Philippa of Luxemburg (md. 1270)
William III d'Avesnes, Count of Hainault and Holland (b. ca 1286 – md. 19 May 1305 – d. 7 June 1337)	+	Jeanne de Valois (b. ca. 1294 – md. 19 May 1305 – d. 7 March 1342)
Edward III, King of England (b. 13 Nov 1312 – md. 24 Jan 1328 – d. 21 June 1377)	+	**Philippa of Hainault** (b. 24 June 1311 – md. 24 Jan 1328 – d. 15 Aug 1369)

Sources: *Dunbar*, Vol. I, p. 355 (under "Guda"); *Stuart:* line 304A, nos. 30 and 29 + line 304, nos. 29 through 27 + line 72, nos. 27 through 25 + line 50, nos. 25 through 22; *Tucker*, Vol. I, pp. 373, 414, and 383; *Weis, AR:* line 100, nos. 27 through 29 + line 168, nos. 30 through 32 + line 103, nos. 33 and 34; *Wells*, pp. 284–285, 305, and 293

St. Aethelbert I, King of Kent

Aethelbert was born around 550 and was the son of Ermenric, King of Kent. After succeeding his father, he married St. Bertha, the daughter of Caribert, King of Paris.

Although Aethelbert was a pagan, he agreed to let his new wife continue to practice her Christian faith. Her sincerity and her other good qualities slowly began to make an impression on him. When Pope Gregory I sent Augustine on a mission to convert the Saxons in 597, Aethelbert allowed Augustine to build a church in Canterbury, to preach freely throughout Kent, and to convert whomever he could.

Around 601, Aethelbert himself was baptized and became the first Saxon king to convert to Christianity. None of his subjects were forced to join the new faith. Aethelbert's belief that conversion should be voluntary and his other enlightened attitudes helped to convert King Saebert of the East Saxons and King Redwald of the East Angles.

Aethelbert also created a code of laws in Kent that was the basis of the later laws of Offa and Alfred. Under him, Kent became the wealthiest and most secure kingdom in Saxon England.

Aethelbert died on 24 February 616 after a reign of more than fifty years. He was the first Saxon king to be venerated as a saint. His daughter Ethelburga also became a saint.

His Line

Husband		Wife
Ermenric, King of Kent (d. 560)	+	**N.N.**
St. Aethelbert (or Ethelbert) I, King of Kent (b. ca. 552 – md. (1) ca. 578 – d. 24 Feb 616)	+	St. Bertha (b. ca. 560 – md. ca. 578 – d. ca. 602)
Eadbald, King of Kent (md. (2) ca. 618 – d. 640)	+	St. Emma (md. ca. 618)
Erconbert (or Eorconbeorht), King of Kent (b. ca. 624 – md. ca. 640 – d. 14 July 664)	+	St. Sexburga (md. ca. 640 – d. 6 July 699)
Egbert, King of Kent (b. ca. 641– d. 4 July 673)	+	N.N.
Wihtread, King of Kent (d. 23 April 725)	+	N.N.
Eadbert, King of Kent (d. 748)	+	N.N.
Aethelbert II, King of Kent (d. 762)	+	N.N.
Eahlmund (or Edmund), King of Kent (b. ca. 758 – d. 786)	+	**N.N.**, a daughter of Aethelbert II, King of Kent
Egbert "the Great," King of Wessex (b. 775 – d. 4 Feb 839)	+	Redburga (or Raedburh) (b. ca. 788)

Aethelwulf, King of Wessex (b. ca. 806 – d. 13 Jan 858)	+	md. (1) Osburh (b. ca. 810 – d. aft. 876)
St. Alfred the Great, King of Wessex (b. 849 – md. 868 – d. 26 Oct 899)	+	St. Eahlswith of Mercia (b. ca. 852 – md. 868 – d. 904)

Sources: *Ashley*, pp. 215–217; *Baring-Gould*, Vol. 2, pp. 406–409; *BBKL*, Vol. 18, cols. 391–392; *Benedictine Monks*, p. 243; *Bentley*, p. 40; *Bunson*, p. 290; *Butler*, Vol. I, pp. 414–415; *CE*, Vol. V, pp. 553–554; *Delaney*, pp. 201–202; *Delaney and Tobin*, p. 384; *HBC*, p. 12; *Holboeck*, pp. 101–103; *Holweck*, pp. 330–331; *Joeckle*, p. 146; *Jones*, p. 84; *Kirby*, p. 179; *NCE*, Vol. 5, p. 566; *O'Malley*, p. 67; *Snodgrass*, p. 82; *Stuart:* line 233A, nos. 49 through 41 + line 233, nos. 42 through 39 (n.b., Stuart adds an additional generation between Wihtread and Aethelbert II); *Wagner*, p. 188; *Weis, AR*, line 1, nos. 12 through 15; *Williams*, p. 359; *Yorke*, p. 36

Bl. Agnes of Franconia

Agnes was born around 1073 and was the daughter of Henry IV of Franconia, Emperor of the West, and his wife Bertha of Maurienne. In 1089, she married her first husband Frederick I, Duke of Swabia, and through their children became one of the founders of the house of Hohenstaufen.

Frederick died in 1105, and in 1106 Agnes remarried. Her second husband was St. Leopold III, Margrave of Austria. This second marriage was an especially happy one. Agnes and Leopold went to mass and read scripture together. They founded the monastery at Klosterneuburg near Vienna. Agnes also took part in most of Leopold's other good works.

Agnes and Leopold had a very large number of children, ten of whom lived to adulthood and perhaps seven more who died in infancy.

After Leopold died in 1136, he became the patron saint of Austria. Agnes survived him by seven years, dying on 24 September 1143.

Her Line

Husband		Wife
Henry IV of Franconia, Emperor of the West (b. 11 Nov 1050 – md. 13 July 1066 – d. 7 Aug 1106)	+	**Bertha of Maurienne** (md. 13 July 1066)
St. Leopold III, Margrave of Austria (b. ca. 1075 – md. (2) 1106 – d. 15 Nov 1136)	+	**Bl. Agnes of Franconia** (b. ca. 1073 – md. (2) 1106 – d. 24 Sept 1143)
Ladislas (or Wladislaw) II, King of Poland (b. 1105 – md. (1) ca. 1126 – d. 30 May 1159)	+	**Agnes of Austria** (md. ca. 1126)
Alfonso VII "El Emperador," King of Castile, Leon, Galicia, Toledo, Zaragoza, and the Asturias (b. 1 March 1105 – md. (2) July 1152 – d. 21 Aug 1157)	+	**Richilde (or Richenza) of Poland** (b. 1130/1140 – md. July 1152 – d. 1166)
Alfonso II, King of Aragon (b. March 1157 – md. (2) 18 Jan 1174 – d. 25 April 1196)	+	**Sancha** (b. 21 Sept 1154 – md. 18 Jan 1174 – d. 9 Nov 1208)
Alfonso, Count of Provence (b. 1180 – md. 1193 – d. Feb 1209)	+	Gersinde of Sabran, heiress of Provence and Forcalquier (md. 1193 – d. aft. 1222)
Raymond Berenger V, Count of Provence and Forcalquier (b. 1198 – md. Dec 1220 – d. 19 Aug 1245)	+	Beatrice of Savoy, Countess of Provence (b. 1198 – md. Dec 1220 – d. Dec 1266)
Henry III, King of England (b. 1 Oct 1207 – md. 14 Jan 1236 – d. 16 Nov 1272)	+	**Bl. Eleanor of Provence** (b. ca. 1223 – md. 14 Jan 1236 – d. 25 June 1291)

Sources: *Dunbar*, Vol. I, p. 30; *Stuart*: line 359, nos. 32 and 31 + line 279, nos. 31 and 30 + line 378, nos. 30 and 29 + line 94, nos. 29 and 28 + line 54, nos. 28 through 25; *Tucker:* Vol. I, pp. 340–341 and 33 + Vol. II, p. 686 + Vol. I, pp. 190–191 and 22 + Vol. II, p. 701; *Weis, AR:* line 45, nos. 23 and 24 + line 147, nos. 26 and 27 + line 116 + line 111, nos. 27 through 30; *WWH*, Vol. 1, p. 115

Bl. Agnes of Poitou

Agnes was born in 1024 and was the daughter of William III "the Great," Count of Poitou, and his third wife Agnes of Burgundy. On 21 November 1043, she married Henry III "the Black," Duke of Bavaria and Swabia. Three years later, Henry became Emperor of the Holy Roman Empire, and Agnes was crowned Empress along with him.

The adult life of Agnes consisted of three parts, and the first part was her years with Henry III. As Henry dealt with the affairs of his realm, he left the operations of his court to Agnes. She became known throughout Europe as a generous patron of writers, painters, and poets. Europe's most creative minds came to Germany, and with them Agnes created a brilliant court. She also had six children with Henry, including his first-born son and heir Henry IV, born in 1050. These happy years ended abruptly when Henry III died in 1056.

When Henry IV succeeded his father, he was only six years old, and the second part of Agnes' life began when she started to rule as regent for her son. Besides her administrative responsibilities, she also acted as chief justice and commander-in-chief of the military. The princes of the empire had approved of her becoming regent and for the first few years were quite satisfied with her performance. They might have remained content for much longer but for the fact that Agnes relied very often on the advice of bishop Henry of Augsburg. The other princes felt that they were losing their own status as advisers to the royal court, and they began to consider how they might usurp the regency. They decided that separating Henry IV from his mother would give them control over the boy and his empire. One day in 1062 while Henry IV was on an island in the Rhine near Cologne, archbishop Anno of Cologne and other princes sailed up in a small ship, seized Henry IV, and kidnapped him.

Agnes' reaction was cool and calculated. Henry IV was twelve when he was abducted but would reach the age of majority just two years later when he turned fourteen. Agnes gave up all the powers she was exercising as regent, moved to Rome, and offered her services to the pope. The second part of her life was over, but the third part was about to begin.

In Rome, Agnes quickly became a close friend of Pope Alexander II, who gave her new ecclesiastical responsibilities and sent her back to Germany on several papal missions. In 1064, Agnes was back in the imperial German court, and she was also present at the ceremony in March 1065 where Henry IV was declared an adult. Her personal intervention was all that prevented Henry IV from taking the sword he had just received and killing archbishop Anno of Cologne.

For the rest of her life Agnes served the pope and the church at the highest diplomatic levels. She made her last trip to Germany in 1074 and then retired to a convent in Rome to pray, fast, and tend the sick. She died on 14 December 1077 and was buried in Rome in the church of Petronilla, which later became part of St. Peter's.

Her Line

Husband		Wife
William III "the Great," Count of Poitou (and as William V Duke of Aquitaine) (b. ca. 969 – md. (3) 1019 – d. 31 Jan 1030)	+	**Agnes of Burgundy** (b. ca. 995 – md. (2) 1019 – d. 10 Nov 1068), daughter of Otto William, King of Lombardy
Henry III "the Black," King of Germany and Emperor of the West (b. 28 Oct 1017 – md. (2) 21 Nov 1043 – d. 5 Oct 1056)	+	**Bl. Agnes of Poitou** (b. 1024 – md. 21 Nov 1043 – d. 14 Dec 1077)
Henry IV of Franconia, Emperor of the West (b. 11 Nov 1050 – md. 13 July 1066 – d. 7 Aug 1106)	+	Bertha of Maurienne (md. 13 July 1066)
St. Leopold III, Margrave of Austria (b. ca. 1075 – md. (2) 1106 – d. 15 Nov 1136)	+	**Bl. Agnes of Franconia** (b. ca. 1073 – md. (2) 1106 – d. 24 Sept 1143)

[For the later generations that connect this line to the kings of England, see the line of Bl. Agnes of Franconia in Part II.]

Sources: *Dunbar*, Vol. I, pp. 28–30; *Stuart:* line 161, nos. 32 and 31 + line 359, nos. 33 through 31; *Tucker*, Vol. I, pp. 18 and 339–341; *Warncke*, pp. 244–245; *Weis, AR*, line 34, nos. 22 through 24; *Wells*, pp. 23 and 270–271; *WWH*, Vol. 1, p. 117

Bl. Aleth of Montbard

Aleth was born around 1070 and was the daughter of Bernard, Lord of Montbard, and his wife Humbeline (or Humberge) de Grancey. Aleth's brother Andre de Montbard was a founding member of the Knights Templar and one of the first Grand Masters. Around 1085, Aleth married Tescelin Sorrel, Lord of Fontaines and Viscount of Dijon. Aleth was considered to be a very holy woman even while she lived, due to her fasts, hospital visits, and other good deeds. Tescelin was a valiant knight and a pious man.

Tescelin and Aleth are remembered today primarily because of their extraordinarily spiritual children. One daughter (Humbeline) and three sons (Gerard, Guy, and Nivard) were beatified. Their son Bernard became St. Bernard of Clairvaux, one of the greatest saints in the history of Christianity.

Aleth died around 1105/1110 and was first buried in the Church of St. Bénigne in Dijon. Because of her son Bernard's extraordinary career, in 1250 her remains were moved to his monastery at Clairvaux.

Her Line

Husband		Wife
Bernard, Lord of Montbard (liv. 1065)	+	**Humbeline de Grancey** (liv. 1065)
Tescelin Sorrel (or Sorus), Lord of Les Fontaines (md. ca. 1085)	+	**Bl. Aleth of Montbard** (b. ca. 1070 – md. ca 1085 – d. 1105/1110)
Anseric II, Sire de Chacenay (d. 1137)	+	md. (1) **Bl. Humbeline de Troyes** (b. 1092 – d. 21 Aug 1141)
Gui, Count of Bar-sur-Seine (d. 1145)	+	**Petronille of Chacenay** (d. 1161)
Theobald I, Count of Bar-le-Duc, Brie, and Luxemburg, Crusader (b. ca. 1160 – md. (3) 1189 – d. 13 Feb 1214)	+	**Ermesinde of Bar-sur-Seine** (md. 1189 – d. ca. 1121)
Henry II, Count of Bar-le-Duc, Luxemburg, and Namur, and Crusader (b. 1190 – md. 1219 – d. 13 Nov 1239)	+	Philippa of Dreux, Dame de Coucy (b. 1192 – md. 1219 – d. 17 March 1242)
Henry III "the Blond," Count of Luxemburg (b.1217 – md. 4 June 1240 – d. 24 Nov 1281)	+	**Mathilde de Bar-le-Duc** (md. 4 June 1240 – d. 23 Nov 1275)
Jean II d'Avesnes, Count of Hainault and Holland (b. 1247 – md. 1270 – d. 22 Aug 1304)	+	**Philippa of Luxemburg** (md. 1270)
William III d'Avesnes, Count of Hainault and Holland (b. ca. 1286 – md. 19 May 1305 – d. 7 June 1337)	+	Jeanne de Valois (b. ca. 1294 – md. 19 May 1305 – d. 7 March 1342)
Edward III, King of England (b. 13 Nov 1312 – md. 24 Jan 1328 – d. 21 June 1377)	+	**Philippa of Hainault** (b. 24 June 1311 – md. 24 Jan 1328 – d. 15 Aug 1369)

Sources: *Baring-Gould*, Vol. 9, pp. 196–197*; *Benedictine Monks*, p. 31; *Bunson*, p. 61; *Butler*, Vol. III, p. 360*; *CE*, Vol. II, p. 498*; *Delaney*, p. 101*; *Delaney and Tobin*, p. 30; *Dunbar*, Vol. I, pp. 12–13 (under "Adelaide"); *Holboeck*, pp. 151–155; *Holweck*, p. 153*; *Joeckle*, p. 69*; *NCE*, Vol. 2, p. 335*; *One Hundred Saints*, p. 188*; *Stuart:* line 385 + line 384, nos. 29 and 28 + line 383, nos. 28 through 26 + line 36, nos. 27 through 25 + line 71, nos. 25 and 24 + line 50, nos. 24 through 22; *Wells*, pp. 144, 48, 47, 361, 305, and 293 (sources marked with a * are accounts of the life of St. Bernard of Clairvaux which mention his parents by name)

St. Alfred the Great, King of Wessex

Alfred was born around 849 and was the son of Aethelwulf, King of Wessex, and his first wife Osburh. Since Alfred had three older brothers, no one ever expected him to become king, and he was educated for a career in the church.

Slowly, the likely succession to the throne began to change. Aethelbald, Alfred's oldest brother, became king when Aethelwulf abdicated in 855 but then died in 860. Aethelbert, the next brother, was crowned immediately but then died in late 865 or early 866. Aethelred, Alfred's last older brother, ruled next but was badly wounded in the battle of Meredune and died on 23 April 871.

In 868 Alfred had married St. Ealhswith of Mercia. They would eventually have five children and a very happy marriage, but it would first be necessary for him to save not only his family but also his country.

Wessex seemed doomed when Alfred became king. By the spring of 871, Danish Vikings had already burned half of its towns to ashes. The other half were the last unconquered part of the last Anglo-Saxon kingdom still holding out against the Vikings. By fighting one battle a month from the spring until the end of the year, Alfred brought the Danish invasion to a standstill. As part of a negotiated truce, he then paid the Danes to leave Wessex alone for the next five years.

In retreating, the Danes simply withdrew across the borders of Wessex into the neighboring British kingdoms that they had already conquered. The question was not whether they would return to Wessex but when. During the five-year truce, Alfred devoted himself to strengthening his defenses and building up his army.

A Danish army returned to Wessex in the spring of 876, and for the next two years Alfred was in several battles. The war did not end until the battle of Ethandune in 878. Alfred's triumph there was so complete that it ended the war. Alfred and the men of Wessex had won.

Apart from a brief skirmish with the Danes in 885, Wessex was at peace for the next fifteen years. During this time, Alfred showed that he was much more than a very capable war leader. He gathered scholars at his court and turned it into a center of learning. He personally translated several works from Latin into Old English, including the first 50 Psalms, the *Consolation of Philosophy* by Boethius, the *Ecclesiastical History of the English People* by Bede, *Pastoral Care* by Gregory the Great, the *Soliloquies* of St. Augustine, and the *World History* of Orosius. Alfred was determined that all sons of freemen would learn to read and write. His scriptoria produced manuscripts for use in education, and public schools were started.

Alfred was generous to the church and anxious to rule his people justly. He took the law codes of earlier rulers such as Offa of Mercia and Ine of Wessex and used them to create a new legal system for his kingdom. He founded two new monasteries at Athelny and Shaftesbury and also rebuilt other religious communities that had been destroyed during the wars with the Vikings. Alfred himself attended mass daily and was a deeply pious man.

As he did all these things, Alfred never forgot about the Danes. During the long peace that began in 878, Wessex ceased to be a plunderland for Vikings and became a formidable military power thanks to the efforts of Alfred. He built a network of twenty-five fortified boroughs that covered the whole country. He refortified London. He started a system of troop rotations, where half of his army would be armed and ready at all times while the other half would be dispersed. For designing ships to halt a sea-borne invasion, Alfred has been called the father of the British navy.

All these preparations would be tested when the Danes in East Anglia marched against Wessex in 893 and started a new war. The new defenses of Wessex held, the Viking force accomplished nothing more than raids against villages, and after four years of fighting with very little to show for it, their army simply melted away.

Seen at the end of his reign as the "Leader of the Christians," the "Saviour of the Saxons," and the model of a Christian ruler, Alfred died on 26 October 899 and was buried in Winchester, which was his capital.

In different ways, Alfred's status as a saint has been acknowledged throughout most of the Christian world. In the east, he is venerated as a saint by the Orthodox Church, and his feast day is October 26th. In his own country and in other parts of the Anglican Communion, he is regarded as a hero of the Christian Church and appears very often in the stained glass windows of Anglican churches. In both historical and theological works by Protestant authors, he has been called a saint. See C. L. Engström, *The Millenary of Alfred the Great, Warrior and Saint, Scholar and King* (1901) and C. W. Stubbs, *King Alfred, Patron Saint of England* (1901) and the work *Celebrating the Saints* cited below. For works by Catholic scholars which number him among the saints, see the books by Bunson and Walsh cited below.

His Line

Husband		**Wife**
Aethelwulf, King of Wessex (b. ca. 806 – d. 13 Jan 858)	+	md. (1) **Osburh** (b. ca. 810 – d. aft. 876)
St. Alfred the Great, King of Wessex (b. 849 – md. 868 – d. 26 Oct 899)	+	St. Eahlswith of Mercia (b. 852 – md. 868 – d. 904)
Edward "the Elder," King of England (b. 895 – md. (3) 919 – d. 924)	+	Eadgifu (md. 919 – d. 961)
Edmund I "the Magnificent," King of England (b. ca. 920 – murdered 26 May 946)	+	md. (1) St. Elgiva (d. 944)

Sources: *Ashley*, pp. 319–321; *Baring-Gould*, Vol. 16, p. 265; *BBKL*, Vol. 1, cols. 115–116; *Bunson*, pp. 66–67; *CE*, Vol. I, pp. 309–310; *CS*, pp. 628–631; *Delaney and Tobin*, p. 37; *Guiley*, pp. 9–10; *HBC*, pp. 23–26; *Snodgrass*, pp. 17–18; *Stuart*, line 233, nos. 40 through 37; *Walsh*, p. 27; *Weir*, pp. 9–11; *Weis, AR:* line 1, nos. 14 through 17; *Wells*, pp. 203–204; *Williamson*, pp. 18–19; *Woodruff*, pp. 36–37, 129, and 183

St. Arddun "Benasgell"

Arddun was the daughter of St. Pabo "Post Prydyn," a ruler of northern Britain. She was also the sister of Saints Dunawd Fawr and Sawyl Benisel. After St. Pabo and his family moved to northern Wales, Arddun married Brochwel "Ysgithrog," son of the king of Powys. In time, Brochwel became both king of Powys and a saint.

Brochwel and Arddun were the parents of St. Tysilio (or Suliau). Her nickname "Benasgell" means "wing-headed."

Her Line

Husband		Wife
St. Pabo "Post Prydyn" (the Pillar of Northern Britain) (b. ca. 430 – d. ca. 510)	+	**N.N.**
St. Brochwel "Ysgithrog," King of Powys (b. ca. 502 – d. ca. 560)	+	**St. Arddun "Benasgell"**
Cynan Garwyn	+	N.N.
Eiludd	+	N.N.
Beli	+	N.N.
Gwylog	+	N.N.
Elise	+	N.N.
Brochwel	+	N.N.
Cadell (d. 808)	+	N.N.
Gwriad ab Elidir (b. ca. 770)	+	**Nest ferch Cadell**
Merfyn "Frych" (the Freckled) (d. 844)	+	Esyllt ferch Cynan Dindaethwy
Rhodri "Mawr" (the Great), King of Wales (d. 878)	+	md. (1) Angharad ferch Meurig
Anarawd, Prince of Gwynedd (d. 916)	+	N.N.
Idwal Foel "the Bald," King of Gwynedd (d. 942)	+	Merddon ferch Cadwr
Meurig ab Idwal Foel (d. 986)	+	N.N.
Idwal ap Meurig ab Idwal Foel (d. 996)	+	N.N.
Iago ab Idwal, King of Gwynedd (d. 1039)	+	Afandreg ferch Gwair
Cynan ab Iago, King of Gwynedd (d. ca. 1060)	+	Ragnhildr (or Raguell)
Gryffudd ap Cynan, King of Gwynedd (b. ca. 1055 – md. (1) 1095 – d. 1137)	+	Angharad ferch Owain ab Edwin (md. (1) 1095 – d. 1162)
Owain I Gwynedd, King of North Wales (b. ca. 1100 – d. 28 Nov 1170)	+	md. (1) Gwladus ferch Llywarch ap Trahaearn (d. 1081)
Iorwerth Drwyndwn "the Flat Nosed," Prince of North Wales (d. ca. 1174)	+	Margred ferch Madog ap Maredudd

Llywelyn ab Iorwerth "the Great," Prince of North Wales (b. 1173 – d. 11 April 1240)	+	N.N.
Donald, 6th Earl of Mar (d. aft. 25 July 1297)	+	**Helen** (her 2nd marriage)
Robert I the Bruce, King of Scots (b. 11 July 1274 – md. (1) ca. 1295 – d. 7 June 1329)	+	**Isabel (or Isabella) of Mar** (md. ca. 1295 – d. bef. 1302)

Sources: *Baring-Gould and Fisher*, Vol. 1, pp. 167–168; *Boyer:* nos. 3 and 24 on pp. 63 and 65–66 + nos. 1, 2, 3, 5, 9, 13, 17, 20, 22, 24, 29, and 36 on pp. 281–283, 285–287, 289–294, 296, and 300–302; *Dunbar*, Vol. I, p. 83; *Holweck*, p. 102; *Rees*, p. 101; *Weis, AR:* line 176, nos. 5 through 7 + line 239, nos. 4 through 6 + line 252, no. 30

St. Arnulf,
Bishop of Metz

Arnulf was born on 13 August 582 and was the son of St. Bodegeisel, Governor of Aquitaine, and his wife St. Oda. Dode was the name of Arnulf's own wife, whom he married around 596.

In his youth Arnulf served King Theodebert II of Austrasia. He was admired as much for his valor in battle as for his wise counsel to the king. He became Mayor of the Palace and began to play a major role in public life. After king Theodebert died in 612, a power struggle broke out among all those who hoped to succeed him. The empty throne was almost taken by the descendants of Brunhilde, who had been one of the most conspicuously murderous players in local politics ever since 568. Arnulf along with Bl. Pepin of Landen and other members of the local nobility led a successful revolt against Brunhilde's party and put King Clotaire II of Neustria on the Austrasian throne.

After the revolt Arnulf and his wife Dode both decided to enter the religious life. She became a nun and entered a convent. He was on the point of entering a monastery when in 614 he was made bishop of Metz, the capital of Austrasia. For the next several years, he had both civil and ecclesiastical responsibilities. In addition, in 622 Clotaire II made Arnulf the tutor and chief adviser to Clotaire's son Dagobert I.

Around 627, Arnulf finally resigned all his duties and retired with his friend Romaric to a hermitage in the Vosges Mountains, which today is the abbey of Remiremont. Arnulf died in his hermitage on 16 August 640 and was taken back to Metz to be buried in the church named after him.

Arnulf was the father of St. Clodulf. Through his other son Ansgise, Arnulf would become an ancestor of the Carolingians. He is the patron saint of Metz.

His Line

Husband		Wife
St. Bodegeisel II, Governor of Aquitaine (murdered 588)	+	**St. Oda**, a Suevian (b. ca. 567 – d. ca. 640)
St. Arnulf (or Arnoul), Mayor of the Palace in Austrasia and Bishop of Metz (b. 13 Aug 582 – md. ca. 596 – d. 16 Aug 640)	+	Dode (or Clothilde) (b. ca. 586 – md. ca. 596)
Ansgise (or Ansegisel), Mayor of the Palace in Austrasia (b. 602 – md. bef. 639 – murdered 685)	+	St. Begga (b. ca. 613 – md. bef. 639 – d. ca. 698)
Pepin (or Pippin) of Heristal, Mayor of the Palace in Austrasia (b. ca. 635 – d. 16 Dec 714)	+	Aupais, a concubine (b. ca. 654)
Charles Martel "the Hammer," Mayor of the Palace in Austrasia, King of the Franks, and victor at the battle of Poitiers (b. ca. 688 – d. 22 Oct 741)	+	md. (1) Chrotrude (or Rotrou), Duchess of Austrasia (d. 724)

Pepin (or Pippin) III, "the Short," Mayor of the Palace in Austrasia and King of the Franks (b. 715 – md. ca. 740 – d. 24 Sept 768)	+	Bertha (or Bertrada) "Bigfoot" (b. ca. 720 – md. ca. 740 – d. 12 July 783)
Bl. Charlemagne, King of the Franks and First Emperor of the West (b. 2 April 747 – md. (2) 771 – d. 28 Jan 814)	+	Bl. Hildegarde, Countess of Vinzgau (b. 758 – md. 771 – d. 30 April 783)
Louis I "the Fair," King of France and Emperor of the West (b. Aug 778 – md. (2) 819 – d. 20 June 840)	+	Judith of Altdorf (or Judith of Bavaria) (b. ca. 800 – md. 819 – d. 19 April 843)
Charles II "the Bald," King of France and Italy, Emperor of the West (b. 13 June 823 – md. 13 Dec 842 – d. 6 Oct 877)	+	Ermentrude of Orleans (b. 29 Sept 830 – md. 13 Dec 842 – d. 6 Oct 869)
Baldwin I "Bras de Fer," Count of Flanders (md. 862 – d. 879)	+	**Judith** (b. ca. 844 – md. (3) 862 – d. aft. 870)
Baldwin II "the Bald," Count of Flanders (b. 863/865 – md. 884 – d. 918)	+	Aelfthryth (b. ca. 877 – md. 884 – d. 7 June 929), daughter of St. Alfred the Great
Arnulf (or Arnold) I "the Old," Count of Flanders and Artois (b. 885/890 – md. (2) 934 – d. 27 March 964)	+	Adelaide (or Adela or Alix) de Vermandois (b. ca. 915 – md. 934 – d. 958/960)
Baldwin III, Count of Flanders (b. ca. 940 – md. 961 – d. 1005)	+	Mathilda of Saxony (md. 961 – d. 1005)
Arnulf (or Arnold) II "the Young," Count of Flanders (b. 961/962 – md. 968 – d. 30 March 987)	+	Rosela (or Susanna), Princess of Italy (b. ca. 950 – md. 968 – d. 7 Feb or 13 Dec 1003)
Baldwin IV de Lille "the Bearded," Count of Flanders and Valenciennes (b. ca. 980 – md. (1) ca. 1012 – d. 30 May 1035)	+	Ogive (or Otgiva) of Luxemburg (b. ca. 995 – md. ca. 1012 – d. 21 Feb 1030)
Baldwin V de Lille, Count of Flanders (b. ca. 1013 – md. 1028 – d. 1 Sept 1067)	+	St. Adela (md. (2) 1028 – d. 8 Jan 1078/1079), daughter of Robert II, King of France
William I the Conqueror, Duke of Normandy and King of England (b. 1027/1028 – md. 1053 – d. 1087)	+	**Mathilde of Flanders** (b. 1032 – md. 1053 – d. 3 Nov 1083)

Sources: *Baring-Gould*, Vol. 8, pp. 435–436; *Benedictine Monks*, p. 83; *Bunson*, p. 122; *Butler*, Vol. III, p. 139; *CE*, Vol. I, p. 752; *Delaney and Tobin*, pp. 73–74; *Guiley*, p. 32; *Holweck*, p. 106; *NCE*, Vol. 1, p. 848; *Stuart:* line 171, nos. 47 through 39 + line 250 + line 235, nos. 38 through 36 + line 141; *Tucker:* Vol. I, pp. 182–186 and 313–315 + Vol. II, pp. 615–616; *Wagner*, p. 189; *Weis, AR:* line 190, nos. 7 through 13 + line 148, nos. 13 through 15 + line 162; *Wells*, pp. 135–137, 247–248, and 206

St. Ashken

Ashken was the daughter of Ashkhadar, King of Alania. Around 298/299, she married Tiridates "the Great," King of Armenia.

Miraculously cured of madness by St. Gregory "the Illuminator," Tiridates was baptized by Gregory, and so was Ashken. They both thus became the world's first Christian monarchs. Along with Tiridates, Ashken founded the Ripsimeyan Marturia, which commemorated several nuns martyred during earlier campaigns of persecution.

Later in life, Ashken decided to become a nun. She entered a convent along with Tiridates' sister St. Khosrowidukht, who had also become a nun. Both remained there the rest of their lives.

Tiridates and Ashken both became saints and are still mentioned in hymns of the Armenian church.

Her Line

Husband		Wife
Ashkhadar, King of Alania (or Ossetia)	+	N.N.
St. Tiridates "the Great," King of Armenia (b. ca. 280 – md. 298/299 – assassinated 330)	+	**St. Ashken** (md. 298/299)
Chosroes (or Khosrow) III, King of Armenia (d. 338)	+	N.N.
Athenagenes	+	**Bambishu** (b. 315)
St. Nerses (or Narces or Narses) I "the Great," Gregorid Prince and Bishop of Armenia (b. 335 – d. 373)	+	Samdukht
St. Isaac (or Sahak) I "the Great," Gregorid Prince and Bishop of Armenia (b. ca. 352 – d. 7 Sept 439)	+	N.N.
Hamazasp I, Prince of the Mamikonids and High Constable of Armenia (b. 345 – d. 416)	+	**Sahakanoysh**, the Gregorid heiress
St. Hmayeak Mamikonian, General and ambassador to Constantinople (b. 410 – d. 2 June 451 in battle)	+	Dzoyk, daughter of Vram, Prince of Rshtuni
Vard, Mamikonian Viceroy of Armenia (b. 450 – d. aft. 509)	+	N.N.
Hmayeak, Mamikonian Viceroy (d. 593)	+	N.N.
Moushegh I, Mamikonian Viceroy and High Constable of Armenia	+	N.N.
Vahan II, Mamikonian prince of Taraun (b. 555 – d. ca. 600)	+	N.N.
Dawith, a Mamikonian	+	N.N.

Hamazasp III, a Mamikonian maezpan and curopalate (b. 610 – d. 658)	+	N.N., a daughter of Theodore I, Prince of Rshtuni
Artavazd, a Mamikonian patrician (b. 650/655)	+	N.N.
Hmayeak, a Mamikonian patrician (b. 700 – d. ca. 788)	+	N.N.
Artavazd, a Mamikonian patrician (b. 740 – d. ca. 778)	+	N.N.
Hmayeak, a Mamikonian prince (b. 755 – d. 780/797)	+	N.N., a daughter of Leo V "the Armenian," Emperor of Byzantium
Konstantinos (b. 785), an officer at the court of Emperor Michael III	+	Pancalo
Bardas, magistros (b. 835 – d. ca. 867), brother of Emperor Basil I	+	N.N.
Basileos, rector	+	N.N.
Niketas Skleros, patrician (b. ca. 885 – liv. 921)	+	**Gregoria**
Konstantin Skleros, patrician at Constantinople (b. ca. 920 – md. ca. 950 – d. aft. 980)	+	Sophia Phokas (b. ca. 936 – md. ca. 950 – d. aft. 980)
Otto II, King of Italy and Emperor of the West (b. 955 – md. (2) 14 April 972 – d. 7 Dec 983)	+	**St. Theophano Skleros** (b. 956 – md. 14 April 972 – d. 15 Sept 991)

[For the later generations that connect this line to the kings of England, see the line of St. Adelaide of Burgundy in Part II.]

Sources: *Dowling*, pp. 53 and 55; *Holweck*, p. 111; *Kaloustian*, p. 17; *Koushagian*, p. 5; *Stone*, Chapter 8, Chart 80; *Stuart:* line 416, nos. 58 through 53 + line 322; *Wagner*, p. 194

St. Bathildis

Even among the saints, the life of St. Bathildis is remarkable.

A Christian girl born somewhere in Britain around the year 630, Bathildis' ancestry is unknown. When she was about 11, she was kidnapped by Vikings, taken across the Channel, and sold into slavery in the kingdom of Neustria, which would later become the northern part of France.

Bathildis was bought as a household slave by Erchinoald, who was mayor of the palace to the Neustrian king Clovis II. As Bathildis grew, Clovis—who was only slightly older than she was—not only noticed her but fell in love with her. He married her in 648 and made her his queen. They had three sons who would all become kings.

As queen, Bathildis was responsible for managing the royal court and distributing charitable funds. She founded monasteries and convents and enlarged the shrines of several saints. She also bought and freed many people who had been sold into slavery.

After almost nine years of marriage, Clovis died in 657, and Bathildis became regent for their son Clothaire III. As such, she was the de facto ruler of Neustria for several years until Clothaire finally came of age. As regent, she suppressed simony among the clergy, appointed several new bishops, and was genuinely interested in the reform of the Merovingian church. She also took steps to improve the lives of the less fortunate. Tax burdens on the poor were reduced. Christians could no longer be sold into slavery. Laws governing other slaves were made less harsh.

Once Clothaire assumed the throne, Bathildis became a Benedictine nun and entered a convent she had founded at Chelles near Paris. Refusing all honors and privileges, she worked for several years at menial jobs with other nuns. In her long final illness, she was often in intense pain which she bore with great patience. She died in January 680 and was buried in the convent.

Her Line

Husband		Wife
N.N.	+	**N.N.**
Clovis II, King of Neustria and Burgundy (md. 649 – d. insane ca. 657)	+	**St. Bathildis** (b. ca. 630 – md. 649 – d. Jan 680)
Theoderic III, King of Neustria and of all Franks (d. 691)	+	Clothilde
Martin of Laon	+	**Bertrada**
Caribert, Count of Laon (liv. 720–747)	+	Bertrada
Pepin (or Pippin) III "the Short," Mayor of the Palace in Austrasia and King of the Franks (d. 715 – md. ca. 740 – d. 24 Sept 768)	+	**Bertha (or Bertrada) "Bigfoot,"** (b. ca. 720 – md. ca. 740 – d. 12 July 783)
Bl. Charlemagne, King of the Franks and First Emperor of the West (b. 2 April 747 – md. (2) 771 – d. 28 Jan 814)	+	Bl. Hildegarde, Countess of Vinzgau (b. 758 – md. 771 – d. 30 April 783)

[For the later generations that connect this line to the kings of England, see the line of St. Arnulf, Bishop of Metz in Part II.]

Sources: *Benedictine Monks*, p. 108; *Bentley*, p. 26; *Bunson*, pp. 150–151; *Butler*, Vol. I, pp. 204–205; *CE*, Vol. II, pp. 348–349; *Chervin*, pp. 180–181; *Delaney*, p. 92; *Dunbar*, Vol. I, pp. 105–106; *Englebert*, p. 41; *Holweck*, p. 142; *Klaniczay*, pp. 77–78; *NCE*, Vol. 2, p. 164; *Parbury*, pp. 22–23; *Scherman*, *Birth of France*, pp. xi and 238; *Snodgrass*, p. 35; *Stuart:* line 123, nos. 47 through 45 + line 214, nos. 45 through 42 (no. 46 in this line is an error) + line 171, nos. 42 and 41; *Wood*, pp. 198–202; *WWH*, Vol. 2, p. 121

St. Begga

Begga was born in 613 and was the daughter of Bl. Pepin of Landen, Mayor of the Palace in Austrasia, and his wife Bl. Itta. Around 632, Begga married Duke Ansgise, who also became Mayor of the Palace.

Around 685/690, Ansgise died violently. Some sources say it was a hunting accident. Others say he was murdered. After his death, Begga went on a pilgrimage to Rome. When she returned, she built seven chapels representing the seven principal churches of Rome. These chapels were at Andenne on the river Meuse in Belgium. She also built a convent there, then became a nun, joined her own convent, and became its abbess.

Begga died on 17 December 694/695 and is buried in Andenne at St. Begga's Collegiate Church.

Begga was a sister of St. Gertrude of Nivelles. One of the sons of Ansgise and Begga was Pepin of Heristal, who is considered to be the founder of the Carolingian dynasty.

Her Line

Husband		Wife
Blessed Pepin (or Pippin) of Landen "the Old," Mayor of the Palace in Austrasia (b. ca. 585 – d. 640)	+	Bl. Itta (d. 652)
Angise (or Ansegisel), Mayor of the Palace in Austrasia (b. 602 – md. ca. 632 – murdered 685/ 690)	+	**St. Begga** (b. ca. 613 – md. ca. 632 – d. 17 Dec 694/695)
Pepin (or Pippin) of Heristal, Mayor of the Palace in Austrasia (b. ca. 635 – d. 16 Dec 714)	+	Aupais, a concubine (b. ca. 654)
Charles Martel "the Hammer," Mayor of the Palace in Austrasia, King of the Franks, and victor at the battle of Poitiers (b. ca. 688 – d. 22 Oct 741)	+	md (1) Chrotrude (or Rotrou), Duchess of Austrasia (d. 724)

[For the later generations that connect this line to the kings of England, see the line of St. Arnulf, Bishop of Metz in Part II.]

Sources: *Baring-Gould*, Vol. 15, p. 207; *BBKL*, Vol. 1, col. 459; *Benedictine Monks*, p. 110; *Bentley*, p. 241; *Bunson*, pp. 153–154; *Butler*, Vol. IV, p. 579; *Delaney*, p. 94; *Delaney and Tobin*, p. 117; *Dunbar*, Vol. I, pp. 111–112; *Holweck*, p. 145; *NCE*, Vol. 2, p. 224; *O'Malley*, pp. 41, 72, and 92; *Stuart:* line 260 + line 171, nos. 45 through 43; *Tucker*, Vol. I, pp. 182–183; *Wagner*, p. 189; *Weis, AR*, line 190, nos. 9 through 11; *Wells*, p. 135; *WWH*, Vol. 6, 180

St. Bertha

Bertha was born around 560 and was the daughter of Caribert I, King of Paris, and his wife Ingoberga. Around 578, Bertha married Aethelbert I, King of Kent.

Bertha is the person who actually began the conversion of England to Christianity. Bertha had been raised a Christian, but when she married Aethelbert, he was still a pagan. Their marriage contract provided that she could continue to practice her religion in pagan Kent and that she could bring her own chaplain with her. Once she was in England, Bertha's piety and other amiable qualities made a great impression on Aethelbert, who welcomed Christian missionaries in 597 and who finally asked to be baptized himself in 601.

There is a letter written by Pope Gregory I to Bertha in 601 in which he compliments her highly on her education and faith. He says that the conversion of the people of Kent was mostly due to her and urges her to continue the work of spreading Christianity.

Bertha died around 602 and was buried in Canterbury at the church of St. Martin's. Aethelbert died in 616 and was buried next to her. Like Bertha, he also became a saint.

Her Line

Husband		Wife
Caribert, King of Paris (liv. 520–575)	+	**Ingoberga** (d. 589)
St. Aethelbert (or Ethelbert) I, King of Kent (b. ca. 552 – md. ca. 578 – d. 24 Feb 616)	+	**St. Bertha** (b. ca. 560 – md. ca. 578 – d. ca. 602)
Eadbald, King of Kent (md. (2) ca. 618 – d. 640)	+	St. Emma (md. ca. 618)
Erconbert (or Eorconbeorht), King of Kent (b. ca. 624 – md. ca. 640 – d. 14 July 664)	+	St. Sexburga (md. ca. 640 – d. 6 July 699)

[For the later generations that connect this line to the kings of England, see the line of St. Aethelbert I, King of Kent in Part II.]

Sources: *Ashley*, pp. 215–217*; *Baring-Gould*, Vol. 2, pp. 406–409; *BBKL*, Vol. 1, col. 549; *Benedictine Monks*, p. 243*; *Bunson*, p. 165; *Butler*, Vol. I, pp. 414–415*; *Delaney and Tobin*, p. 137; *Dunbar*, Vol. I, p. 117; *HBC*, p. 12; *Holweck*, pp. 330–331*; *Joeckle*, p. 146*; *O'Malley*, p. 67*; *Stuart:* line 233A, no. 48 + line 233B, no. 48; *Wagner*, p. 188; *Wells*, p. 325; *Williamson*, p. 359; *WWH*, Vol. 2, p. 513 (sources marked with a * are accounts of the life of St. Aethelbert I which mention St. Bertha)

Bl. Blanche of Castile

Blanche was born on 4 March 1188 and was the daughter of Alfonso IX "the Noble," King of Castile, and his wife Eleanor, daughter of King Henry II of England. In the spring of 1200, Blanche's grandmother Eleanor of Aquitaine came to visit King Alfonso and his wife to help decide which one of their unmarried daughters would make a better bride for Prince Louis, son of King Louis VII of France. Blanche was selected, and Eleanor took her away to be married. On 23 May 1200, the thirteen-year-old Blanche married the twelve-year-old Louis.

Surprisingly, Louis and Blanche became the best of friends almost immediately, and their marriage was a very happy one. They had twelve children, seven of whom died young. Among the surviving children, their daughter Isabel would become Bl. Isabel, and their oldest son would become St. Louis IX of France.

Following his marriage, Blanche's husband spent most of his life waiting to become king. In 1223, he finally ascended the throne as Louis VIII of France. His reign would be short. After conducting a long siege in the summer of 1226 during the first crusade against the Cathars (which became known as the First Albigensian Crusade), Louis VIII was on his way back to Paris. Blanche and the twelve-year-old Louis IX had set out from Paris to meet him halfway. What began as a happy journey ended in tragedy. Before the family was reunited, Louis VIII contracted dysentery and died. In his final moments, he had appointed Blanche to be regent of France during the minority of Louis IX.

After receiving the terrible news, Blanche was mad with grief and even attempted suicide. Then she rallied. Realizing that it would be eight years until Louis IX reached the age of majority in 1234, she began to come to grips with the task of ruling France.

Contemporaries described Blanche as beautiful and even magnificent. She was also a very private person who had taught her children to pray frequently, protect their souls, and avoid sin. During the years she ruled alone, she was sustained by her love for her children and her deep spirituality. She collected relics, had close ties to several religious orders, and was very generous to the Church.

For the first four years of her regency, Blanche had to deal with constant conspiracies and revolts among the French nobles, who each believed that he could do a better job of running the country than Blanche. During this period, Blanche proved herself to be an able politician and an astute administrator. When force was necessary, she also organized and led military expeditions. In 1230, she finally broke the back of the nobles' rebellion.

Four years later in 1234, Blanche's son Louis IX married Margaret of Provence and began to rule in his own right. Although her regency officially ended, Blanche remained at her son's side as a virtual co-ruler. In the ten years of peace and prosperity that followed, Louis IX became the first king in Paris who could truly be called the "King of France."

By 1244, Blanche was fifty-six years old and looking forward to some form of retirement. Any such hope was definitely shattered when Louis IX announced that he had decided to personally lead a new Crusade to the Holy Land. In the four years that were needed to make all the necessary preparations, Blanche tried very hard to talk him out of it, but Louis believed it was his duty to God. Taking his wife Margaret with him, he departed in 1248 on the Seventh Crusade, leaving the sixty-year-old Blanche to rule in his absence.

Blanche kept the kingdom together and even raised a king's ransom to free Louis after he was captured by the Moslems, but she never saw her son again. Feeling that her life was almost over, in the fall of 1252 Blanche went to the Cistercian abbey of Maubuisson near Pontoise, put on a nun's habit, and lay down to die. On 27 November 1252 at the age of sixty-four, Blanche finally laid her burden down and was buried at Maubuisson. Louis did not learn of his mother's death until the summer of 1253, and he did not return to France until 1254, after an absence of six years.

For fourteen of the first twenty-six years of the reign of Louis IX, Blanche had been the actual ruler of France. It is no overstatement to say that Louis IX owed his realm to his mother. Without her, it is very debatable whether Louis IX would have been anything more than a child-king overthrown during his minority, let alone one of the greatest saints of medieval Europe.

Her Line

Husband		Wife
Alfonso IX "the Noble," King of Castile, Toledo, and Extramadura and victor at the battle of Los Navas de Tolosa (b. 11 Nov 1155 – md. 1170 – d. 5 Oct 1214)	+	**Eleanor** (b. 13 Oct 1162 – md. 1170 – d. 25 Oct 1214), daughter of Henry II, King of England
Louis VIII "the Lion," King of France (b. 5 Sept 1187 – md. 23 May 1200 – d. 8 Nov 1226)	+	**Bl. Blanche of Castile** (b. 4 March 1188 – md. 23 May 1200 – d. 27 Nov 1252)
Louis IX (known as "St. Louis"), King of France and Crusader (b. 25 April 1215 – md. 27 May 1234 – d. 25 Aug 1270 during the Eighth Crusade)	+	Margaret of Provence (b. 1221 – md. 27 May 1234 – d. 20/21 Dec 1295
Philip III "the Bold," King of France (b. 1 May 1245 – md. (1) 28 May 1262 – d. 5 Oct 1285)	+	Isabella (b. 1243 or 1247 – md. 28 May 1262 – d. 28 Jan 1271), daughter of James I "the Conqueror," King of Aragon
Philip IV "the Fair," King of France (b. 1268 – md. 16 Aug 1284 – d. 29 Nov 1314)	+	Jeanne of Navarre (b. Jan 1272 – md. 16 Aug 1284 – d. 2 April 1305)
Edward II, king of England (b. 25 April 1284 – md. 25 Jan 1308 – murdered 21 Sept 1327)	+	**Isabella** (b. 1292 – md. 25 Jan 1308 – d. 27 Aug 1357)

Sources: *BBKL*, Vol. 17, cols. 127–128; *Dunbar*, Vol. I, pp. 123–125; *Klaniczay*, pp. 235–236 and Appendix B, Geneal. Table 10; *NCE*, Vol. 2, p. 602; *O'Callaghan*, p. 253; *Pernoud*; *Snodgrass*, p. 42; *Stuart:* line 83, no. 27 + line 88, nos. 28 and 27; + line 70, nos. 27 through 25 + line 51, nos. 25 through 23; *Tucker*, Vol. I, pp. 191 and 175–177; *Weis, AR:* line 113, nos. 27 and 28 + line 101, nos. 27 through 31; *Wells*, pp. 141 and 256–257; *WWH*, Vol. 2, pp. 608–614

St. Bodegeisel II, Governor of Aquitaine

Bodegeisel II was the son of St. Gondolfus, Bishop of Tongres, and his wife Palatina of Troyes. He married St. Oda, a Suevian. Their son was St. Arnulf, Bishop of Metz.

Bodegeisel served the state and the Church. He was first appointed to be governor of Aquitaine. On the Meuse River near Metz, he also founded the monastery of St. Martin-aux-Chênes, where later in life he became a monk and then the abbot. While returning from a diplomatic mission to Constantinople, he was murdered at Carthage in 588.

His Line

Husband		Wife
St. Gondolfus, Bishop of Tongres (liv. 599)	+	**Palatina of Troyes**
St. Bodegeisel II, Governor of Aquitaine (murdered 588)	+	St. Oda, a Suevian (b. ca. 567 – d. ca. 640)
St. Arnulf (or Arnoul), Mayor of the Palace in Austrasia and Bishop of Metz (b. 13 Aug 582 – md. ca. 596 – d. 16 Aug 640)	+	Dode (or Clothilde) (b. ca. 586 – md. ca. 596)
Ansgise (or Ansegisel), Mayor of the Palace in Austrasia (b. 602 – md. bef. 639 – murdered 685)	+	St. Begga (b. ca. 613 – md. bef. 639 – d. ca. 698)
Pepin (or Pippin) of Heristal, Mayor of the Palace in Austrasia (b. ca. 635 – d. 16 Dec 714)	+	Aupais, a concubine (b. ca. 654)
Charles Martel "the Hammer," Mayor of the Palace in Austrasia, King of the Franks, and victor at the battle of Poitiers (b. ca. 688 – d. 22 Oct 741)	+	md. (1) Chrotrude (or Rotrou), Duchess of Austrasia (d. 724)

[For the later generations that connect this line to the kings of England, see the line of St. Arnulf, Bishop of Metz in Part II.]

Sources: *Baring-Gould*, Vol. 15, pp. 220–221; *Benedictine Monks*, p. 127; *Delaney and Tobin*, p. 150; *Holweck*, p. 163; *Stuart*, line 171, nos. 48 through 43; *Wagner*, p. 189; *Weis, AR*, line 190, nos. 6 through 11

St. Boris I,
Khan of the Bulgars

Boris was the son of Presnian, a military leader in Bulgaria. Boris married Marija and became the ruler of Bulgaria in 852. At the beginning of his 47-year reign, Bulgaria was still a pagan country. In the wider world, the rivalry between Rome and Constantinople that would ultimately lead to the great schism between Western and Eastern Christianity was just beginning to heat up.

Born a pagan, Boris's interest in Christianity was not shared by most of Bulgaria's nobility. In 864, Boris, his family, and some of Bulgaria's nobles were baptized by priests from Constantinople. The rest of the pagan nobility revolted against Boris, and this revolt only ended when Boris executed most of the rebels and their families.

For the rest of his reign, Boris asked for advice from the West and from the East about how to build a national church in a newly Christian nation. The national church he ultimately created was independent of both Rome and Constantinople. Both Catholic and Byzantine priests were allowed into the country to baptize and bless people. Religious educators who wanted to establish permanent centers of instruction were particularly welcome and were generously subsidized by Boris. The Slavonic language used by many of the missionaries that came to Bulgaria and the Cyrillic alphabet in which they wrote soon became the first written language of Bulgaria.

In 889, Boris abdicated in favor of his son Vladimir and went off to live in a monastery. When Vladimir tried to reestablish the old pagan religion, Boris came out of his monastery in 893, defeated Vladimir on the battlefield, and blinded him. Boris then made his other son Simeon the ruler of Bulgaria and returned to his monastery. Boris came out of retirement one more time around 895 to help Simeon beat back an invasion of Magyars and Byzantines.

Boris died on 2 May 907 and became the first saint of the national church that he had created. Simeon would go on to become Simeon "the Great," the first ruler of Bulgaria's golden age.

Boris is also known as Boris-Mikhail.

His Line

Husband		Wife
Presnian, a military leader (d. 849)	+	**N.N.**
St. Boris I, Khan of the Bulgars (d. 2 May 907)	+	Marija
Nikola Kumet, Count in West Bulgaria	+	Ripsimija
Aaron Amitopulos of Bulgaria (liv. 988)	+	N.N.
John Wladislaw, Tsar of West Bulgaria (slain in 1018)	+	Marie of Byzantium, a "girdled Patrician"
Troianos (or Trajan), Tsar of West Bulgaria	+	N.N., a niece of John I Tzimisces, Emperor of Byzantium

Andronikos Doukas, protovestiarios (b. by 1045 – md. bef. 1066 – d. 14 Oct 1077)	+	**Maria of Bulgaria** (md. bef. 1066 – d. by 1118)
Alexius I (Alexios I Komnenos), Emperor of Byzantium (b. ca. 1048 – d. 15 Aug 1118)	+	md. (2) **St. Irene Doukaina** (b. 1066 – d. 19 Feb 1127)
Konstantinos Angelos, a general of Byzantium in the war with the Normans	+	**Theodora Komnene** (b. ca. 1070 – d. 20 Feb 1116)
Andronikos Angelos Doukas, a general in the civil and Moslem wars and Ambassador to Jerusalem (md. by 1155 – blinded 1182/1183 – d. by Dec 1185)	+	Euphrosyne Kastamonitissa (md. by 1155 – d. 1185/1195)
Isaac (or Isaakios) II Angelos, Emperor of Byzantium (b. ca. 1155 – blinded and executed by his brother in 1204)	+	md. (1) Eirene Komnena, daughter of Andronicus I Comnenus, Emperor of Byzantium
Philip von Hohenstaufen, Duke of Tuscany and Swabia and Emperor of Germany (b. 1176 – md. 25 May 1197 – murdered 21 June 1208)	+	**Eirene (or Maria) Angelina** (b. ca. 1181 – md. (2) 25 May 1197 – murdered 27 Aug 1208)
Henry II "the Courageous," Duke of Brabant and Lorraine (b. 1207 – md. (1) by 22 Aug 1215 – d. 1 Feb 1248)	+	**Maria von Hohenstaufen** (b. 1201 – md. by 22 Aug 1215 – d. 1235)
Robert I, Count of Artois and Crusader (b. Sept 1216 – md. 14 June 1237 – slain 9 Feb 1250 while crusading in Egypt with his brother St. Louis)	+	**Matilda of Brabant** (md. 14 June 1237 – d. 29 Sept 1288)
Henry I, King of Navarre (b. ca. 1244 – md. (2) 1269 – d. 22 July 1274)	+	**Blanche of Artois** (b. ca. 1248 – md. (1) 1269 – d. 2 May 1302)
Philip IV "the Fair," King of France (b. 1268 – md. 16 Aug 1284 – d. 29 Nov 1314)	+	**Jeanne of Navarre** (b. Jan 1272 – md. 16 Aug 1284 – d. 2 April 1305)
Edward II, King of England (b. 25 April 1284 – md. 25 Jan 1308 – murdered 21 Sept 1327)	+	**Isabella** (b. 1292 – md. 25 Jan 1308 – d. 27 Aug 1357)

Sources: *Holweck*, p. 168; *Klaniczay*, pp. 99–100; *NCE*, Vol. 2, p. 710; *Poulos*, Vol. 2, pp. 123–124; *Snodgrass*, pp. 45–46; *Stuart:* line 309, nos. 39 through 33 + line 215, no. 33 through 28 + line 125, nos. 28 through 26 + line 147, nos. 26 and 25 + line 81, nos. 25 and 24 + line 51, nos. 24 and 23; *Wells*, pp. 104, 121, 123, 124, 272, 89, 36, 424, and 257

St. Brochwel "Ysgithrog," King of Powys

Brochwel was born around 502 and was the son of Cyngen Glodrydd, King of Powys, and his wife Tudclyd. He married St. Arddun "Benasgell," daughter of St. Pabo "Post Prydyn," and was the father of St. Tysilio.

Brochwel succeeded his father as king of Powys. His capital was at Shrewsbury, and his palace was on the spot where St. Chad's Church now stands.

In old Welsh poetry, Brochwel is called a warrior hero. His nickname "Ysgithrog" can be translated as "of the tusk," "of the canine teeth," or "of the fangs." It may refer to his own very large teeth, or to horns on his helmet, or to his aggressiveness as a warrior.

Brochwel died around 560.

His Line

Husband		Wife
Cyngen Glodrydd, King of Powys	+	**Tudclyd**
St. Brochwel "Ysgithrog," King of Powys (b. ca. 5o2 – d. ca. 560)	+	St. Arddun "Benasgell"
Cynan Garwyn	+	N.N.
Eiludd	+	N.N.
Beli	+	N.N.
Gwylog	+	N.N.
Brochwel	+	N.N.
Cadell (d. 808)	+	N.N.
Gwriad ab Elidir (b. ca. 770)	+	**Nest ferch Cadell**
Merfyn "Frych" (the Freckled) (d. 844)	+	Esyllt ferch Cynan Dindaethwy
Rhodri "Mawr" (the Great), King of Wales (d. 878)	+	md. (1) Angharad ferch Meurig

[For the later generations that connect this line to the kings of Scotland, see the line of St. Arddun "Benasgell" in Part II.]

Sources: *Baring-Gould and Fisher*, Vol. 1, pp. 301–303; *Boyer:* no. 3 on p. 63 + no. 24 on pp. 65–66 + nos. 1 and 2 on pp. 281–282; *Butler*, Vol. IV, p. 296 (under "Tysilio"); *Holweck*, pp. 172 and 991 (under "Tudclyd"); *Rees*, pp. 101 and 103

St. Brychan, Ruler of Brecknock

Brychan was born around 480/490 and was the son of Anlach, an Irish prince, and his wife St. Marchell. Brychan was born in Ireland, but his parents moved from Ireland to Wales while he was still quite young.

Brychan was the founder of the Welsh kingdom of Brycheiniog (or Brecknock). This kingdom continued until about 940, when it became part of the kingdom of Deheubarth. In 1093, Deheubarth itself disappeared from the map when Bernard de Neufmarché conquered it and made it a part of his new marcher lordship.

Brychan was a pious king and a patron of the Church, but there are several factual disputes about his life that are unlikely to ever be resolved.

One such dispute is about the number and identity of his wives (perhaps 3). There is an even greater dispute over the number of his children. The total number suggested by scholars varies from twelve to sixty-three. What is certain is that many of the people who have been called children of Brychan became saints. Another certainty is that there are many churches dedicated to people who have been called children of Brychan in Wales, southeastern Ireland, Cornwall, and Brittany. Some of his children are mentioned so often in the ancient records that they and their parents have been called "one of the three saintly clans of Britain" (the children of St. Cunedda and St. Caw are the others).

Some sources say that Brychan lived to a very old age, became a monk, and died a hermit. Others say that he was slain by Saxons at Mertyr Tydvil in Wales. He may be buried in Wales on Ynys Brychan (Lundy Island).

His Line

Husband		Wife
Anlach, an Irish prince	+	**St. Marchell**
St. Brychan, ruler of Brecknock in South Wales (b. 480/490)	+	N.N.
St. Gabran mac Domangart, King of Dalriada (b. ca. 500 – md. bef. 532 – d. ca. 559)	+	**St. Lleian** (md. bef. 532)
Aidan (or Aedan) mac Gabran (b. 532 – d. 606), crowned King of Dalriada by St. Columba of Iona	+	N.N.
Eochaid Buide, King of the Picts and of Dalriada (d. 629)	+	N.N.
Domnall Brec, King of Dalriada (d. ca. 642 in the battle of Strathcarron)	+	N.N., daughter of Widfroith
Domangart (or Domongart), did not rule (d. prob. 673)	+	N.N.

Eochaid II "Crooked Nose," King of Dalriada (killed in battle ca. 697 after ruling ca. 3 years)	+	Spondana, a Pictish princess
Eochaid III, King of Dalriada (d. 733)	+	N.N.
Aed Find "the White," King of Dalriada (liv. 778)	+	N.N.
Eochaid IV "the Poisonous," King of Dalriada (d. 789)	+	Fergusa, daughter of Fergus, King of Dalriada
Alpin mac Eochaid, King of Dalriada (b. ca. 778 – killed 20 July 841 in battle)	+	N.N.
Kenneth MacAlpin (or Cinaed), King of the Picts and Scots (b. ca. 810 – d. 859)	+	N.N.
St. Constantine I, King of Scotland (b. ca. 836 – slain 877 in battle with the Norsemen)	+	N.N.
Donald (or Domnall), King of Scotland (b. ca. 862 – d. 900)	+	N.N.
Malcolm I, King of Scotland (killed 954 by the men of Moray)	+	N.N.
Kenneth (or Cinead), King of Scotland (b. ca. 954 – murdered 995 by his own men)	+	N.N.
Malcolm II, King of Scotland (b. ca. 954 – murdered 25 Nov 1034)	+	N.N.
Crinan the Thane, Earl of Strathclyde and Lord of the Isles (b. 978 – md. ca. 1000 – slain 1045)	+	**Bethoc** (b. ca. 984 – md. ca. 1000)
Duncan I (or Duncan mac Crinan), King of Scotland (b. ca. 1001/1005 – md. ca. 1030 – murdered 14 Aug 1040 by Macbeth)	+	Sibil (b. ca. 1009 – md. ca. 1030)
Malcolm III Canmore, King of Scotland (b. ca. 1031 – md. (2) 1068/1069 – d. in battle 13 Nov 1093 while besieging Alnwick Castle)	+	St. Margaret of Scotland (b. ca. 1045 – md. 1068/1069 – d. 16 Nov 1093)
Henry I, King of England (b. 1070 – md. (1) 11 Nov 1100 – d. 1 Dec 1135)	+	**Mathilda (or Eadgyth) of Scotland** (b. 1079 – md. 11 Nov 1100– d. 1 June 1118)

Sources: *Ashley*, pp. 158 and 197; *Baring-Gould*, Vol. 16, p. 129; *Baring-Gould and Fisher*, Vol. 1, pp. 303–321; *Delaney and Tobin*, p. 183; *Holweck*, p. 174; *Rees*, pp. 151–158; *Stuart*, line 165, nos. 49 through 30; *Weis, AR*, line 170, nos. 4 through 21; *Wells*, p. 177

St. Cadwalader, King of Gwynedd

Cadwalader was born around 633 and was the son of Cadwallon, King of Gwynedd, and his wife Alcfrith. Cadwallon died in battle around 634, but Cadwalader did not succeed him until about 655.

Like earlier Welsh rulers, Cadwalader assumed the title "King of the Britons." Like them he fought against the Saxon invaders who were trying to establish themselves in Britain. His efforts in this struggle became the stuff of legend. In his *History of the Kings of Britain*, Geoffrey of Monmouth calls Cadwalader the last native ruler of Britain. He is remembered in Welsh texts almost like another Arthur. His standard was the red dragon, which was later adopted by Henry VII of England, who claimed descent from him.

Among his own people, Cadwalader was highly regarded as a good and pious ruler. He established at least three religious foundations in Gwynedd and was called Cadwalader "Fendigaid" (the Blessed). There are many churches dedicated to him.

Cadwalader died in a plague around 682 and is believed to be buried in Wales in Llangadwaldr Church ("the Church of Cadwaladr") on Ynys Mon in Anglesey. According to his legend, he will return one day to lead the Britons to victory over their enemies.

His Line

Husband		Wife
Cadwallon ap Cadfan ab Iago ap Beli, King of Gwynedd (killed in battle 634)	+	**Alcfrith**, a sister of Penda, King of Mercia
St. Cadwalader "Fendigaid," King of Gwynedd (b. ca. 633 – d. 682)	+	N.N.
Idwal Iwrch (b. ca. 670)	+	N.N.
Rhodri Molwynog (d. 754)	+	N.N.
Cynan Dindaethwy, Prince of the island of Anglesey (d. 816)	+	N.N.
Merfyn "Frych" (the Freckled) (d. 844)	+	**Esyllt ferch Cynan Dindaethwy**
Rhodri "Mawr" (the Great), King of Wales (d. 878)	+	md. (1) Angharad ferch Meurig

[For the later generations that connect this line to the kings of Scotland, see the line of St. Arddun "Benasgell" in Part II.]

Sources: *Ashley*, pp. 146–147; *Baring-Gould*, Vol. 16, p. 280; *Baring-Gould and Fisher*, Vol. 2, pp. 43–46; *Benedictine Monks*, p. 139; *Boyer:* nos. 24, 27, 30, 33, and 35 on pp. 70–71 + nos. 1 and 2 on pp. 281–282; *Delaney and Tobin*, p. 193; *Holweck*, p. 176; *Tucker*, Vol. II, p. 886

Bl. Carloman,
Mayor of the Palace in Austrasia

Carloman was born in 707 and was the eldest son of Charles Martel and his first wife Chrotrude. When Charles died in 741, Carloman succeeded Charles as ruler of Austrasia. Carloman's brother Pippin the Short became ruler of Neustria.

Toward real or perceived opponents, Carloman could be ruthless. He fought successful wars against the Saxons, the Swabians, the Bavarians, and the dukes of Aquitaine. In 746 at Cannstatt, he convened an assembly of the leaders of the Alamanni, then arrested all of them for treason, and executed them.

Carolman was more than a war leader. He founded several abbeys and helped St. Boniface, the "Apostle to the Germans," in his efforts to spread Christianity in central Europe. Most notably, on 15 August 747 Carloman abdicated in favor of his brother Pippin and became a monk. He received his habit from the hand of Pope Zacharias and entered a monastery.

Carloman's final home was the monastery at Monte Cassino, where he worked as a shepherd and in the kitchen. He died on 17 August 754 and is buried at Monte Cassino.

When Carloman abdicated, Pippin's son Charlemagne was not yet six months old. Pippin himself died in 768, and the age of Charlemagne began.

His Line

Husband		Wife
Charles Martel, "the Hammer," Mayor of the Palace in Austrasia, King of the Franks, and victor at the battle of Poitiers (b. ca. 688 – d. 22 Oct 741)	+	md. (1) **Chrotrude (or Routrou)**, Duchess of Austrasia (d. 724)
Bl. Carloman, Mayor of the Palace in Austrasia (b. 707 – d. 17 Aug 754)	+	N.N.
Girard, Count of Paris (liv. 743–755)	+	**Rotrou**
Begue, Count of Paris (d. 816)	+	Aupais (or Alpis), a daughter of Charlemagne
Hunroch (or Unruoch), Margrave of Friuli and Count of Ternois (d. 853)	+	**Engeltrude (or Engeltron)**
Amadeus, Count of Burgundy (d. aft. 827)	+	N.N.
Anscar II "the Burgundian," Count of Orcheret and Marquis of Ivrea (d. 891/898)	+	Giselle
Adalbert I, Marquis of Ivrea (b. 880/885 – md. (1) bef. 900 – d. 923/925)	+	Gisela of Friuli, Princess of Italy (b. 880/890 – md. bef. 900 – d. 13 June 910)
Berenger II, Marquis of Ivrea and King of Italy (md. 936 – d. 6 July 966)	+	Willa of Arles (md. 936 – d. aft. 966)

Arnulf (or Arnold) II "the Young," Count of Flanders (b. 961/962 – md. 968 – d. 30 March 987)	+	**Rosela (or Susanna)**, Princess of Italy (b. ca. 950 – md. 968 – d. 7 Feb or 13 Dec 1003)

[For the later generations that connect this line to the kings of England, see the line of St. Arnulf, Bishop of Metz in Part II.]

Sources: *Benedictine Monks*, p. 149; *Delaney and Tobin*, p. 212; *Holweck*, p. 190; *NCE*, Vol. 3, pp. 111–112; *Stuart*: line 269, nos. 44 through 40 + line 332, nos. 40 through 35; *Warncke*, pp. 148–149; Weis, *AR:* line 191, nos. 11 through 15 + line 146, nos. 17 through 19

St. Ceneu

Ceneu was the son of St. Coel Hen, a ruler of northern Britain, and his wife Ystradwel ferch Gadeon. He lived from about 400 to 450.

When Coel died, Ceneu inherited the portion of his father's kingdom that was located around York. Like his father Coel and like his own son St. Pabo "Post Prydyn" (the Pillar of Northern Britain), Ceneu not only defended his people against invaders but also maintained their Roman Christian beliefs against the invaders' heathen gods.

Also like his father, Ceneu did not escape the attention of the mythmakers. Geoffrey of Monmouth wrote about how Ceneu attended the coronation of King Arthur. In the novel *The Coming of the King* written almost a thousand years later, the author Nikolai Tolstoy begins his story with a meeting between Ceneu and Merlin.

His Line

Husband		Wife
St. Coel Hen (or Coel Godebog), a ruler of northern Britain (b. ca. 370 – d. 420/430)	+	**Ystradwel ferch Gadeon**
St. Ceneu, a ruler of northern Britain (b. ca. 400 – d. ca. 450)	+	N.N.
St. Pabo "Post Prydyn" (the Pillar of Northern Britain) (b. ca. 430 – d. ca. 510)	+	N.N.
St. Brochwel "Ysgithrog," King of Powys (liv. 570)	+	**St. Arddun "Benasgell"**

[For the later generations that connect this line to the kings of Scotland, see the line of St. Arddun "Benasgell" in Part II.]

Sources: *Ashley*, pp. 96–99; *Baring-Gould and Fisher*, Vol. 2, p. 156; *Boyer*, nos. 1, 2, and 3 on p. 63; *Holweck*, p. 202; *Stuart*, line 405A, no. 57

St. Ceolwald

Ceolwald was born around 622 and was the son of a war leader in Wessex named Cutha.

For most of his life, Ceolwald was a pagan and a warrior in Wessex. In the early 680's, the throne of the country became vacant, and several claimants stepped forward. Ceolwald was one of them. Starting in 685, he and his followers decided to win the throne of Wessex by going to war with the other contenders.

A period of savage fighting ensued. During his first campaign, Ceolwald managed to kill the reigning claimant but was then driven out of the country. When he returned to begin his second campaign, Ceolwald triumphed against all of his opponents, and all of Wessex was his.

After consolidating his hold on Wessex, Ceolwald began to expand his realm by warring on his neighbors. He took Sussex first and then Kent, and then he attacked the Isle of Wight.

While fighting on the Isle of Wight, Ceolwald was severely wounded. As he convalesced, he began to reflect on all the suffering caused by his wars. After several conversations with St. Wilfrid, he came to a remarkable decision. In the summer of 688, Ceolwald gave up all his captured territories, abdicated his throne, and set out for Rome to be baptized there.

Ceolwald reached Rome and on Holy Saturday in 689 was baptized in the presence of Pope Sergius. He fell ill almost immediately and died ten days later on 20 April 689, still wearing his white baptismal gown.

Ceolwald is also known as Cadwalla, Caedwalla, and Ceadwalla. He is buried in Rome in the crypt of St. Peter's Basilica.

His Line

Husband		Wife
Cutha (or Cuthwulf), a war leader in Wessex	+	**N.N.**
St. Ceolwald, a war leader in Wessex (b. ca. 622 – d. 20 April 689)	+	N.N.
Cenred, a war leader in Somerset (liv. 644–694)	+	N.N.
Ingild (b. ca. 680 – d. 718)	+	N.N.
Eoppa	+	N.N.
Eafa (b. ca. 732)	+	N.N.
Eahlmund (or Edmund), King of Kent (b. ca. 758 – d. 786)	+	N.N., a daughter of Aethelbert II, King of Kent
Egbert "the Great," King of Wessex (b. 775 – d. 4 Feb 839)	+	Redburga (or Raedburh) (b. ca. 788)
Aethelwulf, King of Wessex (b. ca. 806 – d. 13 Jan 858)	+	md. (1) Osburh (b. ca. 810 – d. aft. 876)

St. Alfred the Great, King of Wessex (b. 849 – md. 868 – d. 26 Oct 899)	+	St. Eahlswith of Mercia (b. ca. 852 – md. 868 – d. 904)

Sources: *Benedictine Monks*, p. 156; *Butler*, Vol. II, p. 134; *Cruz*, pp. 121–123; *Holweck*, p. 199; *Stuart*, line 233, nos. 48 through 39; *Weis, AR*, line 1, nos. 6 through 15

Bl. Charlemagne, King of the Franks and First Emperor of the West

Later known as Carolus Magnus, Charlemagne, or Charles the Great, Charles was born on 2 April 747. He was the eldest son of Pepin III "the Short," King of the Franks, and his wife Bertha "Bigfoot." Of his childhood and upbringing nothing is known. He was crowned king of the Franks in 768, and he became the greatest European monarch of the Middle Ages.

Charles the Man

Charles stood out in a crowd. Measurements of his skeleton in 1861 confirmed that he was six feet four inches tall, which was an extraordinary height among medieval men. His head was round and well-formed. He had very large and animated eyes, fair hair, and a merry, cheerful face. His voice was a little high. Although he had a paunch, he was very athletic and liked to go riding, hunting, and swimming. He enjoyed excellent health throughout his life.

Mentally, Charles was also far above average. During his main meal of the day, he liked to have a book read aloud or to hear music. His patronage attracted the leading scholars in Europe to his court. No one is certain what his native language was. It may have been Old Low Franconian or an Old High German dialect. He definitely read and spoke Latin, and he also knew some Greek. Although he never learned to write any of his languages, his speech could make a profound impression. Long before the word charisma was invented, he seemed to possess an abundance of it.

Married four times, Charles also had six known concubines and was the father of at least sixteen children. In order, his wives were Desiderata (married 770 – annulled 771), Hildegarde (married 771 – died 783), Fastrada (married 784 – died 794), and Luitgard (married 794 – died ca. 800). Charles loved all his children and took pains to educate them. As his court moved regularly from one palace to another, his entire family would come with him.

Charles the Warrior

Charles inherited one of the major kingdoms of the Dark Ages and turned it into medieval Europe's greatest state. The early death of his brother Carloman made Charles the sole heir of his father, and what he received was modern France, the western part of Germany, and also Belgium, Luxemburg, and the Netherlands. Under his leadership, his armies would increase his inheritance substantially.

Charles enjoyed combat, and he made warfare a national institution of the Franks. From 773 until 805, Charles was almost continuously at war on many fronts and with a few exceptions was usually successful. The three campaigns that did the most to expand his realm were the conquest of the Saxons which began in 772 and would take thirty years to complete, the conquest of the Avars which began in 791 and was completed in 805, and the conquest of Lombardy which began in 773 and was completed in

774. By the end of the Saxon war, Charles controlled all of modern Germany. From the Avars, he took most of modern Austria. From the Lombards, he acquired northern and central Italy.

Charles the Ruler

In governing his realm, Charles was startlingly modern. He divided his empire into counties and hundreds. He appointed counts and hundredmen to govern their respective districts. Four times a year, royal inspectors travelled through their assigned territories and reported back directly to the court of Charles. Each spring, temporal and spiritual lords from the whole empire would gather at an annual parliament to discuss imperial affairs. At the conclusion of each parliament, Charles would issue decrees that were to be followed throughout the empire. Its regions were otherwise free to follow their own traditional laws, which Charles was very interested in codifying.

Apart from a revolt in 785 by a Thuringian noble named Hadrad and another revolt in 792 by Charles' illegitimate son Pippin, Charles never had great cause to complain about any of the men who ruled regions of the empire on his behalf. By dividing up and distributing conquered territories and sharing the other spoils of war, Charles gradually gained the loyalty of a warrior class consisting of 250 to 300 counts and their followers. By the early 800's, Charles' abilities as a leader and a warrior had made him the preeminent figure in Europe.

Charles and the Church

The pope in Rome—and perhaps Christianity in Europe—was saved more than once by the armies of Charles.

Charles first rescued the pope and the church just a few years after his coronation in 768. From his father Pepin, Charles had inherited the duty to protect the rights and lands of the Papacy, and in the early 770's this was no small promise. The pope's lands bordered on the kingdom of Lombardy. The Lombard king Desiderius coveted the pope's territories and in 772 launched an invasion. Pope Adrian I avoided being captured and appealed to Charles for help. In 773, Charles led an army south, and after a year of war, Desiderius was vanquished, and Charles was the new king of Lombardy. On Easter Sunday 774, Pope Adrian I consecrated Charles as the champion of the Catholic Church.

The next crisis in the life of the church began on 25 April 799. Adrian I had died, Leo III had been elected the new pope, and relatives of Adrian who had hoped to keep the papacy in their own family were very unhappy that Leo had been chosen. One day Leo III was making his way through Rome in a street procession when several men rushed forward from the crowd, attacked him, beat him severely, and then imprisoned him. While he was locked up, Leo recovered from his wounds, escaped from his prison, and went straight to Charles. In November 800, Charles and his troops escorted Leo back to Rome. In a great council held on December 23, the parties to the conspiracy were found guilty. At Leo's request, their death sentences were commuted to exile.

As for the future, Leo was much more hard-headed. Similar conspiracies could not be allowed to arise again. Leo thought that sovereign rule over the city of Rome needed to be entrusted to a neutral party who would have no vested interest in any future struggles for the papal throne that might arise between local families. Leo believed that most Romans would only accept a new Roman emperor as their ultimate ruler. The Byzantine emperor ruling in Constantinople was unsatisfactory for several reasons. There was one other possibility, however, and it was Charles, whose military conquests had created a new empire in the West. So it was that during mass on 25 December 800, Leo placed a crown on Charles' head and said, "Hail to Charles the Augustus, crowned of God, the great and peace-bringing Emperor of the Romans." At this moment, a new political formation arose in Europe which historians would later call the Holy Roman Empire, and Charles had been crowned its first emperor.

How to care for the spiritual needs of his people was a subject that always preoccupied Charles. In war he saw his army as God's instrument. Before doing battle with the Avars in 791, the Frankish army prayed and fasted for three days. As it headed into battle, its clergy walked barefoot before it singing psalms. Back in his palace between campaigns, Charles took an active part in the settlement of theological questions and issued many rules governing the lives of the clergy. He built hundreds of churches and other ecclesiastical buildings. Dismayed over the number of priests who could not read the Bible, he established schools to make them literate and other programs of religious instruction for the laity.

The Legacy of Charles

After a reign of forty-seven years and a brief illness, Charles died on 28 January 814 and was buried in the octagonal Pfalz Chapel in Aachen. Immediately hailed as one of the great men of history, the end of his mortal life was the beginning of his immortality.

The extent to which he unified Europe into a single state captured the imaginations of later kings, conquerors, and political leaders almost from the moment of his death down to the present day.

The flowering of art, architecture, literature, and scholarship that occurred during his reign and the era that followed were called the Carolingian Renaissance.

Christianity remembered Charles as the soldier of God, the champion of the faith, and the builder of a vast number of churches throughout his empire. Pronounced holy by a court bishop soon after his death, he continued to receive religious honors for the next several centuries. Within a few decades of his death, his name appeared in a calendar of saints, and popular veneration of him grew rapidly, especially in Germany and France. He was ultimately so highly regarded in Germany that he was once again pronounced a saint there about 350 years after his death. Specifically, on 29 December 1165 relics of his body were brought into the Marien-kirche in Cologne, and archbishop Rainald of Dassel presided at a high mass where Charlemagne was proclaimed a saint. Several days later on 8 January 1166, Emperor Frederick Barbarossa issued a decree making the same proclamation. In 1167 in Rome, Charlemagne's saintly status was confirmed by Pascal III. Two centuries later Charlemagne received similar honors in France. King Charles V (b. 1338 – d. 1380) declared him to be the patron saint of France, and still later King Louis XI (b. 1423 – d. 1483) ordered that Charlemagne was to be venerated throughout the land. By the later Middle Ages, Charlemagne was regarded throughout Europe not only as a saint but also as a crusader and an ideal lawgiver.

Almost a thousand years after Charlemagne was born, he attracted the scholarly attention of Cardinal Prospero Lambertini, who would eventually become Pope Benedict XIV and who is widely regarded as one of the very greatest scholar-popes. In his major work on what were by then the separate concepts of beatification and canonization, the future pope wrote how Charlemagne was Blessed and should be remembered forever for his services to the faith. Even today, there are modern Catholic scholars who are as impressed by Charlemagne as the medievals were and state that he should not be placed among the beati (or Blesseds) but numbered among the saints.

Charlemagne's feast day is January 28.

His Line

Husband		Wife
Pepin (or Pippin) III, "the Short," Mayor of the Palace in Austrasia and King of the Franks (b. 715 – md. ca. 740 – d. 24 Sept 768)	+	**Bertha (or Bertrada) "Bigfoot"** (b. ca. 720 – md. ca. 740 – d. 12 July 783)
Bl. Charlemagne, King of the Franks and First Emperor of the West (b. 2 April 747 – md. (2) 771 – d. 28 Jan 814)	+	Bl. Hildegarde, Countess of Vin gau (b. 758 – md. 771 – d. 30 April 783)
Louis I "the Fair," King of France and Emperor of the West (b. Aug 778 – md. (2) 819 – d. 20 June 840)	+	Judith of Altdorf (or Bavaria) (b. ca. 800 – md. 819 – d. 19 April 843)

[For the later generations that connect this line to the kings of England, see the line of St. Arnulf, Bishop of Metz in Part II.]

Sources: *Baring-Gould,* Vol. I, pp. 437–438; *BBKL,* Vol. 3, cols. 1125–1130; *Becher,* pp. 136–142; *Benedictine Monks,* pp. 159–160; *Bunson,* pp. 203–204; *Butler,* Vol. I, pp. 188–189; *CE,* Vol. III, pp. 610–618; *Delaney,* pp. 144–145; *Englebert,* p. 38; *Holweck,* p. 205; *Joeckle,* pp. 93–95; *Klaniczay,* pp. 171–172; *Lambertini,* Liber Primus, Caput Nonum [Book One, Chapter Nine], pp. 45–49; *Snodgrass,* p. 53; *Stuart,* line 171, nos. 42 through 40; *Walsh,* p. 118; *Weis, AR:* line 50, nos. 12 and 13 + line 148, nos. 13 and 14; *Wells,* pp. 136–137; *Wolf,* pp. 24–25

St. Clodulf,
Bishop of Metz

Clodulf was born in 605 and was the son of St. Arnulf, Bishop of Metz, and his wife Dode. Clodulf's wife was named Hilda.

Like his father Arnulf, Clodulf held several positions of responsibility in the palace of the kings of Austrasia. After serving both Dagobert I and Sigebert I, Clodulf became a priest and in 656 was made bishop of Metz, a post which his father had also held.

During his forty years as bishop, Clodulf performed several notable works of charity. He died on 8 June 696 and is buried near Nancy in the church of Lay-Saint-Christophe.

A biography of St. Arnulf written by Clodulf survives.

His Line

Husband		Wife
St. Arnulf, Mayor of the Palace in Austrasia and Bishop of Metz (b. 13 Aug 582 – md. ca. 596 – d. 16 Aug 640)	+	**Dode (or Clothilde)** (b. ca. 586 – md. ca. 596)
St. Clodulf (or Clodoule or Cloud), Bishop of Metz (b. 605 – d. 8 June 696)	+	Hilda
St. Guerin (or Warinus), Count of Poitiers (d. 677)	+	**Kunza** (d. 690)
Lambert of Hesbaye (liv. 725)	+	N.N.
Robert, Count of Hesbaye (b. ca. 700 – liv. 750)	+	Williswinda
Guerin, Count in the Thurgovie (d. 20 May 772)	+	Adelindis
Bouchard "the Constable" Minur Dominicur in Corsica	+	N.N.
Aubri "the Burgundian," Count of Fezensac	+	N.N.
Bouchard, Prefect of the Royal Hunt	+	N.N.
Geoffrey	+	N.N.
Aubri "Dux," Vicomte d'Orleans (liv. 886)	+	N.N.
Geoffrey, Vicomte d'Orleans and Count in the Gatinais (liv. 933–942)	+	N.N.
Aubri, Vicomte d'Orleans and Count in the Gatinais (liv. 957–966)	+	N.N.
Geoffrey, Count in the Gatinais (liv. 975–987)	+	N.N.

Aubri, Count in the Gatinais (liv. 990)	+	N.N.
Geoffrey "Ferreol," Count in the Gatinais and Chateau-Landon (liv. 990)	+	Beatrice of Macon
Geoffrey II "Ferreol," Count in the Gatinais and Chateau-Landon (b. ca. 1004 – md. 1035 – d. 1043/ 1046)	+	Ermengarde of Anjou (called Blanche) (b. ca. 1018 – md. (1) 1035 – d. 21 March 1076)

[For the later generations that connect this line to the kings of England, see the line of St. Adela, Princess of Austrasia in Part II.]

Sources: *Baring-Gould*, Vol. 6, p. 82; *Benedictine Monks*, p. 170; *Bunson*, p. 214; *Butler*, Vol. II, p. 503; *Delaney*, p. 152; *Delaney and Tobin*, p. 263; *Holweck*, p. 207; *NCE*, Vol. 3, pp. 619–620; *Stuart*: line 35 + line 2, nos. 45 through 31; *Tucker*, Vol. I, pp. 182–183 and 331–332; *Wells*, pp. 135, 303–304, and 267

St. Clothilde

Clothilde was born around 470/475 and was the daughter of Chilperic II, King of the Burgundians, and his wife Caretana. In 492, she married Clovis I "the Great," King of the Salic Franks. At the time of their marriage, Clothilde was a Catholic, but Clovis was still a pagan and had already been king of the Franks for twelve years.

After four years of marriage, Clovis converted to Christianity, but exactly what brought him to this decision will never be definitely known. Many give most of the credit to Clothilde. It is said that the two of them were a loving couple, that she acquired great influence over him, and that she converted him by her prayers and example. Other accounts say that late in 496 at Tolbiac Clovis and his army were in a battle with the Alemanni and that the Franks were on the point of breaking and fleeing from the field. At that moment Clovis prayed to "Clothilde's God" and promised that he would convert if God would give him victory. The tide of battle turned, the Alemanni fled, and the Franks triumphed. Whatever the reason, Clovis and many of his soldiers all became Christians on Christmas Day 496.

Since the kingdom of Clovis included southwestern Germany and most of France, his conversion resulted in a major expansion of Christianity in Europe. Clovis moved his capital from Soissons to Paris. There he and Clothilde founded the church of the apostles Peter and Paul, which was later renamed for their friend St. Geneviève. When Clovis died in 511, he was buried there.

Clothilde surely needed the strength of a saint as her land descended into chaos. After the death of Clovis, their three surviving sons—along with a son of Clovis from his first marriage—immediately divided the realm into four small, extraordinarily quarrelsome kingdoms. For the rest of her life, Clothilde had to watch as her children and her stepson feuded, warred, and murdered over their inheritance. They frequently faced each other in battle and did not hesitate to kill each other's relatives.

Clothilde finally retired to Tours and spent the rest of her life helping the sick and the poor. Surviving her husband by 34 years, she finally died on 3 June 545 and was buried next to Clovis.

After her death, Clothilde was immediately considered a saint. St. Clothilde at prayer was a popular theme in medieval art.

Her Line

Husband		Wife
Chilperic II, King of the Burgundians (died in battle 491/492)	+	**Caretana**
Clovis I "the Great," King of the Salic Franks (b. 466 – md. (2) 492 – d. 27 Nov 511)	+	**St. Clothilde** (b. 470/475 – md. 492 – d. 3 June 545)
Clothaire I, King of Soissons, Orleans, and France (b. 500 – d. 561)	+	md. (4) Arnegundis (or Aregonde or Aregund)
Chilperic I, King of Neustria (b. 523 – d. 584)	+	md. (3) Fredegunde "one of the most bloodthirsty women in history" (b. 543 – d. 597)

Clothaire II, King of Neustria and the Franks (b. 584 – d. 629), signed the "Perpetual Constitution" 614/615, an early Magna Charta	+	Haldetrude (d. 604)
Dagobert I, King of Austrasia and the Franks, greatest of the Merovingian kings (b. 602 – d. 639)	+	md. (4) Berthilde
St. Sigebert III, King of Austrasia (b. 630 – d. 656)	+	Hymnegilde
St. Dagobert II, King of Austrasia and Metz (b. 652 – murdered 23 Dec 678)	+	Mechtilde
Alberic	+	**St. Adela**, Princess of Austrasia (d. 734/735)

[For the later generations that connect this line to the kings of England, see the line of St. Adela, Princess of Austrasia in Part II.]

Sources: *Baring-Gould*, Vol. 6, pp. 23–27; *Benedictine Monks*, p. 170; *Bunson*, p. 214; *Butler*, Vol. II, pp. 462–463; *CE*, Vol. IV, pp. 66–67; *Chervin*, pp. 178–180; *Cruz*, pp. 153–155; *Delaney*, p. 152; *Delaney and Tobin*, p. 263; *Dunbar*, Vol. I, pp. 191–193; *Englebert*, p. 215; *Giorgi*, pp. 332–333; *Guiley*, p. 78; *Holboeck*, pp. 95–100; *Holweck*, p. 207; *Klaniczay*, pp. 70 and 197; *NCE*, Vol. 3, p. 962; *Scherman, Birth of France*, frontispiece and p. 149; *Snodgrass*, p. 59; *Stuart:* line 349, nos. 52 and 51 + line 303, nos. 51 through 44; *Wells*, pp. 109 and 384–385; *WWH*, Vol. 3, pp. 855-858. N.B.: Stuart mistakenly claims that Rodegunda is the mother of Chilperic I. For confirmation that Arnegundis is Chilperic's mother, see ***fmg.ac>Projects>Medieval Lands>Medieval Lands – data by region> France>Kings & early nobility> Merovingian Kings>Clotaire 511–561, Charibert 561–567, Gontran 561–592***.

St. Coel Hen

Coel Hen (or Coel "the Old") came from Ayshire and was the son of a local ruler named Godebog. He lived from about 370 to 420/430 and married a woman named Ystradwel ferch Gadeon. He may have been the last of the Roman *Duces Brittanniarum* (Dukes of the Britons).

Once the Romans withdrew in 410/412 and left the British to fend for themselves, Coel became a leader of his own people. Besides northern England, his territory included southern Scotland, then known as Rheged. His capital was probably at York.

Coel protected the people of the north against the Picts and the Irish and was frequently at war with them. He beat back several attacks in the area around Hadrian's Wall and provided strong leadership in a time of considerable unrest. One legend says that Coel died fighting the Irish near Tarbolton in Ayshire.

The historic Coel is frequently confused with other men named Coel who are purely legendary. One such legend was started by Geoffrey of Monmouth, who wrote about a Coel who was a duke of Colchester and whose daughter Helena became the mother of the Roman emperor Constantine. There is another legend about a still earlier figure named Coel ap Mor.

One of Coel Hen's children is St. Ceneu. Coel Hen is also the "Old King Cole" of the nursery rhyme.

His Line

Husband		Wife
Godebog, a ruler of northern Britain	+	**N.N.**
St. Coel Hen (or Coel Godebog), a ruler of northern Britain (b. ca. 370 – d. 420/430)	+	Ystradwel ferch Gadeon
St. Ceneu, a ruler of northern Britain (b. ca. 400 – d. ca. 450)	+	N.N.
St. Pabo "Post Prydyn" (the Pillar of Northern Britain) (b. ca. 430 – d. ca. 510)	+	N.N.
St. Brochwel "Ysgithrog," King of Powys (b. ca. 502 – d. ca. 560)	+	**St. Arddun "Benasgell"**

[For the later generations that connect this line to the kings of Scotland, see the line of St. Arddun "Benasgell" in Part II.]

Sources: *Ashley*, pp. 97–100; *Baring-Gould and Fisher*, Vol. 2, pp. 155–156; *Boyer*, nos. 1, 2, and 3 on p. 63; *Holweck*, p. 221; *Stuart*, line 405A, no. 57; *Williamson*, p. 83

St. Constantine I, King of Scotland

Constantine (or Causantin) was born around 836 and was the son of Kenneth MacAlpin, King of the Picts and Scots. Constantine became king in 863.

Frequent Viking raids turned Constantine into a warrior king. Early in his reign, he defeated the armies of Olaf the White and Thorsten the Red. He also occasionally made alliances with his enemies. After Constantine defeated Olaf the White, his sister married Olaf, and cooperation between Olaf and Constantine later resulted in their conquest of the neighboring kingdom of Strathclyde.

About two years later in 877, Constantine's luck with the Vikings ran out. Another Viking army led by Halfdan, the brother of Ivar the Boneless, met Constantine and his men at the battle of the Black Cove in Angus. Constantine was killed and buried on Iona.

Since he died fighting the heathen, Constantine was remembered as a martyr.

His Line

Husband		Wife
Kenneth MacAlpin (or Cinead), King of the Picts and Scots (b. ca. 810 – d. 859)	+	**N.N.**
St. Constantine I, King of Scotland (b. ca. 836 – slain 877 in battle with the Norsemen)	+	N.N.
Donald (or Domnall), King of Scotland (b. ca. 862 – d. 900)	+	N.N.
Malcolm I, King of Scotland (killed 954 by the men of Moray)	+	N.N.
Kenneth (or Cinead), King of Scotland (murdered 995 by his own men)	+	N.N.

[For the later generations that connect this line to the kings of England, see the line of St. Brychan in Part II.]

Sources: *Ashley*, p. 384; *Benedictine Monks*, p. 178; *Bunson*, p. 222; *Delaney and Tobin*, p. 280; *Holweck*, p. 233; *Stuart*, line 165, nos. 39 through 35; *Weir*, pp. 167–175; *Weis, AR*, line 170, nos. 13 through 17; *Williamson*, pp. 87 and 379

St. Cunedda Wledig

Cunedda was born around 400 and was the son of Edern ap Padarn "Beisrudd" (of the Scarlet Cloak). He married Gwawl, a daughter of St. Coel Hen.

Cunedda's fame rests on his deeds as a war leader and a king. Around 430, he became the leader of the northern British tribes who were resisting invasions by the Picts in the area around Hadrian's Wall. His deeds in battle earned him the name "Cunedda the Lion." After securing this area, he and his family went to north Wales around 450 and created what would become the kingdom of Gwynedd. His court was at Caer Liwelydd (i.e., Carlisle). To secure his new Welsh kingdom, he and his nine warrior sons drove Irish invaders out of Gwynedd, slaughtering so many that the Irish never returned.

Cunedda may have lived into his late 60's. He was remembered as one of the founders of Wales.

His Line

Husband		Wife
Edern ap Padarn "Beisrudd" (of the Scarlet Cloak), a Romano-British war leader	+	**N.N.**
St. Cunedda Wledig, founder of the kingdom of Gwynedd (b. ca. 400 – d. 460/470)	+	Gwawl, daughter of St. Coel Hen
Ceredig	+	N.N.
Corun	+	Teithfallt, daughter of Nynnian of Gwent
Budic I, King of Brittany	+	**N.N.**, a daughter of Corun
Hoel I "the Great," King of Brittany (b. ca. 491 – d. ca. 545)	+	St. Pompeja
Hoel II, King of Brittany (murdered 547)	+	Rimo
Judicael I, King of Brittany (b. 535)	+	N.N.
Hoel III, King of Brittany (d. 612)	+	Pritelle
St. Judicael II, King of Brittany (b. ca. 590 – d. 17 Dec 658)	+	N.N.
Alain II de Long, King of Brittany (d. 690)	+	N.N.
Ivor	+	N.N.
Daniel Dremrost "the Red-Eyed," King of Brittany (d. 703)	+	N.N.
Budic II, King of Brittany	+	N.N.
N.N. (perh. Melieu)	+	N.N.
Erispoe I	+	N.N.
Nominoe, Duke of Brittany (d. 8 June or 22 Aug 851)	+	Argentael

Erispoe II, Duke of Brittany (d. Nov 857)	+	N.N.
Gurwand, Count of Rennes (d. 876/877)	+	**N.N.**
Berenger, Count of Rennes (d. 890)	+	N.N.
Paskwitan II, Count of Rennes (d. 903)	+	**N.N.**
Juhel Berenger, Count of Rennes (liv. 931 – d. 970)	+	Gerberga
Conan I "le Tort," Count of Rennes and Duke of Brittany (killed 27 June 992)	+	Ermengarde of Anjou
Richard II "the Good", Duke of Normandy (md. ca. 1000 – d. 28 Aug 1027)	+	**Judith of Brittany** (b. 982 – md. ca. 1000 – d. 16 June 1017)
Robert I "the Devil," Duke of Normandy and Crusader (b. ca. 1000 – d. ca. July 1035)	+	Herleve (b. ca. 1003)
William I the Conqueror, Duke of Normandy and King of England (b. 1027/1028 – md. 1053 – d. 9 Sept 1087)	+	Mathilde of Flanders (b. 1032 – md. 1053 – d. 3 Nov 1083)

Sources: *Ashley*, pp. 141–142; *Baring-Gould and Fisher*, Vol. 2, pp. 191–192; *Boyer*: no. 1 on p. 63 + nos. 1 and 2 on pp. 66–67; *Holweck*, p. 247; *Kirby*, pp. 58 and 72; *Stuart:* line 405A, nos. 56 through 53 + line 405, nos. 53 through 37 + line 334, nos. 37 through 35 + line 167, nos. 34 and 33 + line 89, nos. 32 through 30; *Wells*, pp. 95–96 and 433

St. Dagobert II,
King of Austrasia

Dagobert was born in 652 and was the son of St. Sigebert III, King of Austrasia, and his wife Hymnegilde.

While Sigebert was still childless, Grimoald, his mayor of the palace, had persuaded him to adopt Grimoald's son Childeric as his own son. After the adoption Dagobert was born. When Sigebert then died in 656, Grimoald had the four-year-old Dagobert carried off to a monastery in Ireland and kept there while Childeric was named king. It was not until Childeric was murdered about twenty years later in 675 that Dagobert was brought back from Ireland and proclaimed king of Austrasia.

Dagobert was a good king, but his reign was short. Ebroin was his mayor of the palace, and it was henchmen of Ebroin that murdered Dagobert near Verdun on 23 December 678 while he was out hunting.

While he was in exile, Dagobert had married Mechtilde, and they became the parents of St. Adela of Austrasia. During his short reign, Dagobert founded religious establishments and the circumstances of his death caused him to be remembered as a martyr. His relics are at Stenay-sur-Meuse.

His Line

Husband		Wife
St. Sigebert III, King of Austrasia (b. 630 – d. 656)	+	**Hymnegilde**
St. Dagobert II, King of Metz and Austrasia (b. 652 – murdered 23 Dec 678)	+	Mechtilde
Alberic	+	**St. Adela**, Princess of Austrasia (d. 730/734)
Aubri I, Count of Blois	+	N.N.
Aubri II, Count of Blois	+	N.N.
Gainfroi, Count of Sens	+	**Theidlindis** (liv. 795)

[For the later generations that connect this line to the kings of England, see the line of St. Adela, Princess of Austrasia in Part II.]

Sources: *BBKL*, Vol. 23, cols. 252–253; *Benedictine Monks*, p. 192; *Bunson*, p. 238; *Butler*, Vol. IV, p. 601; *Cruz*, pp. 166–167; *Delaney*, p. 171; *Delaney and Tobin*, pp. 307–308; *Holweck*, p. 259; *Klaniczay*, p. 69; *NCE*, Vol. 4, p. 611; *Stuart*, line 303, nos. 46 through 41; *Wells*, pp. 385 and 75; *Wood*, p. 349

St. David I,
King of Scotland

David was born around 1084 and was the youngest son of Malcolm III Canmore, King of Scotland, and his second wife St. Margaret of Scotland.

David spent much of his youth at the court of Henry I of England. After his father's death, David had several relatives whose claim to the Scottish crown was higher than his. As the crown was passed from one relative to another, David was made king of the Scottish lowlands in 1107. During this period, David also married Maud of Huntingdon, widow of Simon de St. Liz, in 1113. In 1124 when he was fifty, David finally became king of all Scotland.

According to some scholars, David improved so much of his kingdom that he became the real creator of the Scotland we know today. He created counties which lasted until the reorganization of local government in 1975. Several towns were developed into major trading centers. A stable monetary system and a new legal code were introduced. David had a deep respect for the idea of fair play. He improved the operation of the law courts and introduced trial by jury to Scotland.

David ruled with great justice, was very charitable to the poor, and with his own piety gave a very good example to everyone. He founded five new monasteries—which were all architecturally superb—and five new sees.

In the war for the crown of England between Matilda, daughter of Henry I, and Stephen, son of Stephen III of Blois, David intervened on the side of Matilda. In 1135, he invaded northern England and fought well for three years until he was defeated by Stephen at the battle of the Standard in 1138.

The reign of David gave Scotland a cohesiveness which it had not attained under any earlier monarch. Even while he lived, David's people regarded him as a saint. He died on 24 May 1153 and was buried at Dumfermline Abbey.

His Line

Husband		Wife
Malcolm III Canmore, King of Scotland (b. ca. 1031 – md. (2) 1068/1069 – d. in battle 13 Nov 1093 while besieging Alnwick Castle)	+	**St. Margaret of Scotland** (b. ca. 1045 – md. 1068/1069 – d. 16 Nov 1093)
David I "the Saint," King of Scotland (b. ca. 1084 – md. 1113 – d. 24 May 1153)	+	Matilda of Huntington (md. (2) 1113 – d. 1130/1131)
Henry of Huntingdon, Earl of Huntingdon and Northumberland (b. ca. 1115 – md. ca. 1139 – d. 12 June 1152)	+	Adelaide (or Ada) de Warenne (b. ca. 1120 – md. 1139 – d. 1178)
Florenz III, Count of Holland (France) and West Sealand, Crusader (b. ca. 1138 – md. 28 Aug 1161/1162 – d. 1 Aug 1190 at Antioch on the 3rd Crusade)	+	**Ada de Huntingdon**, (b. ca. 1146 – md. 28 Aug 1161/1162 – d. 11 Jan 1216/ 1222)

William I, Count of Holland (France) and East Friesland, Crusader (b. c. 1174 – md. 1198 – d. 2 July 1222)	+	Adelaide of Guelders (b. ca. 1186 – md. 1198 – d. 4 Feb 1218)
Florenz IV, Count of Holland (France) and Sealand (b. 24 June 1210 – d. 19 July 1234)	+	Matilda of Brabant (d. 12 Dec 1267)
Jean I d'Avesnes, Count of Hainault and Holland (b. 1 May 1218 – md. 9 Oct 1246 – d. 12 Dec 1257)	+	**Adelaide of Holland** (b. ca. 1225 – md. 9 Oct 1246 – d. 1284)
Jean II d'Avesnes, Count of Hainault and Holland (b. 1247 – md. 1270 – d. 22 Aug 1304)	+	Philippa of Luxembourg (md. 1270)
William III d'Avesnes, Count of Hainault and Holland (b. ca. 1286 – md. 19 May 1305 – d. 7 June 1337)	+	Jeanne de Valois (b. ca. 1294 – md. 19 May 1305 – d. 7 March 1342)
Edward III, King of England (b. 13 Nov 1312 – md. 24 Jan 1328 – d. 21 June 1377)	+	**Philippa of Hainault** (b. 24 June 1311 – md. 24 Jan 1328 – d. 15 Aug 1369)

Sources: *Ashley*, pp. 403–405; *Bentley*, p. 98; *Bunson*, p. 242; *Butler*, Vol. II, pp. 383–384; *CS*, p. 24; *Delaney*, pp. 173–174; *Delaney and Tobin*, p. 313; *HBC*, p. 57; *NCE*, Vol. 4, p. 657; *O'Malley*, pp. 51, 65, and 124–125; *Snodgrass*, p. 66; *Stuart:* line 72 + line 50, nos. 25 through 22; *Tucker:* Vol. II, pp. 761–763 + Vol. I, pp. 414 and 383; *Weir*, pp. 191–192; *Weis, AR:* line 170, nos. 21 through 23 + line 100 + line 168, nos. 30 through 32 + line 103, nos. 33 and 34; *Wells*, pp. 519–520, 305, 44, and 293

St. Ealhswith of Mercia

Born around 852, Ealhswith (also called Ealswitha and Etheldwitha) was the daughter of Aethelred Mucil, Earl of Mercia, and his wife Eadburh. In 868 she married Alfred, the youngest son of King Aethelwulf of Wessex. No one expected Alfred to ever become king, but after all of his older brothers died, he was crowned in 871, and Ealhswith became queen. Alfred would become known to history as Alfred the Great, King of Wessex, Saint, and one of the greatest rulers in the history of his nation.

With Alfred, Ealhswith worked to rebuild religious communities that had been destroyed during the Danish invasions. With him, she also founded St. Mary's Abbey in Winchester. Originally a convent for Benedictine nuns, it became one of the foremost centers of art and learning in England.

Alfred and Ealhswith had five children that survived infancy, including their daughter St. Ethelgiva. After Alfred died in 899, Ealhswith became a nun and entered St. Mary's, where she died around 903/905.

Originally buried in the church in Winchester known as Old Minster, for the next several centuries eternal rest was the last thing that Alfred and Ealhswith enjoyed. When the Old Minster was replaced by a later church called New Minster, Alfred and Ealhswith were reinterred there. After the Norman Conquest, the New Minster was demolished and replaced by the building that is Winchester Cathedral today. During the demolition, Alfred and Ealhswith were moved again to Hyde Abbey in Winchester. When Hyde Abbey was dissolved during the reign of Henry VIII, their graves were lost. None of the alleged "rediscoveries" of the graves of Alfred and Ealhswith in later centuries have been generally accepted by historians.

Her Line

Husband		Wife
Aethelred Mucil, Earl of Mercia	+	**Eadburh**
St. Alfred the Great, King of Wessex (b. 849 – md. 868 – d. 26 Oct 899)	+	**St. Ealhswith** (b. ca. 852 – md. 868 – d. 903/905)
Edward "the Elder," King of England (b. 875 – md. (3) 919 – d. 924)	+	Eadgifu (md. 919 – d. 961)
Edmund I "the Magnificent," King of England (b. ca. 920 – murdered 26 May 946)	+	md. (1) St. Elgiva (d. 944)

Sources: *Baring-Gould*, Vol. 16, p. 253; *Benedictine Monks*, p. 244; *Bunson*, p. 290; *HBC*, p. 24; *Holweck*, p. 332; *Parbury*, p. 34; *Stuart*: line 238 + line 233, nos. 39 through 37; *Weir*, pp. 9–17; *Weis, AR*, line 1, nos. 15 through 17; *Wells*, p. 204; *Williamson*, pp. 18–19 and 365

Bl. Eberhard V

Eberhard V was born around 1010 and was the son of Eberhard IV, Count in the Thurgau, and his second wife Hedwig. He married Ida von Alshausen and had eight children.

In 1046, Eberhard V took part in the Italian campaign of Emperor Henry III. Around 1050, he completed two major building projects: the castle of Nellenburg in Baden Wuerttemburg and the All Saints Monastery at Schaffhausen in Switzerland.

In the late 1060's, Eberhard V went on a pilgrimage to Santiago de Compostela and came back so deeply impressed that he decided to become a monk and joined his own monastery. His wife then founded the convent of St. Agnes at Scaffhausen and became a nun there.

Eberhard died in his monastery around 1076/1079.

His Line

Husband		Wife
Eberhard IV, Count in the Thurgau (b. 960/970 – md. (2) ca. 1009 – d. ca. 8 Feb 1041)	+	**Hedwig**
Eberhard V "the Blessed," Count of Nellenburg and Count in the Zurichgau (b. ca. 1010 – d. 1076/1079)	+	Ida von Alshausen (b. 1015 – d. 26 Feb 1106)
Adalbert, Lord of Burgeln	+	**N.N. von Nellenburg**
Adalbert, Count of Morsberg, Kyburg, and Winterthur (d. 1124/1125)	+	Mechtilde of Bar
Meginhard I, Count of Sponheim (md. bef. 1124 – d. 1136/1145)	+	**Mechtilde von Morsberg** (md. bef. 1124)
Simon I, Count of Saarbrucken (b. ca. 1120 – d. 23 June 1181/1182)	+	**Mathilda von Sponheim** (b. ca. 1127)
Henry III "the Old," Duke of Limburg and Count of Arlon (b. ca. 1140 – d. 21 June 1221)	+	**Sophia von Saarbrucken** (b. 1150 – liv. 1215)
Waleran IV, Duke of Monschou and Count in the Ardennesgau (md. (2) May 1214 – d. 2 July 1226)	+	Ermesinde of Namur (b. July 1186 – md. May 1214 – d. 12 Feb 1247)
Henry III "the Blond," Count of Luxemburg (b. 1217 – md. 4 June 1240 – d. 24 Nov 1281)	+	Mathilde de Bar-le-Duc (md. 4 June 1240 – d. 23 Nov 1275)
Jean II d'Avesnes, Count of Hainault and Holland (b. 1247 – md. 1270 – d. 22 Aug 1304)	+	**Philippa of Luxemburg** (md. 1270)
William III d'Avesnes, Count of Hainault and Holland (b. ca. 1286 – md. 19 May 1305 – d. 7 June 1337)	+	Jeanne de Valois (b. ca. 1294 – md. 19 May 1305 – d. 7 March 1342)

Edward III, King of England (b. 13 Nov 1312 – md. 24 Jan 1328 – d. 21 June 1377)	+	**Philippa of Hainault** (b. 24 June 1311 – md. 24 Jan 1328 – d. 15 Aug 1369)

Sources: *Benedictine Monks*, p. 220 (which mistakenly refers to this saint as Eberhard III); *Holweck*, p. 300 (which makes the same mistake); *Stuart:* line 18, nos. 33 through 31 + line 364, nos. 31 through 29 + line 365, nos. 29 and 28 + line 23, nos. 28 and 27 + line 71, nos. 27 through 24 + line 50, nos. 24 through 22

St. Edgar "the Peaceful," King of England

Edgar was born in 943 and was the son of Edmund "the Magnificent," King of England, and his first wife St. Elgiva (or Alfgifu). Before Edgar was four years old, both of his parents were dead. Edgar's relatives governed England during his minority, while Edgar himself was being educated by St. Ethelwold. In 955 at age 12, he became the ruler of Mercia and Northumbria. In 959 at age 16, he also became king of Wessex.

Edgar achieved several things during his reign that would have long-lasting benefits for his realm. Temporarily spared from Viking invasions, he reorganized the English navy, divided England into shires, and created England's first national coinage. He established more than 30 monasteries and revived religious life. Many reforms in the Church suggested by his tutor St. Ethelwold, his friend St. Dunstan (who became Archbishop of Canterbury), and St. Oswald (who became Archbishop of York) were all carried out.

Less than five feet tall, Edgar's private life was not always exemplary. His first wife Ethelfleda died shortly after the birth of their first child, who would become St. Edward the Martyr. Edgar then took a mistress who would become known as St. Wulfthryth. Their child would become St. Edith of Wilton. Edgar's second wife, whom he married in 965, was Elfrida. Elfrida's first husband had died in a hunting accident. It has been suggested but never proved that he was killed by Edgar, who wanted Elfrida for himself.

The coronation ceremony that is still used in Britain today began on 11 May 973 as an exercise to reconfirm the authority of the royal house of Wessex over all England. On that date, Elfrida became the very first woman to be crowned queen of all England. The first man to be crowned king of the whole nation was Edgar.

Edgar died on 8 July 975 and was buried at Glastonbury Abbey beside his father.

His Line

Husband		Wife
Edmund I "the Magnificent," King of England (b. ca. 920 – murdered 26 May 946)	+	md. (1) St. Elgiva (b. 944)
St. Edgar "the Peaceful," King of England (b. 943 – md. (3) 965 – d. 8 July 975)	+	Elfrida (b. 945 – md. 965 – d. ca. 1000)
Aethelred II "the Redeless," King of England (b. 968 – md. (1) 985 – d. 1016)	+	Aelfgiful (or Elgiva or Aethelfleda or Alfflaed) (b. ca. 968 – md. 985), daughter of Thored (or Thorod or Torin) of Northumbria
Edmund "Ironside," King of England (b. 989 – md. (2) Aug 1015 – d. 30 Nov 1016)	+	Ealdgyth (md. (2) Aug 1015), daughter of Morcar, High Reeve of Northumbria

Sources: *Ashley*, pp. 475–476 and 478–486; *Baring-Gould*, Vol. 7, pp. 198–202; *Benedictine Monks*, p. 222; *Bunson*, p. 267; *Cruz*, pp. 183–186; *Holweck*, p. 302; *Snodgrass*, p. 73; *Stuart*, line 233, nos. 37 through 34; *Weir*, pp. 16–17, 19–20, 22–24, and 27–29; *Weis, AR*, line 1, nos. 17 through 20; *Wells*, pp. 204–205

St. Edith of Polesworth

Edith was the daughter of Edward "the Elder," King of England, and his first wife Egwynn. On 30 January 925, she married Sitric I "the Squinty," the Danish king of Dublin and York. Sitric was a pagan Viking who briefly converted to Christianity around the time he married Edith. Before long, he returned to his old religion and was killed in 926.

Widowed, Edith became a nun at Polesworth Abbey. Her death date is uncertain. According to some records, it was around 927—according to others around 962. More than a dozen churches in England are dedicated to her.

Edith was the sister of Athelstan, King of England and the half-sister of St. Edburga of Winchester.

Her Line

Husband		Wife
Edward "the Elder," King of England (b. 875 – d. 924)	+	md. (1) **Egwynn (or Egwina)** (d. ca. 901/902)
Sitric (or Sihtric) I "the Squinty," King of Dublin and King of York (md. 30 Jan 925 – d. 927)	+	**St. Edith** (md. 30 Jan 925)
Olaf "Cuaran," King of Dublin and King of York (d. ca. 981)	+	md. (1) Donnflaith, daughter of Murchad, King of Leinster
Sitric II "of the Silken Beard," King of Dublin (d. 1042)	+	Slani, daughter of Brian Boru, King of Munster and High King of Ireland
Olaf, King of Dublin (d. 1034)	+	Maelcorcre
Cynan ab Iago, King of Gwynedd (d. ca. 1060)	+	**Ragnhildr (or Raguell)**
Gruffudd ap Cynan, King of Gwynedd (b. ca. 1055 – md (1) 1095 – d. 1137)	+ .	Angharad ferch Owain ab Edwin (md. (1) 1095 – d. 1162)

[For the later generations that connect this line to the kings of Scotland, see the line of St. Arddun "Benasgell" in Part II.]

Sources: *Ashley*, pp. 462–465 and 473; *Baring-Gould*, Vol. 10, pp. 267–268; *Butler*, Vol. III, pp. 109–110; *Delaney and Tobin*, p. 363; *HBC*, p. 24; *Holweck*, p. 303; *Klaniczay*, App. 2, Geneal. Table 3; *O'Malley*, p. 123; *Parbury*, pp. 37–38; *Tucker*, Vol. I, pp. 281–282 and 267; *Weir*, p. 12; *Weis, AR*, line 239, nos. 2 through 5; *Wells*, pp. 204, 192–193, and 598

Bl. Ela,
Countess of Salisbury

Ela was born around 1187/1190 and was the only child of William Fitz Patrick, Earl of Salisbury, and his wife Eleanor de Vitré. When William died in 1196, Ela's inheritance made her an extraordinarily wealthy child. In 1198 King Richard the Lionheart gave her in marriage to his half-brother William de Longespee, a natural son of King Henry II.

Ela grew into a woman of strong character. She had 8 children with William, who was a formidable warrior and Crusader but often unscrupulous with his fellow men. After William died in 1226, Ela founded a monastery at Hinton and a convent at Laycock. In 1238, she became a nun, entered her own convent, and became its abbess.

Ela died on 24 August 1261 and is buried at Laycock.

Her Line

Husband		Wife
William Fitz Patrick, Earl of Salisbury (b. ca. 1150 – md. ca. 1184 – d. 17 April 1196)	+	**Eleanor de Vitré** (md. ca. 1184)
William de Longespee (b. ca. 1176 – md. 1198 – d. 7 March 1226), natural son of King Henry II of England and Crusader	+	**Bl. Ela**, Countess of Salisbury (b. 1187/1190 – md. 1198 – d. 24 Aug 1261)
Stephen Longespee, Justiciar of Ireland (md. 1243/1244 – d. 1260)	+	Emeline de Ridelisford (md. 1243/44 – d. 1276)
Roger la Zouche, Baron Zouche of Ashby (md. bef. 1267 – d. bef. 15 Oct 1285)	+	**Ela Longespee** (md. bef. 1267 – d. bef. 19 July 1276)
Alan la Zouche, Baron Zouche of Ashby (b. 9 Oct 1267 – md. ca. 1285 – d. bef. 25 March 1313/1314)	+	Eleanor de Segrave (b. 1270 – md. ca. 1285 – d. 1314)
Robert de Holand, 1st Baron de Holand (md. bef. 1309/ 1310 – d. 7 Oct 1328)	+	**Maude la Zouche** (b. 1289/1290 – md. bef. 1309/1310 – d. 31 May 1349)
Sir Thomas de Holand, K.G., 1st Earl of Kent (md. ca. 1339 – d. 26/28 Dec 1360)	+	Joan Plantagenet (b. ca. 1328 – md. (1) ca. 1339 – d. 8 Aug 1385), the "Fair Maid of Kent" and granddaughter of Edward I, King of England
Sir Thomas de Holand, K.G., 2nd Earl of Kent (md. aft. 10 April 1364 – d. 25 April 1397)	+	Alice Fitz Alan (md. aft. 10 April 1364 – d. 17 March 1415/1416)
John Beaufort, K.G., Marquess of Dorset & Somerset (b. ca. 1370 – md. bef. 28 Sept 1397 – d. 16 March 1409/1410), son of John of Gaunt, Duke of Lancaster	+	**Margaret de Holand** (b. 1385 – md. (1) bef. 28 Sept 1397 – d. 30 Dec 1429)

Sir James Stewart, "The Black Knight of Lorn" (md. bef. 21 Sept 1439 – d. aft. 17 Aug 1451)	+	**Joan Beaufort** (md. (2) bef. 21 Sept 1439 – d. 15 July 1445), widow of James I, King of Scotland
Sir John Steward of Balveny, 1st Earl of Atholl (b. ca. 1440 – md. (2) bef. 19 April 1512)	+	Eleanor Sinclair (b. ca. 1458 – md. bef. 19 April 1475 – d. 21 March 1518), daughter of William Sinclair, 3rd Earl of Orkney, who built Rosslyn Chapel

Sources: *Benedictine Monks*, p. 226; *Dunbar*, Vol. I, pp. 253–254; *Holweck*, p. 307; *Parbury*, pp. 39–40; *Weis, AR:* line 108, nos. 27 and 28 + line 31, nos. 26 through 29 + line 32, nos. 29 and 30 + line 47; *Weis, MCS:* line 142, no. 1 + line 144, nos. 1 through 3 + line 90, nos. 4 through 9 + line 91, nos. 9 and 10 + line 91A, nos. 10 and 11

Bl. Eleanor of Provence

Eleanor was born in 1222 and was the daughter of Raymond Berenger V, Count of Provence, and his wife Beatrice of Savoy. On 14 January 1236 she married Henry III, King of England.

No one today would have expected Eleanor to be happy in her marriage. She was a beautiful and articulate girl. At the age of fourteen she was sent to a foreign land as a child-bride for a king who was twenty-eight. The two of them had never even met. Nevertheless, their first cordial greetings were followed by real fondness for each other and ultimately by love. They had nine children and were faithful to each other until death. Their love and concern for their children never ended. For Eleanor, nothing was more important than her family.

Besides giving Henry heirs for his crown, Eleanor also saved his kingdom for him during the Second Barons War (1264–1267). Two years after Eleanor of Provence married Henry in 1236, Simon de Montfort married Henry's sister—also named Eleanor—in 1238. At first Simon was an advisor to Henry but later became so discontented with him that by 1258 he was the leader of a group of barons who wanted to toss Henry off his throne and govern the country themselves. These barons saw Henry as an inept king who taxed them to the hilt, ignored their counsel, and wasted resources on unsuccessful foreign campaigns. In 1258 Simon and the other barons forced Henry to sign a document called the "Provisions of Oxford," which abolished the monarchy. The power to govern England was to be exercised by a council of fifteen barons and a parliament. Unwilling to actually surrender his throne, Henry obtained a papal bull in 1262 releasing him from everything he had agreed to in the Provisions of Oxford. A civil war known as the Second Barons War broke out immediately. In the first major battle of that war—at Lewes on 14 May 1264—Henry's army was soundly defeated.

For a year following the battle, Eleanor led her family's resistance to Simon and his barons. Her husband Henry, their son Prince Edward (later Edward I of England), and Henry's brother Richard of Cornwall had all been captured at Lewes and were Simon's prisoners. Eleanor fled to the Continent and became the head of a court-in-exile. She worked tirelessly to line up diplomatic support for Henry, starting with her brother-in-law St. Louis, King of France. She raised funds for her husband. She also gathered troops who were ready to fight for him.

In the summer of 1265, her stubborn refusal to surrender her family's cause paid off. Among his barons, Simon had begun to act so much like a king that he began to lose their support. At the end of May 1265 Prince Edward managed to escape from Simon's men and spent two months assembling a new royal army. In the second major battle of the war—at Evesham on 4 August 1265—Edward and his army annihilated Simon's barons army. Simon himself was killed in the battle, and his rebellion was crushed. Simon's remaining royal prisoners were released, and Eleanor returned to England.

After he was restored to his throne, Henry lived for seven more years and finally died on 16 November 1272. In life, he had been a pious, devoted family man and had always tried to seek peace rather than wage war. The English monarchy would go on for another 375 years before it was once again equally close to extinction following Cromwell's 1648 victory in the English civil war.

Eleanor survived Henry by nineteen years and turned to the church. In Wiltshire, she entered the convent of St. Mary at Amesbury as a lay widow in 1276. She took the vows of a professed nun in 1286. She died on 24 June 1291 and was buried at her convent. Her husband Henry is in Westminster Abbey.

Her Line

Husband		Wife
Raymond Berenger V, Count of Provence and Forcalquier (b. 1198 – md. Dec 1220 – d. 19 Aug 1245)	+	**Beatrice of Savoy** (b. 1198 – md. Dec 1220 – d. Dec 1266)
Henry III, King of England (b. 1 Oct 1207 – md. 14 Jan 1236 – d. 16 Nov 1272)	+	**Bl. Eleanor of Provence** (b. 1222 – md. 14 Jan 1236 – d. 24 June 1291)
Edward I, King of England (b. 17 June 1239 – md. (1) 18 Oct 1254 – d. 8 July 1307)	+	Eleanor of Castile (b. 1240 – md. 18 Oct 1254 – d. 28 Nov 1290)
Edward II, King of England (b. 25 April 1284 – md. 25 Jan 1308 – murdered 21 Sept 1327)	+	Isabella (b. 1292 – md. 25 Jan 1308 – d. 17 Aug 1357), daughter of Philip IV "the Fair," King of France
Edward III, King of England (b. 13 Nov 1312 – md. 24 Jan 1328 – d. 21 June 1377)	+	Philippa of Hainault (b. 24 June 1311 – md. 24 Jan 1328 – d. 15 Aug 1369)

Sources: *Holweck*, p. 308; *Stuart:* line 54, nos. 26 and 25 + line 1, nos. 25 through 22; *Weir*, pp. 73–116; *Weis, AR*: line 111, nos. 29 and 30 + line 1, nos. 27 through 30; *WWH*, Vol. 5, pp. 108–114

St. Elgiva

Elgiva's parents are unknown. In 940, she married Edmund I "the Magnificent," King of England. They had three children, one of whom would become St. Edgar "the Peaceful," King of England.

Elgiva had a very sweet nature. She was pious, possessed of the gift of prophecy, and charitable to a fault. She would give her own clothes away to the poor and secretly freed condemned criminals.

Shortly before his own death in 946, Edmund took a second wife named Ethelfleda. The record is unclear as to what became of Elgiva. She may have predeceased Edmund, or she may have survived him and entered a convent at Shaftesbury after his death.

Elgiva is also known as Aelfgifu or Alfgifu. Her relics are at Shaftesbury.

Her Line

Husband		Wife
N.N.	+	**N.N.**
Edmund I "the Magnificent," King of England (b. ca. 920 –md. (1) 940 – murdered 26 May 946)	+	**St. Elgiva** (md. 940)
St. Edgar "the Peaceful," King of England (b. 943 – md. (3) 965 – d. 8 July 975)	+	Elfrida (b. 945 – md. 965 – d. ca. 1000)
Aethelred II "the Redeless," King of England (b. 968 – md. (1) 985 – d. 1016)	+	Aelfgifu (b. ca. 968 – md. 985), daughter of Thored of Northumbria
Edmund "Ironside," King of England (b. 989 – md. (2) Aug 1015 – d. 30 Nov 1016)	+	Ealdgyth (md. (2) Aug 1015), daughter of Morcar, High Reeve of Northumbria

Sources: *Ashley*, pp. 475–476; *Baring-Gould*, Vol. 5, pp. 254–255; *Benedictine Monks*, p. 228; *Bunson*, p. 275; *Delaney and Tobin*, p. 370; *Dunbar*, Vol. I, p. 256; *HBC*, p. 26; *Holweck*, pp. 23 and 310; *Parbury*, p. 41; *Stuart*, line 233, nos. 37 through 34; *Tucker*, Vol. I, pp. 283–285; *Weir*, pp. 16–29; *Weis, AR*, line 1, nos. 17 through 20; *Wells*, pp. 204–205; *Williamson*, pp. 111 and 365; *WWH*, Vol. 5, p. 116

Bl. Emma of Bavaria

Emma was born around 808 and was the daughter of Welf I, Count of Altdorf, and his wife Heilwig of Saxony. In 827, she married Louis II "the German," King of the East Franks. They had seven children, one of whom was Bl. Ermengard, Abbess of Buchan and Chiemsee.

Emma was a woman of uncommon courage who once led an army against the traitor Adelchis of Benevento when he revolted against Louis. She was also very generous to the Church. In 833, Louis gave her Obermuenster Abbey in Regensburg, whose patroness she became.

Emma died on 31 January 876, the same year as Louis. She is buried in Regensburg in St. Emmeram's Abbey. She is also known as Hemma.

Her Line

Husband		Wife
Welf I, Count of Altdorf	+	**Heilwig of Saxony** (b. ca. 775 – d. aft. 833)
Louis II "the German," King of the East Franks (b. 806 – md. 827 – d. 28 Aug 876)	+	**Bl. Emma of Bavaria** (b. ca. 808 – md. 827 – d. 31 Jan 876)
Carloman, King of Bavaria (liv. 820–880)	+	Litwinde of Carinthia
Arnulf, King of the East Franks (i.e., Germany) (liv. 863–899)	+	Oda of Bavaria
Otto "the Illustrious," Duke of Saxony and Count in South Thuringia (b. ca. 836 – md. 869 – d. 30 Nov 912)	+	**Hedwige** (md. 869 – d. 906)
Henry I "the Fowler," Duke of Saxony and Emperor of the West (b. 876 – md. (2) 909 – d. 2 July 936)	+	St. Mathilda of Ringelheim (b. ca. 890/900 – md. 909 – d. 14 March 968)
Giselbert, Duke of Lorraine and Count of Hainault (b. ca. 890 – md. 929 – d. 2 Oct 934)	+	**Gerberge of Saxony** (b. 913/914 – md. (1) 929 – d. 5 May 984)

[For the later generations that connect this line to the kings of England, see the line of St. Adela, Princess of Austrasia in Part II.]

Sources: *Butler*, Vol. III, p. 119 (under "Bd. Ermengard"); *NCE*, Vol. 6, p. 1015; *Stuart:* line 172, nos. 41 through 38 + line 92, nos. 37 through 35; *Warncke*, pp. 270–271; *Weis, AR*, line 141, no. 17; *Wells*, p. 138; *WWH*, Vol. 5, p. 212

St. Emma

Emma was the daughter of Clothaire II, King of Neustria, and his wife Haldetrude. Around 618, she married Eadbald, King of Kent, as his second wife. They were the parents of St. Eanswitha.

Emma founded the convent of Fontaine-de-Burle.

Her Line

Husband		Wife
Clothaire II, King of Neustria and the Franks (b. 584 – d. 629), signed the "Perpetual Constitution" 614/615, an early Magna Charta	+	**Haldetrude**
Eadbald, King of Kent (md. (2) ca. 618 – d. 640)	+	**St. Emma** (md. ca. 618)
Erconbert (or Eorconbeorht), King of Kent (b. ca. 624 – md. ca. 640 – d. 14 July 664)	+	St. Sexburga (md. ca. 640 – d. 6 July 699)
Egbert, King of Kent (b. ca. 641 – d. 4 July 673)	+	N.N.
Wihtread, King of Kent (d. 23 April 725)	+	N.N.

[For the later generations that connect this line to the kings of England, see the line of St. Aethelbert I, King of Kent in Part II.]

Sources: *Ashley*, pp. 212 and 217–222; *HBC*, p. 13; *Holweck*, p. 321 (under "Enimia"); *Stuart:* line 303, no. 48 + line 233A, nos. 47 through 44; *Williamson*, p. 359

Bl. Ermengarde of Orleans

Ermengarde was born around 800 and was the daughter of Hugh "le Méfiant," Count of Tours, and his wife Aba. On 15 October 821, she married Lothar I, King of Italy and Emperor of the West.

Lothar and Ermengarde had four children, and Ermengarde saw to it that they all received an excellent Christian education. Around 850, Ermengarde founded an abbey for noblewomen at Erstein near Strasbourg. Her one daughter Rotrude became its first abbess. On 20 March 851, Ermengarde died at Erstein and is buried there. Her shrine at Erstein was destroyed during the French Revolution.

Ermengarde of Orleans is also known as Ermengarde (or Irmgard) of Tours.

Her Line

Husband		Wife
Hugh "le Méfiant," Count of Tours (b. ca. 765 – d. Sept/ Nov 836)	+	**Aba (or Bava)** (b. ca. 779 – liv. 837)
Lothar I, King of Italy and Emperor of the West (b. 795 – md. 15 Oct 821 – d. 29 Sept 855)	+	**Bl. Ermengarde of Orleans** (b. ca. 800 – md. 15 Oct 821 – d. 20 March 851)
Giselbert, Count in the Maasgau (md. 846 – d. ca. 885)	+	**Ermengarde (or Irmgarde) of Lorraine and Burgundy** (md. 846)

[For the later generations that connect this line to the kings of England, see the line of St. Adela, Princess of Austrasia in Part II.]

Sources: *BBKL*, Vol. 16, cols. 789–790; *Holboeck*, p. 118; *Holweck*, p. 509; *Stuart*, line 302, nos. 40 and 39; *Weis, AR*, line 140, nos. 15 and 16; *Wells*, pp. 562 and 138

Bl. Ermengarde of Zutphen

Ermengarde was born around 1090 and was the daughter of Otto II, Count of Zutphen, and his wife Judith. Ermengarde first married Gerard II, Count of Guelders. Ermengarde's second husband after Gerard died was Conrad II, Count of Luxemburg. Ermengarde had children by both husbands.

Throughout her life, Ermengarde was a very devout and generous person. She and Gerard enlarged a church at Zutphen. She also made three pilgrimages to Rome during which notable miracles are said to have occurred. When she handed the pope a box of relics she had brought from Germany, earth containing the bones of martyrs turned to blood. On another occasion, Ermengarde was praying before a crucifix when the figure of Christ spoke to her and blessed her.

Ermengarde spent the last years of her life ministering to the sick at a hospice near Cologne. She died shortly before 1134 and is buried in Cologne at the Church of the Three Kings.

Her Line

Husband		Wife
Otto II, Count of Zutphen (d. 1113)	+	**Judith of Arnstein** (d. 1118)
Gerard II, Count of Guelders	+	**Bl. Ermengarde of Zutphen** (b. ca. 1090 – d. bef. 1134)
Henry I, Count of Guelders and Zutphen (b. 1117 – md. 1135 – d. 1182)	+	Agnes von Arnstein (md. 1135 – d. 1179)
Otto I, Count of Friesland, Gueders, Holland, Zealand, and Zutphen, Crusader (md. bef. 1188 – d. betw. 30 April and 24 Sept 1207)	+	Richardis von Wittelsbach (md. bef. 1188 – d. 7 Dec 1231)
William I, Count of Holland (France) and East Friesland, Crusader (b. ca. 1174 – md. 1198 – d. 2 July 1222)	+	**Adelaide of Guelders** (b. ca. 1186 – md. 1198 – d. 4 Feb 1218)

[For the later generations that connect this line to the kings of England, see the line of Bl. Adelheid von Odenkirchen in Part II.]

Sources: *Baring-Gould*, Vol. 10, pp. 51–53; *Dunbar*, Vol. I, p. 413; *Stuart:* line 379, no. 31 and 30 + line 304, nos. 30 through 27

St. Fernando III,
King of Castile and Leon

Almost eleven hundred years passed from the fall of the Roman Empire until the discovery of the New World. Of all the European monarchs who led their armies against Islamic foes during that era, no one was more successful than Fernando III.

Fernando was born on 24 June 1198 and was the son of Alfonso IX "el Barboro," King of Leon, and his second wife Berengaria, daughter of Alfonso IX "the Noble," King of Castile. From his father, Fernando inherited the kingdom of Leon, and from his mother he received the kingdom of Castile. At earlier points in Spanish history, these kingdoms had been ruled by the same man, most recently by Alfonso VII (b. 1 March 1105 – d. 21 August 1157). Fernando's greatest domestic achievement was to make their unity permanent. In the history of Spain after Fernando, the two kingdoms were never ruled by different people again. They became the core of the new Spanish nation.

Fernando had two wives. In 1219, he married Elizabeth von Hohenstaufen and had ten children with her. After she died, he married Jeanne de Dammartin in 1237 and had five children with her, one of whom was Bl. Eleanor of Castile who married Edward I of England.

By the time he became king in 1230, Fernando had already been fighting the Moors for six years. Three factors would be the foundation for all of his later successes. One was the reunification of Castile and Leon, which vastly increased the forces available to him. Another was the fact that from 1225 on Fernando and his men went into battle with the Crusaders' indulgence. The pope had declared that any Christian who died fighting for the reconquest of Spain would enter Paradise with all his sins forgiven. The third factor favoring Fernando was that the rulers of the Moslem kingdoms in Iberia intensely disliked their own Almohad overlords in Morocco, who in turn cared very little for the Spanish Moors. Their mutual animosity finally led to a permanent break in relations. In 1226 and afterwards, the Moslem rulers in Iberia received no more military help from Africa and were left to face the Christians by themselves.

Fernando moved quickly to take advantage of all these events. By 1230, he had taken 20 strongholds of the Moors. After a siege in 1233, he took Ubeda. In 1236, Cordoba surrendered to him, and several dependent towns and fortresses also submitted to him.

Fernando consolidated his gains and then continued the crusade he had begun in 1224. By the middle of the 1240's he was once again at the gates of the impregnable fortress of Jaen, which had beaten back earlier attacks in 1225 and 1230. Instead of another frontal assault, this time Fernando burned all the crops in the outlying fields, cut off all avenues of supply, and had his army surround the city. After a seven-month siege, the starving inhabitants surrendered in March 1246. Later the same year, he used the same tactics against Seville, which was the greatest city in Europe at the time. When it surrendered in November 1248, it became Fernando's final conquest. He had recovered more Spanish territory from the Moors than all his predecessors combined. When Granada—the last Moslem kingdom in Iberia—submitted to him without a fight, the reconquest of Spain was complete.

Besides being a great warrior and an outstanding politician, Fernando was a deeply religious man. He lived like a monk. By fasting and praying for hours before he went into battle and by acknowledging that the glory of his victories always belonged to God, he set a good example for his men. After taking new territory, Fernando also took all measures to re-Christianize it. He restored old churches and monasteries and built new ones. He welcomed new orders of monks who had come to re-educate the people.

Fernando was preparing an expedition to attack the Moors in Africa when he contracted his final illness. He died on 30 May 1252 and at his own request was buried in the robe of a lay order of monks which he belonged to. Later attempts by the Moors in Africa to retake parts of Spain all failed. The permanence of Fernando's achievement set him apart from St. Louis of France and all the other Crusader kings of Europe.

Fernando's grave is in Seville at the cathedral.

His Line

Husband		Wife
Alfonso IX "el Barboro," King of Leon (b. 15 Aug 1171 – md. Dec 1197 – d. 24 Sept 1230)	+	**Berengaria** (b. 1180 – md. (2) Dec 1197 – d. 8 Nov 1246), daughter of Alfonso IX "the Noble," King of Castile, Toledo, and Extramadura
St. Fernando III, King of Castile, Galicia, Leon, Toledo, and Extramadura (b. 24 June 1198 – md. (2) 1237 –d. 30 May 1252)	+	Jeanne de Dammartin, Countess of Ponthieu (b. ca. 1208 – md. 1237 – d. 16 March 1279)
Edward I "Longshanks," King of England (b. 17 June 1239 – md. (1) 18 Oct 1254 – d. 8 July 1307)	+	**Eleanor of Castile** (b. 1240 – md. 18 Oct 1254 – d. 28 Nov 1290)

Sources: *Baring-Gould*, Vol. 5, pp. 421–426; *Benedictine Monks*, p. 271; *Bunson*, pp. 320–321; *Butler*, Vol. II, p. 426; *CE*, Vol. VI, p. 42; *Cruz*, pp. 251–253; *Delaney*, pp. 223–224; *Delaney and Tobin*, pp. 413–414; *Englebert*, p. 207; *Holboeck*, pp. 189–191; *Holweck*, p. 376; *NCE*, Vol. 5, pp. 886–887; *Snodgrass*, p. 87; *Stuart*, line 52, nos. 26 through 24; *Weis, AR:* line 109, no. 30 + line 110, nos. 27 through 30

Bl. Frederick of Arras

Frederick was born sometime after 962 and was the oldest son of Godfrey "the Captive," Count of Verdun and Marquis of Antwerp, and his second wife Matilda of Saxony.

For most of his life, Frederick was a worldly Frankish nobleman. In 985 he and his father Godfrey fought at the side of Emperor Otto II in his war against Lothair of France. Both were captured at Verdun but released in 987 by Hugh Capet. Frederick also married, but the name of his wife is unknown.

In his later years, Frederick became a profoundly spiritual man. After giving away his wealth to the archdiocese of Verdun, he went on a pilgrimage to the Holy Land. Once he returned to Europe, he became a monk and entered the Benedictine abbey of St. Vannes at Verdun. After a time, he followed one of his friends to the abbey of St. Vedast at Arras, became the prior there, and died on 6 January 1020. He is also known as Bl. Frederick of St. Vanne.

His Line

Husband		Wife
Godfrey "the Captive," Count of Verdun and Marquis of Antwerp (b. 930/935 – md. (2) aft. 962 – d. aft. 3 Sept 1005)	+	**Matilda of Saxony** (md. aft. 962 – d. 25 May 1005)
Bl. Frederick of Arras, Count of Verdun (b. aft. 962 – d. 6 Jan 1020)	+	N.N.
Louis II, Count of Ivoix and Chiny (d. 1068)	+	**Sophia of Verdun** (d. 1078)
Arnulf II, Count of Ivoix, Chiny, and Warcq (d. 16 April 1106 a monk of St. Hubert)	+	md. (3) Adela of Rameru and Montdidier (d. 1068/1069)
Otto II, Count of Chiny (d. a monk 28 March 1125)	+	md. (2) Adelaide of Namur (b. ca. 1068 – d. 1124)
Godfrey I "the Bearded," Count of Louvain, Margrave of Antwerp, and Duke of Brabant (b. ca. 1060 – md. (1) ca. 1100 – d. 25 Jan 1139)	+	**Ida of Namur and Chiny** (b. 1083 – md. ca. 1100 – d. aft. 1125)

[For the later generations that connect this line to the kings of England, see the line of Bl. Adalbero, Bishop of Liege, in Part III.]

Sources: *Benedictine Monks*, p. 291; *Delaney and Tobin*, p. 447; *Holweck*, p. 403; *Stuart:* line 104, no. 35 + line 65, nos. 34 through 32 + line 120, nos. 31 and 30; *Weis, AR*, line 149, nos. 22A and 23; *Wells*, pp. 583 and 152

St. Gabran mac Domangart, King of Dalriada

Gabran was born around 500 and was the son of Domangart, King of Dalriada, and his wife Feldelm Foltchain, who was a niece of Niall of the Nine Hostages. Sometime before 532, Gabran married St. Lleian, a daughter of St. Brychan, and ascended to the throne in 537.

Gabran's land was a Celtic kingdom created by settlers from Ireland who crossed the water to the western seaboard of Scotland. Its capital moved from Ireland to Scotland during the reign of Gabran's grandfather King Fergus. A fortress built in Scotland on Dunadd Hill became the residence of its monarchs.

Gabran worked to expand his Scottish territory eastward into the land of the Picts and at first was very successful. Under Brude I, however, the Picts struck back, and the Dalriadans were driven out of most of the land won by Gabran. Gabran himself died in battle around 559.

His son and successor Aidan was crowned on Iona by St. Columba and became the greatest of all the kings of Dalriada. The Scottish kings that ruled a united land in later centuries descend from Fergus, Domangart, Gabran, and Aidan.

His Line

Husband		Wife
Domangart, King of Scottish Dalriada (d. ca. 504)	+	**Feldelm Foltchain**, whose father was a half-brother of Niall of the Nine Hostages
St. Gabran mac Domangart, King of Dalriada (b. ca. 500 – md. bef. 532 – d. ca. 559)	+	St. Lleian (md. bef. 532), daughter of St. Brychan
Aidan (or Aedan) mac Gabran (b. 532 – d. 606), crowned King of Dalriada by St. Columba of Iona	+	N.N.
Eochaid Buide, King of the Picts and of Dalriada (d. 629)	+	N.N.
Domnall Brec, King of Dalriada (d. ca. 642 in the battle of Strathcarron)	+	N.N., daughter of Widfroith

[For the later generations that connect this line to the kings of Scotland, see the line of St. Brychan in Part II.]

Sources: *Ashley*, p. 197; *Holweck*, p. 410; *Stuart*, line 165, nos. 50 through 46; *Weis, AR*, line 170, nos. 3 through 7; *Wells*, pp. 176–177; *Williamson*, pp. 159 and 377

St. Geraint, King of Brittany

In a sense, Geraint has suffered from too much attention. There are mythical figures with this name that have been the inspiration for creative works from the Dark Ages down to modern times. There is also more than one actual historical figure with this name. It is not always easy to tell whether source material is folklore or fact.

Most of what has been written deals with the mythological Geraint rather than the man. The Geraint of the myths is a figure in Arthurian legends and various Welsh epics, such as *The Mabiginion* and the poems *Elegy for Gereint* and *Y Gododdin*. When Alfred, Lord Tennyson wrote his *Idylls of the King*, Geraint became a figure in the poems *The Marriage of Geraint* and *Geraint and Enid*. In 1900, Edward Elgar composed an oratorio called *The Dream of Gerontius*, which was inspired by a poem by Cardinal Newman about an allegorical Geraint who is quite different from the Geraint of the King Arthur tales.

The first real Geraint was the son of Cynan Meriadoc, King of Brittany. The name of Cynan's wife was perhaps Darara. Geraint married Enid and succeeded his father as king. Geraint became a saint and had four sons who also became saints—Cado, Cyngar (or Congar), Jestin (or Iestin), and Selyf (or Salamon or Solomon).

There is another actual historical figure named Geraint who lived in the late 600's and early 700's and who was king of Dumnonia, a realm in the southwestern part of modern England. A letter survives which was written to this Geraint by a churchman named Aldhelm regarding the proper date for celebrating Easter. It was during the reign of this Geraint that conflict between Dumnonia and the neighboring kingdom of Wessex began to increase. This Geraint died ca. 710 at the battle of Longport fighting the armies of St. Ina, King of Wessex. His kingdom of Dumnonia was ultimately absorbed by Wessex.

All the Geraints, both mythical and actual, have variously been called Geraint, Gerontius, Gradlonus, and Gratian.

His Line

Husband		Wife
Cynan (or Conan) Meriadoc, King of Brittany	+	**Darara**
St. Geraint, King of Brittany	+	Enid
St. Salamon I "the Handsome," King of Brittany (liv. in the 400's)	+	St. Gwen
Audren, King of Brittany	+	N.N.
Budic I, King of Brittany	+	N.N., a daughter of Corun

[For the later generations that connect this line to the kings of England, see the line of St. Cunedda Wledig in Part II.]

Sources: *Ashley*, pp. 117 and 309 and 727–728; *Baring-Gould*, Vol. 16, pp. 133 and 260–262; *Baring-Gould and Fisher*, Vol. 3, pp. 46–52; *Holweck*, p. 425; *Stuart*, line 405, nos. 57 through 53

St. Germanus,
Bishop of Auxerre

Germanus was born in 378 and was the son of Decimus Rusticus, a Roman prefect of the Gauls, and his wife Artemia.

In the early life of Germanus, there is nothing to suggest that he would be remembered for his work in the Church. His parents raised him in the Christian faith, but as a young man he went to Rome to study law. After finishing his studies, he practiced law in Rome and was very successful. He married a woman named Eustachia and was appointed by Emperor Honorius to be one of the six Roman governors in Gaul, with responsibility for Brittany and the surrounding territory. He was such a capable governor that in 418 when the bishop of Auxerre died, Germanus was named to succeed him.

After assuming his new office, a profound change came over Germanus. He renounced all worldliness and embraced the life of poverty and austerity. He distributed his goods among the poor, washed their feet, and served them with his own hands. He happily embraced all his new responsibilities and devoted all of his talents to his flock.

Germanus was such an excellent bishop that he was selected by Pope St. Celestine I to go to Britain in 429 to combat the Pelagian heresy that was gaining ground among the faithful there. While he was there, he confronted its leaders in public meetings, preached the true faith, performed miracles of healing, and led a native army as it repelled a Saxon invasion.

Germanus' efforts persuaded many people who had been attracted to Pelagianism to renounce it. Believing his work was finished, Germanus went home to Auxerre. A few years later, enough Britons had relapsed into Pelagianism that Germanus returned to Britain in 440. During this second mission, the heresy was finally stamped out.

In the final years of his life, Germanus' flock in Brittany revolted against Rome. In due course, a Roman force was sent to put down the rebellion. Germanus persuaded its commander to hold his men back while Germanus went to Italy to seek a pardon for his people from the emperor. During this journey, Germanus died in Ravenna on 31 July 448.

Germanus was buried in the abbey church at Auxerre. In 1567, his grave was desecrated by Huguenots, and his bones were scattered.

When St. Patrick was young, he spent several years in Auxerre as a student of St. Germanus. It was Germanus who ordained Patrick bishop of Ireland.

His Line

Husband		Wife
Decimus Rusticus, prefect of the Gauls 409-413	+	**Artemia**
St. Germanus, Bishop of Auxerre (b. 378 – d. 31 July 448)	+	Eustachia

Aquilinus, a noble of Lyons (d. aft. 470)	+	N.N.
Rusticus, Bishop of Lyons (d. 25 April 501)	+	N.N.
Florentinus, Bishop of Geneva (d. aft. 513)	+	**Artemia**
Munderic, Lord of Vitry-en-Parthois (b. ca. 500 – d. 532)	+	**Artemia**
St. Gondolfus, Bishop of Tongres (liv. 599)	+	N.N.
St. Bodegeisel II, Governor of Aquitaine (murdered 588)	+	St. Oda, a Suevian (b. ca. 567 – d. ca. 640)

[For the later generations that connect this line to the kings of England, see the line of St. Arnulf, Bishop of Metz in Part II.]

Sources: *Baring-Gould*, Vol. 8, pp. 681–697; *Baring-Gould and Fisher*, Vol. 3, pp. 52–60; *BBKL*, Vol. 2, cols. 225–226; *Benedictine Monks*, p. 310; *Bentley*, p. 53 (under "Patrick"); *Bunson*, pp. 361–362; *Butler*, Vol. III, pp. 251–253; *Castleden*, pp. 100–101; *CE*, Vol. VI, pp. 472–473; *CS*, pp. 427–428; *Delaney*, pp. 253–254; *Delaney and Tobin*, pp. 477–478; *Holweck*, p. 430; *O'Malley*, pp. 279-280; *Stuart:* line 171A + line 171, nos. 49 through 46; *Weis, AR*, line 190, nos. 5 through 7

St. Gertrude of Hamage

Gertrude was the daughter of Theobald, Lord of Douai. She married Ricomer, the Duke of Burgundy. After Ricomer's death, she founded the convent of Hamage near Douai and became its first abbess.

Gertrude is also known as Gertrude the Elder.

Her Line

Husband		Wife
Theobald, Lord of Douai	+	**N.N.**
Ricomer, Duke of Burgundy	+	**St. Gertrude of Hamage**
Leutharius	+	**Gerberge**
Ansaud (b. ca. 570)	+	**N.N.**
Bodilon de Treves	+	**Sigrada** (d. ca. 678)
St. Guerin (or Warinus), Count of Poitiers (d. 677)	+	Kunza (d. 690), daughter of St. Clodulf, Bishop of Metz

[For the later generations that connect this line to the kings of England, see the line of St. Clodulf, Bishop of Metz in Part II.]

Sources: *Baring-Gould*, Vol. 15, p. 70; *Benedictine Monks*, p. 312; *Bunson*, p. 363; *Delaney and Tobin*, p. 479; *Holweck*, p. 432; *O'Malley*, p. 117; *Stuart:* line 236, nos. 46 through 44 + line 2, nos. 46 and 45; *Wells*, pp. 497 and 303

St. Gondolfus, Bishop of Tongres

Gondolfus was born in the mid-500's and was the son of Munderic, Lord of Vitry-en-Parthois, and his wife Artemia. Munderic was the son of Cloderic "the Parricide," King of Cologne. Artemia was the daughter of Florentius, Bishop of Geneva.

Gondolfus married Palatina of Troyes and was the father of St. Bodegeisel II, Governor of Aquitaine.

The town of Tongres in the Netherlands had been destroyed by barbarians, and after becoming bishop in 599 Gondolfus worked to rebuild it. He died 16 July 604 and is buried in Maastricht in the Church of Saint-Servais. He was later made patron of the city of Maastricht.

His Line

Husband		Wife
Munderic, Lord of Vitry-en-Parthois (b. ca. 500 – d. 532)	+	**Artemia**
St. Gondolfus, Bishop of Tongres (b. mid-500's – d. 16 July 604)	+	Palatina of Troyes
St. Bodegeisel II, Governor of Aquitaine (murdered 588)	+	St. Oda, a Suevian (b. ca. 567 – d. ca. 640)
St. Arnulf (or Arnoul), Mayor of the Palace in Austrasia and Bishop of Metz (b. 13 Aug 582 – md. ca. 596 – d. 16 Aug 640)	+	Dode (or Clothilde) (b. ca. 586 – md. ca. 596)

[For the later generations that connect this line to the kings of England, see the line of St. Arnulf, Bishop of Metz in Part II.]

Sources: *Holweck*, p. 441; *Stuart*, line 171, nos. 49 through 46; *Weis, AR*, line 190, nos. 5 through 8

St. Gregory "the Illuminator"

Gregory was born in 256 and was the son of Anak the Parthian and his wife Okohe. While Gregory was still very young, his father quarreled with the king of Armenia, and as a result Gregory's family had to flee to the city of Caesarea in Cappadocia. In Caesarea, Gregory was raised a Christian and married a woman named Maria.

Around 298/299, a new king came to the throne in Armenia: Tiridates IV. Around the same time, Gregory—who was now in his early 40's—returned to Armenia and found work at the royal court.

At the time Tiridates took the throne, Christianity had already been preached in Armenia but had never really taken root there. Tiridates was a pagan who did not care for Christians or their faith.

After Gregory had become attached to the court, Tiridates was leading a worship service to his gods when Gregory refused to sacrifice to them. Highly displeased, Tiridates threw Gregory into prison. Later on while Gregory was still confined, Tiridates began a general persecution of Christians. On 5 October 301 outside the city of Valarshabad, several nuns were murdered in their convent. Shortly after this deed, Tiridates went mad. His ravings baffled and frightened his whole court, and no one could do anything to help him.

Later in 301 while the king was still out of his mind, it is written that his sister Khosrowidukht had a dream in which she was told to release Gregory from prison and to bring him to Tiridates. When this was done, Gregory put his hands on Tiridates and prayed for him, and by a miracle the king was suddenly cured. Restored to his reason, Tiridates converted to Christianity and made it the official religion of his kingdom.

The king's action made Armenia the world's first Christian nation. In 302 Gregory became the first Katholikos or bishop of Armenia. He built schools, churches, and the cathedral at Etchmiadzin, which is in Yerevan and still the mother church of Armenian Christianity. He wrote prayers and church services and established canon laws. He preached Christianity everywhere.

After several years of hard work, in 318 Gregory appointed his son Aristakes to be the next bishop of Armenia. Gregory then retired to spend his last years living in the mountains and contemplating God. He died in 326.

Gregory is often called "the apostle of Armenia" and has been its patron saint from his own time down to the present. His sons Aristakes and Vardanes became saints. So did Tiridates, the king he converted.

His Line

Husband		Wife
Anak the Parthian	+	**Okohe**
St. Gregory "the Illuminator" (b. 256 – d. 326)	+	Maria
St. Vardanes (d. 339/341)	+	N.N.
St. Yusik I (martyred ca. 344)	+	N.N., a daughter of St. Tiridates "the Great," King of Armenia

Athenagenes	+	Bambishu (b. 315)
St. Nerses (or Narces or Narses) I "the Great," Gregorid Prince and Bishop of Armenia (b. 335 – d. 373)	+	Samdukht

[For the later generations that connect this line to the kings of England, see the line of St. Ashken in Part II.]

Sources: *Baring-Gould*, Vol. 10, pp. 442–449; *BBKL*, Vol. 2, col. 331; *Benedictine Monks*, p. 324; *Bunson*, p. 376; *CE*, Vol. VIII, pp. 23–25; *CS*, pp. 561–562; *Delaney and Tobin*, p. 510; *Dowling*, pp. 51–57; *Guiley*, p. 138; *Holweck*, pp. 449–450; *Hovannisian*, p. 81; *Kaloustian*, pp. 14–18; *Koushagian*, pp. 8–9; *NCE*, Vol. 6, pp. 790–791; *Stone*, Chart 80; *Stuart*, line 416, nos. 56 and 57; *Wagner*, p. 195; *Wells*, p. 33

St. Guerin

Guerin was the son of Bodilon de Treves and St. Sigrada. He married Kunza, daughter of St. Clodulf, Bishop of Metz. He was the brother of St. Leodegar.

Guerin lived in the kingdom of Neustria in the mid-600's. For twenty-four years starting in 657, the de facto ruler of Neustria was Ebroin, who made and unmade the puppet kings who nominally governed Neustria and who variously tortured, blinded, and beheaded his opponents.

One of the figures who opposed Ebroin's career of misrule was Guerin's brother St. Leodegar. After Ebroin captured Leodegar, he was determined to make him suffer several different torments before he died. In 677 outside of Arras, France, St. Guerin was tied to a tree by Ebroin's men and stoned to death as Leodegar was made to stand by.

Guerin is also known as Warinus.

His Line

Husband		Wife
Bodilon de Treves	+	**St. Sigrada** (d. ca. 678)
St. Guerin (or Warinus), Count of Poitiers (d. 677)	+	Kunza (d. 690), daughter of St. Clodulf, Bishop of Metz
Lambert of Hesbaye (liv. 725)	+	N.N.
Robert, Count of Hesbaye (b. ca. 700 – liv. 750)	+	Williswinda
Guerin, Count in the Thurgovie (d. 20 May 772)	+	Adelindis

[For the later generations that connect this line to the kings of England, see the line of St. Clodulf, Bishop of Metz in Part II.]

Sources: *Baring-Gould*, Vol. 11, pp. 19–31 (under "St. Leodegar"); *Benedictine Monks*, pp. 722–723; *Bunson*, pp. 360 and 849; *Butler*, Vol. IV, pp. 9–11 (under "St. Leodegarius"); *Delaney and Tobin*, p. 477; *Holweck*, p. 428; *Stuart*, line 2, nos. 46 through 42; *Tucker*, Vol. I, p. 331; *Wells*, p. 303

St. Gwen

Gwen was the daughter of Gwynyr "Ceinfarfog" (Gwynyr the Fair Bearded), Lord of Caer Gawch, and his second wife Anna. She married St. Salamon I "the Handsome," King of Brittany. They became the parents of St. Cybi.

Gwen was known for her prayer life and founded the church of St. Wenn in Cornwall. She was also the sister of St. Non, the mother of St. David of Wales.

Her Line

Husband		Wife
Gwynyr (or Gynyr or Cynyr) "Ceinfarfog" (the Fair Bearded), Lord of Caer Gawch (or Caer Goch) in Pembrokeshire, Wales	+	md. (2) **Anna**, daughter of Gwerthefyr (or Vortimer) "Fendigaid" (the Blessed)
St. Salamon I "the Handsome," King of Brittany (liv. in the 400's)	+	**St. Gwen**
Audren, King of Brittany	+	N.N.
Budic I, King of Brittany	+	N.N., a daughter of Corun
Hoel I "the Great," King of Brittany (b. ca. 491 – d. ca. 545)	+	St. Pompeja

[For the later generations that connect this line to the kings of England, see the line of St. Cunedda Wledig in Part II.]

Sources: *Baring-Gould*, Vol. 16, p. 133; *Baring-Gould and Fisher*, Vol. 3, pp. 166–167; *Benedictine Monks*, pp. 330 and 652*; *Bunson*, pp. 382 and 763*; *Delaney and Tobin*, pp. 524 and 1070*; *Holweck*, pp. 460 and 926*; *Parbury*, pp. 53–54; *Stuart*, line 405, nos. 55 through 52 (references marked with a * are alphabetized under "Solomon I")

St. Harold III "Bluetooth," King of Denmark

Harold was born around 910 and was the son of Gorm "the Old," King of Denmark and his wife Thyra Danebord. During his long reign, Harold's two greatest achievements were preserving the independence of the new Danish nation and the conversion of his country to Christianity. All of this was accomplished over considerable opposition.

The basis of Harold's political achievement was created during the reign of his father. After winning wars with other Danish leaders, Gorm was the first man to rule over all of Denmark. In a war with Emperor Henry I of Germany that started in 934, however, Gorm was defeated. The peace treaty obliged him to do homage to Henry and pay tribute. At the time, it was very uncertain whether Gorm could hold his new realm together and also keep it out of the hands of the German emperors.

As king, Harold saved what Gorm had begun. Thanks to his efforts, the kingdom didn't break up and also didn't disappear into the Germans' Holy Roman Empire. The dynasty begun by Gorm and Harold still rules Denmark today.

During Harold's early life, the conversion of Denmark to Christianity also seemed highly unlikely. Missionaries had already been coming to Denmark for about two hundred years, but none of them had persuaded any significant part of the country's Viking population to give up their pagan beliefs. Harold's father Gorm had been a strong opponent of Christianity who burned churches and killed priests. Harold himself was born a pagan but heard his first favorable accounts of the new religion from his mother Thyra. When German missionaries arrived in Denmark after the war of 934, a major breakthrough was achieved when Harold welcomed them and allowed them to preach throughout the country.

Harold himself was baptized in 965. It is reported that Harold was brought to this decision by witnessing the following miracle. A priest named Poppo had told Harold and his companions that the Christian God was the one true and all-powerful God. Harold asked Poppo if he was willing to let this claim be judged by his God, and Poppo agreed. A bar of iron was heated red hot, and Poppo was asked to pick it up and carry it in his bare hands. Poppo did so and held it until Harold told him to put it down. When Harold looked at Poppo's hands, they had not been burned.

Following his baptism, Harold allowed more missionaries to enter his kingdom. Even then, not all of the Danes were ready to be converted. In the 980's, Harold's son Sweyn Forkbeard led a revolt against his father which was supported in part by some pagan Danes who wanted their old religion reestablished. After reigning for almost fifty years, Harold led his army out to crush the revolt, was wounded in battle, and died on 1 November 985/986.

Harold was buried in the cathedral of St. Lucius in Roskilde, Denmark, which has since become the burial place of Danish kings.

His Line

Husband		Wife
Gorm "the Old," King of Denmark, East Anglia, Seeland, and Jutland (d. aft. 950)	+	**Thyra Danebord** (d. ca. 935)
St. Harold III "Bluetooth," King of Denmark and Norway (b. ca. 910 – d. in battle 1 Nov 985/986)	+	md. (2) Gunhilda
Styrbiorn Olafsson, leader of the Jomsborg Vikings (b. 956 – slain 985 at the battle of Blackfeld)	+	md. (1) **Thyra of Denmark** (d. 18 Sept 1000)
Jarl Thorkill Sprakalaeg	+	N.N.
Godwin, Earldorman of Wessex (md. (2) 1019/1020 – d. 15 April 1053)	+	**Gytha** (md. 1019/1020)
Harold II Godwinsson, King of England (b. ca. 1022 – slain 14 Oct 1066 at the battle of Hastings)	+	Ealdgyth "Swanneshals" (Swan Neck)
St. Vladimir Vsevolodovich Monomach (or Vladimir II "Monomachos"), Grand Prince of Kiev (b. 1053 – md. (1) ca. 1070 – d. 19 May 1125)	+	**Gytha of Wessex** (md. ca. 1070)
St. Mstislav Vladimirovich (or Mstislav I Harold), Grand Prince of Kiev (b. 1076 – md. (2) 1122 – d. 15 April 1132)	+	Lyubawa (md. 1122 – d. 1168), daughter of Dmitri Zaviditsch, Possadnik of Novgorod
Geza II, King of Hungary (b. ca. 1130 – md. 1146 – d. 3 May 1162)	+	**Euphrosyne Mstislava** (b. 1130 – md. 1146 – d. 1175/1176)
Bela III, King of Hungary (b. ca. 1148 – md. 1172 – d. 23 April 1196)	+	Agnes (or Anne) de Chatillon-sur-Loing (b. 1153 – md. 1172 – d. 1184)
Andrew II, King of Hungary (b. 1176 – md. (2) 1215 – d. 21 Sept 1235)	+	Yolande de Courtenay (b. ca. 1194 – md. 1215 – d. 1233)
James I "the Conqueror," King of Aragon (b. 1 Feb 1207 – md. 8 Sept 1235 – d. 25 July 1276)	+	**Yolande** (b. 1213 – md. 8 Sept 1235 – d. 12 Oct 1251)
Philip III "the Bold," King of France (b. 1 May 124 – md. (1) 28 May 1262 – d. 5 Oct 1285)	+	**Isabella of Aragon** (b. 1243 or 127 – md. 28 May 1262 – d. 28 Jan 1271)
Philip IV "the Fair," King of France (b. 1268 – md. 16 Aug 1284 – d. 29 Nov 1314)	+	Jeanne of Navarre (b. Jan 1272 – md. 16 Aug 1284 – d. 2 April 1305)
Edward II, King of England (b. 25 April 1284 – md. 25 Jan 1308 – murdered 21 Sept 1327)	+	**Isabella** (b. 1292 – md. 25 June 1308 – d. 27 Aug 1357)

Sources: *Baring-Gould*, Vol. 13, pp. 28–39; *CE*, Vol. VIII, p. 141; *HBC*, p. 29; *Holweck*, p. 464; *Stuart:* line 369, nos. 39 through 37 + line 368, nos. 34 through 30 + line 240, nos. 30 through 28 + line 51, nos. 29 through 23; *Weis, AR:* line 1B, nos. 22 through 24 + line 242, nos. 7 through 10 + line 103, nos. 27 and 28 + line 105 + line 101, nos. 29 through 31

Bl. Haziga of Diessen

Haziga was the daughter of Frederick II, Count of Diessen, and his wife Ermengarde von Gilching.

Haziga's first two husbands were Hermann IV, Duke of Swabia (d. 28 July 1038) and Hermann von Kastl (d. 1056). In 1057, Haziga married Otto I von Scheyern, Count in the Middle Paar and Crusader. Their descendants became the Wittlesbach Dukes of Bavaria.

In 1077, Haziga founded the monastery of Bayrischzell, now Scheyern. She died on 1 August 1103 and is buried there.

Her Line

Husband		Wife
Frederick II von Diessen, Count of Diessen (liv. 1035 – d. ca. 1075)	+	md. (her 2nd) **Ermengarde von Gilching**
Otto I von Scheyern, Count in the Middle Paar, Crusader (md. (2) 1057 – d. 4 Dec 1072)	+	**Bl. Haziga of Diessen** (md. (3) 1057 – d. 1 Aug 1103)
Otto II von Scheyern, Count in the Paar and in the Kelsgau (md. (2) 1088/2090 – d. ca. 1110)	+	Richardis of Weimar (md. 1088/1090 – d. aft. 16 May 1120)
Otto von Wittlesbach IV, Count of Wittlesbach and Pfalzgraf of Bavaria (md. bef. 13 July 1116 – d. 4 Aug 1156)	+	Heilika von Pettendorf (md. bef. 13 July 1116 – d. 13 Sept 1170)
Otto von Wittlesbach V, Duke of Bavaria, Crusader, and Ambassador to Constantinople (b. ca. 1117 – md. 1159/1167 – d. 1 July 1183)	+	Agnes von Loos (b. ca. 1150 – md. 1159/1167 – d. 26 March 1191)
Otto I, Count of East Friesland, Guelders, Holland, Zealand, and Zutphen, Crusader (md. bef. 1188 – d. betw. 30 April and 24 Sept 1207)	+	**Richardis von Wittlesbach** (md. bef. 1188 – d. 7 Dec 1231)

[For the later generations that connect this line to the kings of England, see the line of Bl. Adelheid von Odenkirchen in Part II.]

Sources: *Holweck*, p. 466; *Stuart:* line 46, nos. 31 and 30 + line 307, nos. 30 through 26; *Wells*, pp. 187, 517, 58, and 285

St. Hereswitha

Also known as Saeware, Hereswitha was the daughter of Prince Hereric of Northumbria and his wife Berguswitha. Hereric was a nephew of St. Edwin, King of Northumbria. Hereric was murdered in 616 shortly after Hereswitha was born, and Hereswitha grew up at the court of her uncle St. Edwin.

Hereswitha's first husband was Anna, King of East Anglia. Five of their children became saints: Erconwald, Ethelburga, Etheldreda, Sexburga, and Withburga.

After Anna died in battle against Penda of Mercia in 653, Hereswith remarried. Most authorities say her second husband was Anna's brother Aethelhere, who became the next king of East Anglia. This marriage produced another daughter Sethrida who would become a saint, and after Aethelhere died in the battle of Winwaed on November 15, 655, Hereswitha was a widow again.

Hereswitha then became a Benedictine nun and retired to a convent in Chelles, France where she died around 680/690. She was a sister of St. Hilda of Whitby.

Her Line

Husband		Wife
Hereric (d. 616), a nephew of St. Edwin, King of Northumbria	+	**Berguswitha**
Anna, King of East Anglia (ruled ca. 641–653, until he died in battle with Penda of Mercia)	+	**St. Hereswitha** (b. shortly bef. 616 – d. 680/690)
Erconbert (or Eorconbeorht), King of Kent (b. ca. 624 – md. ca. 640 – d. 14 July 664)	+	**St. Sexburga** (md. ca. 640 – d. 6 July 699)
Egbert, King of Kent (b. ca. 641 – d. 4 July 673)	+	N.N.
Wihtread, King of Kent (d. 23 April 725)	+	N.N.

[For the later generations that connect this line to the kings of England, see the line of St. Aethelbert I, King of Kent in Part II.]

Sources: *Ashley*, pp. 212 and 219–222; *Benedictine Monks*, pp. 338–339; *Browne*, pp. 84–85 and 87; *Bunson*, p. 391; *Delaney and Tobin*, p. 553; *HBC*, p. 8; *Holweck*, p. 474; *King*, p. 195; *Stuart:* line 437, nos. 47 and 46 + line 233A, nos. 46 through 44; *Wells*, p. 197; *Yorke*, pp. 68 and 36

Bl. Hildegarde, Wife of Bl. Charlemagne

Hildegarde was born around 754 and was the daughter of Gerold, Duke of Allemania and Count in the Vinzgau, and his wife Emma. In 771 at the age of seventeen, she married Bl. Charlemagne, King of the Franks. In 12 years of marriage, they had 9 children.

Hildegarde was a very beautiful woman who befriended monks and nuns, especially St. Lioba. She restored Kempten Abbey and founded several churches. Charlemagne seemed to truly love her.

Hildegarde died on 30 April 783. She was buried in Metz at the church of St. Arnulf, and her tomb became a place of pilgrimage. Some of her relics are also at Kempten.

Her Line

Husband		Wife
Gerold, Duke of Allemania and Count in the Vinzgau (liv. 779)	+	**Emma of Allemania** (d. 798)
Bl. Charlemagne, King of the Franks and First Emperor of the West (b. 2 April 747 – md. (2) 771 – d. 28 Jan 814)	+	**Bl. Hildegarde**, Countess of Vinzgau (b. ca. 754 – md. 771 – d. 30 April 783)
Louis I "the Fair," King of France and Emperor of the West (b. Aug 778 – md. (2) 819 – d. 20 June 840)	+	Judith of Altdorf (or Judith of Bavaria) (b. ca. 800 – md. 819 – d. 19 April 843)

[For the later generations that connect this line to the kings of England, see the line of St. Arnulf, Bishop of Metz in Part II.]

Sources: *BBKL*, Vol. 2, col. 846; *Benedictine Monks*, p. 345; *Butler*, Vol. II, pp. 199–200; *Delaney*, p. 286; *Delaney and Tobin*, p. 562; *Dunbar*, Vol. I, pp. 384–386; *Holweck*, p. 485; *Stuart:* line 262, nos. 42 and 41 + line 171, nos. 41 and 40; *Warncke*, pp. 156–157; *Weis, AR:* line 182, nos. 4 and 5 + line 140, nos. 13 and 14; *Wells*, pp. 9 and 136–137

St. Hmayeak Mamikonian

Hmayeak was born in 410 and was the son of Hamazasp I, Prince of the Mamikonids, and his wife Sahakanoysh. He married Dzoyk of the Rshtuni.

Besides serving as the ambassador of Armenia to the eastern Roman Empire, Hmayeak was also a general. When Persia hoped to force Armenia to abandon Christianity and embrace Zoroastrianism in 451, Hmayeak's brother St. Vardan II, Prince of the Mamikonids, led the Armenian army out to meet the Persians at the battle of Avarayr. Hmayeak was a co-commander with his brother.

The battle on 2 June 451 was one of the defining moments of the Armenian nation. Militarily, it was a Persian victory. Hmayeak, his brother Vardan, and a large number of Armenians were killed. Popular resistance, however, made the Persians abandon their designs on Armenia soon afterwards. All of the Armenians who died at Avarayr were later canonized by the Armenian church.

His Line

Husband		Wife
Hamazasp I, Prince of the Mamikonids and High Constable of Armenia (b. 345 – d. ca. 416)	+	**Sahakanoysh**, the Gregorid heiress
St. Hmayeak Mamikonian, General and Mamikonian ambassador to Constantinople (b. 410 – d. in battle 2 June 451)	+	Dzoyk, daughter of Vram, Prince of Rshtuni
Vard, Mamikonean Viceroy of Armenia (b. 450 – d. aft. 509)	+	N.N.
Hmayeak, Mamikonean Viceroy (d. 593)	+	N.N.
Moushegh I, Mamikonian Viceroy and High Constable of Armenia	+	N.N.

[For the later generations that connect this line to the kings of England, see the line of St. Ashken in Part II.]

Sources: *Kaloustian*, pp. 23–24; *Koushagian*, pp. 18–19; *Stone*, Chart 80; *Stuart*, line 322, nos. 53 through 49; *Wagner*, p. 196

Bl. Humbeline of Troyes

Humbeline was born in 1092 and was the daughter of Tescelin Sorrel, Lord of Les Fontaines, and his wife Bl. Aleth of Montbard. She had several children with her first husband Anseric II, Sire de Chacenay. Her second husband was Gautier II, Count of Brienne.

Humbeline was a beautiful woman with a lovely singing voice. During her first several years of marriage, she lived the life of the nobility of the day and traveled in fine clothes and with many servants. Her spiritual outlook began to change after she visited her brother St. Bernard of Clairvaux at his monastery. He talked with her at great length about the most important things in life. She went away and began to reflect. About two years later with her second husband's consent, she became a nun and entered the convent of Jully-les-Nonnais near Troyes. She lived a life of great austerity, became the abbess there, and died in her brother's arms on 21 August 1141.

She is regarded as the founder of the Cistercian nuns. Her relics are still at the convent.

Her Line

Husband		Wife
Tescelin Sorrel (or Sorus), Lord of Les Fontaines (md. ca. 1085)	+	**Bl. Aleth of Montbard** (b. ca. 1070 – md. ca. 1085 – d. 1105/ 1110)
Anseric II, Sire de Chacenay (d. 1137)	+	md. (1) **Bl. Humbeline de Troyes** (b. 1092 – d. 21 Aug 1141)
Gui, Count of Bar-sur-Seine (d. 1145)	+	**Petronille de Chacenay** (d. 1161)
Theobald I, Count of Bar-le-Duc, Brie, and Luxemburg, Crusader (b. ca. 1160 – md.(3) 1189 – d. 13 Feb 1214)	+	**Ermesinde of Bar-sur-Seine** (md. 1189 – d. ca. 1211)
Henry II, Count of Bar-le-Duc, Luxemburg, and Namur, Crusader (b. 1190 – md. 1219 – d. 13 Nov 1239)	+	Philippa of Dreux, Dame de Coucy (b. 1192 – md. 1219 – d. 17 March 1242)

[For the later generations that connect this line to the kings of England, see the line of Bl. Aleth of Montbard in Part II.]

Sources: *BBKL*, Vol. 20, cols. 394–395; *Benedictine Monks*, p. 353; *Bunson*, p. 403; *Butler*, Vol. III, pp. 360 and 376–377; *Chervin*, pp. 254–256; *Delaney*, pp. 293–294; *Delaney and Tobin*, p. 580; *Dunbar*, Vol. I, pp. 394–395; *Holweck*, p. 495; *NCE*, Vol. 7, pp. 230–231; *O'Malley*, p. 73; *Snodgrass*, p. 123; *Stuart:* line 385 + line 384, nos. 29 and 28 + line 383, nos. 28 through 26; *Wells*, pp. 144, 48, and 47

Bl. Humbert III,
Count of Savoy

Humbert was born on 4 August 1135 and was the son of Amadeus III, Count of Savoy, and his wife Matilda d'Albon.

Humbert was only twelve years old when his father died while on crusade. Humbert nevertheless became the new Count of Savoy and ruled very wisely during his forty-year reign. He was just, pious, and a very good military commander who fought several invaders and won.

It was not until his fourth marriage in 1175 that Humbert managed to produce a male heir. His wives were (1) Faidiva, (2) Gertrude of Flanders, (3) Clementia of Zaehringen, and (4) Beatrice of Macon.

In old age Humbert became a monk and entered the Cistercian abbey of Hautecombe, where he lived in great humility and self-denial. He died on 4 March 1188 and was buried in his monastery, which became the burial place of the counts of Savoy.

His Line

Husband		Wife
Amadeus (or Amadeo) III, Count of Savoy, Marquis of Maurienne, and Crusader (b. 1080/1092 – md. 1133/1134 – d. 30 March 1148 on the 2nd Crusade)	+	**Matilda d'Albon** (md. 1133/1134 – d. aft. Jan 1145)
Bl. Humbert (or Umberto III), Count of Savoy and Marquis of Italy (b. 4 Aug 1136 – md. (4) 1175 – d. 4 March 1189)	+	Beatrice of Macon (b. ca. 1160 – md. 1175 – d. 8 April 1230)
Thomas I, Count of Savoy (b. 20 May 1178 – md. 1196 – d. 1 March 1233)	+	Margaret of Geneva (b. ca. 1180 – md. 1196 – d. 13 April 1236)
Raymond Berenger V, Count of Provence and Forcalquier (b. 1198 – md. Dec 1220 – d. 19 Aug 1245)	+	**Beatrice of Savoy** (b. 1198 – md. Dec 1220 – d. Dec 1266)
Henry III, King of England (b. 1 Oct 1207 – md. 14 Jan 1236 – d. 16 Nov 1272)	+	**Bl. Eleanor of Provence** (b. ca. 1223 – md. 14 Jan 1236 – d. 25 June 1291)

Sources: *BBKL*, Vol. 22, col. 588; *Benedictine Monks*, p. 353; *Butler*, Vol. I, p. 482; *Delaney*, p. 294; *Delaney and Tobin*, p. 580; *Holweck*, p. 495; *Stuart:* line 93, nos. 29 through 26 + line 54, nos. 26 and 25; *Wagner*, p. 203; *Weis, AR*, line 133, nos. 26 and 27; *Wells*, pp. 512 and 482

St. Ida of Herzfeld

Some authorities say that Ida was the daughter of Count Dietrich "the Riparian." Others say that she was the daughter of Duke Bernard, who was an illegitimate son of Charles Martel. The dispute will probably never be resolved.

There is agreement that Ida married Ecbert (or Egbert) "the Loyal," Count in the Ittergau and that she was the mother of Bl. Warin, Abbot of Corvie, Bl. Hedwig, Abbess of Herford, and other children.

Ida was profoundly religious throughout her life. While Ecbert was alive, he and Ida founded a church in Herzfeld. After his death, she founded a convent and began to give most of the revenues of her estate to the poor. In her final years, she was afflicted with a painful illness which she bore with great patience, and her piety and austerities only increased. She died sometime after 21 November 838.

After her death, Ida was first buried in the church in Herzfeld which she and Ecbert had built. Her grave soon became a place of pilgrimage, and on 26 November 980 the bishop of Münster had her remains reburied in a manner befitting a saint.

Her Line

Husband		Wife
N.N.	+	**N.N.**
Ecbert (or Egbert) "the Loyal," Count in the Ittergau (d. aft. 834)	+	**St. Ida of Herzfeld** (d. aft. 21 Nov 838)
Reginhart, son of Walbert, Count of Ringelheim and of the Threkwitigau	+	**Mathilda** (alive in 909)
Dietrich, Count of Ringelheim, Saxony, and the Saxon Hamalant (b. ca. 872 – md. (1) 882 – d. 8 Dec 917)	+	Gisela of Lorraine (b. 860/865 – md. 882 – d. by 26 Oct 907)
Henry I "the Fowler," Duke of Saxony and Emperor of the West (b. 876 – md. (2) 909 – d. 2 July 936)	+	**St. Matilda of Ringelheim** (b. ca. 890/900 – md. 909 – d. 14 March 968)
Giselbert, Duke of Lorraine and Count of Hainault (b. ca. 890 – md. 929 – d. 2 Oct 934)	+	**Gerberga of Saxony** (b. 913/914 – md. (1) 929 – d. 5 May 984)

[For the later generations that connect this line to the kings of England, see the line of St. Adela, Princess of Austrasia in Part II.]

Sources: *BBKL*, Vol. 2, cols. 1249–1250; *Benedictine Monks*, pp. 356–357; *Bunson*, p. 406; *Butler*, Vol. III, p. 486; *Cruz*, p. 331; *Delaney and Tobin*, p. 584; *Holboeck*, pp. 115–116; *Holweck*, p. 500; *NCE*, Vol. 7, p. 335; *Stuart:* line 338 + line 92, nos. 36 and 35; *Weis, AR*, line 42, nos. 17 and 18; *Wells*, pp. 515 and 270. Also see ***fmg.ac>Projects>Medieval Lands>Medieval Lands – data by region>France>Kings & early nobility>Carolingian Nobility>Family of Adalhard and Wala***.

Bl. Ida of Boulogne

Ida was born around 1040 and was the daughter of Godfrey, Duke of Upper and Lower Lorraine and Count of Verdun, and his wife Ida (also known as Oda). In December 1057, Ida became the second wife of Eustace II, Count of Boulogne. The same year, Ida's uncle Frederick became Pope Stephen IX.

Ida's husband and sons all triumphed in war. Her husband was one of the companions of William the Conqueror at the battle of Hastings. In the Crusades, all three of their sons would play major roles. Their son Godfrey of Boulogne would become a leader of the First Crusade and the first Latin king of Jerusalem. Their son Baldwin of Boulogne was also a leader of the First Crusade and succeeded his brother Godfrey as king of Jerusalem. Their son Eustace III accompanied his brothers on the First Crusade and later married Mary, daughter of King Malcolm III Canmore of Scotland and Saint Margaret of Scotland.

Ida was a very pious woman, and her marriage to Eustace was a very happy one. Eustace II and Ida were dedicated to good works, and after he died, Ida spent much of her inheritance on helping the poor. She also built monasteries and the church of Notre Dame in Boulogne. She prayed ardently for the success of the First Crusade and had a vision of her sons' triumphant entry into Jerusalem.

After a long and painful illness, Ida died on 13 April 1113. Her relics are in Bayeux today. She is also known as Ida of Lorraine.

St. Anselm was Ida's spiritual adviser, and some of his letters to her have survived.

Her Line

Husband		Wife
Godfrey (or Geoffrey), Duke of Upper and Lower Lorraine and Count of Verdun (d. 24 Dec 1069)	+	**Ida (or Oda)**
Eustace II "aux Gernons," Count of Boulogne and Lens, fought in the Norman army at Hastings (b. ca. 1030 – md. (2) Dec 1057 – d. 1070/1080)	+	**St. Ida of Boulogne (or Bouillon)** (b. ca. 1040 – md. Dec 1057 – d. 13 April 1113)
Eustace III, Count of Boulogne and Lens, Crusader (b. ca. 1058 – md. 1102 – d. aft. 1125)	+	Mary (md. 1102 – d. 31 May 1116), daughter of Malcolm III Canmore, King of Scotland, and St. Margaret of Scotland
Stephen of Blois, King of England (b. ca. 1095 – md. ca. 1120 – d. 25 Oct 1154)	+	**Mathilda of Boulogne** (b. ca. 1105 – md. ca. 1120 – d. 3 July 1151)
Eustace IV, Count of Boulogne (b. ca. 1129 – d. 10 Aug 1153)	+	N.N., an unknown mistress
Anselm Candavene, Count of St. Pol (d. 1174)	+	md. (her 2nd) **Eustachie de Champagne**

Jean I, Count of Ponthieu and Montreuil, Crusader (b. ca. 1140 – d. 30 June 1191 on the 3rd Crusade)	+	md. (3rd for both) **Beatrice of St. Pol** (b. ca. 1160 – liv. 1204)
William II Talvas, Count of Ponthieu and Montreuil, Commander of the French right wing at Bouvines on the Albigensian Crusade (b. 1179 – md. 20 Aug1195 – d. 6 Oct 1221)	+	Alice of France (b. ca. 1170 – md. 20 Aug 1195 – d. aft. 18 July 1218), daughter of Louis VII, King of France
Simon II de Dammartin, Count of Aumale and Dammartin (b. ca. 1180 – md. Sept 1208 – d. 21 Sept 1239)	+	**Marie,** Countess of Ponthieu and Montreuil (b. 17 April 1199 – md. (1) Sept 1208 – d. Sept 1250)
St. Fernando III, King of Castile, Galicia, Leon, Toledo, and Extramadura (b. 24 June 1198 – md. (2) 1237 – d. 30 May 1252)	+	**Jeanne de Dammartin**, Countess of Ponthieu (b. ca. 1208 – md. 1237 – d. 16 March 1279)
Edward I "Longshanks," King of England (b. 17 June 1239 – md. (1) 18 Oct 1254 – d. 8 July 1307)	+	**Eleanor of Castile** (b. 1240 – md. 18 Oct 1254 – d. 28 Nov 1290)

Sources: *BBKL*, Vol. 2, col. 1249; *Benedictine Monks*, p. 356; *Butler*, Vol. II, p. 85; *Chervin*, pp. 54–55; *Cruz*, pp. 329–330; *Delaney*, p. 296; *Delaney and Tobin*, p. 584; *Dunbar*, Vol. I, p. 400; *Holboeck*, pp. 147–148; *Holweck*, p. 500; *NCE*, Vol. 7, p. 335; *Snodgrass*, pp. 144–145; *Stuart:* line 242, nos. 33 through 28 + line 148, nos. 28 through 26 + line 82, nos. 26 and 25 + line 52, nos. 25 and 24; *Weis, AR:* line 158, nos. 22 through 24 + line 169A + line 109, nos. 27 through 30 + line 110, nos. 29 and 30; *Wells*, pp. 355, 85, 505, 476, 177, and 142; *WWH*, Vol. 7, pp. 650–651

St. Ilduara Eriz

Ilduara was the daughter of Ero Fernandez, Count of Lugo, and his wife Adosinda. She married Gutierre Menendez, Count in Galicia, and was the mother of St. Rosendo.

Ilduara founded a convent near the monastery of Cellanueva in Galicia. After her husband died, she became a nun, entered her convent, and lived under the rule of her own daughter Adosinda.

Ilduara died in 958 and is buried at her convent.

Her Line

Husband		Wife
Ero Fernandez, Count of Lugo	+	**Adosinda**
Gutierre Menendez, Count in Galicia	+	**St. Ilduara Eriz** (d. 958)
Pelayo Gonzalez, Count of Galicia (d. ca. 959)	+	**Hermesenda Gutierrez**
Gonzalo Menendez, Count of Galicia (d. ca. 985)	+	**Ilduara Pelaez** (d. by 985)
Menendo Gonzalez, Count of Galicia	+	md. (1) Totadomna (d. ca. 1022)
Alfonso V, King of Castile and Leon (b. 994 – md. (1) 1015 – slain 7 Aug 1028)	+	**Elvira Menendez** (b. ca. 996 – md. 1015 – d. Dec 1022)

[For the later generations that connect this line to the kings of England, see the line of St. Florentina in Part III.]

Sources: *Dunbar*, Vol. I, p. 404; *Holweck*, p. 503; *Stuart*, line 277, nos. 36 through 33; *Tucker*, Vol. I, pp. 79–80; *Wells*, p. 263

St. Ingegerd

Ingegerd was born around 1000 and was the daughter of the Swedish king St. Olaf III "Skotkonung" (the "Tax King"), and his second wife Astrid of the Obotrites. In February 1019, she married St. Yaroslav I Vladimirovich, who was about 22 years older than Ingegerd and known as "the Wise." After winning a civil war with his brothers the same year, Yaroslav became the sole ruler of Kievan Rus. Yaroslav's realm included most of what later generations would call the Soviet Union west of the Urals.

Yaroslav and Ingegerd's marriage was a very happy one which lasted thirty-one years and produced at least ten children. In history, Yaroslav would prove to be the greatest ruler of Kievan Rus, and his reign would be remembered as a golden age. Determined to turn his capital into a "Byzantium on the Dnieper," Yaroslav built the new city of Kiev. There were several new churches in the new city of Kiev, and many more were built throughout the country. Yaroslav also opened Kievan Rus to Greek evangelists, and by the end of his reign, Russia's conversion to Christianity was complete.

Ingegerd became an important adviser to Yaroslav and sometimes accompanied him on his military campaigns. She was a well educated woman for her time and drew the first sketches of the structure that would become the greatest monument to her and her husband. Located in Kiev and originally called the Cathedral of Holy Wisdom, it still stands today and is known as the Cathedral of St. Sophia.

Near the end of her life, Ingegerd became a nun and entered a convent she had founded in Kiev. She took the new name of Anna and died there on 10 February 1050, four years before her husband. Today, Ingegerd's remains rest together with those of Yaroslav in a large stone sarcophagus in the Cathedral of St. Sophia.

Ingegerd is sometimes called St. Anna of Novgorod and was the first Swedish woman to become a saint. She is also occasionally called Irina, which is an adopted name she took after she arrived in Russia and before she became a nun.

Three of the children of Yaroslav and Ingegerd also became saints: Izyaslav I Yaroslavich, Sviatoslav II Yaroslavich, and Vladimir Yaroslavich.

Her Line

Husband		Wife
St. Olaf III "Skotkonung" (the Tax King), King of Sweden (b. prob. in 960's – d. ca. 1020)	+	md. (2) **Astrid of the Obotrites** (b. ca. 979)
St. Jaroslav I Vladimirovich "the Wise," Grand Prince of Kiev (b. 978 – md. (2) Feb 1019 – d. 20 Feb 1054)	+	**St. Ingegerd**, Princess of Sweden (b. ca. 1000 – md. Feb 1019– d. 10 Feb 1050)
Vsevolod I Jaroslavich, Grand Prince of Kiev and Prince of Perejaslaw (b. ca. 1030 – md. (1) 1046 – d. 13 April 1093)	+	Maria Monomacha (md. 1046), daughter of Konstantinos Monomachos (Constantine IX), Emperor of Byzantium
St. Vladimir Vsevolodovich	+	Gytha of Wessex (md. ca. 1070),

Monomach (a.k.a., Vladimir II "Monomachos"), Grand Prince of Kiev (b. 1053 – md. (1) ca. 1070 – d. 19 May 1125)

daughter of Harold II Godwinsson, King of England

[For the later generations that connect this line to the kings of England, see the line of St. Harold III, King of Denmark in Part II.]

Sources: *Dunbar*, Vol. I, pp. 69–70 (under "Anna"); *Edberg*; *Hist. Rus. Ch.*, Vol. 2, p. 120; *Stuart:* line 143, no. 31 + line 240, nos. 33 through 30; *Walsh*, p. 46 (under "Anna of Novgorod"); *Weis, AR*, line 242, nos. 5 through 7; *Wells*, pp. 549 and 329; *WWH*, vol. 7, p. 69

St. Irene,
Empress of Byzantium

It has been a very long time since anyone prayed to St. Irene.

She was born in 752, and the names of her parents are unknown. Remembered as a startlingly beautiful woman, she married the Byzantine emperor Leo IV in 769. Their son and only child Constantine VI was born 14 January 771 and crowned co-emperor in 776 when he was only five years old. Leo himself died of a fever on 8 September 780 while campaigning against the Bulgarians, and Irene was suddenly regent for the nine-year-old Constantine.

To understand Irene's claim to sanctity, one must know a little of the history of iconoclasm in Byzantium. In the early 700's, some bishops in the East decided that the icons in Christian churches were actually irreligious and should no longer be displayed or venerated. Their views were called iconoclasm. In 726, the Byzantine emperor Leo III began to agree with these views, and in 730, the destruction of icons began. After escalating to actual persecution of iconophiles in the 760's, the movement began to wane in 775 after the death of emperor Constantine V.

Irene had always been an iconophile, and after becoming regent of the empire, she convened the Second Council of Nicea in 787, where iconoclasm as a movement was officially condemned and the veneration of icons was restored. This development plus her patronage of several iconophile clerics and her creation of several hospitals and poor houses was enough to make her a saint in the eyes of many.

This saintly reputation withers greatly, however, when it is compared with Irene's own ambitions for herself and her country. As her son Constantine VI grew older, her relations with him deteriorated dramatically. In December 790 when he was nineteen, Constantine deposed Irene and began to rule alone. He proved to be an ineffectual ruler who wasted two years in fruitless campaigns against the Arabs and the Bulgarians. Forced to recall Irene, the two of them uneasily ruled together for about four years until Irene finally deposed Constantine on 19 April 797 and made her victory permanent by having him blinded. For the next five years, Irene reigned alone as empress and was the first woman in the history of the empire to do so.

In 802, Irene was herself toppled by Nikephoros I and exiled to the island of Lesbos. She died there on 9 August 803. Later in the ninth century her remains were transferred to the church of the Holy Apostles in Constantinople.

The line of descent which connects the kings of England to Irene is one of the longer lines. For example, in the fourth generation after Irene, one finds emperor Michael III "the Drunkard." This book follows the majority view that Michael III was the father of Emperor Leo VI. For details, refer to the chapter on Leo VI.

Her Line

Husband		Wife
N.N.	+	**N.N.**
Leo IV "the Khazar," Emperor of Byzantium (b. 25 Jan 750 – md. 769 – d. 8 Sept 780)	+	**St. Irene** (b. 752 – md. 769 – d. 9 Aug 803)

Constantine VI, Emperor of Byzantium (b. 771 – md. Nov 778 – d. aft. 15 Aug 797)	+	Maria of Amnia (md. Nov 788)
Michael II "the Stammerer," Emperor of Byzantium (b. 770 – md. (2) ca. 823 – d. 2 Oct 829)	+	**Euphrosyne** (md. ca. 823)
Theophilos, Emperor of Byzantium (b. ca. 812 – md. 5 June 830 – d. 20 Jan 842)	+	St. Theodora (b. ca. 815 – md. 5 June 830 – d. 11 Feb 867)
Michael III "the Drunkard," Emperor of Byzantium (b. 840 – d. 24 Sept 867)	+	Eudokia Ingarina (b. ca. 840 – d. 882/883), his mistress and the mother of his son
St. Leo VI "the Philosopher," Emperor of Byzantium (b. 1 Sept 866 – md. (2) 898 – d. 12 May 912)	+	Zoe Tzautzia (md. 898 – d. Dec 899)
Louis III "Beronides" (the Blind), King of Provence and Italy and Emperor of the West (b. ca. 883 – md. (1) ca. 900 – d. 5 June 928)	+	**Anna of Byzantium** (md. ca. 900 – d. 962)
Charles Constantine, Count of Vienne (b. ca. 901 – d. aft. Jan 962)	+	Teutberge de Troyes (d. aft. 960)
Boso II, Count of Provence and Avignon (d. 965/967)	+	**Constance of Provence** (d. 961/965)
William I, Count of Provence and Arles (b. ca. 955 – md. aft. 981 – d. 993/994)	+	Adelaide of Anjou (b. ca. 942 – md. aft. 981 – d. 1026)
Robert II "the Pious," King of France (b. 27 March 972 – md. (3) 998 – d. 20 July 1031)	+	**Constance of Arles, Provence, and Toulouse** (b. 986 – md. 998 – d. 25 July 1032)

[For the later generations that connect this line to the kings of England, see the line of St. Adela, Princess of France in Part II.]

Sources: *BBKL*, Vol. 2, cols. 1328–1330; *Dunbar*, Vol. I, p. 412; *Holweck*, pp. 508–509; *NCE*, Vol. 7, pp. 632–633; *Norwich*, Vol. 1, pp. 366–381; *Snodgrass*, pp. 128–129; *Stuart:* line 322B, nos. 41 and 40 + line 322A, nos. 41 and 40 + line 253, nos. 40 through 38 + line 333, nos. 36 through 34; *Walsh*, p. 281; *Wells*, pp. 118–119 and 481; *WWH*, Vol. 7, pp. 690–694

St. Irene Doukaina

Irene was a very attractive woman with light blue eyes. She was born around 1066 and was the daughter of Andronikos Doukas, a Byzantine general, and his wife Maria of Bulgaria. Around 1078 she married Alexios, who in 1081 would become Alexios I Komnenos, Emperor of Byzantium.

Without Irene, the history of Byzantium would have been vastly different. During the short reigns of Alexios' immediate predecessors, the empire had become very unsettled. It was the support of Irene's family and the Byzantine military generally that put Alexios on the throne. His long reign of 37 years and his unusually wise government brought a much-needed stability.

Strangers when their marriage began, Alexios and Irene became a very loving couple. Irene was alert to plots against Alexios and saved him from danger several times. After their children were born, she would often accompany him on campaigns. As his health began to fail, she cared for him with her own hands. When he began to suffer from severe respiratory problems, she would often try to ease his breathing by holding him propped in her arms throughout the night. During attacks of gout, she would be his nurse.

In addition to everything she did as a wife and mother, Irene was noted for her intellectual accomplishments and for her charity. She enjoyed reading about the saints. She gave generously to monks and to the poor. After Alexios died in 1118, she became a nun and entered the convent of Kecharitomene, which she had founded some years earlier. At her convent, Irene continued to give food to the poor and to educate orphan girls. She died on 19 February 1127.

Irene is also known as Irene Ducas. Her portrait appears in the Pala d'Oro.

Her Line

Husband		Wife
Andronikos Doukas, protovestarios (b. by 1045 – md. bef. 1066 – d. 14 Oct 1077)	+	**Maria of Bulgaria** (md. bef. 1066 – d. by 1118)
Alexius I (Alexios I Komnenos), Emperor of Byzantium (b. ca. 1048 – md. (2) ca. 1078 – d. 15 Aug 1118)	+	md. (2) **St. Irene Doukaina** (b. ca. 1066 – md. ca. 1078 – d. 19 Feb 1127)
Konstantinos Angelos, a general of Byzantium in the war with the Normans	+	**Theodora Komnene** (b. ca. 1070 – d. 20 Feb 1116)

[For the later generations that connect this line to the kings of England, see the line of St. Boris I, Khan of the Bulgars in Part II.]

Sources: *Dunbar*, Vol. I, p. 412; *Oxford Dict. Byz.*, Vol. 2, p. 1009; *Stuart*, line 215, nos. 33 through 31; *Tucker*, Vol. I, pp. 157–159; *Weis, AR*, line 105A, no. 24; *Wells*, pp. 121 and 123–124; *WWH*, Vol. 7, pp. 689–690

St. Isaac I "the Great"

Isaac was born around 350 and was the son of St. Nerses I "the Great" and his wife Samdukht. The name of Isaac's wife is unknown, but she died young. Isaac then became a monk. In 390, he became Katholikos (i.e., bishop or patriarch) of Armenia.

The year 390 was the beginning of the Golden Age of the Armenian church, and Isaac was its guiding force throughout. He saw to it that an Armenian alphabet was invented, and he then used it to translate the bible and writings of the early church fathers into Armenian. He also composed hymns, wrote a national liturgy, and brought the Armenian church under Byzantine canon law. He built churches, hospitals, and schools. He reformed the clergy and ended the practice of married bishops. Many consider Isaac the real founder of the Armenian church and the founder of Armenian literature.

Isaac died in September 439/440 and is buried at Ashtishat. His daughter would become the mother of St. Hmayeak Mamikonian and St. Vardan II.

Isaac is also known as Sahag or Sahak. He is mentioned daily in the Armenian liturgy.

His Line

Husband		Wife
St. Nerses (or Narces or Narses) I "the Great," Gregorid Prince and Bishop of Armenia (b. 355 – d. 373)	+	**Samdukht**
St. Isaac I "the Great," Gregorid Prince and Bishop of Armenia (b. ca. 350 – d. Sept 439/440)	+	N.N.
Hamazasp, Prince of the Mamikonids and High Constable of Armenia (b. 345 – d. ca. 416)	+	**Sahakanoysh**, the Gregorid heiress
St. Hmayeak Mamikonian, general and ambassador to Constantinople (b. 410 – d. in battle 2 June 451)	+	Dzoyk, daughter of Vram, Prince of Rshtuni
Vard, Mamikonian Viceroy of Armenia (b. 450 – d. aft. 509)	+	N.N.

[For the later generations that connect this line to the kings of England, see the line of St. Ashken in Part II.]

Sources: *BBKL*, Vol. 2, cols. 1348–1349; *Benedictine Monks*, p. 362; *Bunson*, p. 414; *Butler*, Vol. III, pp. 512–513; *CE*, Vol. VIII, pp. 175–176; *Delaney*, p. 302; *Delaney and Tobin*, p. 594; *Holweck*, pp. 510–511; *Hovannisian*, pp. 78, 84, 92–93, and 96–98; *Kaloustian*, p. 21; *Koushagian*, p. 14; *NCE*, Vol. 7, p. 662; *O'Malley*, p. 42; *Snodgrass*, p. 129; *Stone*, Chapter 8, Chart 80; *Stuart:* line 416, nos. 55 through 53 + line 322, nos. 53 through 51; *Wagner*, p. 195

Bl. Itta

Itta was born around 597 and was the daughter of St. Arnulf of Metz and his wife Dode. She was the sister of St. Modoald and St. Severa.

Itta married Bl. Pepin of Landen, who would become Mayor of the Palace in Austrasia. They became the parents of St. Begga and St. Gertrude.

At Nivelles, Itta founded a convent for Benedictine nuns, and her daughter St. Gertrude became abbess there. After Pepin died, Itta also became a nun and spent the last years of her life living at Nivelles under her daughter's rule.

Itta died on 8 May 652 and is buried at Nivelles next to Pepin. She is also known as Iduberga, Idaberga, and Ida of Nivelles.

Her Line

Husband		Wife
St. Arnulf (or Arnoul), Mayor of the Palace in Austrasia and Bishop of Metz (b. 13 Aug 582 – md. ca. 596 – d. 16 Aug 641)	+	**Dode (or Clothilde)** (b. ca. 586 – md. ca. 596)
Bl. Pepin of Landen "the Old," Mayor of the Palace in Austrasia (b. ca. 580/585 – d. 640/646)	+	**Bl. Itta** (b. ca. 597 – d. 8 May 652)
Angise (or Ansegisel), Mayor of the Palace in Austrasia (b. 602 – md. bef. 639 – murdered 685)	+	**St. Begga** (b. ca. 613 – md. bef. 639 – d. ca. 698)
Pepin (or Pippin) of Heristal, Mayor of the Palace in Austrasia (b. ca. 635 – d. 16 Dec 714)	+	Aupais, a concubine (b. ca. 654)
Charles Martel "the Hammer," Mayor of the Palace in Austrasia, King of the Franks, and victor at the battle of Poitiers (b. ca. 688 – d. 22 Oct 741)	+	md. (1) Chrotrude (or Rotrou), Duchess of Austrasia (d. 724)

[For the later generations that connect this line to the kings of England, see the line of St. Arnulf, Bishop of Metz in Part II.]

Sources: *Baring-Gould*, Vol. 5, p. 116; *Benedictine Monks*, p. 356; *Butler*, Vol. I, pp. 384–385 (under "Pepin of Landen"); *Delaney and Tobin*, p. 584; *Dunbar*, Vol. I, p. 399; *Holweck*, p. 500 (under "Idaberga"); *NCE*, Vol. 7, pp. 348–349; *Stuart:* line 260 + line 171, nos. 45 through 43; *Wells*, p. 135; *WWH*, Vol. 7, p. 651

St. Izyaslav I Yaroslavich, Grand Prince of Kiev

Izyaslav was born around 1024/1025 and was the first-born son of St. Yaroslav I Vladimirovich "the Wise," Grand Prince of Kiev and ruler of Kievan Rus, and his second wife St. Ingegerd of Sweden. Around 1043 Izyaslav married Gertrude, daughter of King Mieszko II of Poland.

When Yaroslav died in 1054, Izyaslav succeeded him. In the beginning of his reign, Izyaslav promoted the Christianity that had become the national religion of Kievan Rus in his father's time. He built churches, supported ecclesiastical scholarship, abolished the death penalty for a time, and continued the codification of the laws.

Sadly, Izyaslav's piety far surpassed his political abilities. After several failures of leadership, many people began to question whether he was up to the job of ruling his own land. In 1068 a popular revolt broke out. Izyaslav fled to Poland and didn't return until 1069. In 1073 he was attacked by the troops of his brothers Sviatoslav and Vsevolod, who had also become dissatisfied with his rule. Izyaslav fled to Poland again and didn't return until 1076. On both occasions, he only regained his throne with the help of Polish troops. Civil war finally broke out two years later, and during a battle with his relatives, Izyaslav was slain on 3 October 1078.

His Line

Husband		Wife
St. Yaroslav I Vladimirovich "the Wise," Grand Prince of Kiev (b. 978 – md. (2) Feb 1019 – d. 20 Feb 1054)	+	**St. Ingegerd**, Princess of Sweden (b. ca. 1101 – md. Feb 1019 – d. 10 Feb 1050)
St. Izyaslav I Yaroslavich, Grand Prince of Kiev (b. 1024/1025 – md. ca. 1043 – slain 3 Oct 1078)	+	Gertrude (md. ca. 1043), daughter of Mieszko II, King of Poland
Sviatpolk II Izyaslavich, Grand Prince of Kiev, Novgorod, and Turow (b. 1050 – d. 16 Apr 1113)	+	N.N. (d. bef. 1094)
Boleslas III, King of Poland (b. 20 Aug 1086 – md. (1) 1103 – d. 28 Oct 1138)	+	**Zbyslava of Kiev** (md. 1103 – d. 1110/1111)
Ladislas (or Wladislaw) II King of Poland (b. 1105 – md. (1) ca. 1126 – d. 30 May 1159)	+	Agnes of Austria (md. ca. 1126), daughter of St. Leopold III, Margrave of Austria
Alfonso VII "El Emperador," King of Castile, Leon, Galicia, Toledo, Zaragoza, and the Asturias (b. 1 March 1105 – md. d. 1166) (1) July 1152 – d. 21 Aug 1157)	+	**Richilde (or Richenza) of Poland** (b. 1130/1140 – md. July 1152 –

[For the later generations that connect this line to the kings of England, see the line of St. Adelaide of Burgundy in Part II.]

Sources: *Allen*, p. 19; *Hist. Rus. Ch.*, Vol. 2, p. 684; *Hrushevsky*, pp. 80–83; *Stuart:* line 363 + line 378, nos. 31 through 29; *Weis, AR:* line 241, nos. 6 through 8 + line 147, nos. 25 through 27; *Wells*, pp. 329, 330, and 474

St. Judicael II,
King of Brittany

Judicael was born around 590 and was the son of Hoel III, King of Brittany, and his wife Pritelle. He was the brother of St. Judoc.

Judicael's life ranged over a wide canvas. When Hoel died in 612, some of his sons disputed the succession. After being attacked by the forces of his brother Salamon II, Judicael abandoned his own claim to the throne and entered the monastery of Gael near Vannes. According to some writers, he practiced very extreme penances there, such as submerging himself in icy streams in winter.

After Salamon II died around 632, the throne of Brittany was once again vacant. Judicael left his monastery, got married, and was elected king.

As a war leader, Judicael was formidable. One chronicle says,

> "Terror of his name alone was sufficient to keep evil men from violence, for God, who watched over him without ceasing, had made him brave and mighty in battle; it happened more than once that with the aid of the Almighty he was able to put whole troops of the enemy to flight by the strength of his sword-arm alone."

Judicael was also esteemed by his friends and loved by his people. St. Eligius was especially close to him.

After several years on the throne, Judicael abdicated in favor of St. Judoc and returned to the monastery of Gael. He died there on 17 December 658. In addition to his victories in war, Judicael was remembered for the many churches and monasteries he built and for being the only ruler of his country who renounced his throne twice.

In history, Judicael is also known as Josse. His relics are preserved in the parish church of Saint Josse, near Montreuil.

His Line

Husband		Wife
Hoel III, King of Brittany (d. 612)	+	**Pritelle**
St. Judicael II, King of Brittany (b. ca. 590 – d. 17 Dec 658)	+	N.N.
Alain II de Long, King of Brittany (d. 690)	+	N.N.
Ivor	+	N.N.
Daniel Dremrost "the Red Eyed," King of Brittany (d. 703)	+	N.N.

[For the later generations that connect this line to the kings of England, see the line of St. Cunedda Wledig in Part II.]

Sources: *Ashley*, p. 728; *Baring-Gould*, Vol. 15, pp. 173–174; *Benedictine Monks*, p. 410; *Bunson*, p. 464; *Butler*, Vol. IV, p. 550 (under "St. Judoc" – n.b. that Butler mistakenly states that Judicael was both the father and brother of St. Judoc); *Delaney and Tobin*, p. 635; *Holweck*, p. 567; *Jones, Celtic Saints*, pp. 173–174; *NCE*, Vol. 8, p. 40; *Stuart*, line 405, nos. 49 through 45

St. Ladislas, King of Hungary

Ladislas was born on 29 July 1040 and was the second son of Bela I, King of Hungary, and his wife Rixa. In 1077 he married Adelaide of Rheinfelden.

After his older brother Geza succeeded to the throne, Ladislas never expected to become king. Instead, he became Geza's chief adviser and helped him defeat rivals on the battlefield. Yet when Geza died in 1077, the Hungarians proclaimed Ladislas as their new king. He would become one of their greatest national heroes.

The foundation of Ladislas' fame was his greatness as a warrior. From helping Geza to win his own wars, Ladislas went on to repel several invasions by barbaric tribes, to crush Polish, Russian, and Tartar forces, and to repeatedly defeat, forgive, and release rivals who wanted the throne of Hungary for themselves. Inspection of the records of his campaigns very strongly suggests that he was never defeated on a battlefield.

Under the leadership of Ladislas, Hungary also prospered domestically. He added Croatia and Dalmatia to the national territory. All people of good will—including Jews and Moslems—were allowed to freely practice their own religion. In his eighteen-year reign, Hungary became a great state.

Ladislas the man was tall and strong and, in the opinion of everyone, possessed the outward graces and inner virtues of an ideal knight of chivalry. This opinion of him extended far beyond the borders of his own country. When Pope Urban II was organizing the First Crusade, Ladislas was the first person he looked to for help. All the rulers of Europe agreed that Ladislas should lead the First Crusade. It was only his brief sickness and unexpected death on 29 July 1095 near Neutra, Bohemia that prevented him from becoming one of the first great leaders of the Crusading era.

Ladislas was buried in Nagyvrad in the cathedral of Szüs Maria. He was regarded as a saint from the moment of his death and an equal of St. Stephen, who founded the Hungarian monarchy and converted the country to Christianity. There are many popular stories about him.

His Line

Husband		Wife
Bela I, King of Hungary (md. ca. 1040 – d. 1063)	+	**Rixa** (b. 1018 – md. ca. 1040 – d. aft. 1052), daughter of Mieszko II, King of Poland
St. Ladislas I, King of Hungary (b. 29 July 1040 – md. 1077 – d. 29 July 1095)	+	Adelaide of Rheinfelden (md. 1077 – d. 1090)
John II Komnenos, Emperor of Byzantium (md. 1104/1105 – d. 8 April 1143)	+	**St. Prisca** (b. ca. 1088 – md. 1104/1105 – d. 13 Aug 1134)
Andronikos Komnenos, sebastokrator (b. ca. 1108 – d. 1142)	+	Eirene (d. 1150/1151)

Alexies Komnenos, lover of the Empress Maria and Governor during her regency (murdered 1183)	+	Marie Dukaina
William VIII, Seigneur of Montpellier (b. ca. 1158 – md (1) 1178/1179 – d. 1218)	+	**Eudoxia Komnena** (b. ca. 1168 – md. 1178/1179 – d. aft. 4 Nov 1202)
Pedro II, King of Aragon (b. 1176 – md. 15 June 1204 – fell in the battle of Murat 14 Sept 1213)	+	**Marie**, Dame de Montpellier (b. 1182 – md. (3) 15 June 1204 – d. 21 April 1213)
James I "the Conqueror," King of Aragon (b. 1 Feb 1207 – md. 8 Sept 1235 – d. 25 July 1276)	+	Yolande (b. 1213 – md. 8 Sept 1235 – d. 12 Oct 1251)
Philip III "the Bold," King of France (b. 1 May 1245 – md. (1) 28 My 1262 – d. 5 Oct 1285)	+	**Isabella of Aragon** (b. 1243 or 1247 – md. 28 May 1262 – d. 28 May 1262 – d. 28 Jan 1271)
Philip IV "the Fair," King of France (b. 1268 – md. 16 Aug 1284 – d. 29 Nov 1314)	+	Jeanne of Navarre (b. Jan 1272 – md. 16 Aug 1284 – d. 2 April 1305)
Edward II, King of England (b. 25 April 1284 – md. 25 Jan 1308– murdered 21 Sept 1327)	+	**Isabella** (b. 1292 – md. 25 Jan 1308 – d. 27 Aug 1357)

Sources: *Baring-Gould*, Vol. 6, pp. 400–406; *BBKL*, Vol. 4, cols. 967–968; *Benedictine Monks*, p. 423; *Bunson*, p. 478; *Butler*, Vol. II, pp. 654–655; *CE*, Vol. VIII, p. 737; *Cruz*, pp. 398–401; *Delaney*, p. 344; *Delaney and Tobin*, pp. 660–661; *Holweck*, p. 588; *Joeckle*, p. 263; *Klaniczay*, Appendix B, Geneal. Table 6; *NCE*, Vol. 8, p. 311; *Stuart:* line 75, nos. 33 and 32 + line 381, nos. 32 and 31 + line 111, nos. 31 through 28 + line 150, nos. 28 and 27 + line 51, nos. 26 through 23; *Weis, AR:* line 244A + line 105A, nos. 25 through 29 + line 105, nos. 29 and 30 + line 101, nos. 29 through 31; *Wells*, pp. 308, 123, 405, 24, and 257

St. Leo VI "the Philosopher," Emperor of Byzantium

Leo was born on 1 September 866. His mother was Eudokia Ingarina. The identity of his father is a subject of scholarly disagreement. The majority view is that his father was the Byzantine emperor Michael III "the Drunkard" (b. 840 – d. 24 Sept 867). The minority view says that his father was Basil I (b. 830/835 – d. 29 August 886), who was also an emperor of Byzantium and Michael's successor. The majority view will be followed in the present work.

Before and after he ascended the throne in the late summer of 886, Leo had prodigious difficulties in producing a male heir. From his first marriage to St. Theophano in 881/882, one daughter was born. St. Theophano died in 897, and Leo next married Zoe Tzautzina. This second marriage also produced one daughter before Zoe died in 899. Leo's third wife was Eudokia Baiane, who died in 901 giving birth to a son who himself died in infancy. Leo found a fourth wife in Zoe Karbonopsina (or Carbopsina), and in 905 their son Konstantinos was finally born. He would later rule the empire as Emperor Konstantinos VII.

Also known as Leo "the Wise," Leo had several scholarly interests. Legal philosophy was one of them, and it led him to write several of his own legal decrees and to issue collections of civil laws. He also was the author of poems, orations, and even military treatises. Leo was also deeply interested in religion. He composed a number of hymns, sermons, and prayers. In orthodox churches today, hymns attributed to him are still sung on Lazarus Saturday. He also issued collections of canon law.

As emperor, Leo earnestly wanted to end four decades of conflict between previous patriarchs and emperors over church-state relations. Late in 886, Leo's removal of Patriarch Photios and replacement of him with Leo's own half-brother St. Stephen was one of several measures to that end.

In addition to his scholarship and his political decisions, Leo also fought injustice and corruption in a very personal way. He liked to disguise himself as a common person and go out among his people. He would observe how they treated one another. Whoever he saw doing the right thing would be brought to the palace and rewarded. Whoever he saw doing the wrong thing would also be brought to the palace and disciplined.

Leo died on 12 May 912.

His Line

(1) Eudokia Ingarina's long-time lover was:

Michael III "the Drunkard," Emperor (b. 849 – d. 24 Sept 867)

Eudokia Ingarina (b. ca. 840 – d. 882/883). Michael married Eudokia Dekapolitissa while he was still a small child. In his teens, he secretly made Eudokia Ingarina his mistress. By 865, Michael decided that appearances re-

(2) Eudokia Ingarina's husband was:

Basil I "the Macedonian," Emperor of Byzantium (b. ca. 830/835 – md. (2) 865 – d. 29 Aug 886)

quired a more complex arrangement. Michael's friend Basil (later Emp. Basil I) would divorce his own wife and marry Eudokia Ingarina. Eudokia Ingarina, however, would continue to be intimate only with Michael. This sham marriage took place in 865. The secret arrangement continued until 24 September 867, when Michael was assassinated by Basil. The majority view is that the biological father of Leo VI – who was born on 1 September 866 – was Michael III and not Basil I.

St. Leo VI "the Philosopher," Emperor of Byzantium (b. 1 Sept 866 – md. (2) 898 – d. 12 May 912)	+	Zoe Tzautzina (md. 898 – d. Dec 899)
Louis III "Beronides" (the Blind), King of Provence and Italy and Emperor of the West (b. ca. 883 – md. (1) ca. 900 – d. 5 June 928)	+	**Anna of Byzantium** (b. 899 – md. ca. 900 – d. 962)
Charles Constantine, Count of Vienne (b. ca. 901 – d. aft. Jan 962)	+	Teutberge de Troyes (d. aft. 960)

[For the later generations that connect this line to the kings of England, see the line of St. Irene, Empress of Byzantium in Part II.]

Sources: *BBKL*, Vol. 4, cols. 1476–1480**; *Holweck*, p. 601; *Norwich*, Vol. 2, pp. 865–866*; *Oxford Dict. Byz.*, Vol. 2, p. 1210; *Stuart:* line 253, nos. 40 through 38* + line 25, nos. 39 and 38; *Wells*, pp. 119* and 589 (References marked with a * follow the majority view that Michael III was Leo's father. References marked with a ** follow the minority view that Leo's father was Basil I. The persuasiveness of the Oxford Dict. Byz. is undercut by the fact that in one place [see Vol. 2, p. 739], it states that Michael married Eudokia Dekapolitessa. Elsewhere [see Vol. 2, p. 1364], it states that Michael married Eudokia Ingarina [sic!].)

St. Leopold III, Margrave of Austria

Leopold III was born around 1075 and was the son of Leopold II "the Handsome," Margrave of Austria, and his wife Ida von Cham. Leopold III's first wife was a daughter of Walchun von Perg and died before 1105. His second wife was Agnes of Franconia. They married in 1106 and had eighteen children, eleven of whom survived to become adults.

Leopold III succeeded his father as ruler of Austria in 1095, and the growth of his country from a marginal border state to one of the great powers of Europe began during his reign. He defeated two invasions by the Magyars. He encouraged the spread of religious institutions and founded the monasteries of Heiligenkreuz, Klosterneuberg, and Mariazell. He made the Austrian church independent of the Holy Roman Empire. He also encouraged the development of cities, especially Vienna. The most eloquent testimony to his devotion to his country came in 1125, when he had the chance to become the next emperor of the Holy Roman Empire and turned it down.

Leopold died in a hunting accident on 15 November 1136 and was buried in the monastery he founded at Klosterneuberg. He is the patron saint of Austria.

His Line

Husband		Wife
Leopold II "der Schoene" (the Handsome), Margrave of Austria and Crusader (b. 1050 – md. 1065 – d. 12 Oct 1102)	+	**Ida of Cham** (md. 1065 – d. 1101)
St. Leopold III, Margrave of Austria (b. ca. 1075 – md. (2) 1106 – d. 15 Nov 1136)	+	Agnes of Franconia (b. 1072/1073 – md. (2) 1106 – d. 24 Sept 1143), daughter of Henry IV, Holy Roman Emperor
Ladislas (or Wladislaw) II, King of Poland (b. 1105 – md. (1) ca. 1126 – d. 30 May 1159)	+	**Agnes of Austria** (md. ca. 1126)
Alfonso VII "El Emperador," King of Castile, Leon, Galicia, Toledo, Zaragoza, and the Asturias (b. 1 March 1105 – md. (2) July 1152 – d. 21 Aug1157)	+	**Richilde (or Richenza) of Poland** (b. 1130/1140 – md. July 1152 – d. 1166)

[For the later generations that connect this line to the kings of England, see the line of St. Adelaide of Burgundy in Part II.]

Sources: *Baring-Gould*, Vol. 13, pp. 340–341; *BBKL*, Vol. 4, cols. 1507–1510; *Benedictine Monks*, p. 436; *Bunson*, p. 490; *Butler*, Vol. IV, p. 350 (which mistakenly refers to this saint as "Leopold IV"); *Cruz*, pp. 406–407; *Delaney*, p. 357; *Delaney and Tobin*, pp. 695–696; *Holboeck*, pp. 156–158; *Holweck*, p. 606; *NCE*, Vol. 8, p. 663; *Stuart:* line 279, nos. 32 through 30 + line 378, nos. 30 and 29; *Weis, AR*, line 147, nos. 26 and 27; *Wells*, pp. 40 and 474

St. Liévin, Bishop of Trier

Liévin was born around 660/665 and was the son of St. Guerin and his wife Kunza. He married a daughter of Chrodobertus II of Neustria.

Liévin became bishop of Trier and also founded Mettlach Abbey in Germany. He died around 722/724 and is buried at Mettlach.

Liévin is also known as Leutwinus or Liutwin. His daughter Chrotrud married Charles Martel and became an ancestor of the Carolingians.

His Line

Husband		Wife
St. Guerin (or Warinus), Count of Poitiers (d. 677)	+	**Kunza** (d. 690), daughter of St. Clodulf, Bishop of Metz
St. Liévin, Bishop of Trier (or Treves) (b. 660/665 – d. 722/724)	+	N.N., a daughter of Chrodobertus II of Neustria
Count Gui (liv. 706–722)	+	N.N.
Lambert, Count of Hornbach (liv. 783)	+	N.N.
St. William of Gellone, Duke of Toulouse and Margrave of Septimania (b. 755 – d. 28 May 812)	+	md. (2) **Guibour of Hornbach**
Bernard, Count of Autun and Margrave of Septimania (executed 844)	+	Dhoude (b. ca. 804 – d. 2 Feb 843)
Wulgirim, Count of the Palace of King Charles "the Bald," Count of Agen, Angouleme, and Perigord (md. ca. 844 – d. 3 May 886)	+	**Roselinde** (md. ca. 844 – d. 896/901)
William, Count of Agen and Perigord (d. 920)	+	Regilinda
Boso I, Count of la Marche and of la Haute Marche (md. 944)	+	**Emma of Perigord** (md. 944)
Adalbert I, Count de la Haute Marche and Perigord (md. (1) ca. 975 – killed 997)	+	Almode de Limoges (md. (1) ca. 975 – d. 1007/1011)
Bernard I, Count de la Haute Marche and Perigord (b. 986 – d. 1047)	+	Amelia
Pons III, Count of Albi, Dijon, and Toulouse (b. ca. 990 – md. 1044/1045 – d. 1060)	+	**Almode de la Haute Marche** (md. 1044/1045 – murdered 1071/1075)
William IV, Duke of Narbonne, Count of Albi, Carcasson, Dijon, Perigord, Rodez, and Toulouse, Crusader (b. ca. 1040 – md. (2) ca. 1071 – d. 1093 in battle	+	Emma de Mortain (b. ca. 1058 – md. ca. 1071 – liv. 1080)

at Huesca)		
William IX, Duke of Aquitaine (and as William VII Count of Poitou), Crusader (b. ca. 22 Oct 1071 – md. 1094 – d. 10 Feb 1126/1127)	+	**Philippa**, Regent of Toulouse (b. ca. 1073 – md. (2) 1094 – d. 28 Nov 1117)
St. William X, Duke of Aquitaine (and as William VIII Count of Poitou), Crusader (b. 1099 – md. (1) late 1121 – d. 9 April 1137)	+	Eleanore de Chatellerault (b. ca. 1105 – md. late 1121 – d. aft. March 1130)
Henry II, King of England (b. 5 March 1133 – md. 18 May 1152 – d. 6 July 1189)	+	**Eleanor of Aquitaine** (b. 1122 md. (2) 18 May 1152 – d. 31 March 1204)

Sources: *Bunson*, p. 493; *Stuart:* line 330 + line 326, nos. 40 through 36 + line 327, nos. 35 through 32 + line 374, nos. 31 and 30 + line 160, nos. 30 and 29 + line 88, nos. 31 through 29; *Weis, AR:* line 185, nos. 2 and 3 + line 110, nos. 24 through 26

St. Lleian

Lleian was a daughter of St. Brychan of Brecknock. She married St. Gabran mac Domangart, an early ruler of the Celtic kingdom of Dalriada. They lived in Scotland in a fortress built on Dunadd Hill.

The most notable child of Gabran and Lleian was their son Aidan. After Gabran died in battle around 559, Aidan succeeded him and became the greatest of all the kings of Dalriada.

Her Line

Husband		Wife
St. Brychan, ruler of Brecknock in South Wales (b. 480/490)	+	**N.N.**
St. Gabran mac Domangart, King of Dalriada (b. ca. 500 – md. bef. 532 – d. ca. 559)	+	**St. Lleian** (md. bef. 532)
Aidan (or Aedan) mac Gabran (b. 532 – d. 606), crowned King of Dalriada by St. Columba of Iona	+	N.N.
Eochaid Buide, King of Picts and of Dalriada (d. 629)	+	N.N.
Domnall Brec, King of Dalriada (d. ca. 642 in the battle of Strathcarron)	+	N.N., daughter of Widfroith

[For the later generations that connect this line to the kings of England, see the line of St. Brychan in Part II.]

Sources: *Ashley*, p. 197; *Baring-Gould and Fisher*, Vol. 3, pp. 380–381; *Holweck*, p. 630; *Stuart*, line 165, nos. 49 through 46; *Weis, AR*, line 170, nos. 4 through 7; *Wells*, p. 177

St. Louis IX,
King of France

Louis was born on 25 April 1214 and was the son of Louis VIII, King of France, and his wife Bl. Blanche of Castile. On 27 May 1234, he married Margaret of Provence and had eleven children with her, seven of whom survived him. He died on 25 August 1270 while on the Eighth Crusade.

Among the monarchs and saints of Europe, Louis is unique. One of his constant companions wrote such a detailed biography of him that Louis steps forth from the pages of history like no other medieval ruler. For historians and biographers, he will be an eternal and very fertile subject.

Louis the Man

Louis was tall, slim, blond, and blue-eyed. He had a delicate nose, a small mouth, and a rosy complexion. He was athletic and an excellent rider and swimmer. He was also trained in arms.

Various illnesses troubled Louis throughout his life. He had bouts of dysentery and scurvy, and three or four times a year he would be flattened by episodes of erysipelas, also known as "St. Anthony's Fire." A mysterious illness in the 1240's almost killed him and led to his decision to lead the Seventh Crusade.

Louis was a very well educated man who was literate in both French and Latin and who maintained his own library. At table, he almost always asked some other similarly cultivated person to lead the conversation. He eagerly sought out scholars and discussed all subjects with them. As a ruler, he founded the Sorbonne.

Louis and his wife Margaret deeply loved each other, but in family relations he was definitely not a modern man. He was caring, but he expected to be obeyed. Margaret was not allowed to make any decisions without consulting him. Louis loved his children too and personally taught them certain subjects, but bad behavior brought swift discipline.

Louis saw himself as a Christian first and a king second. In any age, a more profoundly religious man would be very hard to find. He lived like a monk. He dressed drably and ate simply. He often gave his own food to others. In abbeys, he would serve meals to the monks and wash their feet. He distributed alms constantly and also washed the feet of the poor. In hospices, he would treat lepers in person and eat with them from the same plate.

Besides his regular weekly confessions, Louis always kept a confessor close by in case he committed a mortal sin and needed to confess immediately. After confession, he would insist that his confessor flagellate him. He had specially made scourges for this purpose which he also kept close at hand but concealed. He would pray on his knees five times every evening, and he steadfastly kept his own schedule of weekly, monthly, and annual devotions. He never hunted. He never had a mistress or an affair. Louis was keenly interested in relics and built Sainte Chapelle (the "Holy Chapel") to house his collection.

If such piety and zeal can produce flaws, the chief one would be Louis' lack of tolerance for the things he considered religious failings. Heretics, atheists, and blasphemers could expect harsh measures—i.e., mutilation or death—from Louis. For the Jews, Louis was definitely not "St. Louis." He held them responsible for the crucifixion, he made them wear bright yellow disks on their clothing, and anyone practicing usury could be expelled and their property confiscated. Louis also found nothing to respect in Islam but did not punish its faithful with the same measures.

Louis the Ruler

The operation of all branches of government in France improved significantly during the reign of Louis.

The greatest change in the executive branch was that, for the first time since the Carolingians, the king's power was felt throughout the realm. For the first time, the king in Paris was in fact the king of France. Louis insisted that no wrong be done in the king's name. He appointed special agents to travel incognito, to watch for any injustices committed by anyone enforcing the king's law, and to report such matters back to him. Under Louis, France became the largest and wealthiest country in continental Europe. He improved the operation of the tax system. His reign saw building and rebuilding on an unprecedented scale.

In the judicial branch the conduct of trials changed vastly. Trial by combat was abolished. So was trial by ordeal (i.e., by fire or by water). They were replaced by an inquest where proof by witnesses was required and where an accused was presumed innocent until proven guilty.

At the time, parliament was the part of the king's court where very important cases were heard and where judgments were pronounced. Their institution also grew under Louis.

Louis was a born arbiter who was frequently called upon to settle other people's differences and keep the peace. At the international level, he was called upon to settle other rulers' disputes from England to Byzantium. Within France, he demanded a 40-day cooling-off period before any barons could settle their differences with each other by force of arms. He usually appointed himself to settle differences between his nobles.

Compared to what France would experience in the fourteenth century—the Black Death, the beginning of the Hundred Years War, and economic decline—the reign of Louis would in hindsight look like a golden age.

Louis the Crusader

In the popular imagination, Louis is primarily remembered as a Crusader. He was the leader of two great military efforts against the Moslems: the Seventh Crusade begun in 1248, and the Eighth Crusade begun in 1270. Both were utter failures. Louis could prepare an army for war as well as anyone, but the only place he ever led his men was to defeat.

Louis first decided to mount a crusade in 1244. His preparations were careful and detailed and took more than four years to complete. Seeing the Egyptian sultans as the main threat to the Latin Kingdom of Jerusalem, Louis and about 25,000 men finally set sail for Egypt rather than Palestine in the spring of 1249. Because of a storm, only half the fleet reached its destination in June 1249.

It would be a fairly short war for Louis. After assembling his army, he marched toward the town of Damietta. As the Crusaders approached, the inhabitants panicked and fled, and Louis's army occupied a deserted city. After waiting several months in Damietta for reinforcements to arrive, Louis next marched toward the Nile and engaged the Egyptians from 8 to 11 February 1250 in the battle of Al Mansurah. During the battle, part of the Crusader army was cut off and wiped out, and the rest retreated in disorder to their own camp, where they were beaten again and forced to begin retreating towards Damietta. A separate Egyptian force then attacked the supply depot in the rear of Louis's army and destroyed most of the Crusaders' provisions. Finally on 6 April 1250 in the battle of Fariskur, most of what was left of Louis's army was wiped out, and Louis himself was captured. Louis had lost every battle since he landed, and his crusade was over.

He was not finished losing money, however. Louis was held about one month by the Egyptians. He wasn't mistreated, but he became very ill. His teeth fell out from scurvy, and he turned white and frail while suffering from dysentery. On payment of a king's ransom, he was released. What was left of his army returned to France. He personally went to the Holy Land and spent four more years there improving the key fortifications at Acre, Caesarea, Jaffa, and Sidon. He finally returned to France in April 1254.

All of France was astounded in 1267 when Louis declared his intent to take up the cross again. Preparations took three years, and this time the target was Tunis. Louis hoped to convert the inhabitants to Christianity and to turn Tunis into a base for operations against Egypt. He landed with his new army on 17 July 1270, and an unidentified epidemic struck the French forces almost immediately. Perhaps it was dysentery. Perhaps it was typhus. Before Louis could fight even one battle, he fell ill and died on 25 August 1270. His final crusade quickly fell apart, and its survivors returned home.

Louis' Memorial

The body of the man who is remembered as the ideal Christian monarch was boiled down to the bones, which were then taken back to France. At St. Denis, they were placed in a magnificent gilt brass monument. Many miracles of healing were reported at his tomb. During the French Revolution, the monument was melted down and the bones scattered.

Louis is the patron saint of France.

His Line

Husband		Wife
Louis VIII "the Lion," King of France (b. 5 Sept 1187 – md. 23 May 1200 – d. 8 Nov 1226)	+	**Bl. Blanche of Castile** (b. 4 March 1188 – md. 23 May 1200 – d. 27 Nov 1252)
St. Louis IX (known as "St. Louis"), King of France and Crusader (b. 25 April 1214 – md. 27 May 1234 – d. 25 Aug 1270 during the Eighth Crusade)	+	Margaret of Provence (b. 1221 – md. 27 May 1234 – d. 20/21 Dec 1295)
Philip III "the Bold," King of France (b. 1 May 1245 – md. (1) 28 May 1262 – d. 5 Oct 1285)	+	Isabella (b. 1243 or 1247 – md. 28 May 1262 – d. 28 Jan 1271), daughter of James I "the Conqueror," King of Aragon

Philip IV "the Fair," King of France (b. 1268 – md. 16 Aug 1284 – d. 29 Nov 1314)	+	Jeanne of Navarre (b. Jan 1272 – md. 16 Aug 1284 – d. 2 April 1305)
Edward II, King of England (b. 25 April 1284 – md. 25 Jan 1308 – murdered 21 Sept 1327)	+	**Isabella** (b. 1292 – md. 25 Jan 1308 – d. 27 Aug 1357)

Sources: *Baring-Gould*, Vol. 9, pp. 284–310; *BBKL*, Vol. 5, cols. 364–366; *Benedictine Monks*, p. 442; *Bentley*, pp. 164–165; *Bradbury*, pp. 201–236; *Bunson*, pp. 496–497; *Butler*, Vol. III, pp. 394–398; *Castleden*, pp. 118–119; *CE*, Vol. IX, pp. 368–370; *Cruz*, pp. 410–420; *Delaney*, pp. 363–364; *Delaney and Tobin*, pp. 712–713; *Englebert*, pp. 325–326; *Giorgi*, pp. 502–503; *Guiley*, pp. 209–212; *Holboeck*, pp. 206–212; *Holweck*, p. 615; *Joeckle*, pp. 279–281; *NCE*, Vol. 8, pp. 1010–1012; *One Hundred Saints*, pp. 213–215; *Snodgrass*, pp. 154–155; *Stuart:* line 70, nos. 27 through 25 + line 51, nos. 25 through 23; *Tucker*, Vol. I, pp. 175–177; *Weis, AR*, line 101, nos. 27 through 31; *Wells*, pp. 256–257

St. Ludmilla, Duchess of Bohemia

Ludmilla was born around 860 and was the daughter of Slawibov, Prince of Psov. By 871, she had married Borivoy I, Duke of Bohemia.

In 871, Borivoy and Ludmilla were both baptized by St. Methodius and thus became the first Christian rulers of Bohemia. They then began the conversion of their people, and at first they were very unsuccessful. A pagan revolt broke out, and Borivoy and Ludmilla had to briefly flee the country. Once the leader of the revolt was slain, the revolt broke up, and Borivoy and Ludmilla returned. At a slower pace, their conversion of their country to Christianity then resumed.

Borivoy died in 894. Around 910 his son Ratislav entrusted the education of his own seven-year-old son Wenceslaus to Ludmilla, who was about fifty. Guided by Ludmilla, Wenceslaus grew up to be a deeply committed Christian.

After Ratislav died fighting the Magyars on 13 February 921, his widow Drahomira became the leader of another pagan reaction against the new religion. After trying and failing to convert Wenceslaus back to the pagan faith, Drahomira resorted to more dramatic measures to end Ludmilla's influence over him. On 15 September 921, assassins sent by Drahomira broke into Ludmilla's residence and strangled her with her own veil.

The effect of this on Wenceslaus was the opposite of what was intended. He had Ludmilla buried in Prague in the church of St. George, redoubled his own efforts to spread Christianity in Bohemia, and ultimately became a saint himself.

Her Line

Husband		Wife
Slawibov, Prince of Psov	+	**N.N.**
Borivoy I, Duke of Bohemia (md. by 871 – d. 894)	+	**St. Ludmilla** (b. ca. 860 – md. by 871 – murdered 15 Sept 921)
Wratislaw I, Duke of Bohemia (md. bef. 910 – d. 13 Feb 921)	+	Drahomir of Stodar (md. bef. 910)
Boleslaw I "the Cruel," Duke of Bohemia (d. 15 July 972)	+	Biagota of Stockow
Boleslaw II "the Pious," Duke of Bohemia (d. 7 Feb 999)	+	Hemma (d. ca. 1005)
Udalrich, Duke of Bohemia (d. 9 Nov 1034)	+	Bozena (d. 1055)
Bretislaw I "the Warrior," Duke of Bohemia, Moravia, and Silesia (b. ca. 1005 – md. ca. 1021 – d. 10 Jan 1055)	+	Judith von Schweinfurt (md. ca. 1021 – d. 2 Aug 1058)
Wratislaw II, King of Bohemia and Hungary and Lord of Olmutz (b. ca. 1035 – md. (2) 1056/1058 – d. 14 Jan 1092)	+	Adelaide (b. ca. 1038/1040 – md. 1056/1058 – d. 27 Jan 1062), daughter of Andrew I, King of Hungary

Ladislas I (or Wladislaw I Hermann), King of Poland (b. ca. 1040 – md. ca. 1080 – d. 4 June 1102)	+	**Judith of Bohemia** (b. ca. 1058 – md. ca. 1080 – d. 25 Dec 1086)

[For the later generations that connect this line to the kings of England, see the line of St. Adelaide of Burgundy in Part II.]

Sources: *Baring-Gould*, Vol. 10, pp. 265–266; *BBKL*, Vol. 17, cols. 869–870; *Benedictine Monks*, p. 448; *Bunson*, p. 501; *Butler*, Vol. III, p. 570; *Chervin*, pp. 181–182; *Cruz*, pp. 429–430; *Delaney*, p. 367; *Delaney and Tobin*, p. 720; *Dunbar*, Vol. I, pp. 475–477; *Holboeck*, pp. 119–121; *Holweck*, p. 624; *Klaniczay*, pp. 100–101, 328, and 353; *NCE*, Vol. 8, pp. 1062–1063; *Snodgrass*, p. 155; *Stuart*, line 362; *Weis, AR*, line 244, nos. 7 and 8; *Wells*, pp. 78–79

St. Marchell

Marchell's parents are unknown. She married an Irish prince named Anlach and became the mother of St. Brychan of Brecknock.

Her Line

Husband		Wife
N.N.	+	**N.N.**
Anlach, an Irish prince	+	**St. Marchell**
St. Brychan, ruler of Brecknock in South Wales (b. 480/490)	+	N.N.
St. Gabran mac Domangart, King of Dalriada (b. ca. 500 – md. bef. 532 – d. ca. 559)	+	**St. Lleian** (md. bef. 532)
Aidan (or Aedan) mac Gabran (b. 532 – d. 606), crowned King of Dalriada by St. Columba of Iona	+	N.N.
Eochaid Buide, King of the Picts and of Dalriada (d. 629)	+	N.N.

[For the later generations that connect this line to the kings of England, see the line of St. Brychan in Part II.]

Sources: *Ashley*, p. 158; *Baring-Gould*, Vol. 16, p. 129; *Baring-Gould and Fisher*, Vol. 3, pp. 436–437; *Holweck*, pp. 174 (under "Brychan") and 651; *Rees*, p. 151; *Stuart*, line 165, nos. 49 through 47; *Weis, AR*, line 170, nos. 4 through 6

St. Margaret of Scotland

Margaret was born around 1046 and was the daughter of Edward "the Exile" and his wife Agatha von Braunschweig. Her earliest years were spent with her parents at the Hungarian court. After her father died around 1057, her mother took her children to the court of Edward the Confessor in England. When William the Conqueror captured the English crown for himself in 1066, the family moved again, this time to the court of Scotland, where Malcolm III Canmore was king. Outwardly, Malcolm was a rough, uncultured man who couldn't read or write. Inwardly, he had a good heart and was deeply impressed by the attractive and well-educated Margaret. The two were married around 1069.

For the next twenty-four years, Margaret initiated a series of ecclesiastical reforms that transformed the religion and cultural life of Scotland. When she first arrived, there were no organized monastic orders in Scotland. Margaret invited the Benedictines in, built churches and monasteries, and brought the practices of the Celtic Scottish church into line with Roman ritual. She organized synods and insisted that the country observe the Sabbath.

Her own life was one of austerities, fasting, prayers, and generosities. She ransomed captives, cared for the sick, and saw to it that her eight children were well schooled in religion and all other subjects. Three of her six sons became kings themselves. Her prayer book is at the Bodelian Library at Oxford and has been reprinted.

Margaret was a very good wife to Malcolm, and when she received the news that he had died in battle on 13 November 1093, she lost all desire to live any longer and died herself on 16 November 1093.

Margaret was buried at Dunfermline and is the patron saint of Scotland. As the Middle Ages were drawing to a close, her remains were removed to the Continent and then lost during periods of religious unrest.

Her Line

Husband		Wife
Edward "the Exile" (b. 1016 – md. ca. 1043 – d. ca. 1057), son of Edmund "Ironside," King of England	+	**Agatha von Braunschweig** (b. ca. 1025 – md. ca. 1043 – d. aft. 1066)
Malcolm III Canmore, King of Scotland (b. ca. 1031 – md. (2) ca. 1069 – d. in battle 13 Nov 1093 while besieging Alnwick Castle)	+	**St. Margaret of Scotland** (b. ca. 1046 – md. ca. 1069 – d. 16 Nov 1093)
Henry I, King of England (b. 1070 – md. (1) 11 Nov 1100 – d. 1 Dec 1135)	+	**Matilda of Scotland** (b. 1079 – md. 11 Nov 1100 – d. 1 June 1118)

Sources: *Baring-Gould*, Vol. 6, pp. 136–138; *BBKL*, Vol. 17, cols. 898–901; *Benedictine Monks*, p. 468; *Bentley*, p. 222; *Bunson*, p. 522; *Butler*, Vol. II, pp. 515–517; *CE*, Vol. IX, pp. 655–656; *Chervin*, pp. 184–185; *Cruz*, pp. 491–495; *CS*, pp. 699–700; *Delaney*, p. 383; *Delaney and Tobin*, p. 752; *Dunbar*, Vol. II, pp. 13–17; *Giorgi*, pp. 674–675; *Guiley*, pp. 220–221; *Holboeck*, pp. 144–146; *Holweck*, p. 655; *Joeckle*, pp. 289–290; *NCE*, Vol. 9, p. 200; *One Hundred Saints*, pp. 182–183; *Parbury*, pp. 63–65;

Snodgrass, p. 161; *Stuart:* line 233, nos. 33 and 32 + line 165, nos. 31 and 30; *Wagner*, p. 206; *Weir*, pp. 184–185 and 46–47; *Weis, AR*, line 1, nos. 21 through 23; *Wells*, pp. 205, 519–520, and 207; *WWH*, Vol. 10, pp. 230–233

St. Matilda of Ringelheim

Matilda was born around 892 and was the daughter of Dietrich, Count of Saxony, and his wife Gisela of Lorraine. She was educated in a convent and married Henry I, Duke of Saxony, in 909 when she was seventeen.

Henry became emperor of the Holy Roman Empire ten years later. Before and after his elevation, Henry was very often away fighting and winning wars, and the day-to-day operations of his court were left to Matilda.

Her court reflected her personality. Matilda was a deeply pious woman who lived austerely, almost like a nun. She built the Benedictine abbeys of Engern, Nordhausen, Poehlde, and Quedlinburg. She comforted the sick, visited prisoners, and always gave very generously to the poor. Even to her servants, she was a loving mother. Her court was quiet, pious, and intellectual, more like a convent than a seat of imperial power.

Although Henry was about sixteen years older than Matilda, they had an exceptionally happy marriage and had several children, including one son who would become St. Bruno the Great, Archbishop of Cologne.

The trials and sufferings of Matilda began after Henry died in 936. Otto was their first-born-son, and their second son also was named Henry. Matilda thought that son Henry would be a better emperor than Otto and supported his claims to the imperial throne. Most of the nobles of the empire preferred Otto, however, and it was he who succeeded to the throne as Emperor Otto I.

Matilda's family then became an extraordinarily unhappy one. Because of her support for Henry, Otto began to profoundly distrust Matilda and started using spies to keep a very close watch on her. Otto's appointment of brother Henry as Duke of Bavaria did little or nothing to soften his unhappiness over not becoming emperor. His subsequent actions earned him the nickname Henry "the Quarrelsome" or Henry "the Wrangler." In the several years following Otto's elevation, Henry led three different revolts against Otto, which were put down with increasing ferocity. Between Henry's revolts, there were temporary reconciliations between Henry and Otto. During these periods, the two of them would unite long enough to accuse their mother of mismanaging the imperial finances by giving far too much money away to the allegedly worthless poor. Matilda was accused of hiding treasure, and accountings of her expenditures were demanded. At one point, Henry and Otto took away most of her revenue-producing lands and banished her from court. Only Henry's death in 955 permanently ended his quarrels with his brother and mother.

After Otto's rule was finally no longer disputed, Otto reconciled with his Matilda to a certain extent, but their original loving relationship was never restored. Matilda became a nun, entered one of her own convents, and continued to give away her possessions. By the time she lay dying on 14 March 968, she had given away everything but her own burial robe. She died owning nothing and was buried at Quedlinburg next to her husband Henry. Immediately after her death, she was venerated as a saint.

Her Line

Husband		Wife
Dietrich, Count of Saxony (b. ca. 872 – md. (1) 882 – d. 8 Dec 917)	+	**Gisela** (b. 860/865 – md. 882 – d. by 26 Oct 907), daughter of Lothar II, King of Lorraine
Henry I "the Fowler," Duke of Saxony and Emperor of the West (b. 876 – md. (2) 909 – d. 2 July 936)	+	**St. Matilda of Ringelheim** (b. ca. 892 – md. 909 – d. 14 March 968)
Otto I "the Great," King of Germany and Italy and Emperor of the West (b. 23 Nov 912 – md. (2) 25 Dec 951 – d. 7 May 973)	+	St. Adelaide of Burgundy (b. 932 – md. (2) 25 Dec 951 – d. 16/17 Dec 999)

[For the later generations that connect this line to the kings of England, see the line of St. Adelaide of Burgundy in Part II.]

Sources: *Baring-Gould*, Vol. 3, pp. 260–265; *BBKL*, Vol. 5, cols. 1015–1016; *Benedictine Monks*, p. 486; *Bentley*, p. 51; *Bunson*, p. 566; *Butler*, Vol. I, pp. 592–593; *CE*, Vol. X, p. 49; *Chervin*, pp. 51–52; *Cruz*, pp. 517–520; *Delaney*, p. 394; *Delaney and Tobin*, p. 770; *Dunbar*, Vol. II, pp. 67–71; *Englebert*, pp. 101–102; *Giorgi*, pp. 162–163; *Holboeck*, pp. 122–125; *Holweck*, p. 682; *Klaniczay*, Appendix B: Geneal. Table 3; *NCE*, Vol. 9, p. 463; *Stuart:* line 338, nos. 37 and 36 + line 321, nos. 37 and 36; *Weis, AR*, line 147, nos. 18 and 19; *Wells*, p. 270; *WWH*, Vol. 10, pp. 623–624

Bl. Matilda of Saxony

Matilda was born in 981 and was the daughter of Otto II, King of Italy and Emperor of the West, and his second wife St. Theophano Skleros.

Matilda's brother was also named Otto and was born one year before her in 980. When their father Otto II died on December 7, 983, Matilda's almost three-year-old brother suddenly became Otto III, the next Holy Roman Emperor, although it would be years before he would rule in his own right. For all the ambitious nobles of the empire, the almost two-year-old Matilda suddenly became an extraordinarily desirable prospective wife.

In the ensuing contest for her hand, the winner was Ezzo (also known as Ehrenfried), Count Palatine of Lorraine. They were married in 991, when Matilda was ten and Ezzo was in his late thirties. According to a widespread legend, Ezzo won Matilda by playing chess with her brother Otto, beating him three games in a row, and then being offered whatever he desired as a reward for his accomplishment. Since at the time of the marriage brother Otto was only eleven years old, it is highly unlikely that such a fateful chess match between a boy and a middle-aged man ever took place.

In 994 Otto III finally reached the age of majority and began to rule the Holy Roman Empire in his own right. Ezzo's fortunes rose dramatically along with those of Otto. Besides the lands he acquired as his wife's dowry, Ezzo received many more in a wide radius all around Cologne. Next to Otto himself, Ezzo became the second most powerful man in the empire.

Notwithstanding the great age difference between Ezzo and Matilda, they had three sons and seven daughters, almost all of whom were honored by the Church. Their son Hermann became archbishop of Cologne, six of their daughters became abbesses, and the only daughter who didn't become an abbess (Richenza) became a saint.

In 1024 Ezzo and Matilda founded the monastery of Brauweiler near Cologne. Matilda died on 4 November 1025 and Ezzo on 21 May 1034. They are both buried there.

Her Line

Husband		Wife
Otto II, King of Italy and Emperor of the West (b. 955 – md. (2) 14 April 972 – d. 7 Dec 983)	+	**St. Theophano Skleros** (b. 956 – md. 14 April 972 – d. 15 Sept 991)
Ezzo, Count Palatine of Lorraine, Lord of Duisburg and Kaiserwerth (b. ca. 955 – md. 991 – d. 21 May 1034)	+	**Bl. Matilda of Saxony** (b. 981 – md. 991 – d. 4 Nov 1025)
Mieszko II, King of Poland (b. ca. 990 – md. 1013 – d. 10 May 1034)	+	**St. Richenza of Pfalz-Lorraine** (b. ca. 1000 – md. (1) 1013 – d. 21 March 1063)

[For the later generations that connect this line to the kings of England, see the line of St. Adelaide of Burgundy in Part II.]

Sources: *Dunbar*, Vol. II, pp. 71–72; *Stuart*, line 237, nos. 36 through 34; *Weis, AR*, line 147, nos. 20 through 22; *Wells*, p. 83; *WWH*, Vol. 10, p. 624

St. Meurig ap Tewdrig, King of Gwent and Glywysing

Meurig was born in the mid 500's and was the son of St. Tewdrig, King of Gwent in south Wales, and his wife Enynny ferch Cynfarch Oer. Enynny was a sister of Urien, King of Rheged.

Meurig married Onbrawst, who was the daughter of Gwrgan Fawr "the Great," King of Ergyng in Wales.

Meurig was an impulsive man with a strong temper. When his father abdicated to enter a monastery, Meurig first became king of Gwent but later added Glywysing to his dominions. His enlarged realm was later known as the kingdom of Morgannwg and is today called Glamorgan.

Meurig was a warrior king. Besides enlarging his state, Meurig also saved it from destruction more than once. With his father, he led a Welsh army against the Saxons and soundly defeated them near Tintern ca. 584 at the battle of the Saxon Bridge. One of his sons was Athrwys ap Meurig. As early as 1796, scholars suggested that the legends of King Arthur were based on the real life of Athrwys, and this speculation continues to this day.

Like his father, Meurig continued to donate to Llandaff Cathedral, where he is buried.

His Line

Husband		Wife
St. Tewdrig ap Llywarch, King of Gwent (b. early 500's)	+	**Enynny ferch Cynfarch Oer**
St. Meurig ap Tewdrig, King of Gwent and Glywysing (b. mid 500's)	+	Onbrawst ferch Gwrgan Fawr
Athrwys ap Meurig (b. ca. 570)	+	N.N.
Morgan, King of Glywysing (d. 665)	+	Rhiceneth
Rhys ap Morgan (b. ca. 655)	+	N.N.
Brochwel ap Rhys (b. ca. 700)	+	N.N.
Gwriad ap Brochwel (b. ca. 730)	+	Ceingar ferch Maredudd (d. 796)
Arthfael ap Gwriad (b. ca. 770)	+	Brawstudd ferch Gloud
Rhys ap Arthfael (b. ca. 800)	+	N.N.
Hywel ap Rhys (d. ca. 886)	+	Lleucu
Owain ap Hywel (d. ca. 930)	+	Nest ferch Rhodri Mawr
Morgan Mar ap Owain (also known as Morgan Hen), King of Morgannwg (d. 974)	+	Lleucu ferch Enflew
Seferws ap Cadwr, Lord of Buallt and Maes Yfed	+	**Lucy ferch Morgan Hen**
Ifor ap Seferws, Lord of Buallt and Maes Yfed	+	Isabell ferch Tryffin

Cuhelyn ap Ifor, Lord of Buallt and Maes Yfed	+	Rheingar ferch Gronwy
Elystan Glodrydd ap Cuhelyn, Lord of Buallt and Maes Yfed (b. 933 – liv. 1010)	+	Gwenllian ferch Einion
Cadwgon ap Elystan Glodrydd, Lord of Radnor, Maes Yfed, and Buallt (b. ca. 970)	+	N.N.
Iorwerth ap Cadwgon, Lord of Cedewain (b. ca. 1000)	+	N.N.
Llywarch ap Trahaearn, Lord of Arwystli (d. ca. 1129)	+	**Dyddgu ferch Iorwerth**
Owain I Gwynedd, King of North Wales (b. ca. 1100 – d. 28 Nov 1170)	+	md. (1) **Gwladus ferch Llywarch** ap Trahaearn (d. 1081)
Iorwerth Drwyndwn "the Flat Nosed," Prince of North Wales (d. ca. 1174)	+	Margred ferch Madog ap Maredudd
Llywelyn ap Iorwerth "the Great," Prince of North Wales (b. 1173 – d. 11 April 1240)	+	N.N.
Donald, 6th Earl of Mar (d. aft. 25 July 1297)	+	**Helen** (her 2nd marriage)
Robert I the Bruce, King of Scots (b. 11 July 1274 – md. (1) ca. 1295 – d. 7 June 1329)	+	**Isabel (or Isabella) of Mar** (md. 1295– d. bef. 1302)

Sources: *Ashley*, pp. 104–105, 122, and 125; *Baring-Gould*, Vol. 16, p. 139; *Baring-Gould and Fisher*, Vol. 3, pp. 481–483; *Boyer*: nos. 4 through 15 on pp. 160–161 + nos. "1–14," 15, and 19 on pp. 137–139 + no. 18 on p. 347 + no. 24 on pp. 292–294 + no. 29 on p. 296 + no. 36 on pp. 300–302; *CE*, Vol. XIV, p. 52 (under "Tewdrig"); *Holweck*, p. 709 and p. 951 (under "Tewdrig"); *Weis, AR:* line 176, nos. 4 through 7 + line 252, no. 30

St. Mstislav I Vladimirovich "the Great," Grand Prince of Kiev

Mstislav was born in 1076. He was the son of St. Vladimir Vsevolodovich Monomach, Grand Prince of Kiev and ruler of Kievan Rus, and his first wife Gytha of Wessex. Mstislav had two wives. In 1095, he married Christine, daughter of King Inge I of Sweden. In 1122, he married Lyubawa, daughter of Dmitri Zaviditsch, Possadnik of Novgorod.

Like his father, Mstislav was a warrior who fought the enemies of Kievan Rus for most of his adult life. He led a dozen campaigns against the Cumans, the Estonians, the Lithuanians, and the Princedom of Polotsk. When his father died in 1125, Mstislav succeeded him as Grand Prince of Kiev. Among his people, Mstislav was known for his mercifulness and his gift of prayer. He ordered the "Mstislav Gospel" to be written. He also founded many churches and was a friend to the poor.

Mstislav died on 14 April 1132. Because he was a grandson of King Harold Godwinsson of England through his mother, Mstislav was also known as "Mstislav I Harold." Two of his sons by his first wife Christine—Rostislav I Mstislavich and Vsevolod Mstislavich of Pskov—would also be remembered as saints.

Mstislav was the last ruler of Kievan Rus as a united kingdom. After his death the land would be torn apart.

His Line

Husband		Wife
St. Vladimir Vsevolodovich Monomach (a.k.a. Vladimir II "Monomachos"), Grand Prince of Kiev (b. 1053 – md. (1) ca. 1070 – d. 19 May 1125)	+	**Gytha of Wessex** (md. ca. 1070), daughter of Harold II Godwinsson, King of England
St. Mstislav Vladimirovich (a.k.a., Mstislav I Harold), Grand Prince of Kiev (b. 1076 – md. (2) 1122 – d. 15 April 1032)	+	Lyubawa (md. 1122 – d. 1168), daughter of Dmitri Zaviditsch, Possadnik of Novgorod
Geza II, King of Hungary (b. ca. 1130 – md. 1146 – d. 3 May 1162)	+	**Euphrosyne Mstislavna** (b. 1130 – md. 1146 – d. 1175/1176)
Bela III, King of Hungary (b. ca. 1148 – md. 1172 – d. 23 April 1196)	+	Agnes (or Anne) de Chatillon-sur-Loing (b. 1153 – md. 1172 – d. 1184)
Andrew II, King of Hungary (b. 1176 – md. (2) 1215 – d. 21 Sept 1235)	+	Yolande de Courtenay (b. ca. 1194 – md. 1215 – d. 1233)

[For the later generations that connect this line to the kings of England, see the line of St. Harold III "Bluetooth," King of Denmark in Part II.]

Sources: *Fedotov*, p. 92; *Golubinskii*, p. 58; *Holweck*, p. 724; *Stuart:* line 240, nos. 30 through 28 + line 51, nos. 29 through 27; *Tucker:* Vol. II, pp. 732–733 + Vol. I, pp. 425–427; *Wagner*, p. 206; *Weis, AR:* line 242, nos. 7 through 10 + line 103, nos. 27 and 28

St. Nerses I "the Great"

Nerses was born around 333/337 and was the son of Athenagenes and his wife Bambishu. He married the princess Samdukht and began his career as a soldier and then as chamberlain to Arshak II, King of Armenia.

After Samdukht died young, Nerses became a priest and in 353 was made Katholikus (i.e., Bishop or Patriarch) of Armenia. He did so much to enlarge the Church there that he was also called Nerses "the Builder." He reformed the clergy, convened a synod (the Council of Ashdishad) in 364–65, and built many churches, schools, hospitals, and monasteries.

Nerses did not suffer sinners gladly. When Arshak II had his own wife murdered, Nerses denounced him so vigorously that Arshak exiled him. In 369 after Arshak died in battle, Nerses was invited to return to Armenia by Arshak's son King Pap. Nerses did so but then refused to allow King Pap to enter Nerses' church until he reformed his evil life. Invited to a banquet in 373 to hopefully resolve their differences, Nerses was poisoned by King Pap.

Nerses is regarded as a martyr and is mentioned daily in the Armenian liturgy. One of his children with Samdukht would grow up to be St. Isaac "the Great."

His Line

Husband		Wife
Athenagenes	+	**Bambishu** (b. 315)
St. Nerses (or Narces or Narses) I, Gregorid Prince and Bishop of Armenia (b. 333/337 – d. 373)	+	Samdukht
St. Isaac (or Sahak or Sahag) I "the Great," Gregorid Prince and Bishop of Armenia (b. 345/352 – d. 7 Sept 439)	+	N.N.
Hamazasp I, Prince of the Mamikonids and High Constable of Armenia (b. 345 – d. ca. 416)	+	**Sahakanoysh**, the Gregorid heiress
St. Hmayeak Mamikonian, General and Ambassador to Constantinople (b. 410 – d. in battle 2 June 451)	+	Dzoyk, daughter of Vram, Prince of Rshtuni

[For the later generations that connect this line to the kings of England, see the line of St. Ashken in Part II.]

Sources: *BBKL*, Vol. 6, cols. 619–620; *Benedictine Monks*, p. 519; *Bunson*, p. 602; *CE*, Vol. X, p. 754; *Delaney*, p. 421; *Delaney and Tobin*, p. 845; *Holweck*, p. 734; *Hovannisian*, pp. 83, 86, and 90–91; *Koushagian*, pp. 11–12; *NCE*, Vol. 10, p. 342; *O'Malley*, pp. 42, 52, and 66; *Stone*, Chap. 8, Chart 80; *Stuart:* line 416, nos. 56 through 53 + line 322, nos. 53 and 52; *Wagner*, p. 195

St. Oda

Oda was born around 567. Her parents are unknown, but she is called "a Suevian." During Roman times, the Suevians were a confederation of tribes who lived in Germany. As the Roman Empire fell, they rode out of their homelands to conquer new territories and ultimately reached Spain.

Oda married St. Bodegeisel, Governor of Aquitaine. They were the parents of St. Arnulph, Bishop of Metz.

After Bodegeisel's death, Oda spent the rest of her life aiding the poor. She died around 640 and is buried at the church of St. Ouen.

Her Line

Husband		Wife
N.N.	+	**N.N.**
St. Bodegeisel II, Governor of Aquitaine (murdered 588)	+	**St. Oda**, a Suevian (b. ca. 567 – d. ca. 640)
St. Arnulf (or Arnoul), Mayor of the Palace in Austrasia and Bishop of Metz (b. 13 Aug 582 – md. ca. 596 – d. 16 Aug 641)	+	Dode (or Clothilde) (b. ca. 586 – md. ca. 596)
Ansgise (or Ansegisel), Mayor of the Palace in Austrasia (b. 602 – md. bef. 639 – murdered 685)	+	St. Begga (b. ca. 613 – md. bef. 639 – d. ca. 698)
Pepin (or Pippin) of Heristal, Mayor of the Palace in Austrasia (b. ca. 635 – d. 16 Dec 714)	+	Aupais, a concubine (b. ca. 654)

[For the later generations that connect this line to the kings of England, see the line of St. Arnulf, Bishop of Metz in Part II.]

Sources: *Bunson*, p. 614; *Dunbar*, Vol. II, p. 113; *Holweck*, p. 751; *Stuart*, line 171, nos. 47 through 44; *Tucker*, Vol. I, pp. 182–183; *Wagner*, p. 189; *Weis, AR*, line 190, nos. 7 through 10; *Wells*, p. 135; *WWH*, Vol. 4, p. 690

St. Olaf II,
King of Norway

Olaf was born around 995 and was the son of Harald Granske "Greenlander," a Norwegian lord, and his wife Asta Gudbrandsdatter.

At the age of twelve, Olaf joined the Vikings. For about the next eight years, he took part in Viking expeditions to the Baltics, to France, and to England. During this time, his own country of Norway was just a collection of petty kingdoms that were mostly in the hands of the Danes and the Swedes.

Olaf began his career as a ruler in 1015. Landing in Norway with enough men to conquer three of the petty kingdoms, he was crowned the new king of Norway. His ambition was to unite all of its parts into one realm ruled by him. To this end, he incited popular rebellions against the Danish and Swedish overlords in Norway. He also continued his fight against the Norwegian lords who were unwilling to submit to his rule. After several early victories, in February 1019 he married Astrid, daughter of St. Olaf III, King of Sweden.

Next to winning on the battlefield, Olaf thought that the best way to encourage political unity was to achieve religious unity. Olaf himself had been baptized at 15, and almost all of the rulers of the Norwegian lands since Hakon the Good (c. 920-961) had been Christians. Yet most of the people who were Christian lived along the coast. In the interior of the country, the old pagan religion was still very much alive.

Olaf decided to complete the conversion of his country, by force if necessary. Building new churches nationwide, sending for missionaries from England and Germany, and establishing the Norwegian state church in 1024 were among his more peaceful measures. Pagans who still refused to convert might have their farms burned down, their hands hacked off, or their eyes gouged out.

Not everyone agreed with Olaf's goals or methods, and those who didn't went to their old overlords the Danes for help. In 1028, an army led by King Canute the Great landed in Norway and was joined by the forces of the Norwegian lords who were resisting Olaf. Olaf himself fled the country and spent two years in exile in Kievan Rus. In 1030, Olaf returned to Norway with a new army and met his opponents on 29 July 1030 in the battle of Stiklestadt. By the end of the day, Olaf was dead. He was buried in Trondheim in the Nidaros Cathedral.

With Olaf gone, the next political developments were not exactly what his opponents had expected. The Norwegian church immediately declared Olaf a martyr and a saint. Canute sent his son Svein to rule in Norway, but the Norwegian Christians turned Olaf into a national symbol around which opponents of the Danes could rally. Danish rule came to be regarded as foreign oppression, and when Olaf's son Magnus arrived with a new Norwegian army in 1035, Svein fled.

As the first ruler of a united realm, Olaf is remembered as the "eternal king of Norway" and became its patron saint.

His Line

Husband		Wife
Harald Granske "Greenlander," ruler of Vigulmark, Vestfold, and Agdir (b. ca. 952 – murdered ca. 995)	+	**Asta Gudbrandsdatter**
St. Olaf Haraldsson (a.k.a. Olaf II), King of Norway (b. ca. 995 – md. Feb 1019 – slain 29 July 1030 in the battle of Stiklestadt)	+	Astrid (md. Feb 1019), daughter of St. Olaf III, King of Sweden
Ordulf, Duke of Saxony (b. ca. 1020 – md. (1) Nov 1042 – d. 28 March 1072)	+	**Ulfhild** (b. ca. 1023 – md. (2) Nov 1042 – d. 24 May 1071)
Magnus, Duke of Saxony (b. ca. 1045 – md. (2) ca. 1071 – d. 23 Aug 1106)	+	Sophia (md. ca. 1071 – d. 18 June 1095), daughter of Bela I, King of Hungary
Henry I "the Black," Duke of Bavaria (b. 1074 – md. 1095/ 1100 – d. 13 Dec 1126)	+	**Ulfhild of Saxony** (b. ca. 1071 – md. 1095/1100 – d. 29 Dec 1126)
Frederick II von Hohenstaufen, Duke of Swabia (b. 1090 – md. 1121 – d. 4/6 April 1147)	+	**Judith of Bavaria** (b. ca. 1100 – md. 1121 – d. 22 Feb 1130/ 1135)
Frederick III Barbarosa, Duke of Swabia, Emperor of Germany and the West, Crusader (b. 1122 – md. 10/16 June 1156 – drowned 10 June 1190 while on the 3rd Crusade)	+	Beatrice of Burgundy (b. ca. 1145 – md. 10/16 June 1156 – d. 15 Nov 1184)
Philip von Hohenstaufen, Duke of Tuscany and Swabia and Emperor of Germany (b. 1176 – md. 25 May 1197 – murdered 21 June 1208)	+	Eirene (or Maria) Angelina (b. ca. 1181 – md. (2) 25 May 1197 – murdered 27 Aug 1208), daughter of Isaac II Angelos, Emperor of Byzantium

[For the later generations that connect this line to the kings of England, see the line of St. Boris I, Khan of the Bulgars in Part II.]

Sources: *Baring-Gould*, Vol. 8, pp. 636–676; *BBKL*, Vol. 6, cols. 1175–1176; *Benedictine Monks*, p. 533; *Bunson*, p. 616; *Butler*, Vol. III, pp. 208–209; *CE*, Vol. XI, p. 234; *Cruz*, pp. 568–573; *Delaney*, pp. 435–436; *Guiley*, p. 263; *Holweck*, p. 754; *NCE*, Vol. 10, p. 671; *One Hundred Saints*, pp. 174–175; *Snodgrass*, p. 177; *Stuart:* line 28, nos. 35 through 31 + line 43, nos. 31 and 30 + line 40, nos. 30 and 29 + line 125, nos. 29 and 28; *Tucker:* Vol. II, pp. 626 and 753 + Vol. I, pp. 56–57 and 341–342; *Weis, AR:* line 243A, nos. 20 through 23 + line 166, nos. 24 and 25 + line 45, nos. 25 through 27; *Wells*, pp. 439, 516, 57–58, and 271–272

St. Olaf Bjornsson, King at Uppsala

Olaf was the son of Bjorn Eriksson, King at Uppsala. He married Ingelberg of Sula.

When Olaf was born, Sweden was neither a Christian country nor a united realm. The first Christian missionary (Ansger) arrived in 829, only to be attacked by Vikings and robbed of all his possessions. For most of the next 200 years, similar missions met with little success. Sweden did not become one realm until around 1075.

Prior to unification, the most important sub-kingdom in Sweden was Uppsala. Its king was called the "king at Uppsala." Around 950, two sons of Bjorn Eriksson were crowned joint-kings at Uppsala: Olaf Bjornsson and his brother Erik Segersall, whose son Olaf would become a Christian himself and begin the conversion of Sweden.

Olaf Bjornsson was interested in Christianity, and this interest played an unclear role in his death around 964. According to some sources, he was murdered by his subjects for refusing to sacrifice to pagan gods. According to others, he was killed by poisoned drink which was offered to him during a meal. Whatever his form of death, he is remembered as an early martyr of Swedish Christianity.

His Line

Husband		Wife
Bjorn, King at Uppsala (b. 868 – d. ca. 956)	+	**N.N.**
St. Olaf Bjornsson, King at Uppsala (slain 964)	+	Ingelberg, daughter of Thraud, Earl (Jarl) of Sula
Styrbiorn Olafsson, leader of the Jomsborg Vikings (b. 956 – slain 985 at the battle of Blackfeld)	+	md. (1) Thyra of Denmark (d. 18 Sept 1000)
Jarl Thorkill Sprakalaeg	+	N.N.
Godwin, Earldorman of Wessex (md. (2) 1019/1020 – d. 15 April 1053)	+	**Gytha** (md. 1019/1020)
Harold II Godwinsson, King of England (b. ca. 1022 – slain 14 Oct 1066 at the battle of Hastings)	+	Ealdgyth "Swanneshals" (Swan Neck)

[For the subsequent generations that connect this line to the later kings of England, see the line of St. Harald III "Bluetooth," King of Denmark in Part II.]

Sources: *Benedictine Monks*, p. 533; *Delaney and Tobin*, p. 872; *Holweck*, p. 754; *Stuart*, line 368, nos. 36 through 31; *Tucker:* Vol. II, p. 818 + Vol. I, pp. 258 and 450–451; *Weis, AR*, line 1B, nos. 22 through 24

St. Olaf III "Skotkonung" (the Tax King), King of Sweden

Olaf was born around 980 and was the son of Erik "Segersall," King of Sweden and Denmark, and his wife Sigrid "Starrade." Shortly before 1001, he married Astrid, princess of the Obotrites.

At the time of their marriage, Astrid was a Christian, but Olaf was still a pagan. In the next several years, Astrid worked to give Olaf a more favorable view of Christianity, and her work was not in vain. When he was baptized around 1008, Olaf became the first Christian ruler of all Sweden.

After becoming a Christian, Olaf tried to convert his country too and met sharp opposition. He was killed around 1021/1022 and is remembered as a martyr.

Olaf was buried at Husaby. He and Astrid were the parents of St. Ingegerd.

His Line

Husband		Wife
Erik "Segersall" (the Victorious), King of Sweden and Denmark (b. ca. 935)	+	**Sigrid "Starrade" (the Proud)** (b. ca. 950)
St. Olaf III "Skotkonung" (the Tax King), King of Sweden (b. ca. 980 – md. (2) bef. 1001 – d. 1021/1022)	+	Astrid, a princess of the Obotrites (b. ca. 979 – md. bef. 1001)
St. Yaroslav I Vladimirovich "the Wise," Grand Prince of Kiev (b. 978 – md. (2) Feb 1019 – d. 20 Feb 1054)	+	**St. Ingegerd**, Princess of Sweden (b. ca. 1001 – md. Feb 1019 – d. 10 Feb 1050)

[For the later generations that connect this line to the kings of England, see the line of St. Ingegerd, Princess of Sweden in Part II.]

Sources: *Bunson*, pp. 616–617; *CS*, pp. 100–101 (under "Sigfrid"); *Delaney*, p. 436; *Delaney and Tobin*, p. 872; *Moncrieffe*, p. 113; *Stuart*, line 240, nos. 34 and 35; *Tucker*, Vol. II, p. 818; *Weis, AR*, line 241, no. 5; *Wells*, p. 549

St. Olga,
Princess of Izborsk

Olga was the daughter of Oleg, Danish Prince of Kiev. Around 930/935, she married Igor, Grand Prince of Kiev.

Olga first stepped onto the pages of history in 945. Igor had gone to collect taxes from the Derevlians, one of the Slavic tribes living in his kingdom. Instead of paying, they killed him. Assuming the role of regent for their young son Sviatoslav, Olga's response was swift. The first Derevlian prisoners she took were buried alive. The next group was offered a chance to bathe, then locked in the bathhouse and burned to death. A very large third group was offered a banquet and then massacred while they ate. Finally, she surrounded Derevlian villages with her troops and then burned them and their inhabitants to ashes.

After these reprisals, there were no more revolts in Olga's kingdom. She continued to rule on behalf of her son Sviatoslav, established a system of uniform taxes, and initiated other administrative and fiscal reforms.

The moment when Olga made religious history occurred in 957, when she traveled to Constantinople to be baptized a Christian. She was the first Russian ruler to embrace the new religion. She wanted to lead her country out of its pagan faith and brought back the first Christian missionaries. The hoped-for national conversion did not occur, however. It had to wait two more generations until the time of Olga's grandson St. Vladimir.

Olga remained regent for her son Sviatoslav until he came of age around 957. She died on 11 July 969 and was buried in Kiev. Sviatoslav—who never converted—was killed in battle three years later.

In 1240 Olga's tomb was destroyed by the Mongol army of Batu Khan.

Her Line

Husband		Wife
Oleg (or Helgi II), Danish Prince of Kiev (slain in 912)	+	**N.N.**
Igor (or Ingvar), Grand Prince of Kiev and Novgorod (b. 910/920 – md. 930/935 – slain 945)	+	**St. Olga** (md. 930/935 – d. 11 July 969)
Sviatoslav I Igorevich, Grand Prince of Kiev and Novgorod (b. ca. 940 – killed in battle 972)	+	md. (2) Maloucha (d. 1002)
St. Vladimir I Sviatoslavich "the Great," Grand Prince of Kiev and Novgorod (b. ca. 955 – d. 15 July 1015)	+	md. (3) Rognieda of Polotsk (b. ca. 956 – d. 1002)
St. Yaroslav I Vladimirovich "the Wise," Grand Prince of Kiev (b. 978 – md. (2) Feb 1019 – d. 20 Feb 1054)	+	St. Ingegerd (b. ca. 1001 – md. Feb 1019 – d. 10 Feb 1050), daughter of St. Olaf III "Skotkonung," King of Sweden

[For the later generations that connect this line to the kings of England, see the line of St. Izyaslav I Yaroslavich, Grand Prince of Kiev in Part II.]

Sources: *BBKL*, Vol. 6, cols. 1201–1202; *Benedictine Monks*, p. 533; *Bunson*, p. 617; *Butler*, Vol. III, p. 72; *Chervin*, pp. 332–333; *Cruz*, pp. 574–575; *Delaney*, p. 436; *Delaney and Tobin*, p. 873; *Dunbar*, Vol. II, pp. 117–119; *Englebert*, pp. 266–267; *Fedotov*, pp. 74 and 88; *Holweck*, p. 754; *NCE*, Vol. 10, p. 679; *Tucker*, Vol. II, pp. 731–732; *Weis, AR*, line 241, nos. 2 through 5; *Wells*, pp. 328–329; *WWH*, Vol. 12, pp. 88–92. Also see ***fmg.ac>Projects>Medieval Lands>Medieval Lands – data by region>Russia>Rurikids>Rurik [862–879], Oleg [879–912], Igor [912]–945, Sviatoslav I 957–972, Iaropolk I 972–980, Vladimir I 980–1015, Sviatopolk I 1015–1019***.

St. Pabo "Post Prydyn"

Pabo was the son of St. Ceneu, a ruler of northern Britain. Pabo lived from about 430 to 510.

When St. Ceneu died, Pabo had to defend his inherited kingdom against invading Picts, Irish, and Saxons. His several victories against them are the basis for his being called "Post Prydyn" (the Pillar of Northern Britain).

After being defeated in battle by the Picts, Pabo and his family moved to north Wales, where Pabo became a monk and founded the monastery of Llanbabo in the Welsh county of Anglesey. One tradition says he's buried at Llanbabo, and there is a tomb there with his name and a striking full-length medieval image carved onto the lid. In this image, he is dressed in the clothing of royalty.

Three of Pabo's children also became saints: his daughter Arddun Benasgell, his son Dunawd, and his son Sawyl Benisel.

His Line

Husband		Wife
St. Ceneu, a ruler of northern Britain (b. ca. 400)	+	**N.N.**
St. Pabo "Post Prydyn" (the Pillar of Northern Britain) (b. ca. 430 – d. ca. 510)	+	N.N.
St. Brochwel "Ysgithrog," King of Powys (liv. 570)	+	**St. Arddun "Benasgell"**
Cynan Garwyn	+	N.N.
Eiludd	+	N.N.
Beli	+	N.N.

[For the later generations that connect this line to the kings of Scotland, see the line of St. Arddun Benasgell in Part II.]

Sources: *Baring-Gould*, Vol. 16, p. 302; *Baring-Gould and Fisher*, Vol. 4, pp. 38–39; *Benedictine Monks*, p. 539; *Boyer*, nos. 2 and 3 on p. 63; *Bunson*, p. 624; *Delaney and Tobin*, p. 887; *Holweck*, p. 763; *Rees*, p. 101

Bl. Pepin of Landen,
Mayor of the Palace in Austrasia

Pepin's early life is obscure. He was born around 580/585. He came from Landen in eastern Belgium. The names of his parents are unknown.

By the early 600's, Pepin was one of the most prominent men in the kingdom of Austrasia. In the revolution of 613, he helped Bishop Arnulf of Metz, some members of the local nobility, and King Clothaire II of Neustria overthrow Brunhilda, the tyrannical and murderous ruler of Austrasia. For his role, Pepin was made Mayor of the Palace in Austrasia and served its next three kings: Clothaire II, Dagobert I, and St. Sigebert III. Contemporaries praised him for his good government and wise counsel, and he was seen as one of the leading statesmen of his time.

Pepin did many things to help the Church. He saw to it that more capable bishops were appointed to the diocese of Austrasia. He defended Christian towns from heathen invaders. He founded the Church of St. Mary in Landen. He also worked to spread Christianity.

Pepin's wife Itta and his two daughters Begga and Gertrude all became saints. His descendants through St. Begga became the Carolingian dynasty.

Pepin died around 640/646 and is buried in Nivelles next to his wife St. Itta and his daughter St. Gertrude of Nivelles. Because several of his descendants have the same name, he is sometimes called Pepin "the Old."

His Line

Husband		Wife
N.N.	+	**N.N.**
Bl. Pepin of Landen "the Old," Mayor of the Palace in Austrasia (b. 580/585 – d. 640/646)	+	Bl. Itta (b. ca. 597 – d. 8 May 652)
Ansguise (or Ansegisel), Mayor of the Palace in Austrasia (b. 602 – md. bef. 639 – murdered 685)	+	**St. Begga** (b. ca. 613 – md. bef. 639 – d. ca. 698)
Pepin (or Pippin) of Heristal, Mayor of the Palace in Austrasia (b. ca. 635 – d. 16 Dec 714)	+	Aupais, a concubine (b. ca. 654)
Charles Martel "the Hammer," Mayor of the Palace in Austrasia, King of the Franks, and victor at the battle of Poitiers (b. ca. 688 – d. 22 Oct 741)	+	md. (1) Chrotrude (or Rotrou), Duchess of Austrasia (d. 724)

[For the later generations that connect this line to the kings of England, see the line of St. Arnulf, Bishop of Metz in Part II.]

Sources: *Baring-Gould*: Vol. 2, pp. 360–361, and Vol. 16, p. 150; *Benedictine Monks*, p. 556; *Bunson*, p. 648; *Butler*, Vol. I, pp. 384–385; *Cruz*, pp. 601–603; *Delaney*, p. 455; *Holweck*, p. 789; *Stuart:* line 260 + line 171, nos. 45 through 43; *Wagner*, p. 189; *Weis, AR*, line 190, nos. 9 through 11; *Wells*, p. 135

St. Peter Orseolo I, Doge of Venice

Peter Orseolo was born in 928 and was the son of a wealthy Venetian nobleman who was also named Peter Orseolo. In 946, he married Felicita, the daughter of the Conti de Malpiero.

Peter's public life began in 948 when he was made commander of the Venetian fleet and fought several successful campaigns against Dalmatian pirates in the Adriatic sea.

His military success ultimately translated into political prominence. In 976 there was a popular revolt in Venice. Doge Peter Candiano IV was murdered, and a fire broke out which destroyed a large part of the city. Peter became the next Doge on 12 August 976 and immediately began to restore the city. He paid for the reconstruction of St. Mark's and the Doge's Palace with his own money and supervised the rebuilding of hundreds of homes. He was also very generous to the poor.

After two years of service in which he led Venice out of the political crisis that nearly destroyed it, Doge Peter Orseolo I disappeared during the night of 1 September 978. Months later he reappeared at the Benedictine abbey of Cuxa in the Pyrenees. He had taken holy orders and become a monk. At the abbey he always sought the most menial tasks and usually gave himself severe penances. In the final years of his life, he left the abbey and lived a hermit's life.

Peter died on 10 January 987. He is the only canonized Doge of Venice. His son Peter II also became Doge and is considered to be the real founder of the Venetian state.

His Line

Husband		Wife
Peter Orseolo	+	**N.N.**
St. Peter Orseolo I, Doge of Venice (b. 928 – md. 946 – d. 10 Jan 987)	+	Felicita (md. 946)
Peter Orseolo II, Doge of Venice (b. ca. 961 – md. bef. 983 – d. 1008)	+	Maria Candiana (md. bef. 983), daughter of Vitale Candiano, Doge of Venice
Ottone Orseolo, Doge of Venice (b. bef. 980 – md. aft. 1005 – d. 1032)	+	Grimelda (or Maria) (b. 989 – md. aft. 1005 – d. 1026), a sister of St. Stephen I, King of Hungary
Adalbert I "the Victorious," Margrave of Austria (md. (2) bef. 1027 – d. 26 May 1053)	+	**Frowila Orseolo (also known as Adela of Austria)** (b. ca. 1012 – md. bef. 1027 – d. 17 Feb 1071)
Ernst "the Bold," Margrave of Austria (b. ca. 1027 – slain 9 June 1075)	+	Adelaide (or Maud) von Eilenburg (b. ca. 1040 – d. 26 Jan 1071)
Leopold II "der Schoene" (the Handsome), Margrave of Austria and Crusader (b. 1050 – md. 1065 – d. 12 Oct 1102)	+	Ida of Cham (md. 1065 – d. 1101)

[For the later generations that connect this line to the kings of England, see the line of St. Leopold III, Margrave of Austria in Part II.]

Sources: *ADB*, Vol. 1, pp. 65–66; *Benedictine Monks*, p. 559; *Butler*, Vol. I, pp. 64–65; *CE*, Vol. XI, p. 776; *Delaney*, p. 463; *Delaney and Tobin*, p. 920; *Hantsch*, p. 52; *Holweck*, p. 792; *Klaniczay*, p. 435; *MI*, Vol. 2, p. 802; *NCE*, Vol. 11, pp. 225–226; *NDB*, Vol. 1, p. 45; *Stuart*, line 279, nos. 34 through 30 (N.B.: At generation no. 34, Stuart erroneously states that Frowila Orseolo was not the mother of Ernst "the Bold" in generation no. 33. The German-language authorities cited in this note state that she was.); *Weis, AR*, line 147, nos. 26 and 27; *Wells*, pp. 581–582 and p. 40; *Zoellner*, Tafel I at pp. 676–677

St. Pompeja

Pompeja's parents and birth date are unknown. She married Hoel I "the Great," King of Brittany.

When the Frisians invaded Brittany, Hoel and his family sought refuge in Wales. Hoel later reconquered Brittany but then died around 545. After Hoel died, Pompeja became a nun and entered a convent in Brittany along with her daughter St. Sève.

Pompeja's tomb is in Brittany in a church at Langoat near Tréguier. There are several bas-reliefs on it with scenes from her life. Relics of her are in a reliquary above the tomb.

Hoel and Pompeja were the parents of St. Leonorius, St. Sève, and St. Tugdual.

Pompeja is also known as Alma Pompaea, Alma Pompa, and Aspasia.

Her Line

Husband		Wife
N.N.	+	**N.N.**
Hoel I "the Great," King of Brittany (b. ca. 491 – d. ca. 545)	+	**St. Pompeja**
Hoel II, King of Brittany (murdered 547)	+	Rimo
Judicael I, King of Brittany (b. 535)	+	N.N.
Hoel III, King of Brittany (d. 612)	+	Pritelle

[For the later generations that connect this line to the kings of England, see the line of St. Cunedda Wledig in Part II.]

Sources: *Ashley*, p. 728; *Baring-Gould*, Vol. 16, p. 138; *Baring-Gould and Fisher*, Vol. 4, pp. 106–107; *Dunbar*, Vol. I, p. 206 (under "Copagia"); *Holweck*, p. 823; *Stuart*, line 405, nos. 52 through 49

St. Prisca

Prisca was born around 1088 and was the daughter of St. Ladislas I, King of Hungary, and his wife Adelaide of Rheinfelden. Around 1105 she married John II Komnenos, the Emperor of Byzantium.

Historians of the era have sometimes called Prisca's husband "John the Beautiful." This description does not refer to his body—he was short and unusually ugly, with a complexion so dark that he was known as "the Moor." It refers instead to his soul. His piety and personal purity caused a notable improvement in the manners of his age. His reign was so just that he has been called the Byzantine Marcus Aurelius.

In the Byzantine court, Prisca was gentle, pious, and charitable. She lived more like a nun than an empress and set an example of moderation in a society that had carried luxury to excess. She also founded the monastery of the Saviour at Constantinople.

After having eight children with John, Prisca died on 13 August 1134 and was buried at her monastery. Her portrait—together with those of her husband and son, the future emperor Manuel I Komnenos—is in a mosaic on the wall of the Haga Sophia on Constantinople.

Her Line

Husband		Wife
St. Ladislas I, King of Hungary (b. 29 July 1040 – md. 1077 – d. 27 July 1095)	+	**Adelaide of Rheinfelden** (md. 1077 – d. 1090)
John II Komnenos, Emperor of Byzantium (b. 13 Sept 1087 – md. ca. 1105 – d. 8 April 1143)	+	**St. Prisca** (b. ca. 1088 – md. ca. 1105 – d. 13 Aug 1134)
Andronikos Komnenos, sebastokrator (b. ca. 1108 – d. 1142)	+	Eirene (d. 1150/1151)
Alexies Komnenos, lover of the Empress Maria and Governor during her regency (murdered 1183)	+	Marie Dukaina
William VIII, Seigneur of Montpellier (b. ca. 1158 – md. 1178/1179 – d. 1218)	+	**Eudoxia Komnena** (b. ca. 1168 – md. 1178/1179 – d. aft. 4 Nov 1202)

[For the later generations that connect this line to the kings of England, see the line of St. Ladislas I in Part II.]

Sources: *Baring-Gould*, Vol. 9, pp. 134–136; *Dunbar*, Vol. I, pp. 412–413; *Holweck*, p. 509 (under "Irene"); *Klaniczay*, pp. 182–183 and Appendix B, Geneal. Table 6; *Stuart:* line 381, nos. 32 and 31 + line 111, nos. 31 through 28; *Weis, AR:* line 244A, nos. 7 and 8 + line 105A, nos. 25 through 27; *Wells*, pp. 308, 123, and 405

St. Ragnald III,
Earl of Orkney and Caithness

Ragnald (who was originally called Kali) was born around 1100 and was the son of Kol, who was the son of Kali Saebjarnarson. The name of Ragnald's wife is unknown.

Ragnald is described as a well-set man who was fair-haired, strong-limbed, and extremely likable. He was also a very successful self-made man. He started out as a merchant and during his travels happened to become a friend of Gillechrist, who was the brother of King Sigurd I of Norway. Soon Ragnald was an official at Sigurd's court. In 1129, Sigurd made Ragnald the earl of Orkney. Ragnald's title was revoked in 1130 by the next king Magnus IV but then restored in 1135 by Harald IV, who was Ragnald's old friend Gillechrist and who had defeated Magnus in battle and ascended to the throne himself. Further fighting in the Orkneys in 1136–1137 finally put Ragnald in possession of his new domain. He immediately began construction of a cathedral dedicated to his uncle St. Magnus.

After several years in the Orkneys, in 1151 Ragnald decided to go on a pilgrimage to the Holy Land. Setting out with fifteen ships, he reached Spain first, then the Barbary Coast, and was in Acre by 1153. On the return voyage, he spent 1154 in Constantinople and then visited Rome before returning home.

Landing in the Orkneys in December 1155, Ragnald was less than pleased to find himself in the middle of a local war for control of the islands. Ragnald joined in the fight and on 20 August 1158 was murdered by one of the defeated rebels. He was buried in the cathedral of St. Magnus and venerated as a martyr.

His Line

Husband		Wife
Kol, son of Kali Saebjarnarson	+	**Gunnhild (or Gunnhilda)**, sister of St. Magnus, Earl of Orkney
St. Ragnald III, Earl of Orkney and Caithness (b. ca. 1100 – murdered 20 Aug 1158)	+	N.N.
Erik Slagbrellir (or Stagbrellr) (md. 1156)	+	**Ingigerd (or Ingrid)** (md. 1156)
Gilchrist (or Gillbride), Earl of Angus	+	md. (2) **Elin**
Gilchrist, Earl of Angus (witnessed a charter of Arbroath Abbey in 1198 – d. 1207/1211)	+	N.N.
Walter, 3rd Great Steward of Scotland, Justiciar of Scotland, and first to assume the surname of "Stewart" (d. 1241)	+	**Beatrix (or Bethoc)**, daughter of Gilchrist, Earl of Angus
Alexander Stewart, 4th Great Steward of Scotland and Crusader (d. 1283)	+	Jean (or Jane), daughter of James, Lord of Bute

James Stewart, 5th Great Steward of Scotland (b. ca. 1243 – d. 16 July 1309), who fought for William Wallace in 1297 at the battle of Stirling Bridge	+	Egidia (or Jill), daughter of Walter de Burgh, 1st Earl of Ulster
Walter Stewart, 6th Great Steward of Scotland and Regent of the kingdom (b. 1291 – md. (1) 1315 – d. 9 April 1327)	+	Marjorie (md. 1315 – d. 2 March 1316), daughter of Robert I the Bruce, King of Scotland
Robert II Stewart, King of Scotland (b. 2 March 1315/1316 – md. (1) 22 Nov 1347 – d. 19 April 1390)	+	Elizabeth (md. 22 Nov 1347), daughter of Sir Adam Muir of Rowallan
Robert III Stewart, King of Scotland (b. 1337 – md. on or bef. 1367 – d. 4 April 1406)	+	Annabella (md. on or bef. 1367), daughter of John Drummond of Stobhall

Sources: *Ashley*, pp. 448 and 453–545; *Baring-Gould*, Vol. 9, pp. 215–220*; *Bunson*, p. 723*; *Burke's:* Vol. I, p. 469 + Vol. II, pp. 1985 and 1989–1990; *Delaney and Tobin*, p. 1003*; *Holweck*, p. 867*; *Skene*, pp. 571–576 (All references marked with a * are alphabetized under "Ronald.") Also see ***fmg.ac> Projects>Medieval Lands>Medieval Lands – data by region>British Isles>Scotland, nobility>Norwegian Jarls of Orkney [1030]–1156***. In addition, see ***fmg.ac>Projects>Medieval Lands>Medieval Lands – data by region>British Isles>Scotland, nobility>Earls of Angus***.

Raymond Berenger IV "the Saint," Count of Barcelona

Raymond was born around 1113 and was the son of Raymond Berenger III "el Grande," Count of Barcelona, and his third wife Dulce di Gievaudun.

From an early age, Raymond prospered. When his father Raymond III died in 1131, he inherited the county of Barcelona. Later, King Ramiro II "the Monk" wanted an outlet to the sea for his neighboring landlocked kingdom of Aragon. In 1137, a long negotiation with Raymond IV began. When it was over, Raymond IV was betrothed to Ramiro's two-year-old daughter Petronilla, and when Ramiro abdicated later on in 1137, Raymond IV became the de facto ruler of Aragon. It was not until 1150 that the wedding of Raymond IV and Petronilla took place.

The fame of Raymond IV rested on his victories against the infidels. In a series of successful military campaigns in 1147–1149, he expanded the amount of Spanish territory reconquered from the Moors. During his prolonged siege of Tortosa, Pope Eugene III gave Raymond IV and his army the Crusaders' Indulgence, thus making their campaign the first true crusade in Europe. To honor the Spanish women who had initially defended Tortosa against the Moors, Raymond created a special military order of knighthood for them called the Order of the Hatchet (Orden de la Hacha).

Raymond IV was en route to meet with the Emperor Frederick Barbarosa when he died on 6 August 1162. He was buried in the monastery he had founded at Poblet.

His Line

Husband		Wife
Raymond Berenger III "el Grande," Count of Barcelona and Provence (b. 11 Nov 1080 – md. (3) 3 Feb 1112 – d. 19 Aug 1131)	+	**Dulce di Gievaudun** (b. ca. 1095 – md. 3 Feb 1112 – d. 1127/1130)
Raymond Berenger IV "the Saint," Count of Barcelona and Crusader against the Moors in Spain (b. ca. 1113 – md. 1150 – d. 6 Aug 1162)	+	Petronilla of Aragon (b. 1135 – md. 1150 – d. 17 Oct 1174), daughter of Ramiro II "the Monk," King of Navarre and Aragon
Alfonso II, King of Aragon (b. March 1157 – md. (2) 18 Jan 1174 – d. 25 April 1196)	+	Sancha, Princess of Castile and Leon (b. 21 Sept 1154 – md. 18 Jan 1174 – d. 9 Nov 1208)
Alfonso, Count of Provence (b. 1180 – md. 1193 – d. Feb 1209)	+	Gersinde de Sabran, heiress of Forcalquier (md. 1193 – d. aft. 1222)
Raymond Berenger V, Count of Provence and Forcalquier (b. 1198 – md. Dec 1220 – d. 19 Aug 1245)	+	Beatrice of Savoy (b. 1198 – md. Dec 1220 – d. Dec 1266)
Henry III, King of England (b. 1 Oct 1207 – md. 14 Jan 1236 – d. 16 Nov 1272)	+	**Eleanor of Provence** (b. ca. 1223 – md. 14 Jan 1236 – d. 25 June 1291)

Sources: *CE*, Vol. III, p. 428 (under "Catalonia"); *O'Callaghan*, pp. 224–225 and 231–232; *Stuart*, line 54, nos. 30 through 25; *Wagner*, p. 202; *Weis, AR*, line 111, nos. 26 through 30; *Wells*, pp. 49–50, 24, and 482

St. Reginlink

Reginlink was born around 885/890 and was the daughter of Eberhard, Margrave of Friuli, and his wife Gisela. She married Burkhard II, Duke of Swabia, and became the mother of St. Alaricus and St. Wiltrudis.

After Burkhard died in 926, Reginlink became a nun and entered the convent of Saints Felix and Regula in Zurich.

Reginlink suffered greatly in her final years. She died of leprosy on the island of Ufnau in 959. A chapel is dedicated to her there.

Her Line

Husband		Wife
Eberhard, Margrave of Friuli (md. 836 – d. 16 Dec 862)	+	**Gisela** (b. 818/822 – md. 836 – d. 1 July 874), daughter of Louis I "the Fair," Emperor of the West
Burkhard II, Duke of Swabia (b. ca. 885 – md. bef. 911 – slain in battle 29 April 926)	+	**St. Reginlink** (b. 885/890 – md. (1) bef. 911 – d. 959)
Berthold, Duke of Bavaria in Karinthia (b. ca. 900 – d. 23 Feb 947)	+	**St. Wiltrudis (or Biletrud)** (d. ca. 986)
Ulrich (or Udalrich), Count in the Schweinachgau (liv. 947–970)	+	**Kunigunde**
Berthold I, Count in the Lurngau (md. 980)	+	Himiltrude (md. 980)
Thiemo (or Dietmar), Count in the Quinziggau (liv. 1025–1040)	+	N.N.
Frederick, Count of Formbach (b. ca. 1020 – slain 1059)	+	Gertrude, heiress of Haldensleben (d. 21 Feb 1116)
Dietrich I of Alsace, Duke of Upper Lorraine (md. (1) ca. 1075 – d. 23 Jan 1115)	+	**Hedwig von Formbach** (b. 1058 – md. (2) ca. 1075 – d. 1095/1100)
Simon I of Alsace, Duke of Upper Lorraine (b. ca. 1076 – d. 13 Jan 1138)	+	Adelaide of Lorraine (d. ca. 1158)
Reynold (or Renaud), Count of Macon and Burgundy (b. ca. 1090 – md. 1130 – d. 22 Jan 1148)	+	**Agatha of Alsace** (md. 1130)
Frederick III Barbarosa, Duke of Swabia, Emperor of Germany and the West, Crusader (b. 1122 – md. 10/16 June 1156 – drowned 10 June 1190 while on the 3rd Crusade)	+	**Beatrice of Burgundy** (b. ca. 1145 – md. 10/16 June 1156 – d. 15 Nov 1184)
Philip von Hohenstaufen, Duke of Tuscany and Swabia and Emperor of Germany (b. 1176 – md. 25 May 1197 – murdered 21 June 1208)	+	Eirene (or Maria) Angelina (b. ca. 1181 – md. (2) 25 May 1197 – murdered 27 Aug 1208), daughter of Isaac II Angelos, Emperor of Byzantium

[For the later generations that connect this line to the kings of England, see the line of St. Boris I, Khan of the Bulgars in Part II.]

Sources: *Holweck*, p. 851 (under "Regulinda"); *Stuart*: line 345, no. 38 + line 41A, nos. 37 and 36 + line 41, nos. 36 through 29 + line 125, nos. 29 and 28; *Weis, AR*, line 45, nos. 26 and 27; *Wells*, pp. 483, 253, 356, 369, and 271–272

St. Richenza of Pfalz-Lorraine

Richenza was born around the year 1000 and was the daughter of Ezzo, Count Palatine of Lorraine and his wife Bl. Matilda of Saxony. She was the oldest of their seven daughters. In 1013, she married Mieszko II, King of Poland.

Mieszko was a very well educated man for his time. He could read and write and knew both Greek and Latin. He and his wife had a happy marriage, and Richenza acquired a great reputation for charity.

Discontented nobles assassinated Mieszko in 1034, and in the "pagan revolt" that followed, churches and monasteries were burned, and many priests, monks, and knights were killed by peasants who had never really converted to Christianity.

Richenza fled the country and found refuge at the court of the German Emperor Conrad II. After becoming a nun in her final years, she died on 21 March 1063. Today her remains are in the cathedral at Cologne.

Her Line

Husband		Wife
Ezzo, Count Palatine of Lorraine and Lord of Duisburg and Kaiserwerth (b. ca. 955 – md. 991 – d. 21 May 1034)	+	**Bl. Matilda of Saxony** (b. 981 – md. 991 – d. 4 Nov 1025), daughter of Otto II, Emperor of the West
Mieszko II, King of Poland (b. ca. 990 – md. 1013 – d. 10 May 1034)	+	**St. Richenza of Pfalz-Lorraine** (b. ca. 1000 – md. 1013 – d. 21 March 1063)
Casimir "the Great," King of Poland (b. 25 July 1016 – md. 1041/1042 – d. 19 March 1058)	+	Dobronega Maria of Kiev (b. aft. 1012 – md. 1041/1042 – d. 1087), daughter of St. Vladimir I Sviatoslavich "the Great"
Ladislas I (or Wladislaw I Hermann), King of Poland (b. ca. 1040 – md. ca. 1080 – d. 4 June 1102)	+	Judith of Bohemia (b. ca. 1058 – md. ca. 1080 – d. 25 Dec 1086)

[For the later generations that connect this line to the kings of England, see the line of St. Adelaide of Burgundy in Part II.]

Sources: *BBKL*, Vol. 20, cols. 1220–1221; *Dunbar*, Vol. II, pp. 190–192; *Holweck*, p. 857; *Stuart:* line 237, nos. 35 and 34 + line 378, nos. 34 through 32; *Tucker:* Vol. I, p. 295 + Vol. II, pp. 685–686; *Weis, AR*, line 147, nos. 21 through 24; *Wells*, pp. 83 and 474; *WWH*, Vol. 13, p. 282

St. Salamon I "the Handsome," King of Brittany

Also known as Salomon or Solomon or Selyf, this saint was the son of St. Geraint, King of Brittany, and his wife Enid. He was nicknamed "the Handsome," and his wife was St. Gwen. Saints Cado, Cyngar, and Jestin were his brothers.

Like his father Geraint, Salamon has sometimes been made into a mythical figure or confused with other real men with the same name. In *The Legends of Charlemagne* by Thomas Bulfinch, for example, "Salomon, King of Brittany" becomes one of the twelve Paladins (i.e., the most illustrious knights) of Charlemagne.

It is hard to find any kernel of truth in this legend. Brittany had three kings named Salamon, and Salamon I is sometimes insufficiently distinguished from Salamon II and Salamon III. Salamon I was a man of the 400's, but Salamon II was the son of King Hoel III and a man of the 600's. Since Charlemagne was born in the year 747, Salamon I and Salamon II never knew him. Charlemagne also died in January 814. Since Salamon III was king of Brittany from 857 until his own death in 874, it is also safe to assume that he and Charlemagne never met. Salamon III was also the last king of Brittany before it was overrun by Vikings and thrown into a prolonged period of chaos.

Little else is known about Salamon I. He had a reputation as a military leader and was slain by pagans among his own people during a revolt. It is said that he was killed while praying in church and is therefore considered a martyr. His son Cybi also became a saint.

His Line

Husband		Wife
St. Geraint, King of Brittany	+	**Enid**
St. Salamon I "the Handsome," King of Brittany (liv. in the 400's)	+	St. Gwen
Audren, King of Brittany	+	N.N.
Budic I, King of Brittany	+	N.N., a daughter of Corun

[For the later generations that connect this line to the kings of England, see the line of St. Cunedda Wledig in Part II.]

Sources: *Ashley*, p. 728; *Baring-Gould*, Vol. 16, pp. 133 and 261; *Baring-Gould and Fisher*, Vol. 4, pp. 180–182; *Benedictine Monks*, p. 652; *Bunson*, p. 763; *Butler*, Vol. IV, p. 295 (under "St. Cybi"); *Delaney and Tobin*, p. 1070; *Holweck*, pp. 425 (under "Geraint") and 895; *Parbury*, pp. 53–54 (under "St. Gwen"); *Stuart*, line 405, nos. 56 through 53

St. Sexburga

Sexburga was the oldest daughter of Anna, King of East Anglia, and his wife St. Hereswitha. Around 640 Sexburga married Erconbert (also known as Eorconbeorht), King of Kent and had several children with him.

Sexburga was a very devout woman who completed the conversion of Kent to Christianity by persuading Erconbert to take down the last pagan idols there. After Erconbert died in 664, Sexburga ruled Kent as regent for their son Egbert for the next four years.

After Egbert came of age, Sexburga became a nun. She entered the monastery of Minster-in-Sheppey which she had founded with Erconbert, became its abbess, and lived there for several years. After her sister St. Etheldreda founded a monastery at Ely, Sexburga left Minster-in-Sheppey and moved to Ely. When Sexburga died on 6 July 699, she was buried at Ely next to Etheldreda.

Two of Sexburga's daughters—Ercongota and Ermenilda—also became saints. Sexburga's shrine at Ely survived until the Reformation.

Her Line

Husband		Wife
Anna, King of East Anglia (ruled ca. 641–653 – died in battle with Penda of Mercia)	+	**St. Hereswitha (or Saeware)** (b. shortly bef. 616 – d. 680/690)
Erconbert (or Eorconbeorht), King of Kent (b. ca. 624 – md. ca. 640 – d. 14 July 664)	+	**St. Sexburga** (md. ca. 640 – d. 6 July 699)
Egbert, King of Kent (b. ca. 641 – d. 4 July 673)	+	N.N.
Whitread, King of Kent (d. 725)	+	N.N.
Aethelbert II, King of Kent (d. 762)	+	N.N.

[For the later generations that connect this line to the kings of England, see the line of St. Aethelbert I, King of Kent in Part II.]

Sources: *Ashley*, pp. 239 and 242; *Baring-Gould*, Vol. 7, pp. 158–160 and Vol. 12, pp. 438–440; *BBKL*, Vol. 9, cols. 1530–1531; *Benedictine Monks*, p. 641; *Bunson*, p. 749; *Butler*, Vol. III, pp. 25–26; *CE*, Vol. XIII, p. 747; *Delaney*, p. 518; *Delaney and Tobin*, p. 1052; *Dunbar*, Vol. II, pp. 222–223; *HBC*, pp. 8 and 13; *Holweck*, p. 908; *O'Malley*, pp. 64, 73, and 98; *Parbury*, p. 81; *Snodgrass*, p. 215; *Stuart*: line 437, nos. 47 and 46 + line 233A, nos. 46 through 42; *Wagner*, p. 188; *Wells*, pp. 197 and 325; *Williamson*, p. 35; *WWH*, Vol. 14, pp. 158–159

St. Sigebert III,
King of Austrasia

Sigebert was born in 630 and was the son of Dagobert I, King of Austrasia and the greatest of all the Merovingian kings, and his fourth wife Berthilde. In 633 at the age of three, he married Hymnegilde (also called Himnechildis). Sigebert's education was entrusted to Bl. Pepin of Landen but ended perhaps too soon in 639 when Dagobert died and the nine-year-old Sigebert succeeded him.

Morally, Sigebert led a just and spotless life. He endowed monasteries, churches, and hospitals, he was generous with the poor, and he prayed often and at great length. One of his sons would become St. Dagobert II, King of Austrasia.

When viewed through the lens of Dark Ages realpolitik, Sigebert was definitely an overwhelmed child king who fought one war, lost it, and sat in his saddle crying when he learned he had lost the critical battle. The decline and eventual fall of the Merovingian dynasty began during his reign and continued during the reign of later child-monarchs.

Sigebert died at the age of 25 on 1 February 656. His relics are in the church of Our Lady in Nancy, France.

His Line

Husband		Wife
Dagobert I, King of Austrasia and King of the Franks (b. 602 – d. 639)	+	md. (4) **Berthilde**
St. Sigebert III, King of Austrasia (b. 630 – d. 1 Feb 656)	+	Hymnegilde
St. Dagobert II, King of Austrasia (b. 652 – murdered 23 Dec 678)	+	Mechtilde
Alberic	+	**St. Adela**, Princess of Austrasia (d. 734/735)
Aubri I, Count of Blois	+	N.N.
Aubri II, Count of Blois	+	N.N.
Gainfroi, Count of Sens	+	**Theidilindis** (liv. 795)

[For the later generations that connect this line to the kings of England, see the line of St. Adela, Princess of Austrasia in Part II.]

Sources: *Baring-Gould*, Vol. 2, pp. 24–25; *BBKL*, Vol. 10, cols. 266–267; *Benedictine Monks*, p. 642; *Bunson*, p. 752; *Butler*, Vol. I, p. 229; *Cruz*, pp. 676–677; *Delaney*, p. 520; *Delaney and Tobin*, p. 1058; *Holweck*, p. 910; *Klaniczay*, p. 69; *NCE*, Vol. 13, p. 204; *Stuart*, line 303, nos. 47 through 41; *Wells*, pp. 385 and 75

St. Sigismund, King of Burgundy

Sigismund was the son of Gundobald, King of Burgundy. He first married Theodogotho, daughter of Theodoric I "the Great" of the Ostrogoths.

While he was still a prince of Burgundy, Sigismund had converted from Arian Christianity to Catholicism. In 515 at the burial place of St. Maurice, he founded the monastery of St. Maurice at Aguane, which became one of the most prestigious of the early medieval monasteries. He saw to it that the "laus perennis" or perpetual chant was sung there to insure that praise was offered unceasingly to God. After Gundobald died in 516, Sigismund ascended the throne.

Sigismund's Christianity was far from perfect, however. By 522 Theodogotho was dead, and Sigismund's second wife was a woman who had once been one of his servants. She wanted Sigismund's first-born son Sigistrix dead and managed to convince Sigismund that his son was plotting against him. One night while Sigistrix slept, he was strangled in his bed by assassins sent by Sigismund.

Sigismund instantly regretted this crime, threw himself on the body of his dead son, and wept without ceasing. He then retired to the monastery of St. Maurice to pray for forgiveness. It is written that he asked God to punish him in this world rather than in the next.

In 523 after Sigismund emerged from his monastery, his country was invaded by Chlodomer, King of Orleans. In the battle that followed, Sigismund was defeated. He was taken prisoner along with his second wife and their children. Chlodomer took his royal prisoners to Orleans, executed all of them, and had their dead bodies thrown into a well. Since Sigismund had done much penance and reformed his life before he was executed, his death was seen as martyrdom, and Sigismund became the first martyr king of medieval Europe.

Sigismund was buried in the monastery of St. Maurice. In 1354, his body was moved to the cathedral at Prague by Emperor Charles IV.

His Line

Husband		Wife
Gundobald, King of Burgundy (liv. 473–516)	+	**N.N.**
St. Sigismund, King of Burgundy (reigned 516–523)	+	Theodogotho, daughter of Theodoric I of the Ostrogoths
Wacho, King of the Lombards	+	Austigusa, princess of the Gepidae
Garibald I, Duke of Bavaria (553–592)	+	**Waldrada**
Gundwald, Duke of Asti (d. ca. 614)	+	N.N.
Aripert I, King of the Lombards (reigned 653–661)	+	N.N.

Godepert, Prince of the Lombards (liv. 662)	+	N.N.
Reginpert, Duke of Turin	+	N.N.
Aripert II (liv. 712)	+	N.N.
Vislas I, King of the Obotrites (liv. 700)	+	**Petrussa of the Lombards**
Aribert I of the Obotrites (liv. 724)	+	Mandana
Billung I of the Obotrites	+	Hildegarde
Billung II of the Obotrites	+	Jutta
Mieceslas I of the Obotrites	+	Antonia
Rodigastus of the Obotrites (liv. 840)	+	N.N.
Mistui I of the Obotrites (liv. 869)	+	N.N.
Mieceslas II of the Obotrites (liv. 885)	+	N.N.
Mistui II, Prince of the Obotrites (liv. 919–999)	+	N.N.
Mieceslas III, Prince of the Obotrites	+	N.N.
St. Olaf III "Skotkonung" (the Tax King), King of Sweden	+	**Astrid**, princess of the Obotrites

[For the later generations that connect this line to the kings of England, see the line of St. Ingegerd, Princess of Sweden in Part II.]

Sources: *Baring-Gould*, Vol. 5, pp. 17–20; *BBKL*, Vol. 10, cols. 274–277; *Benedictine Monks*, p. 643; *Bentley*, p. 84; *Bunson*, pp. 752–753; *Butler*, Vol. II, pp. 209–210; *Giorgi*, pp. 262–263; *Holweck*, p. 911; *Joeckle*, p. 406; *Klaniczay*, pp. 67–68; *Stuart*, line 380, nos. 52 through 33; *Wood*, pp. 51–52

St. Sigrada

Sigrada was the daughter of Ansaud of Dijon and his wife, who was a daughter of Leutharius of Metz. Sigrada married Bodilon de Treves. St. Guerin and St. Leodegarius were their sons.

After Bodilon died, Sigrada became a nun and entered the convent of Notre Dame at Soissons. She died around 678 shortly after the martyrdom of her sons, who were barbarically put to death by Ebroin, Mayor of the Palace in Austrasia.

Her Line

Husband		Wife
Ansaud (b. ca. 570)	+	**N.N.**
Bodilon de Treves	+	**St. Sigrada** (d. ca. 678)
St. Guerin (or Warinus) Count of Poitiers (d. 677)	+	Kunza (d. 690), daughter of St. Clodulf, Bishop of Metz
Lambert of Hesbaye (liv. 725)	+	N.N.
Robert, Count of Hesbaye liv. 750)	+	Williswinda
Guerin, Count in the Thurgovie (d. 20 May 772)	+	Adelindis

[For the later generations that connect this line to the kings of England, see the line of St. Clodulf, Bishop of Metz in Part II.]

Sources: *Baring-Gould*, Vol. 11, p. 20 (under "St. Leodegar"); *Benedictine Monks*, p. 643; *Bunson*, p. 753; *Delaney and Tobin*, p. 1060; *Dunbar*, Vol. II, pp. 224–225; *Holweck*, p. 911; *Stuart:* line 236, nos. 45 and 44 + line 2, nos. 46 through 42; *Tucker*, Vol. I, p. 331; *Wells*, p. 303

St. Tewdrig ap Llywarch, King of Gwent

Tewdrig was born in the early 500's and was the son of Llywarch (Teithfall), King of Gwent in south Wales. His mother's name is unknown.

Tewdrig married into a very prominent family. His wife Enynny was the sister of Urien, King of Rheged in northern England. Urien's exploits were so famous in his day that some scholars have called him a source for the legends of King Arthur.

Tewdrig was a warrior too, and his valor as a prince of Gwent gained him considerable prestige. He established Gwent as the most powerful kingdom in south Wales and fought several successful battles against invaders.

As king, Tewdrig gave liberally to the cathedral at Llandaff. After several years on the throne, he decided to devote himself to religion and contemplation, abdicated in favor of his son St. Meurig, and retired to an abbey near Tintern.

When King Ceolwulf crossed the Severn with an army of heathen Saxons, however, Tewdrig came out of retirement and joined his son Meurig at the head of the Welsh army. The battle of the Saxon Bridge was a brilliant victory for the Welsh, but Tewdrig was mortally wounded. As he was being carried from the battlefield back to his home, he died near a spring known today as St. Tewdrig's Well. In the opinion of his people, he had died a martyr's death.

Near this spot, his son St. Meurig built a church where he buried his father. A village grew up around the church, which was originally called "Merthyr Tewdrig." That village still exists in Wales and is called Mathern.

While Merthyr Tewdrig was being repaired in the early 1600's, Tewdrig's bones were found. A plaque marks the spot.

His Line

Husband		Wife
Llywarch (Teithfall) ap Nynnio ab Erb, King of Gwent	+	**N.N.**
St. Tewdrig ap Llywarch, King of Gwent	+	Enynny ferch Cynfarch Oer
St. Meurig ap Tewdrig, King of Gwent and Glywysing (b. ca. 530)	+	Onbrawst ferch Gwrgan Fawr
Athrwys ap Meurig (b. ca. 570)	+	N.N.
Morgan, King of Gwent and Glywysing (d. 615)	+	Rhiceneth

[For the later generations that connect this line to the kings of Scotland, see the line of St. Meurig ap Tewdrig in Part II.]

Sources: *Ashley*, pp. 104–105 and 125; *Baring-Gould*, Vol. 16, p. 137; *Baring-Gould and Fisher*, Vol. 4, pp. 252–254; *Boyer*, nos. 3 through 7 on pp. 159–160; *CE*, Vol. XIV, p. 542; *Holweck*, p. 951

St. Theodora,
Empress of Byzantium

Theodora was born around 815 and was the daughter of Marinus, Toumarque of Paphlogonia, and his wife Theoktiste Phlorina.

Theodora was a woman of startling beauty who was chosen at a bride show to be the wife of Theophilos, Emperor of Byzantium. The two were married on 5 June 830 and ultimately had seven children.

To understand Theodora's claim to sanctity, we must return to the chapter on St. Irene and specifically to its brief treatment of the movement in the eastern church known as iconoclasm. The Second Council of Nicea which St. Irene convened in 787 and which restored the veneration of icons was not exactly a final victory over the iconoclasts, who saw icon veneration as a form of idolatry. During the reign of emperor Leo V (crowned 813—died 820), a weakened form of iconoclasm once again became imperial policy. The next two emperors after Leo V—Michael II and Theophilos—were also half-hearted iconoclasts. Theodora, however, had always secretly been an iconophile. When Theophilos died on 20 January 842, Theodora suddenly became regent for Theophilos' two-year-old son and heir Michael III.

The dispute over icons ended once and for all on 11 March 843 when Theodora led a triumphal procession to the Hagia Sophia and celebrated a liturgy where icons were again venerated as they once were and iconoclasm was forever rejected. Even down to the present day, the eastern church calls this event the "Triumph of Orthodoxy" and celebrates it on the first Sunday of Lent. After more than 125 years, the controversy was finally over.

This final restoration of icon veneration was the chief achievement of Theodora's regency. In 856 when her son Michael III was sixteen, he deposed Theodora and began to rule in his own right. Theodora lived in the palace for two years and was then sent to the monastery of Gastria, where she died sometime after 24 September 867.

Her Line

Husband		Wife
Marinus, Toumarque of Paphlogonia (b. 780 – d. 815/830)	+	**Theoktiste Phlorina,** a titled patrician in Paphlogonia (b. 795 – d . ca. 831)
Theophilos, Emperor of Byzantium (b. ca. 812 – md. 5 June 830 – d. 20 Jan 842)	+	**St. Theodora** (b. ca. 815 – md. 5 June 830 – d. aft. 24 Sept 867)
Michael III "the Drunkard," Emperor of Byzantium (b. 840 – d. 24 Sept 867)	+	Eudokia Ingarina (b. ca. 840 – d. 882/883), his mistress and the mother of his child
St. Leo VI "the Philosopher," Emperor of Byzantium (b. 1 Sept 866 – md. (2) 898 – d. 12 May 912)	+	Zoe Tzautzina (md. 898 – d. Dec 899)

[For the later generations that connect this line to the kings of England, see the line of St. Irene, Empress of Byzantium in Part II.]

Sources: *Baring-Gould*, Vol. 2, p. 275; *BBKL*, Vol. 11, cols. 924–929; *Benedictine Monks*, p. 671; *Bunson*, p. 786; *Dunbar*, Vol. II, pp. 255–256; *Holweck*, p. 958; *NCE*, Vol. 14, p. 15; *Norwich*, Vol. 2, pp. 32 and 46–60; *Stuart:* line 322A, nos. 42 through 40 + line 253, nos. 40 and 39; *Wells*, pp. 118–119; *WWH*, Vol. 15, pp. 359–360

The question of who is the father of St. Leo VI is dealt with in Leo's chart in part II.

St. Theophano Skleros

Theophano was born in 956 and was the daughter of Konstantin Skleros, a Byzantine patrician, and his wife Sophia Phokas. On 14 April 972, she married Otto II, Emperor of the West.

Otto and Theophano had five children, and when Otto II died unexpectedly in December 983, Theophano became regent for their son Otto III. She ruled in that capacity for the next eight years until her own death.

Theophano was a capable regent, and she was also very concerned for the salvation of her husband's soul. She had many prayers said for him, and she also gave generously to the church and the poor.

Theophano died on 15 September 991 and was buried in Cologne at the church of St. Pantaleon.

Besides the higher elements of Byzantine culture which Theophano brought to Otto's court, she is also credited with introducing the fork to Europe. Earlier generations of Europeans had eaten with their hands.

Her Line

Husband		Wife
Konstantin Skleros, patrician at Constantinople (b. ca. 920 – md. ca. 950 – d. aft. 980)	+	**Sophia Phokas** (b. ca. 936 – md. ca. 950)
Otto II, King of Italy and Emperor of the West (b. 955 – md. (2) 14 April 972 – d. 7 Dec 983)	+	**St. Theophano Skleros** (b. 956 – md. 14 April 972 – d. 15 Sept 991)
Ezzo, Count Palatine of Lorraine, Lord of Duisburg and Kaiserwerth (b. ca. 955 – md. 991 – d. 21 May 1034)	+	**Bl. Matilda of Saxony** (b. 981 – md. 991 – d. 4 Nov 1025)
Mieszko II, King of Poland (b. ca. 990 – md. 1013 – d. 10 May 1034)	+	**St. Richenza of Pfalz-Lorraine** (b. ca. 1000 – md. (1) 1013 – d. 21 March 1063)
Casimir "the Great," King of Poland (b. 25 July 1016 – md. 1041/1042 – d. 19 March 1058)	+	Dobronega Maria of Kiev (b. aft. 1012 – md. 1041/1042 – d. 1087), daughter of St. Vladimir I Sviatoslavich "the Great"

[For the later generations that connect this line to the kings of England, see the line of St. Adelaide of Burgundy in Part II.]

Sources: *BBKL*, Vol. 11, cols. 1026–1028; *Holweck*, p. 970; *Stuart:* line 219, no. 37 + line 322, nos. 37 and 36 + line 237, nos. 36 through 34 + line 378, nos. 34 and 33; *WWH*, Vol. 15, pp. 365–366

Bl. Theudelinde

Theudelinde was born in 568 and was the daughter of Garibald I, Duke of Bavaria and his wife Waldrada. On 15 May 589 she married Authari, King of the Lombards. After Authari was assassinated in September 590, Theudelinde was allowed to choose her next husband from the local nobility. In November 590 she married Agilulf, who became the next king of the Lombards.

At the time, the Arian heresy (which denied the divinity of Jesus) was the religion of the Lombards. Theudelinde, however, was a friend of the Roman pope St. Gregory the Great, who completed her conversion to true (i.e., Nicene) Christianity. Theudelinde in turn managed to convert her husband Agilulf and to have their children raised in the same faith.

After Agilulf died in 616, Theudelinde ruled as regent for their son. She built several churches, including the Basilica of St. John the Baptist in Monza and the octagonal Baptistery of St. John in Florence. She was known for caring for the poor and for other charitable work. She also completed the conversion of the Lombards to true Christianity.

Theudelinde died on 22 January 628. Her relics are in Monza in the Basilica of St. John the Baptist.

Theudelinde is also known as Theodelinda.

Her Line

Husband		Wife
Garibald I, Duke of Bavaria (d. 592)	+	**Waldrada**, daughter of Wacho, King of the Lombards
Agilulf, King of the Lombards (md. Nov 590 – d. 616)	+	**Bl. Theudelinde** (md. (2) Nov 590 – d. 22 Jan 628)
Chrodaold "Agilolingo" (Nimble-Tongued) (d. 624)	+	N.N., daughter of Gisulf
N.N.	+	**Fara** (d. 611)
Theodo II, Duke of Bavaria (d. 716)	+	Regintrude, illegitimate daughter of Dagobert I, King of Austrasia
Godefried, Duke of Allemania (d. 708/709)	+	**N.N.**
Nebi-Huoching (or Theutbold), Duke of Allemania (d. 727)	+	Hersuinda
Nebi (or Huabi), Duke of Allemania and Count in the Vinzgau (d. 788)	+	N.N.
Gerold, Duke of Allemania and Count in the Vinzgau (liv. 779)	+	**Emma of Allemania** (d. 798)
Bl. Charlemagne, King of the Franks and First Emperor of the West (b. 2 April 747 – md. (2) 771 – d. 28 Jan 814)	+	**Bl. Hildegarde**, Countess in Linzgau (b. 758 – md. 771 – d. 30 April 783)

[For the later generations that connect this line to the kings of England, see the line of St. Arnulf, Bishop of Metz in Part II.]

Sources: *Dunbar*, Vol. II, pp. 251–253; *Holweck*, p. 957; *Snodgrass*, pp. 223–224; *Stuart*, line 262, nos. 50 through 41; *Warncke*, pp. 32–33; *Weis, AR*, line 182; *Wells*, p. 5; *WWH*, Vol. 15, p. 346

St. Tiridates "the Great," King of Armenia

Tiridates was born around 280 and was the son of Chosroes II "the Valiant," King of Western Armenia. After Chosroes was assassinated in 287, Tiridates was taken to Rome and educated there. With Roman help, he regained the throne of his murdered father in 298/299, and he married Ashken, daughter of the king of Alania.

Following the martyrdom of Ripsime, Gaiana, and other nuns during Tiridates' persecution of Christians in 301, the great king went mad. Nothing suggested by anyone in his court helped him. Finally his sister Khosrowidukht said that St. Gregory "the Illuminator" should be released from prison and brought to her brother. By a miracle, St. Gregory cured Tiridates, who was baptized and who then turned his country into the world's first Christian nation. He subsequently made several large donations for the construction of churches and has been called "the Armenian Constantine."

Tiridates died violently. Like his father, in 330 he was assassinated by Armenian nobles who were friendly to Persia.

Tiridates' name is mentioned daily in the Armenian mass.

His Line

Husband		Wife
Chosroes (or Khosrow) II "the Valiant," King of Western Armenia (b. ca. 236 – assassinated 287)	+	**N.N.**
St. Tiridates "the Great," King of Armenia (b. ca. 280 – assassinated 330)	+	St. Ashken, daughter of Ashkhadar, King of Alania
Chosroes (or Khosrow) III, King of Armenia	+	N.N.
Athenagenes	+	**Bambishu** (b. 315)
St. Nerses I, Gregorid Prince and Bishop of Armenia (b. 335 – d. 373)	+	Samdukht
St. Isaac (or Sahak) I "the Great," Gregorid Prince and Bishop of Armenia (b. ca. 352 – d. 7 Sept 439)	+	N.N.

[For the later generations that connect this line to the kings of England, see the line of St. Ashken in Part II.]

Sources: *Holweck*, p. 986; *Hovannisian*, pp. 74–75, 81–82, and 94; *Kaloustian*, pp. 15–18; *Koushagian*, p. 5; *NCE*, Vol. 14, p. 171; *Stone*, Chapter 8, Chart 80; *Stuart*, line 416, nos. 59 through 54; *Wagner*, p. 194

St. Vardanes

Vardanes was the first-born son of St. Gregory "the Illuminator" and his wife Maria. His brother was St. Aristakes.

After Aristakes was martyred in 333, Vardanes became the third bishop of Armenia and worked to establish Christianity in the provinces which were still pagan. After narrowly escaping martyrdom himself, Vardanes died in 342.

His Line

Husband		Wife
St. Gregory the Illuminator (b. 240 – d. 330/332)	+	**Maria**
St. Vardanes (d. 342)	+	N.N.
St. Yusik I (martyred ca. 344)	+	N.N., a daughter of St. Tiridates "the Great," King of Armenia
Athenagenes	+	Bambishu (b. 315)
St. Nerses I, Gregorid Prince and Bishop of Armenia (d. 373)	+	Samdukht

[For the later generations that connect this line to the kings of England, see the line of St. Ashken in Part II.]

Sources: *Baring-Gould*, Vol. 10, p. 443*; *Delaney and Tobin*, p. 510*; *Dowling*, p. 52; *Holweck*, pp. 449–450* and p. 1011; *Hovannisian*, p. 85; *Kaloustian*, p. 15*; *Koushagian*, p. 9* and pp. 19 and 21; *NCE*, Vol. 6, p. 790*; *Stone*, Chapter 8, Chart 80; *Stuart*, line 416, nos. 56 and 55; *Wagner*, p. 195 (information on pages marked with a * is all alphabetized under Gregory the Illuminator)

St. Vladimir I Sviatoslavich, Grand Prince of Kiev

Vladimir was born around 955 and was the son of Sviatoslav I Igorievich, Grand Prince of Kiev, and his second wife Maloucha. He was the youngest of their three sons and in 969 was appointed by his father to rule Novgorod.

When Sviatoslav died in 972, all suddenly seemed lost for Vladimir. A bloody civil war broke out between Vladimir's brothers Oleg and Yaropolk. Vladimir fled to Scandinavia, and the civil war continued until Yaropolk slew Oleg and became the next ruler of all of Kievan Rus.

Vladimir then assembled a force of Viking warriors, returned with his army to Kievan Rus, and began to march toward the capital. It would be years before he got there. Along the way, any city that did not submit to him was taken by force and its ruler slain. One such city was Polotsk. After conquering it in 977 and slaying its ruler Rogvolod, Vladimir married Rogvolod's daughter Rognieda.

By 980, Vladimir and his army had reached Kiev, the capital. Yaropolk fled but then returned to negotiate with Vladimir and was treacherously murdered. Vladimir was now the sole ruler of Kievan Rus. His realm stretched from the Black Sea to the Baltics and included most of what later generations would call European Russia.

The more noble deeds for which Vladimir is remembered today began after he divorced Rognieda in 986. A pagan from birth, Vladimir began to think that his country's pagan gods could be improved on. He sent out envoys to study the religions of neighboring nations. The only enthusiastic reports he received were from the envoys who went to Constantinople and observed the rites of the Greek Orthodox Church. It so happened that in 987 the Byzantine emperor Basil II was facing uprisings in Anatolia and Bulgaria and needed Russian help to put them down. Vladimir sent Basil enough men to put down the revolts and in return was offered the emperor's sister Anna as a new wife. There was one condition, and it was that Vladimir convert to Christianity. Vladimir agreed, was baptized in 988, and married Anna of Byzantium the same year.

What Vladimir did next testified to the sincerity of his conversion. He welcomed evangelists. He began to give generously to the poor and spared many criminals from execution. All the pagan idols in Kievan Rus were taken down, and churches and schools were built in their place. In a classic case of conversion from the top, Vladimir at first ordered and eventually forced his subjects to accept baptism. Vladimir also did not exempt himself from the more uncomfortable commandments of the new faith. While he was a pagan, chronicles had called Vladimir a "fornicator immensus," but after his conversion, he gave up his many concubines.

In the years following Vladimir's conversion, both Greek Orthodox ritual and Byzantine culture generally were imported into his kingdom on a vast scale. After his wife Anna died around 1011, Vladimir married Adela von Öhningen but then died on 15 July 1015 as he was readying his troops to suppress a rebellion.

The Russian Orthodox Church today refers to Vladimir as "Equal to the Apostles." Boris and Gleb—two of his sons by Anna—also became saints.

His Line

Husband		Wife
Sviatoslav I Igorievich, Grand Prince of Kiev, Novgorod, and Perejaslaw (b. 915/927 – slain 972)	+	**Maloucha** (d. 1002)
Vladimir I Sviatoslavich "the Great," Grand Prince of Kiev and Novgorod (b. ca. 955 – d. 15 July 1015)	+	md. (3) Rognieda of Polotsk (b. ca. 956 – d. 1102)
St. Yaroslav I Vladimirovich "the Wise," Grand Prince of Kiev (b. 978 – md. (2) Feb. 1019 – d. 20 Feb 1054)	+	St. Ingegerd, Princess of Sweden (b. ca. 1001 – md. Feb 1019 – d. 10 Feb 1050)
St. Izyaslav I Yaroslavich, Grand Prince of Kiev (b. 1025 – md. ca. 1043 – slain 3 Oct 1078)	+	Gertrude (md. ca. 1043), daughter of Mieszko II, King of Poland

[For the later generations that connect this line to the kings of England, see the line of St. Izyaslav I Yaroslavich, Grand Prince of Kiev in Part II.]

Sources: *Allen*, pp. 11–14; *Baring-Gould*, Vol. 7, pp. 360–369; *BBKL*, Vol. 17, cols. 1506–1507; *Benedictine Monks*, p. 718; *Bunson*, p. 844; *Butler*, Vol. III, pp. 110–111; *CE*, Vol. XV, pp. 497–498; *Cruz*, pp. 725–730; *Delaney*, p. 578; *Delaney and Tobin*, pp. 1175–1176; *Fedotov*, p. 74; *Guiley*, pp. 346–347; *Holweck*, p. 1041; *Hrushevsky*, pp. 63–74; *Klaniczay*, Appendix B, Geneal. Table 2; *NCE*, Vol. 14, p. 734–735; *O'Malley*, p. 118; *One Hundred Saints*, pp. 176–177; *Poulos*, Vol. 3, pp. 35–36; *Snodgrass*, pp. 236–237; *Tucker*, Vol. II, pp. 731–732; *Weis, AR*, line 241, nos. 3 through 6; *Wells*, pp. 328–330

St. Vladimir Vsevolodovich Monomach, Grand Prince of Kiev

Vladimir was born in 1053. He was the son of Vsevolod I Yaroslavich, Grand Prince of Kiev, and his first wife Maria Monomacha.

Vladimir was a gifted military leader who spent his life battling the enemies of Kievan Rus. In his day, the most troublesome enemy of the Russians was a nomadic Turkish people known by three different names: the "Cumans," also known as the "Polovtsy," also known as the "Kipchaks." After Yaroslav "the Wise"—who was Vladimir's grandfather and the ruler of Kiev—died in 1054, the Cumans believed that Kievan Rus would soon become unstable and open to attack, and they began to make their plans.

At first, things went exactly the way the Cumans hoped. Yaroslav "the Wise" was succeeded by his son St. Izyaslav I Yaroslavich, who was a good man but a weak ruler and a worse general. In 1068 the first popular revolt against Izyaslav began after he fought a battle against the Cumans just outside of Kiev and lost. Further disasters were temporarily avoided by paying the Cumans not to attack Kiev again.

After Izyaslav was slain in a battle with his own relatives in 1078, Vladimir's father Vsevolod succeeded him. Vladimir was now twenty-five, and Vsevolod entrusted the defense of the kingdom to him. Vladimir's measures protected Kiev until Vsevolod's own death in 1093, when he was succeeded by Izyaslav's son Svyatopolk.

The Cumans thought that the death of Vsevolod would begin a new period of instability in Kievan Rus, and shortly after Svyatopolk ascended the throne, they rode in from the steppes. Instead of paying them tribute, Svyatopolk rashly started a war with them before sufficient Russian forces could be marshaled to stop them. A disastrous series of battles followed.

In desperation, the leaders of Kiev turned to Vladimir, who called councils of the Russian leaders in 1097 and 1100 to plan a great campaign against the Cumans. The final details of this effort were worked out by Svyatopolk and Vladimir in 1103. The great campaign was then launched. Vladimir attacked the Cumans with a large army and, after fighting nineteen wars against them, finally wiped them out.

Besides his series of wars against the Cumans, Vladimir also led the Russians against the Chuds, the Estonians, the Lithuanians, the Poles, and the Volga Bulgars. When Svyatopolk died in 1113, Vladimir succeeded him and became the next ruler of Kiev.

Under Vladimir's rule, his country regained the power and prestige it had enjoyed under Yaroslav "the Wise." At home Vladimir continued the work of his fathers in codifying the laws. He also abolished usurious interest rates and a creditor's right to enslave a non-paying debtor.

Vladimir married three times. His first wife was Gytha of Wessex, an illegitimate daughter of King Harold Godwinsson of England, whom he married around 1070. The names of his second and third wives are unknown.

Vladimir died on 19 May 1125 and was buried in Kiev in the cathedral of St. Sophia. By his own count, he had led 83 military campaigns, and he was remembered as a hero who saved his country in an era when foreign enemies almost overwhelmed it.

His Line

Husband		Wife
Vsevolod I Yaroslavich, Grand Prince of Kiev and Prince of Perejaslaw (b. ca. 1030 – md. (1) 1046 – d. 13 April 1093)	+	**Maria Monomacha** (md. (1) 1046), daughter of Constantine IX Monomachos, Emperor of Byzantium
St. Vladimir Vsevolodovich Monomach (a.k.a., Vladimir II "Monomachos") Grand Prince of Kiev (b. 1053 –md. (1) ca. 1070 – d. 19 May 1125)	+	Gytha of Wessex (md. ca. 1070), daughter of Harold II Godwinsson, King of England
St. Mstislav Vladimirovich (a.k.a., Mstislav I Harold), Grand Prince of Kiev (b. 1076 – md. (2) 1122 – d. 15 April 1132)	+	Lyubawa (md. 1122 – d. 1168), daughter of Dmitri Zaviditsch, Possadnik of Novgorod
Geza II, King of Hungary (b. ca. 1130 – md. 1146 – d. 3 May 1162)	+	**Euphrosyne Mstislavna** (b. 1130 – md. 1146 – d. 1175/1176)

[For the later generations that connect this line to the kings of England, see the line of St. Harold III, King of Denmark in Part II.]

Sources: *Allen*, pp. 20–22; *Fedotov*, p. 87; *Hrushevsky*, pp. 83–85; *Orth. Encyc.*, Vol. 8, pp. 681–688; *Stuart*, line 240, nos. 31 through 28; *Tucker*, Vol. II, pp. 732–733; *Wagner*, p. 206; *Weis, AR*, line 242, nos. 6 through 8; *Wells*, p. 329

St. Waltheof II,
Earl of Huntingdon and Northampton

Waltheof was born in 1045 and was the son of Siward Biornsson, Earl of Huntingdon and Northampton, and his first wife Aelflaed II of Northumberland. Waltheof's family was a very important one in Saxon England, and in 1066 he fought beside King Harold at the battle of Hastings.

In 1069 when Svein II invaded northern England, Waltheof and his men joined the Danish force in its attack on the Normans at York. After the defeated Danes left, Waltheof submitted to William, was forgiven and restored to his possessions, and was even offered William's niece Judith of Lens as a wife, whom he married in 1070.

In 1075, Waltheof became involved in the Revolt of the Earls against William. Although Waltheof did not take up arms, he did not go back to William to seek more forgiveness until it became clear that the rebellion would fail. Upon presenting himself to William a second time, Waltheof was not so lucky as before. William threw him into prison, kept him there for almost a year, and then had him brought out and beheaded on 31 May 1076. Waltheof was buried at Croyland Abbey.

An extraordinary number of Saxons saw Waltheof as a martyr for their liberty. Miracles were reported at his tomb, and his people began to honor him as a saint. When his grave was opened in 1092 so that his remains could be moved to a more splendid tomb, his body was found to be incorrupt.

His Line

Husband		Wife
Siward (or Sigurd) Biornsson, Earl of Huntingdon, Northampton, and Northumbria (b. ca. 1020 – d. 1055)	+	**Aelflaed II of Northumberland**
St. Waltheof II, Earl of Huntingdon, Northampton, and Northumberland (b. 1045 – md. 1070 – beheaded 31 May 1076)	+	Judith of Lens (b. 1054 – md. 1070 – liv. aft. 1086)
David I "the Saint," King of Scotland (b. ca. 1080 – md. 1113/1114 – d. 24 May 1153)	+	**Matilda of Huntingdon** (md. (2) 1113/1114 – d. 1130/1131)

Sources: *HBC*, p. 57; *Holweck*, p. 1031; *Stuart*, line 221, nos. 33 through 31; *Wagner*, p. 206; *Weir*, p. 192; *Weis, AR*, line 148, nos. 23 and 24; *Wells*, p. 520

Bl. Widukind,
Duke of Saxony

Widukind was the son of Warnechin, Duke of Engern, and his wife Kunhilde of Rugen. Widukind married Geva, the daughter of the Norwegian ruler Eystein of Westfold.

Widukind stepped onto the pages of history shortly after Charlemagne began his long series of campaigns against the Saxons, who were still pagans and the only Germanic people who were not yet a part of Charlemagne's empire. After early victories by the Franks in 774 and 775, Widukind rallied the Saxons and counterattacked. He became a folk hero who proved that he could beat the Franks on the battlefield and who united the Saxon tribes by his own dynamic personality. From 779 to 785, the military situation remained very volatile, with the Franks and the Saxons each winning several battles. The decisive battle of the wars between Charlemagne and Widukind was fought at Osnabrück in 785, and Widukind was finally defeated. He then acknowledged that the Christian God was stronger than Odin and was baptized, with Charlemagne acting as his godfather.

Charlemagne's difficulties with the Saxons were not exactly over. There would be more revolts, but Widukind would take no part in them. He spent the last several years of his life building churches in Saxony, and he and Charlemagne became friends.

After his death around 804, Widukind became a legendary German hero. He is buried in Engern.

His Line

Husband		Wife
Warnechin, Duke of Engern	+	**Kunhilde of Rugen**
Bl. Widukind, Duke of the Westphalian Saxons (d. ca. 804)	+	Geva of Vestfold
Wicibert, Count in Westphalia (d. 843/851)	+	Ordrad
Walbert, Count in the Threkwitigau (occ. in charters 834–872 – d. by 891)	+	Altburg of Savoy
N.N. of the Threkwitigau	+	Mathilda (liv. in 909)
Dietrich, Count of Saxony (b. ca. 872 – md. (1) 882 – d. 8 Dec 917)	+	Gisela of Lorraine (b. 860/865 – md. 882 – d. by 26 Oct 907)
Henry I "the Fowler," Duke of Saxony and Emperor of the West (b. 876 – md. (2) 909 – d. 2 July 936)	+	**St. Mathilda of Ringelheim** (b. ca. 890/900 – md. 909 – d. 14 March 968)
Otto I "the Great," King of Germany and Italy and Emperor of the West (b. 23 Nov 912 – md. (2) 25 Dec 951 – d. 7 May 973)	+	St. Adelaide of Burgundy (b. 932 – md. (2) 25 Dec 951 – d. 16/17 Dec 999)

[For the later generations that connect this line to the kings of England, see the line of St. Adelaide of Burgundy in Part II.]

Sources: *CE*, Vol. 15, p. 618; *Delaney*, p. 592; *Delaney and Tobin*, p. 1210; *Stuart:* line 339, nos. 41 through 38 + line 338, nos. 38 through 36 + line 321, nos. 37 and 36; *Weis, AR:* line 141, no. 18 + line 147, nos. 18 and 19; *Wells*, pp. 608, 515, and 270

St. William of Gellone

William was born in 755 and was the son of Theuderic, Count of Autun, and his wife Alda. William's first wife was Kunigunde, and his second wife was Gilbour of Hornbach.

William began his career at the court of Charlemagne, where he held various offices. In 789, Charlemagne made him count of Toulouse. Shortly after his appointment, William put down a revolt among the Gascons. A few years later in 793, the Moslems in Spain made their final attempt to invade France. Their army met a Frankish army led by William in a pitched battle at the Orbiel River. Moslem losses were so great that they withdrew south of the Pyrenees and never came back to France. Several years later around 801, William led an army of Franks into Spain with the goal of besieging and capturing Barcelona. After the city fell, he returned to France in triumph.

William's own conduct during these campaigns was remembered as an exemplary display of chivalry. He was called an ideal Christian knight and became the hero of several epic poems. Under the names William *au court-nez*, William Firebrace, and William of Orange, he appears in *La geste de Garin de Monglane*, *La prise d'Orange*, and other works.

In old age, the real William founded a Benedictine monastery and convent at Gellone. He later became a monk, entered his own monastery, and died there on 28 May 812. In his honor, the monastery was renamed *Saint-Guilhelm-du-Désert* (or St. William in the Wilderness).

One of the hotly disputed questions in medieval genealogy today is whether or not William's father Theuderic is a provable descendant of a line of ancestors that goes back into antiquity and ultimately to the kings of ancient Israel, including King David, King Solomon, and several of their successors. If this line ever wins scholarly acceptance, genealogical catalogs of saintly medieval ancestors will have to be enlarged to include several very well known Old Testament figures. The names of St. William and many other men and women of the medieval era may then gain added luster from the acknowledgment that they are all "of the house of David."

His Line

Husband		Wife
Theuderic (or Thierry), Count of Autun, and Exilarch of Narbonne (Septimania) (liv. 771–793)	+	**Alda (or Aldana or Aude)**
St. William of Gellone, Duke of Toulouse and Margrave of Septimania (b. 755 – d. 28 May 812)	+	md. (2) Gilbour of Hornbach
Bernard, Count of Autun and Margrave of Septimania (executed 844)	+	Dhoude (b. ca. 804 – d. 2 Feb 843)

[For the later generations that connect this line to the kings of England, see the line of St. Liévin, Bishop of Trier in Part II.]

Sources: *Benedictine Monks*, p. 727; *Bunson*, p. 855; *Butler*, Vol. II, p. 411; *CE*, Vol. 15, p. 633; *Delaney*, p. 588; *Delaney and Tobin*, p. 1202; *NCE*, Vol. 14, pp. 920–921; *Stone*, Chapter 7, Chart 72; *Stuart*, line 326, nos. 41 through 39; *Tucker*, Vol. II, p. 836; *Wells*, pp. 560 and 422

St. William I "Longsword," Duke of Normandy

William was born around 900 and was the son of Rollo (or Hrólfr Ketilsson), leader of the Vikings of Rouen, and his concubine Poppa of Bayeaux. Around 911, Rollo and his men landed in France and began to take possession of the land around the mouth of the Seine. Though they were unaware of it at the time, they were starting the history of Normandy and its ruling house.

Rollo ruled his new possession for several years after he landed and managed to have his right to it recognized in the Treaty of St. Claire signed by the French king Charles III "the Simple." Rollo died after a long illness sometime between 927 and 932.

Rollo's son and successor William preferred to be seen as a European prince rather than the son of a Viking chief. He did many things to cast off his Viking heritage and become a part of what was seen as the civilized world. He was baptized a Christian and welcomed back monks who had fled the abbeys in Normandy in his father's time. With the help and encouragement of the Church in France, William began to call himself "Count of Rouen" and to see himself as a Christian prince with all the corresponding obligations: peacemaking, defending the weak, helping the poor, and so on. In 934, William forcefully put down a revolt by some of his own men who were not pleased with their ruler's abandonment of Viking ways and adoption of Frankish ones.

William's transformation was completed on 17 December 943 but not in a way that he intended. Without first asking for hostages and without taking along any means of self-defense, he met Count Arnulf of Flanders on an island in the River Somme to arrange a peaceful settlement of their differences regarding the territory around Montreuil. As the meeting was ending, William was attacked by several of Arnulf's men and hacked to death. In the view of many, he died as a martyr for peace.

William is buried in the cathedral at Rouen. By a concubine named Sprote de Bretagne, he had a son who would be called Richard I "the Fearless," the third Duke of Normandy, Rollo having been the first and William the second.

His Line

Husband		Wife
Rollo "the Viking," first Duke of Normandy (b. ca. 870 – md. (2) 891 – d. 927/932)	+	**Poppa de Bayeaux** (b. ca. 872 – md. 891)
St. William "Longsword," Duke of Normandy (b. ca. 900 – murdered 17 Dec 943)	+	md. (1) Sprote de Bretagne
Richard I "the Fearless," Duke of Normandy (b. ca. 932 – md. (2) ca. 978 – d. 20 Nov 996)	+	Gunnora de Crepon (b. ca. 936 – md. ca. 978 – d. 1027/1031)
Richard II "the Good," Duke of Normandy (md. ca. 1000 – d. 28 Aug 1027)	+	Judith of Brittany (or Rennes) (b. 982 – md. ca. 1000 – d. 16 June 1017)

Robert I "the Devil," Duke of Normandy and Crusader (b. ca. 1000 – d. 22 July 1035)	+	Herleve de Falaise (b. ca. 1003)
William I "the Conqueror," Duke of Normandy and King of England (b. 1027/1028 – md. 1053 – d. 9 Sept 1087)	+	Matilda (or Maud) of Flanders (b. 1032 – md. 1053 – d. 1083)

Sources: *Baring-Gould*, Vol. 15, pp. 212–217; *Holweck*, p. 1037; *Stuart:* line 166, nos. 35 through 33 + line 89, nos. 33 through 30; *Weis, AR:* line 121E, nos. 18 through 22 + line 121, nos. 23 and 24; *Wells*, pp. 432–433

St. William X, Duke of Aquitaine

William was born in 1099. His father was William IX, Duke of Aquitaine (and as William VII Count of Poitou), and his mother was Philippa, Regent of Toulouse.

William came from a uniquely dysfunctional family. Aimery I, the Vicomte de Chatellerault, was one of his father's vassals. Aimery's wife was Dangerose, and by 1115, William's father had conceived a violent passion for her. With no recorded protest by Dangerose, one night William's father abducted her from her own castle and installed her in her new home, which was his own bedchamber.

When William's mother Philippa returned from a visit to Toulouse and discovered the new arrangements, she was stunned. She begged the Church for help, and the papal legate did threaten her husband with excommunication but all to no avail. Philippa retired in grief to Fontevrault and died there on 28 November 1117.

Not long after Philippa's death, Dangerose prevailed upon her lover William to arrange a marriage between his son William X and Eleanor de Chatellerault, who had been born to Aimery I and Dangerose around 1105! This marriage took place late in 1121. Remarkably, it is recorded that this event ended most of William X's resentment over the way his father had treated his mother Philippa in 1115.

As a man, William X was very tall, broad, robust, and possessed of a huge appetite. He had inherited some of his father's charm but also his violent temper. When William IX died after a short illness on 10 February 1126, William X also inherited all of his father's domains, which together amounted to about 25% of present-day France. At the time, these domains were larger than those ruled by the king of France. Thanks to an inherited title, William X of Aquitaine also became William VIII, Count of Poitou.

Like his father, William X was both a lover of the arts and a warrior. He was extraordinarily well educated for his time and continued his father's patronage of literature, music, and troubadours. At the head of his army, William X fought in Normandy and elsewhere in France. Within his own realm, he also crushed a revolt led by Hugh VII of Lusignan and the lord of Parthenay.

Also like his father, William X's reign was marred by difficulties with the Church. Early in 1130, factional rivalry in Rome had grown so bad that after Pope Honorius II died, two different men were elected on February 23 to succeed him. One became Pope Innocent II, and the other became the Antipope Anacletus II. Most of Europe's lords and monarchs supported Innocent II, but the most important supporter of Anacletus II was William X of Aquitaine. The resulting schism lasted for years. William did not abandon Anacletus until 1135, and then only because of the personal efforts of St. Bernard of Clairvaux.

William's saintly honors owe much to the manner of his death and also to what became of his children. William resolved to make a penitential pilgrimage to Santiago de Compostela early in 1137. Just as he arrived on April 9th—which happened to be Good Friday—he became violently ill after eating some tainted fish and died the same day. He was buried inside the shrine at the foot of the high altar.

William X's most famous child was his daughter Eleanor. Louis VII of France was her first husband. Henry II of England was her second.

His Line

Husband		Wife
William IX, Duke of Aquitaine (and as William VII Count of Poitou) and Crusader (b. ca. 22 Oct 1071 – md. (2) 1094 – d. 10 Feb 1126)	+	**Philippa**, Regent of Toulouse (b. ca. 1073 – md. (2) 1094 – d. 28 Nov 1117)
St. William X, Duke of Aquitaine (and as William VIII Count of Poitou) (b. 1099 – md. late 1121 – d. 9 April 1137)	+	Eleanor de Chatellerault (b. ca. 1105 – md. late 1121 – d. aft. March 1130)
Henry II, King of England (b. 5 March 1133 – md. 18 May 1152 – d. 6 July 1189)	+	**Eleanor of Aquitaine** (b. 1122 – md. (2) 18 May 1152 – d. 31 March 1204)

Sources: *Holweck*, pp. 1037–1038; *Stuart*, line 88, nos. 31 through 29; *Weir*, pp. 58–59; *Weis, AR*, line 110, nos. 24 through 26; *Wells*, p. 23

St. William VI, Lord of Montpellier

William VI was born around 1100 and was the son of William V, Lord of Montpellier and Crusader, and his wife Ermesende de Melgueil. After returning from a pilgrimage to the Holy Land, William VI married Sibel de Vasto di Savona in August 1129.

William VI and Sibel loved each other deeply and had eight children. Inconsolable after her death, William VI became a Cistercian monk and entered the monastery at Grandselve near Toulouse. He died there in 1162.

His Line

Husband		Wife
William V, Seigneur de Montpellier and Crusader (b. ca. 1065/1069 – md. (2) 1086/1087 – d. ca. 1122)	+	**Ermesende de Melgueil** (md. 1086/1087)
St. William VI, Seigneur de Montpellier (b. ca. 1100 – md. Aug 1129 – d. 1162)	+	Sibel de Vasto di Savona (md. Aug 1129 – d. bef. 1146)
William VII, Duke of Montpellier and Seigneur de Tortosa (b. ca. 1130 – md. 25 Feb 1157 – d. aft. May 1173)	+	Mathilda of Burgundy (b. ca. 1130 – md. 25 Feb 1157 – d. bef. 29 Sept 1172)
William VIII, Seigneur de Montpellier (b. ca. 1158 – md. (1) 1178/1179 – d. 1218)	+	Eudoxia Komnena (b. ca. 1168 – md. 1178/1179 – d. aft. 4 Nov 1202)
Pedro II, King of Aragon (b. 1176 – md. 15 June 1204 – fell in the battle of Murat 14 Sept 1213)	+	**Marie,** Dame de Montpellier (b. 1182 – md. (3) 15 June 1204 – d. 21 April 1213)

[For the later generations that connect this line to the kings of England, see the line of St. Ladislas I, King of Hungary in Part II.]

Sources: *Holweck*, p. 1038; *Stuart*, line 150, nos. 31 through 27; *Tucker*, Vol. II, pp. 559–560; *Weis, AR*, line 105A, nos. 27 and 28; *Wells*, pp. 405 and 24

St. Wiltrudis

Wiltrudis was the daughter of Burkhard II, Duke of Swabia, and his wife St. Reginlink. She was the sister of St. Alaricus.

Wiltrudis married Berthold, Duke of Bavaria in Karinthia, and had several children with him. After Berthold died in 947, Wiltrudis became a nun. In 976, she founded the Benedictine convent of Bergen near Neuberg, Germany and became its first abbess. She died there around 986.

In life, Wiltrudis was widely known for her goodness and her skill in handicrafts.

Her Line

Husband		Wife
Burkhard II, Duke of Swabia (b. ca. 885 – slain in battle 29 April 926)	+	**St. Reginlink**
Berthold, Duke of Bavaria in Karinthia (d. 23 Feb 947)	+	**St. Wiltrudis (or Biletrud)** (d. ca. 986)
Ulrich, Count in the Schweinachgau (liv. 947–970)	+	**Kunigunde**
Berthold I, Count in the Lurngau (md. 980)	+	Himiltrude (md. 980)

[For the later generations that connect this line to the kings of England, see the line of St. Reginlink in Part II.]

Sources: *Benedictine Monks*, p. 731; *Bunson*, p. 859; *Butler*, Vol. I, p. 42; *Delaney*, p. 591; *Delaney and Tobin*, p. 1206; *Holweck*, p. 1039; *NCE*, Vol. 14, p. 953; *Stuart:* line 41A, nos. 37 and 36 + line 46, nos. 36 and 35

St. Yaroslav I Vladimirovich "the Wise," Grand Prince of Kiev

Yaroslav was born in 978. He was the son of St. Vladimir I Sviatoslavich, Grand Prince of Kiev and ruler of Kievan Rus, and Vladimir's third wife Rognieda of Polotsk.

While Vladimir lived, Yaroslav was given Rostov and then Novgorod to rule. After Vladimir died in 1015, a war broke out among his sons over who would be the ultimate ruler of Kievan Rus. After four years of bloody struggle, Yaroslav won the war in 1019 and became the sole ruler of Vladimir's realm. In 1019, he also married St. Ingegerd of Sweden as his second wife.

At home, Yaroslav encouraged learning, codified the laws, and built magnificent churches, including the cathedral of St. Sophia in Kiev. He broke Byzantine domination of the Russian Church by appointing Hilarion, a Russian monk, to be the patriarch of Kiev. Many people in Kievan Rus were still pagan when Yaroslav took the throne in 1019, but by the end of his reign, Christianity had become the established faith.

Physically, Yaroslav was partly lame from an arrow wound he had received in the wars of his youth. Intellectually, he was a shrewd statesman who consolidated the power and prestige of Kievan Rus. He died on 20 February 1054. He is buried in the St. Sophia Cathedral in Kiev.

His Line

Husband		Wife
St. Vladimir I Sviatoslavich "the Great," Grand Prince of Kiev and Novgorod (b. ca. 955 – d. 15 July 1015)	+	md. (3) **Rognieda of Polotsk** (b. ca. 956 – d. 1002)
St. Yaroslav I Vladimirovich "the Wise," Grand Prince of Kiev (b. 978 – md. (2) Feb 1019 – d. 20 Feb 1054)	+	St. Ingegerd, Princess of Sweden (b. ca. 1001 – md. Feb 1019 – d. 10 Feb 1050)
St. Izyaslav I Yaroslavich, Grand Prince of Kiev (b. 1025 – md. ca. 1043 – slain 3 Oct 1078)	+	Gertrude (md. ca. 1043), daughter of Mieszko II, King of Poland
Sviatpolk II Izyaslavich, Grand Prince of Kiev, Novgorod, and Turow (b. 1050 – d. 16 April 1113)	+	N.N. (d. bef. 1094)

[For the later generations that connect this line to the kings of England, see the line of St. Izyaslav I Yaroslavich, Grand Prince of Kiev in Part II.]

Sources: *Allen*, pp. 15–18; *BBKL*, Vol. 2, col. 1566; *Fedotov*, p. 87; *Golubinskii*, p. 579; *His. Rus. Ch.*, Vol. 2, p. 120; *Hrushevsky*, pp. 74–79; *Stuart*, line 363, nos. 34 through 32; *Tucker*, Vol. II, pp. 731–732; *Weis, AR*, line 241; *Wells*, pp. 328–330

St. Yusik,
Bishop of Armenia

Born around 305, Yusik was the son of St. Vardanes, Katholikos of Armenia. The name of Yusik's wife is unknown, but she was a daughter of St. Tiridates "the Great," King of Armenia. She and Yusik were married around 317.

In 342 after the death of his father, Yusik was made the fourth Katholikos of Armenia. At the time, Tiran I was the king.

Yusik resisted royal intervention in ecclesiastical affairs and repeatedly called on the king to observe his Christian duties. This led to a serious conflict between church and state, which came to a head when the king decided to put a picture of the emperor Julian the Apostate in one of the major churches. Yusik refused to allow this and around 348 was clubbed to death by assassins sent by the king.

Yusik is also known as Hesychius, Hoosig, and Hussik. He was the brother of St. Grigoris.

In 350, King Tiran perhaps regretted his treatment of Yusik. Embroiled in a dispute with the Persians, he was captured by them and blinded.

His Line

Husband		Wife
St. Vardanes (d. 339/341)	+	**N.N.**
St. Yusik I (b. ca. 305 – martyred ca. 348)	+	N.N., a daughter of St. Tiridates "the Great," King of Armenia
Athenagenes	+	Bambishu (b. 315)

[For the later generations that connect this line to the kings of England, see the line of St. Ashken in Part II.]

Sources: *Holweck*, p. 496; *Hovannisian*, p. 86; *Koushagian*, p. 5; *Stuart*, line 416, no. 56; *Wagner*, p. 195

PART III

Saints Who Are Aunts and Uncles

Contents for Part III

Aunts and Uncles

St. Abban

Abban was the son of Cormac mac Airt, King of Leinster, and the brother of St. Illogan.

Abban founded so many churches in the Irish counties of Wexford and Ferns that he is called "the Apostle of Wexford." His main monastery was Magher-anoidhe in Adamstown.

His Line

	Husband		Wife
	Cormac mac Airt, King of Leinster	+	**N.N.**
Cairpre's brother: ***St. Abban***	**Cairpre Liphechair**	+	N.N.
	Fiachu Sraptine	+	N.N.
	Muiredach Tirech	+	N.N.
	Echu (or Eochaid) Muigmedon	+	N.N.
	Niall Noigiallach (or "Niall of the Nine Hostages"), High King of Ireland (liv. 400)	+	Ine, daughter of Dubtach
	Eogan, King of Ailech (converted to Christianity ca. 442 and d. 465)	+	Indorb Finn ("the White")
	Muiredach, King of Ailech (d. ca. 480)	+	Eirc, daughter of Loarn Mor
	Muircheartach mac Earca ("Eirc's son"), High King of Ireland (d. 534)	+	Duaibhsech, daughter of Duach Teangumha ("Brazen Tongued"), King of Connaught
	Domnall Ilcealgach ("The Deceitful") (d. 566), Joint High King of Ireland with his brother Fergus	+	N.N.
	Aedh Uairidhnach ("Of the Ague"), High King of Ireland (d. 612)	+	N.N.
	Maelfithrig, King of Ailech (killed in battle 630)	+	N.N.
	Maelduin, King of Ailech (killed 681 at the battle of Leathairbhe)	+	Cacht, daughter of Maelcobha, King of Tir Conaill and High King of Ireland
	Fergal, High King of Ireland (killed in battle 722)	+	md. (2) Athiocht, daughter of Cian, King of Keenaght (or Connaught)

Niall Frasach ("Of the Showers"), High King of Ireland, who abdicated, became a monk at Iona, and died 778	+	Eithne (d. 768), daughter of Breasal of Brega
Aed Oirdnidhe ("The Dignified"), High King of Ireland (d. 819)	+	Maedhbh, daughter of Inreachtach of Connaught
Niall Caille, High King of Ireland	+	Gormfhlaith (d. 860), daughter of Dunchad mac Domhnaill
Aedh Finnliath ("White Hair"), High King of Ireland (d. 879)	+	Maelmuire, daughter of Kenneth Mac Alpin, King of the Picts and Scots
Niall Glundubh ("Black Knee"), High King of Ireland (killed 15 Sept 919 near Dublin in battle against the Vikings)	+	Gormfhlaith (d. 947), daughter of Flann Sionna ("The Fox"), High King of Ireland
Muircheartach na Cochall Craicenn ("Of the Leather Cloaks"), King of Ailech	+	md. (1) Flann (d. 940), daughter of Donnchadh, High King of Ireland
Brian Boru, High King of Ireland (killed 1014 at the battle of Clontarf)	+	**Donnfhlaith (or Gormflaith)** (d. 1030), who md. (1) Domnall, King of Meath, and (2) Olaf Cuaran, Danish King of Northumbria and Dublin. Brian Boru was her 3rd husband.
Donnchad, King of Munster (d. 1064 on a pilgrimage to Rome)	+	N.N.
Diarmait MacMael Nam Bo, King of Hy Kinsale (d. 23 Feb 1072)	+	**Darbforgaill** (d. 1080)
Murchad (d. 8 Dec 1070)	+	Sadb, daughter of MacBricc
Donnchad Macmurchada, King of Dublin (killed in battle against Domnall Ua Brian 1115)	+	Orlaith
Diarmait Macmurchada, King of Leinster (b. 1100 – d. 1 Jan 1171)	+	Mor (d. 1164), daughter of Muir-chertach Ua Tuathail

Richard de Clare "Strongbow," 2nd Earl of Pembroke and Justiciar of Ireland (b. ca. 1130 – md. ca. 26 Aug 1171 – d. ca. 20 April 1176)	+	**Aoife (or Eve) of Leinster** (md. ca. 26 Aug 1171 – liv. 1186)
William Marshall, 3rd Earl of Pembroke, Regent of England, and the greatest knight in English history (b. ca. 1146 – md. Aug 1189 – d. 14 May 1219)	+	**Isabel de Clare** (md. Aug 1189 – d. 1220)
Gilbert de Clare, 7th Earl of Clare, Magna Charta Surety (b. ca. 1180 – md. 9 Oct 1217 – d. 25 Oct 1230)	+	**Isabel Marshall** (md. (1) 9 Oct 1217 – d. 17 Jan 1239/ 1240)
Robert Bruce, Lord of Annandale (b. 1210 – md. (1) May 1240 – d. 31 March 1295)	+	**Isabel de Clare** (b. 2 Nov 1226 – md. May 1240 – d. aft. 10 July 1264)
Robert Bruce, Lord of Annandale (b. July 1243 – md. (1) 1271 – d. March 1304)	+	Margaret (or Marjorie) (md. (2) 1271 – d. 1292), daughter of Neil, 2nd Earl of Carrick
Robert I the Bruce, King of Scotland (b. 11 July 1274 – md. (1) ca. 1295 – d. 7 June 1329)	+	Isabel of Mar (md. ca. 1295 – d. bef. 1302)

Sources: *Bunson*, p. 24; *Burke's*, Vol. II, pp. 2151–2152; *Byrne*, p. 280; *Holweck*, p. 2; *Jaski*, p. 302; *Weis, AR:* line 175 + line 66, nos. 26 and 27 + line 63, no. 28 + line 252, nos. 28 through 30; *Weis, MCS:* line 145, nos. 1 and 2 + line 41, nos. 2 through 5

St. Adalard

Adalard was born around 751 and was the son of Duke Bernard and his first wife N.N., a daughter of Caribert, Count of Laon. A half-brother of St. Wala, Adalard was educated at the court of Pepin "the Short" and at age 20 decided to become a monk. Admitted to the monastery at Corvey, he later became the abbot there.

Adalard's life of seclusion did not last very long. His cousin Charlemagne made him one of his chief advisers. In 796 Adalard was appointed to act as prime minister to Charlemagne's son Pepin I, King of Italy. When Pepin I died in 810, Adalard became regent of Italy until Pepin's very young son Bernard came of age.

After Charlemagne himself died in 814, his son and successor Louis "the Pious" stripped all of his father's advisors of their offices and power. Adalard was sent to the monastery of St. Filebert. While he was at St. Filebert's, Adalard wrote a treatise on government for Louis and was eventually rehabilitated.

On 22 December 825, Adalard fell violently ill, and on 2 January 826 he died. He was buried in the monastery chapel at Corvey, later known as New Corvey.

Adalard was variously called "the Augustine, Anthony, and Jeremiah of his age." He is the patron saint of many towns in France. In Germany along the lower Rhine, there are many churches dedicated to him. He is also known as Adalhard.

His Line

Husband		Wife	
Duke Bernard (d. ca. 784), a natural son of Charles Martel	+	md. (2) **"a Saxon woman"**	
N.N.	+	**Theoderada (or Theodrada)**	Theoderada's half-brother: ***St. Adalard*** (Duke Bernard's son by his first wife)
Pepin (or Pippin) I, King of Italy (b. 767 – d. 8 July 810)	+	**Chrothais**	
Bernard, King of Italy (b. 797 – d. 17 April 818)	+	Cunegunde (d. ca. 835)	
Pepin, Count of Senlis, Peronne, and St. Quentin (b. 817/818 – d. aft. 840)	+	N.N.	
Herbert I, Count of Vermandois (b. ca. 840 – murdered 900/908)	+	Liegardis	
Herbert II, Count of Vermandois (b. 887 – md. bef. 907 – d. 943)	+	Hildebrande of Neustria (b. 887 – md. bef. 907 – d. 943)	
Arnulf (or Arnold) I "the Old," Count of Flanders and Artois (b. 885/890 – md. (2) 934 – d. 27 March 964)	+	**Adelaide (or Adela or Alix)** de Vermandois (b. ca. 915 – md. 934 – d. 958/960)	
Baldwin III, Count of Flanders (b. ca. 940 – md. 961 – d. 1005)	+	Mathilda of Saxony (md. 961 – d. 1005)	

[For the later generations that connect this line to the kings of England, see the line of St. Arnulf, Bishop of Metz in Part II.]

Sources: *Baring-Gould*, Vol. 1, pp. 34–36; *BBKL*, Vol. 13, col. 164 (under "Wala"); *Benedictine Monks*, p. 7; *Bibliotheca Sanctorum*, Vol. 1, columns 170-171; *Bunson*, p. 32; *Butler*, Vol. I, pp. 22–23; *Cabaniss*, pp. 3-4; *CE*, Vol. I, p. 126; *Delaney*, p. 25; *Delaney and Tobin*, p. 8; *Holweck*, p. 14; *McKitterick*, p. 134; *Settipani*, pp. 170–172, 211–227, 355–358, "Tableau 4: Les Pippinides," and "Tableau 8: Les Descendants de Pippin d'Italie"; *Stuart:* line 231, no. 40 through 36 + line 169, ns. 36 and 35 + line 141, nos. 36 and 35; *Weis, AR:* line 50, nos. 14 through 18 + line 48, nos. 19 and 20 + line 162, nos. 18 and 19 (According to Weis, Pepin I King of Italy married a daughter of Duke Bernard. Settipani persuasively argues that Pepin I's wife Chrothais was actually a granddaughter of Duke Bernard and that her mother was Duke Bernard's daughter Theoderada.) Also see ***fmg.ac>Projects>Medieval Lands>Medieval Lands – data by region>France>Kings & early nobility>Carolingian nobility>Family of Adalhard and Wala***. In addition, see ***fmg.ac>Projects>Medieval Lands>Medieval Lands – data by region>Italy>Emperors & Kings> Kings of Italy 774–887 (Carolingians)***.

St. Adalbero,
Bishop of Wuerzburg

Adalbero was born in 1010 and was the son of Arnold II, Count of Wels-Lambach on the Traun. In 1045, Emperor Henry III made him bishop of Wuerzburg.

In his diocese, Adalbero continued the construction of the new cathedral of Wuerzburg. He also carried out significant reforms in the ecclesiastical life at several monasteries.

Nationally, after the death of Henry III, Adalbero became deeply involved in synods and in councils of the court and the empire. In 1066, he performed the marriage ceremony between the new emperor Henry IV and Bertha of Saxony and often acted as the new emperor's counselor.

When the investiture dispute between Henry IV and Pope St. Gregory VII began in the mid-1070's, however, Adalbero strongly defended papal authority against Henry IV's efforts to diminish it. In 1077, Adalbero even worked with other nobles to set up Rudolf of Rheinfelden as anti-king to Henry IV.

In retaliation, Henry IV removed Adalbero from his post in Wuerzburg in 1085. Adalbero returned to his family estate in Lambach, which had been turned into a monastery, and died there on 6 October 1090.

His Line

Husband		Wife	
Arnold II, Count of Wels-Lambach on the Traun and in the Chiemgau	+	**N.N.**	
Ottokar V, Count in the Chiemgau (d. ca. 1020)	+	**N.N.**, daughter of Arnold II	N.N.'s brother: ***St. Adalbero, Bishop of Wuerzburg***
Ottokar VI, Count in the Chiemgau (d. 1075)	+	md. (2) Willibirg von Eppenstein	
Ottokar VII, Count in the Chiemgau (md. bef. 1082 – d. 28 Nov 1122)	+	Elizabeth (md. bef. 1082 – d. 16 Oct 1107/1114), daughter of Leopold II "der Schoene" ("the Handsome"), Margrave of Austria and Crusader	
Eckbert II, Count of Formbach-Puttin and Neuburg (md. bef. 1134 – d. bef. 1140)	+	**Willibirg von Steirermark** (md. bef. 1134 – d. 18 Jan 1145)	
Berthold V, Count of Andechs and Margrave of Istria (b. 1122/1123 – md. 1152 – d. ca. 1188)	+	**Hedwig von Formbach-Puttin** (md. (1) 1152 – d. 16 July 1174)	

Berthold VI, Count of Andechs, Margrave of Istria, and Duke of Croatia; Crusader (b. ca. 1152 – md. 1170 – d. 12 Aug 1204)	+	Agnes von Groitzsch-Rochlitz (md. 1170 – d. 25 March 1195)
Andrew II, King of Hungary (b. 1176 – md. (1) bef. 1203 – d. 21 Sept 1235)	+	**Gertrude von Meran** (md. bef. 1203 – d. 8 Sept 1213)
Bela IV, King of Hungary (b. 1206 – md. 1218 – d. 3 May 1270)	+	Maria Laskarina (b. ca. 1206 – md. 1218 – d. 1270), daughter of Theodore I Lascaris, Emperor of Byzantium
Stephen V, King of Hungary (b. Dec 1239 – md. 1253 – d. 1 Aug 1272)	+	Elizabeth (md. 1253 – d. aft. 1290), daughter of Kuthen, Khan of the Kumans
Charles II "le Boiteux" ("the Lame"), King of Naples and Prince of Salerno (b. 1254 – md. 1270 – d. 5 June 1309)	+	**Maria** (b. ca. 1257 – md. 1270 – murdered 25 March 1323)
Charles of Valois (b. 12 March 1270/1271 – md. 16 Aug 1290 – d. 16 Dec 1325), son of Philip III "the Bold," King of France	+	**Marguerite** (b. ca. 1273 – md. 16 Aug 1290 – d. 31 Dec 1299)
William III d'Avesnes, Count of Hainault and Holland (b. ca. 1286 – md. 19 May 1305 – d. 7 June 1337)	+	**Jeanne de Valois** (b. ca. 1294 – md. 19 May 1305 – d. 7 March 1342)
Edward III, King of England (b. 13 Nov 1312 – md. 24 Jan 1328 – d. 21 June 1377)	+	**Philippa of Hainault** (b. 24 June 1311 – md. 24 Jan 1328 – d. 15 Aug 1369)

Sources: *BBKL*, Vol. 1, cols. 23–24; *Benedictine Monks*, p. 8; *Bunson*, p. 32; *Delaney*, p. 24; *Delaney and Tobin*, p. 7; *Holweck*, p. 12; *NCE*, Vol. 1, pp. 111–112; *Stuart:* line 12, nos. 34 through 31 + line 9, nos. 31 and 30 + line 7, nos. 30 through 28 + line 78 + line 88, nos. 25 and 24 + line 70, nos. 24 and 23 + line 50, nos. 23 and 22; *Weis, AR*, line 103, nos. 28 through 34; *Wells*, pp. 381, 309, 421, 257, 293

Bl. Adalbero, Bishop of Liège

Adalbero was the son of Henry II, Count of Louvain, and his wife Adelaide of the Betuwe. After being a canon at Metz, he was made bishop of Liège, held that post for the rest of his life, and died on 1 January 1128.

His Line

	Husband		Wife
	Henry II, Count of Louvain (b. ca. 1020 – d. 1078/1079)	+	**Adelaide of the Betuwe** (b. ca. 1045 – d. aft. 1086)
Godfrey I's brother: ***Bl. Adalbero, Bishop of Liège***	**Godfrey I "the Bearded,"** Count of Louvain, Margrave of Antwerp, and Duke of Brabant (b. ca. 1060 – md. (1) c. 1100 – d. 25 Jan 1139)	+	Ida of Namur and Chiny (b. 1083 – md. ca. 1100 – d. aft. 1125)
	Godfrey II, Count of Louvain and Duke of Brabant (b. ca. 1108 – md. ca. 1139 – d. 1142)	+	Luitgarde von Sulzbach (b. ca. 1120 – md. ca. 1139 – d. aft. 1162)
	Godfrey III, Count of Louvain and Duke of Brabant (b. 1142 – md. (1) bef. 1155 – d. 10 Aug 1190)	+	Margaret von Limburg (b. ca. 1139 – md. bef. 1155 – d. 1172/1173)
	Henry I, Count of Louvain and Duke of Brabant (b. 1165 – md. (1) 1179 – d. 5 Sept 1235)	+	Matilda of Alsace and Flanders (md. 1179)
	Henry II "the Courageous," Duke of Brabant and Lorraine (b. 1207 – md. (1) by 22 Aug 1215 – d. 1 Feb 1248)	+	Maria von Hohenstaufen (b. 1201 – md. by 22 Aug 1215 – d. 1235)

[For the later generations that connect this line to the kings of England, see the line of St. Boris I, Khan of the Bulgars in Part II.]

Sources: *Benedictine Monks*, p. 8; *Delaney and Tobin*, p. 24; *Delaney and Tobin*, p. 7; *Holweck*, p. 12; *Stuart*, line 68, nos. 32 through 27; *Wagner*, p. 159; *Weis, AR*, line 155, nos. 22 through 27; *Wells*, pp. 357 and 89

St. Adeloga

Adeloga was the daughter of Charles Martel, King of the Franks, and possibly Swanhilde, his second wife.

Adeloga became a nun, founded the great Benedictine abbey at Kitzingen, and became its first abbess. She was very well known for her learning and charitable work.

Adeloga died around 745. Her relics at Kitzingen were destroyed in 1525 during a peasants' revolt. She is also known as Hadeloga.

Her Line

	Husband		Wife
	Charles Martel "the Hammer," Mayor of the Palace in Austrasia, King of the Franks, and the victor at the battle of Poitiers (b. ca. 688 – d. 22 Oct 741)	+	md. (1) **Chrotrude (or Rotrou),** Duchess of Austrasia (d. 724)
Pepin's sister: ***St. Adeloga***	**Pepin (or Pippin) III "the Short,"** Mayor of the Palace in Austrasia and King of the Franks (b. 715 – md. ca. 740 – d. 24 Sept 768)	+	Bertha (or Bertrada) "Bigfoot" (b. ca. 720 – md. ca. 740 – d. 12 July 783)
	Bl. Charlemagne, King of the Franks and First Emperor of the West (b. 2 April 747 – md. (2) 771 – d. 28 Jan 814)	+	Bl. Hildegarde, Countess of Vinzgau (b. 758 – md. 771 – d. 30 April 783)

[For the later generations that connect this line to the kings of England, see the line of St. Arnulf, Bishop of Metz in Part II.]

Sources: *Baring-Gould*, Vol. 2, pp. 42–44; *BBKL*, Vol. 17, col. 554; *Benedictine Monks*, p. 11; *Bunson*, p. 36; *Delaney*, p. 27; *Delaney and Tobin*, p. 10; *Holweck*, pp. 16–17; *Stuart*, line 171, nos. 43 through 41; *Tucker*, Vol. I, pp. 183–184; *Wagner*, p. 189; *Weis, AR*, line 50, nos. 11 through 13; *Wells*, pp. 135–136; *WWH*, Vol. 10, p. 462

St. Aidan of Ferns

Aidan was born around 558 and was the son of Setnae, a prince in Ulster, and his wife Eithne.

To insure the loyalty of Setnae's family to the High King of Ireland, Aidan was held hostage as a small boy. He then went to Wales to become a monk and studied under St. David of Wales. Returning to Ireland as a missionary to Wexford, he founded several churches and was made the first bishop of Ferns around 598.

Aidan died around 626/632, and many miracles were attributed to him. His bell, satchel, and shrine are in the National Museum in Dublin. There is a cathedral dedicated to him in Enniscarthy.

His Line

	Husband		Wife
	Setnae, a prince in Ulster	+	**Eithne**
Ainmere's brother: ***St. Aidan of Ferns***	**Ainmere mac Setnae**, High King of Ireland (d. 569)	+	N.N.
	Aed mac Ainmerech, High King of Ireland (d. 598)	+	N.N.
	Maelcobha, King of Tir Conaill and High King of Ireland (d. 615)	+	N.N.
	Maelduin, King of Ailech (killed 681 at the battle of Leathairbhe)	+	**Cacht**

[For the later generations that connect this line to the kings of England, see the line of St. Abban in Part III.]

Sources: *Baring-Gould*, Vol. I, pp. 471–472; *Baring-Gould and Fisher*, Vol. 1, p. 118; *Benedictine Monks*, p. 23; *Bunson*, p. 51; *Burke's*, Vol. II, p. 2151; *Byrne*, p. 283; *CE*, Vol. IX, p. 520 (under "Maedoc"); *CS*, p. 69; *Delaney and Tobin*, p. 19; *Jaski*, p. 306; *Tucker*, Vol. I, p. 444; *Williamson*, p. 387

St. Alaricus

Alaricus was the son of Burkhard II, Duke of Swabia, and his wife St. Reginlink. He was educated in Switzerland at the monastery of Einsiedeln, where he became a monk. He ultimately went to live as a hermit on the island of Uffnau, which is on the lake at Zurich. He died on 29 September 975.

Alaricus is also known as Adalrai.

His Line

Husband		Wife	
Burkhard II, Duke of Swabia (b. ca. 885 – md. bef. 911 – d. in battle 29 April 926)	+	**St. Reginlink** (b. 885/890 – md. (1) bef. 911 – d. 959)	
Berthold, Duke of Bavaria in Carinthia (b. ca. 900 – d. ca. 947)	+	**St. Wiltrudis (or Biletrud)** (d. ca. 986)	Wiltrudis' brother: ***St. Alaricus***
Ulrich (or Udalrich), Count in the Schweinachgau (liv. 947–970)	+	**Kunigunde**	

[For the later generations that connect this line to the kings of England, see the line of St. Reginlink in Part II.]

Sources: *Benedictine Monks*, p. 25; *Delaney*, p. 35; *Delaney and Tobin*, p. 21; *Holweck*, pp. 14 and 851 (under "Regulinda"); *Stuart:* line 345, no. 38 + line 41A, nos. 37 and 36; *Wells*, p. 545

St. Albert of Louvain, Bishop of Liège

Albert was born in 1166 and was the son of Godfrey III, Count of Louvain and Duke of Brabant, and his wife Margaret von Limburg. In 1178, Albert was made a canon of Liège but resigned that priestly honor in 1187 to become a knight.

The way of the sword and the way of the cross are two very different paths, and the truth was that Albert was drawn to both of them. After being knighted, Albert also took the Crusader's oath. Yet instead of leaving for the Holy Land, he continued to think about what God really wanted from him. In the end, the cross prevailed over the sword. After asking to be released from his Crusader's oath and knightly vows, Albert was allowed to become a canon at Liège again. If he had any inkling that he would still die by the sword one day, it is not recorded.

The events for which Albert is remembered began in 1191. The office of bishop for the diocese of Liège was a politically powerful position, and the noble houses of Brabant and Hainault were struggling with each other over which one of them would control it after the old bishop died in 1191. Brabant's candidate was Albert of Louvain. Hainault's candidate was Albert of Rethel. On 8 September 1191, Albert of Louvain was elected, but Albert of Rethel then appealed to his relative Emperor Henry VI. The emperor responded by appointing his own man Lothaire of Bonn to the post.

This imperial power grab did not please Albert of Louvain, who then disguised himself as a servant to avoid being taken by the emperor's men and set out for Rome to appeal directly to Pope Celestine III. The pope decided to make Albert both the bishop of Liège and a cardinal, and Albert was consecrated at Rheims on 29 September 1192.

The next act in the power struggle occurred on 24 November 1192, when a small group of the emperor's knights walked up to Albert of Louvain, drew their swords, and murdered him in cold blood. His martyrdom closely resembled that of Thomas à Becket, who had died in England 22 years earlier in a similar conflict between church and state.

Following Albert's murder, Lothaire of Bonn was excommunicated, and Henry VI was forced to do public penance. In Albert's life, the final victory of the cross over the sword occurred when Albert, like Becket, was made a saint.

Albert's relics are in the cathedral of Liège and also in the church of the Carmelite convent in Brussels.

His Line

Husband		Wife
Godfrey III, Count of Louvain and Duke of Brabant (b. 1142 – md. (1) bef. 1155 – d. 10 Aug 1190)	+	**Margaret von Limburg** (b. ca. 1139 – md. bef. 1155 – d. 1172/1173)

Henry I's brother: ***St. Albert of Louvain, Bishop of Liège***	**Henry I**, Count of Louvain and Duke of Brabant (b. 1165 – md. (1) 1179 – d. 5 Sept 1235)	+	Matilda of Alsace and Flanders (md. 1179)
	Henry II "the Courageous," Duke of Brabant and Lorraine (b. 1207 – md. (1) by 22 Aug 1215 – d. 1 Feb 1248)	+	Maria von Hohenstaufen (b. 1201 – md. by 22 Aug 1215 – d. 1235)

[For the later generations that connect this line to the kings of England, see the line of St. Boris I, King of the Bulgars in Part II.]

Sources: *BBKL*, Vol. 1, col. 82; *Benedictine Monks*, p. 28; *Bunson*, pp. 55–56; *Butler*, Vol. IV, pp. 400–402; *CE*, Vol. I, p. 261; *Delaney*, pp. 37–38; *Delaney and Tobin*, p. 24; *Holweck*, p. 40; *Stuart*, line 68, nos. 29 through 27; *Weis, AR*, line 155, nos. 25 through 27; *Wells*, pp. 357 and 89

St. Alburga

Alburga was the daughter of Eahlmund, King of Kent, and a wife whose name is unknown but who was the daughter of Aethelbert II, King of Kent. Alburga married Wulstan, Earl of Wiltshire, who founded a monastery at Wilton.

Alburga displayed piety at an early age. After her husband died, she transformed his monastery into a convent, became a nun, and remained there until she died ca. 810.

Her Line

	Husband		Wife
	Eahlmund (or Edmund), King of Kent (b. ca. 758 – d. 786)	+	**N.N.,** a daughter of Aethelbert II, King of Kent
Egbert's sister: ***St. Alburga***	**Egbert "the Great,"** King of Wessex (b. 775 – d. 4 Feb 839)	+	Redburga (or Raedburh) (b. ca. 788)
	Aethelwulf, King of Wessex (b. ca. 806 – d. 13 Jan 858)	+	md. (1) Osburh (b. ca. 810 – d. aft. 876)
	St. Alfred the Great, King of Wessex (b. 849 – md. 868 – d. 28 Oct 899)	+	St. Eahlswith of Mercia (b. ca. 852 – md. 868 – d. 904)

Sources: *Baring-Gould*, Vol. 16, p. 324; *Benedictine Monks*, p. 29; *Bunson*, p. 59; *Delaney*, p. 39; *Delaney and Tobin*, p. 27; *Dunbar*, Vol. I, p. 39; *Holweck*, p. 42; *Stuart*, line 233, nos. 42 through 39; *Weis, AR*, line 1, nos. 12 through 15; *Wells*, pp. 203-204

St. Anna of Kiev

Anna was the daughter of Vsevolod I Jaroslavich, Grand Prince of Kiev, and his second wife Anna of the Cumans. In 1087 Anna became a nun and entered the St. Andrew's convent near Kiev. Among the nuns there, she encouraged learning and the development of a deeper spiritual life. She died at the convent around 1112/1116.

Her Line

Vsevolod I Yaroslavich,
Grand Prince of Kiev and Prince of Perejaslaw (b. ca. 1030 – d. 13 April 1093)

md. (1) ca. 1046 **Maria Monomacha**, daughter of Constantine IX Monomachos, Emperor of Byzantium

md. (2) Anna of the Cumans

Son of Vsevolod and Maria:		Daughter of Vsevolod and Anna:
St. Vladimir Vsevolodovich Monomach (a.k.a. Vladimir I "Monomachos"), Grand Prince of Kiev (b. 1053 – md. (1) ca. 1070 – d. 19 May 1125)	+	Gytha of Wessex (md. ca. 1070), daughter of of Harold II Godwinsson, King of England
St. Mstislav Vladimirovich (a.k.a., Mstislav I Harold), Grand Prince of Kiev (b. 1076 – md. (2) 1122 – d. 15 April 1132)	+	Lyubawa (md. 1122 – d. 1168), daughter of Dmitri Zaviditsch, Possadnik of Novgorod

St. Anna of Kiev

[For the later generations that connect this line to the kings of England, see the line of St. Harold III "Bluetooth," King of Denmark in Part II.]

Sources: *Holweck*, p. 80; *Stuart*, line 240, nos. 31 through 29; *Wagner*, p. 206; *Weis, AR*, line 242, nos. 6 through 8; *Wells*, p. 329

St. Anthusa

Anthusa was born in 757 and was the daughter of Constantine V Copronymus, Emperor of Byzantium, and his third wife Eudokia. After Constantine V died in 775, Anthusa gave all her property to the poor and became a nun.

Entering the convent of Homonia in Constantinople, Anthusa became an example of humility. She carried water, served her sisters during meals, cleaned the church, and did many other kinds of hard manual labor. She died around 809/811.

Her Line

Constantine V Copronymus, Emperor of Byzantium (b. 718 – d. 14 Sept 775)

md. (1) 731/732 **Tzitzak** (bapt. "Irene" – d. 750), daughter of Bihar, Khan of the Khazars

Constantine and Tzitzak's son:

md. (3) ca. 753 Eudokia

Constantine and Eudokia's daughter:

St. Anthusa

Leo IV "the Khazar," Emperor of Byzantium (b. 25 Jan 750 – md. 769 – d. 8 Sept 780)	+	St. Irene (b. 752 – md. 769 – d. 9 Aug 803)
Constantine VI, Emperor of Byzantium (b. 771 – md. Nov 788 – d. aft. 15 Aug 797)	+	Maria of Amnia (md. Nov 788)

[For the later generations that connect this line to the kings of England, see the line of St. Irene, Empress of Byzantium in Part II.]

Sources: *Holweck*, p. 84; *Norwich*, Vol. 1, "The Family of Leo III" in the "Family Trees" section; *Stuart*, line 322B, nos. 41 and 40; *Wells*, p. 118

St. Aristakes,
Bishop of Armenia

Aristakes was the younger son of St. Gregory "the Illuminator" and his wife Maria.

At first, Aristakes was an aide and representative of St. Gregory as Gregory worked to establish Christianity in Armenia. In 318 when Gregory retired, Aristakes became the country's second bishop and represented it at the Council of Nicea in 325.

Continuing his father's work in Armenia, Aristakes was martyred in 333 by Archelaus, a local prince whose wickedness Aristakes had denounced.

The name of Aristakes is mentioned daily in the Armenian mass. He was the brother of St. Vardanes.

His Line

	Husband		Wife
	St. Gregory "the Illuminator," (b. 240 – d. 330/332)	+	**Maria**
Vardanes' brother: ***St. Aristakes, Bishop of Armenia***	**St. Vardanes** (d. 339/341)	+	N.N.
	St. Yusik I (martyred ca. 344)	+	N.N., a daughter of St. Tiridates "the Great," King of Armenia
	Athenagenes	+	Bambishu (b. 315)

[For the later generations that connect this line to the kings of England, see the line of St. Ashken in Part II.]

Sources: *Baring-Gould*, Vol. 10, p. 443*; *Delaney and Tobin*, p. 510*; *Dowling*, p. 52; *Holweck*, pp. 449–450* and p. 104; *Hovannisian*, pp. 84–85; *Kaloustian*, p. 15*; *Koushagian*, pp. 9*, 4, and 21; *NCE*, Vol. 6, p. 790*; *Wagner*, p. 195 (information on pages marked with a * is alphabetized under Gregory the Illuminator)

St. Attalia

Attalia was born around 687/690 and was the daughter of Adalbert, Duke of Alsace and his wife Gerlinde. She was raised in a convent by Adalbert's sister St. Odilia. After becoming a Benedictine nun, she was made the first abbess of St. Stephen's convent in Strasbourg, which Adalbert had founded in 717.

Attalia was an example of piety and charity and was so deeply loved by her nuns and the people of Strasbourg that when she died in December 741 her funeral lasted five weeks. Her relics remained in Strasbourg until they disappeared during the French Revolution.

Attalia's sisters Eugenia and Gudelindis also became saints.

Her Line

	Husband		Wife
	Adalbert, Duke of Alsace (d. 722)	+	**Gerlinde**
Luitfride's sister: ***St. Attalia***	**Luitfride I**, Duke of Alsace (d. 767)	+	Edith
	Luitfride II, Count of Upper Alsace (d. 802)	+	Hiltrude
	Hugh "le Méfiant," Count of Tours (b. ca. 765 – d. Sept/ Nov 836)	+	Aba (or Bava) (b. ca. 779 – liv. 837)
	Rupert IV (called "Robert the Strong"), Count of Paris, Tours, and Wormsgau (md. (2) ca. 864 – slain 25 July 866)	+	**Adelaide of Alsace and Tours** (md. ca. 864)
	Robert I, Count of Paris and Poitiers, anti-king of France (b. posthumously in 866 – died in battle 15 June 923)	+	md. (2) Aelis
	Herbert II, Count of Vermandois, Troyes, Meaux, and Soissons (b. 887 – md. bef. 907 – d. 27 March 964)	+	**Hildebrande of Neustria** (b. 887 – md. bef. 907 – d. 943)
	Arnulf (or Arnold) I "the Old," Count of Flanders and Artois (b. 885/890 – md. (2) 934 – d. 27 March 964)	+	**Adelaide (or Adela or Alix) de Vermandois** (b. ca. 915 – md. 934 – d. 958/960)

[For the later generations that connect this line to the kings of England, see the line of St. Arnulf, Bishop of Metz in Part II.]

Sources: *Baring-Gould*, Vol. 15, p. 20 and Vol. 16, p. 152; *BBKL*, Vol. 15, cols. 44–45; *Benedictine Monks*, p. 89; *Bunson*, p. 120; *Dunbar*, Vol. I, p. 89; *Holweck*, pp. 115–116; *NCE*, Vol. 5, p. 627 (under "St. Eugenia"); *Stuart:* line 224, nos. 41 through 37 + line 169, nos. 38 through 35; *Weis, AR:* line 181, nos. 2 through 6 + line 48, nos. 17 through 20; *Wells*, pp. 9–10, 613, 586, and 248

Bl. Ayrald

Ayrald was the son of William II "the Great," Count of Burgundy and Macon, and his wife Stephanie of Longwy.

Ayrald joined the Carthusian monks at Portes and became prior there. He was later appointed bishop of Maurienne and died ca. 1146.

Ayrald's ability to serve God was magnified by the fact that he was the brother of Pope Callistus II, whose given name was Guy of Burgundy.

His Line

	Husband		Wife
	William II "the Great," Count of Burgundy and Macon (b. ca. 1024 – md. 1049/1057 – d. 12 Nov 1087)	+	**Stephanie of Longwy** (b. ca. 1035 – md. 1049/ 1057 – d. aft. 1088)
Raymond's brother: ***Bl. Ayrald***	**Raymond of Burgundy and Ivrea**, Count of Castile, Galicia, Coimbra, and d'Amous, went to Spain on a Crusade against the Moors (b. ca. 1070 – md. ca. 1095 – d. 13/20 Sept 1107)	+	Urraca (b. ca. 1082 – md. ca. 1095 – d. 8 March 1126), daughter of Alfonso VI, King of Castile and Leon
	Alfonso VII, King of Castile, Leon, Galicia, Toledo, Zaragoza, and the Asturias (b. 1 March 1105 – md. (2) July 1152 – d. 21 Aug 1157)	+	Richilde (b. 1130/ 1140 – md. July 1152 – d. 1166), daughter of Wladislaw II, King of Poland
	Alfonso II, King of Aragon (b. March 1157 – md. (2) 18 Jan 1174 – d. 25 April 1196)	+	**Sancha**, Princess of Castile and Leon (b. 21 Sept 1154 – md. 18 Jan 1174 – d 9 Nov 1208)
	Alfonso, Prince of Aragon and Count of Provence (b. 1180 – md. 1193 – d. Feb 1209)	+	Gersinde of Sabran, heiress of Provence and Forcalquier (md. 1193 – was a nun in 1222 – d. aft. 1222)
	Raymond Berenger V, Count of Forcalquier and Provence (b. 1198 – md. Dec 1220 – d. 19 Aug 1245)	+	Beatrice of Savoy (b. 1198 – md. Dec 1220 – d. Dec 1266)
	Henry III, King of England (b. 1 Oct 1 207 – md. 14 Jan 1236 – d. 16 Nov 1272)	+	**Eleanor of Provence** (b. ca. 1223 – md. 14 Jan 1236 – d. 25 June 1291)

Sources: *Delaney*, p. 82; *Delaney and Tobin*, p. 88; *Stuart:* line 94, nos. 31 through 28 + line 54, nos. 38 through 25; *Weis, AR:* line 132, nos. 24 and 25 + line 113, nos. 24 and 25 + line 116 + line 111, nos. 27 through 30

St. Balderic

Balderic was the son of Sigebert (or Sigibert) I, King of Metz (Austrasia), and his wife Brunhilda, daughter of Athanagildo, King of the Visigoths.

Balderic became a monk. He founded the convent of St. Peter's in Rheims and made his sister St. Bova its first abbess. Later in life, he founded the monastery of Montfacon in Champagne, became its first abbot, and spent the rest of his life there.

Balderic and Bova constantly encouraged each other in virtue. From time to time, Balderic would go to visit his sister at her convent. It was during one such visit that he died. Today his relics are at his monastery in Champagne.

Ingudis, another sister of Balderic, became the wife of St. Hermenegild. In the histories of the saints, Balderic is also known as Baudry.

His Line

Husband		Wife	
Sigebert I, King of Metz (Austrasia) (murdered 575)	+	**Brunhilda (or Brunechildis)**	
Recaredo (or Recared) I, King of the Visigoths in Spain (d. 601)	+	**Chlodesindis (or Clodoswindis)**	Chlodesindis' brother: ***St. Balderic***
Suintila (or Suintilo), King of the Visigoths in Spain (deposed in 631)	+	Theodora, daughter of Sisebuto, King of the Visigoths in Spain	
Ervigio, King of the Visigoths in Spain (d. 687)	+	**Liubigotona**	

[For the later generations that connect this line to the kings of England, see the line of St. Florentina in Part III.]

Sources: *Baring-Gould*, Vol. 12, pp. 427–428; *Benedictine Monks*, p. 99; *Bunson*, p. 141; *Delaney and Tobin*, p. 94; *Holweck*, p. 129; *NCE*, Vol. 2, p. 740 (under "Bova"); *Scherman, Birth of France*, frontispiece; *Tucker:* Vol. II, p. 26 + Vol. I, p. 79; *Wagner*, p. 188; *Wells*, p. 593. Also see ***fmg.ac>Projects>Medieval Lands>Medieval Lands – data by region>Iberia>Vandals, Suevi & Visigoths>Recaredo I 586–601, Liuva II 601–603***. In addition, see ***fmg.ac>Projects>Medieval Lands>Medieval Lands – data by region>Iberia>Vandals, Suevi & Visigoths>Suintila 621–633***.

St. Benedict of Aniane

Originally named Witiza, Benedict was born around 750 and was the son of Aigulf, Count of Maguelone in southern France. Benedict was educated at the royal Frankish court and was first a cupbearer to Pepin the Short. He then joined Charlemagne's army and went on a campaign in Lombardy. Near Pavia, Italy, he almost drowned while trying to rescue his brother in a river. After returning home, Benedict reflected further on the profession of arms and became a monk.

It was not Benedict's destiny to be an ordinary monk. After a few years in the Benedictine monastery of St.-Seine, in 779 he built a hermitage on his own estate at Aniane and lived there for years in isolation. He was gradually joined by so many like-minded men that he turned his hermitage into a new monastery which became a model for monastic reform.

It was under Charlemagne's successor Louis and Pious that Benedict's influence reached its height. Louis made him a personal adviser and appointed him overseer of all the monasteries in the Carolingian empire. Benedict wrote many homilies and new monastic rules. At a meeting in Aachen of all the abbots of the empire in 817, Benedict's rules for the restoration of monastic discipline were adopted.

Benedict died on 11 February 821. He is remembered as the great restorer of monasticism in the West.

His Line

	Husband		Wife
	Aigulf, Count of Maguelone (Substantion) (liv. ca. 752)	+	**N.N.**
Amic's brother: ***St. Benedict of Aniane***	**Amic**, Count in the Council of Narbonne	+	N.N.
	Robert, Count of Substantion (liv. 819)	+	N.N.
	N.N. of Substantion	+	Guillenette (liv. 899)
	Bernard I, Count of Melgueil and Substantion	+	N.N.
	Berenger of Melgueil Bernard II,	+	Giselo
	Count of Melgueil (d. ca. 989)	+	Senegunde (d. 989)
	Berenger (d. bef. 985)	+	N.N.
	Bernard III, Count of Melgueil (liv. 989 – d. ca. 1055)	+	Adele
	Raymond I, Count of Melgueil (md. bef. 1055 – d. ca. 1079)	+	Beatrix of Poitou
	Pierre, Count of Melgueil (md. ca. 1065 – liv. 1085)	+	Almode of Toulouse (md. ca. 1065 – liv. 1132)

William V, Seigneur de Montpellier and Crusader (b. ca. 1065/1069 – md. (2) 1086/1087 – d. ca. 1122)	+	**Ermesende de Melgueil** (md. 1086/1087)
St. William VI, Seigneur de Montpellier (b. ca. 1100 – md. Aug 1129 – d. 1162)	+	Sibel de Vasto di Savona (md. Aug 1129 – d. bef. 1146)

[For the later generations that connect this line to the kings of England, see the line of St. William VI, Lord of Montpellier in Part II.]

Sources: *Baring-Gould*, Vol. 2, pp. 284–285; *BBKL*, Vol. 1, cols. 493–494; *Benedictine Monks*, p. 111; *Bunson*, p. 155; *Butler*, Vol. I, pp. 309–310; *CE*, Vol. II, p. 467; *Delaney*, p. 97; *Delaney and Tobin*, p. 125; *Holweck*, p. 146; *Stuart:* line 203 + line 142, nos. 30 and 29 + line 150, nos. 31 and 30; *Wells*, pp. 380 and 405

Bl. Berengaria

Berengaria was born in 1228 and was the daughter of St. Fernando III, King of Castile, and his first wife Elisabeth, daughter of Philip von Hohenstaufen, Emperor of Germany. Berengaria became a nun, entered the royal monastery of Las Huelgas de Burgos, and died in 1288.

Her Line

St. Fernando III, King of Castile, Galicia, Leon, Toledo, and Extramadura (b. 24 June 1198 – d. 30 May 1252)

md. (1) 1219 Elisabeth (b. 1203 – d. 1235), daughter of Philip von Hohenstaufen, Emperor of Germany

md. (2) 1237 **Jeanne de Dammartin**, Countess of Ponthieu (b. ca. 1208 – d. 16 March 1279)

Daughter of Fernando and Elisabeth: ***Bl. Berengaria***

Edward I "Longshanks," King of England (b. 17 June 1239 – md. (1) 18 Oct 1254 – d. 8 July 1307) + **Eleanor of Castile** (b. 1240 – md. 18 Oct 1254 – d. 28 Nov 1290)

Sources: *Dunbar*, Vol. I, p. 116; *Stuart*, line 52, nos. 25 and 24; *Weis, AR:* line 109, no. 30 + line 110, nos. 29 and 30; *Wells*, p. 142

St. Bernard of Clairvaux, Doctor of the Church

Bernard was born in 1090 and was the son of Tescelin Sorrel, Lord of Les Fontaines, and his wife Bl. Aleth of Montbard. Martin Luther considered him to be the greatest of all the fathers of the Church. He was at the very least the leading personality in the Western Church in the twelfth century. His writing fills eight modern volumes, is never out of print, and is still studied today.

Bernard and the Cistercians. How He Fostered the Templars and Chose a Pope.

The career of this extraordinary man began in 1112 when he decided to become a monk and entered a new Benedictine abbey at Citeaux. This was the first monastery that was dedicated to a new, stricter interpretation of the Benedictine rule. The ideas taught at Citeaux were called "Cistercian," and they impressed Bernard profoundly. In 1115, Bernard and other monks from Citeaux were sent to found a new monastery at Clairvaux. Bernard would become the first abbot of Clairvaux and held that position for the rest of his life. His written and spoken eloquence led to the creation of hundreds of daughter houses of Clairvaux all across Europe. Along with the Benedictines and the Carthusians, the white-robed Cistercians would become one of the three major monastic orders of the Middle Ages. The first half of the twelfth century—when the Cistercians grew much faster than any other order—would later be called the golden age of Christian monasticism.

As the Cistercians became more prominent, so did Bernard. After nine Crusading knights founded the Knights Templar in Jerusalem in 1119, Bernard took a keen interest in their new organization as well. He was instrumental in obtaining church recognition for them in 1128 at the Council of Troyes and became a very effective recruiter for them. The Templars would go on to become the most famous of all the Christian military orders.

A no less important achievement was Bernard's resolution of the schism of 1130–1138. In the conclave of cardinals that followed the death of Pope Honorius II on 14 February 1130, Anacletus II was elected by a narrow margin. Many influential cardinals supported Innocent II, however, who was then banished by Anacletus. Innocent II took refuge in France, and King Louis VI convened a national council of French bishops. The bishops summoned Bernard to act as judge between the rival popes. Bernard decided in favor of Innocent II, who was then recognized by almost all of the great powers of Europe. Bernard then began the work of converting the holdouts, and when Anacletus died on 25 January 1138 and his successor Victor IV abdicated in favor of Innocent II, most of the credit for reuniting the Western church belonged to Bernard.

Bernard vs. Abelard

Not all of Bernard's efforts on behalf of the Church would be applauded today. One of Bernard's contemporaries was Peter Abelard, whose written works declaring the supremacy of human reason had led to more than one conflict with the

Church. Abelard's resumption of his university lectures in 1139 got him charged with heresy. At the Council of Sens in 1141, Bernard argued the case against Abelard. Believing that the Council would condemn him no matter what he said, Abelard would not answer any of the questions that were put to him. After the Council found him guilty, Abelard said he would appeal directly to the Pope, but before he even left France, Bernard reached the pope first. The pope rescinded the excommunication of Abelard but otherwise affirmed the finding of heresy and ordered Abelard to remain silent. Once Abelard died in 1142, the first victories of human reason over unquestioning faith had to wait until the writings of Dante (1265–1321) and Petrarch (1304–1374) and the paintings of Giotto (1267–1337) began a movement in Florence that history would call the Renaissance.

Bernard and the Second Crusade

In the contest with Abelard, Bernard's faith had wrestled with reason, and faith had won. In Bernard's next great cause, a vast number of Christian soldiers went to war with Moslems in the East, with a very different outcome. On the eastern end of the Mediterranean, the Latin County of Edessa had fallen to the Moslems in 1144. Pope Eugene III decided that a new Crusade was required and gave Bernard the job of rousing the Europeans to action. Although popular enthusiasm for the project was low at first, the effect of Bernard's eloquence was extraordinary, and for the first time two European monarchs—Louis VII of France and Conrad III of Germany—raised the necessary armies. Unfortunately, the two armies did not unite while they were still in Europe but crossed into modern-day Turkey separately and were each mauled by the Moslems in separate battles. Louis and Conrad finally joined forces once they were in the Holy Land, but they then made a very ill-advised attack on Damascus, where they were soundly defeated. Louis and Conrad then returned to Europe, taking what was left of their armies with them. The Second Crusade, which Bernard had so passionately argued for, was a failure.

Remarkably, everyone attributed this to the Crusaders' own sins and selfish motives. Nobody blamed Bernard. At a council called in 1150 to immediately plan a new Crusade that would succeed where Louis and Conrad had failed, Bernard himself was elected to lead the next army that would be sent to the Holy Land. Citing his age and ill health, Bernard declined the honor, and the expedition ultimately known as the Third Crusade would not be launched until 1189.

Bernard's Legacy

In his final years, Bernard turned his attention back to Europe and with his usual eloquence fought the latest manifestation of heresy, which was the Cathars, also known as the Albigensian heresy. Bernard was not able to stamp out the Cathars and their teaching in his own lifetime. That task would be left to the greatest French saint of the next century, King Louis IX.

After almost forty years where Bernard had been both the abbot at Clairvaux and an adviser to kings, popes, and councils, he finally died on 20 August 1153. Besides his personal achievements, he left a written legacy consisting of many treatises, more than 300 sermons, and more than 500 letters. He was buried at Clairvaux, and after the abbey was dissolved during the French Revolution, his remains were transferred to the church of Ville-sou-la-Ferte. Canonized in 1174, he was declared a Doctor of the Church in 1830.

Bernard was the brother of Bl. Gerard, Bl. Guy, Bl. Humbeline, and Bl. Nivard, all of whom were also honored by the Church. "On Loving God"—Bernard's most popular work—is one of the greatest devotional classics of all time.

His Line

Husband		Wife	
Tescelin Sorrel (or Sorus), Lord of Les Fontaines (md. ca. 1085)	+	**Bl. Aleth of Montbard** (b. ca. 1070 – md. ca. 1085 – d. 1105/1110)	
Anseric II, Sire de Chacenay (d. 1137)	+	md. (1) **Bl. Humbeline de Troyes** (b. 1092 – d. 21 Aug 1141)	Humbeline's brother: ***St. Bernard of Clairvaux, Doctor of the Church***
Gui, Count of Bar-sur-Seine (d. 1145)	+	**Petronille de Chacenay** (d. 1161)	

[For the later generations that connect this line to the kings of England, see the line of Bl. Aleth of Montbard in Part II.]

Sources: *Baring-Gould*, Vol. 9, pp. 196–215; *BBKL*, Vol. 1, cols. 530–532; *Bentley*, p. 160; *Bunson*, pp. 61 (under "Aleth") and 162–163; *Butler*, Vol. III, pp. 360–366; *Castleden*, pp. 116–117; *CE*, Vol. II, pp. 498–501; *CS*, pp. 477–479; *Delaney*, pp. 101–102; *Delaney and Tobin*, pp. 30 (under "Aleth") and 132; *Englebert*, p. 319; *Giorgi*, pp. 492–493; *Guiley*, pp. 47–49; *Holweck*, pp. 153–154; *Joeckle*, pp. 69–71; *NCE*, Vol. 2, pp. 335–338; *O'Malley*, pp. 99–100; *One Hundred Saints*, pp. 188–191; *Snodgrass*, pp. 40–41; *Stuart:* line 385 + line 384, nos. 29 and 28; *Wells*, p. 144; *Wolf*, pp. 104–105

Bl. Boniface of Savoy, Archbishop of Canterbury

Boniface was born ca. 1207. His father was Thomas I, Count of Savoy, and his mother was Margaret of Geneva. Boniface was handsome enough to be nicknamed "the Absalom of Savoy," and he entered the Church at a very young age.

The daughters of his sister Beatrice of Savoy found husbands whose stature did no harm to Boniface's own career. Beatrice's daughter Margaret married St. Louis IX, King of France. Beatrice's daughter Eleanor married Henry III, King of England. The youngest daughter, also named Beatrice, married Charles I, Count of Anjou, King of Naples and Sicily, and Crusader.

After Boniface served as a prior at Mantua, then as an administrator of the diocese of Belley in Burgundy, and finally as the bishop of Valence, he was appointed in 1240 to succeed St. Edmund as the 46th archbishop of Canterbury. The subsequent deaths of two popes delayed his confirmation until 1243.

When Boniface first arrived in England in 1244, he found his archdiocese deeply in debt. He instituted several reforms which paid off these debts over the next 25 years. The necessary austerities made him very unpopular with many of the English clergy, however. During a visit to St. Paul's in London, for example, Boniface was attacked by the priests there and had to be rescued by his own bodyguards.

The royal relatives of Boniface had a much higher opinion of him. King Henry III of England appointed Boniface regent of England while he was abroad. He also took Boniface to France to assist him in negotiations there. When Henry's wife Eleanor and son Edward (the future Edward I) went to Spain in 1254 for Edward's marriage to Eleanor of Castile, Boniface went with them. In 1269, Boniface also set out with Edward on a crusade but died in Savoy on 14 July 1270 before he reached the Holy Land.

Personally, Boniface was extraordinarily kind to the poor, and he saved his archdiocese from financial ruin. He is buried with his ancestors in the monastery at Hautecombe.

His Line

Husband		Wife	
Thomas I, Count of Savoy (b. 20 May 1178 – md. 1196 – d. 1 March 1233)	+	**Margaret of Geneva** (b. ca. 1180 – md. 1196 – d. 13 April 1236)	
Raymond Berenger V, Count of Provence and Forcalquier (b. 1198 – md. Dec 1220 – d. 19 Aug 1245)	+	**Beatrice of Savoy**, Countess of Provence (b. 1198 – md. Dec 1220 – d. Dec 1266)	Beatrice's brother: ***Bl. Boniface of Savoy, Archbishop of Canterbury***

Henry III, King of England (b. 1 Oct 1207 – md. 14 Jan 1236 – d. 16 Nov 1272)	+	**Bl. Eleanor of Provence** (b. ca. 1223 – md. 14 Jan 1236 – d. 25 June 1291)

Sources: *Benedictine Monks*, p. 130; *Butler*, Vol. III, pp. 102–104; *Delaney and Tobin*, pp. 158–159; *Holweck*, p. 167; *NCE*, Vol. 2, p. 674; *Stuart:* line 93, nos. 27 and 26 + line 54, nos. 26 and 25; *Wagner*, p. 203; *Weis, AR:* line 133, nos. 26 and 27 + line 11, nos. 29 and 30; *Wells*, pp. 512 and 482

St. Boris the Passion-Bearer, Prince of Kiev

Boris was born around 990/994. St. Vladimir I "the Great," Grand Prince of Kiev and ruler of Kievan Rus was his father. Anna, daughter of the Byzantine Emperor Romanos II, was his mother.

From his youth, Boris was noted for his devotion to the new Christian faith that his father had made the state religion of Kievan Rus. When Boris was old enough to begin assuming state responsibilities, Vladimir made him the ruler of the province of Rostov, and Boris worked hard to convert pagans there.

Even while Vladimir was alive, some of his twelve sons had begun to fight with each other over who would inherit the kingdom. On July 15, 1015, Vladimir finally died, and his son Sviatpolk "the Accursed" decided to settle all questions of succession by murdering all of his brothers. The events that would make Boris a saint had thus been set into motion.

After fighting with the Pechenegs, Boris was returning to Kiev with his father's troops when riders from the city met him near the Alta River. They told him of Vladimir's death and Sviatpolk's seizure of power. They told him that men sent by Sviatpolk to kill Boris were on their way and would be arriving soon. The troops Boris was leading were outraged and were ready to start a civil war on the spot by going to war with Sviatpolk's men. Boris decided to avoid civil war by sacrificing his own life instead and sent his men away. He then went into his tent to pray and await his fate.

Late in the night of 23/24 July 1015, Sviatpolk's men finally arrived. They entered the tent of Boris and attacked him as he blessed them. Believing him to be dead, they threw his body in a wagon and headed for Kiev. Several hours later when they discovered that Boris was still breathing, they finished him off.

Civil war broke out anyway between Sviatpolk and most of the other sons of Vladimir and did not end until 1019, when Sviatpolk was routed by Boris's half-brother St. Jaroslav I Vladimirovich "the Wise," who became the next ruler of Kievan Rus.

A large number of miracles were attributed to Boris after his death. Jaroslav moved Boris's body to a specially constructed church in Vyshgorod. Called a "Passion-Bearer"—that is, an innocent man who accepts death in the unresisting spirit of Christ—Boris was one of the very first saints canonized by the Russian Church. He was so highly esteemed that his feast was celebrated six times a year. He is the patron saint of Moscow and is sometimes called "Romanus" after his Byzantine grandfather Romanus II. He is often pictured with his martyred brother St. Gleb.

His Line
St. Vladimir I Sviatoslavich "the Great," Grand Prince of Kiev and Novgorod (b. ca. 955 – d. 15 July 1015)

md. (3) **Rognieda of Polotsk**			md. (7) Anna, daughter of Romanus II, Emperor of Byzantium
Son of Vladimir and Rognieda:			
St. Yaroslav I Vladimirovich "the Wise," Grand Prince of Kiev (b. 978 – md. (2) Feb 1019 – d. 20 Feb 1054)	+	St. Ingegerd, Princess of Sweden (b. ca. 1001 – md. Feb 1019 – d. 10 Feb 1050)	Son of Vladimir and Anna: ***St. Boris, the Passion-Bearer***
St. Izyaslav I Yaroslavich, Grand Prince of Kiev (b. 1025 – md. ca. 1043 – slain 3 Oct 1078)	+	Gertrude (md. ca. 1043), daughter of Mieszko II, King of Poland	

[For the later generations that connect this line to the kings of England, see the line of St. Izyaslav I Yaroslavich, Grand Prince of Kiev in Part II.]

Sources: *Baring-Gould*, Vol. 10, pp. 75–76; *Benedictine Monks*, p. 613; *Bunson*, pp. 174–175; *Butler*, Vol. III, pp. 175–176; *Cruz*, pp. 102–105; *Delaney and Tobin*, p. 161; *Fedotov*, p. 72; *Guiley*, p. 52; *Holweck*, p. 168; *Klaniczay*, pp. 109–113 and Appendix B, Geneal. Table 2; *O'Malley*, pp. 90–91; *One Hundred Saints*, pp. 178-179; *Snodgrass*, p. 46; *Tucker*, Vol. II, pp. 731–732; *Weis, AR*, line 241, nos. 4, 5^2, and 6^2; *Wells*, pp. 328–330

St. Bova

Bova was the daughter of Sigebert (or Sigibert) I, King of Metz (Austrasia), and his wife Brunhilda, daughter of Athanagildo, King of the Visigoths.

After Bova became a nun, her brother St. Balderic founded the convent of St. Peter's in Rheims and made her its first abbess.

Her Line

Husband		Wife	
Sigebert I, King of Metz (Austrasia) (murdered 575)	+	**Brunhilda (or Brunechildis)**	
Recaredo (or Recared) I, King of the Visigoths in Spain (d. 601)	+	**Chlodesindis (or Clodoswindis)**	Chlodesindis' sister: ***St. Bova***
Suintila (or Suintilo), King of the Visigoths in Spain (deposed in 631)	+	Theodora, daughter of Sisebuto, King of the Visigoths in Spain	
Ervigio, King of the Visigoths in Spain (d. 687)	+	**Liubigotona**	

[For the later generations that connect this line to the kings of England, see the line of St. Florentina in Part III.]

Sources: *Baring-Gould*, Vol. 12, pp. 427–428 (under "Balderic"); *Benedictine Monks*, p. 132; *Bunson*, p. 175; *Delaney and Tobin*, p. 168; *Dunbar*, Vol. I, p. 130; *Holweck*, p. 169; *NCE*, Vol. 2, pp. 740–741; *Scherman, Birth of France*, frontispiece; *Tucker:* Vol. II, p. 526 + Vol. I, p. 79; *Wagner*, p. 188; *Wells*, p. 593. Also see ***fmg.ac>Projects>Medieval Lands>Medieval Lands – data by region>Iberia>Vandals, Suevi & Visigoths>Recaredo I 586–601, Liuva II 601–603***. In addition, see ***fmg.ac>Projects>Medieval Lands>Medieval Lands – data by region>Iberia>Vandals, Suevi & Visigoths>Suintila 621–633***.

St. Bruno the Great, Archbishop of Cologne

Bruno was born in 925 and was the son of Henry I "the Fowler," Duke of Saxony and Emperor of the West, and his wife St. Matilda of Ringelheim. From childhood, Bruno was devoted to learning and at age 4 was sent to the cathedral school at Utrecht.

When Henry I died in 936, Bruno's oldest brother Otto became the next Holy Roman Emperor. Appointments of Bruno to important posts in the state and the church soon followed. In 940, Bruno became Otto's confidential secretary and later his chancellor. In 950, Bruno was also ordained a priest and made the abbot of the monasteries at Lorsch and Corvey.

After Otto's son Liudolf and son-in-law Conrad started a rebellion against Otto in 951 that would last for four years, the emperor's dependence on Bruno only increased. He was appointed archbishop of Cologne in 953. After the rebellious Conrad was removed from his position as Duke of Lotharingia, Otto appointed Bruno to succeed him. Bruno thus became one of the most influential men in the empire, second only to his brother the emperor.

Otto's reliance on his youngest brother was not misplaced. Bruno was one of the most educated men in the realm. He was also a very capable statesman and a good man. He devoted himself to improving the lives of his flock. He founded many schools and also raised the standards of education for the clergy. He was a generous benefactor to many churches and monasteries and set a high example of personal goodness and devotion.

Bruno died on 11 October 965 and was buried in Cologne at the church of St. Pantaleon.

His Line

	Husband		Wife
	Henry I "the Fowler," Duke of Saxony and Emperor of the West (b. 876 – md. (2) 909 – d. 2 July 936)	+	**St. Matilda of Ringelheim** (b. ca. 890/900 – md. 909 – d. 14 March 968)
Otto I's brother: ***St. Bruno the Great, Archbishop of Cologne***	**Otto I "the Great,"** King of Germany and Italy and Emperor of the West (b. 23 Nov 912 – md. (2) 25 Dec 951 – d. 7 May 973)	+	St. Adelaide of Burgundy (b. 932 – md. (2) 25 Dec 951 – d. 16/17 Dec 999)
	Otto II, King of Italy and Emperor of the West (b. 955 – md. (2) 14 April 972 – d. 7 Dec 983)	+	St. Theophano Skleros (b. 956 – md. 14 April 972 – d. 15 Sept 991)

[For the later generations that connect this line to the kings of England, see the line of St. Adelaide of Burgundy in Part II.]

Sources: *BBKL*, Vol. 1, cols. 772–773; *Benedictine Monks*, pp. 136–137; *Bentley*, p. 200; *Bunson*, p. 180; *Butler*, Vol. IV, pp. 88–89; *CE*, Vol. III, pp. 13–14; *Delaney and Tobin*, p. 182; *Holweck*, p. 174; *Klaniczay*, Appendix B, Geneal. Table 3; *NCE*, Vol. 2, pp. 837–838; *O'Malley*, p. 42; *Stuart:* line 338, no. 36 + line 321, nos. 37 and 36 + line 237, nos. 37 and 36; *Weis, AR*, line 147, nos. 18 through 20; *Wells*, p. 270

St. Cado

Cado was the son of St. Geraint, King of Brittany, and his wife Enid. He was a man of the 400's and became Duke of Cornwall. He was a hero of the war against the West Saxons, who tried to conquer Cornwall during his lifetime.

His Line

	Husband		Wife
	St. Geraint, King of Brittany	+	**Enid**
Salamon's brother: ***St. Cado***	**St. Salamon I "the Handsome,"** King of Brittany (liv. in the 400's)	+	St. Gwen
	Audren, King of Brittany	+	N.N.
	Budic I, King of Brittany	+	N.N., a daughter of Corun

[For the later generations that connect this line to the kings of England, see the line of St. Cunedda Wledig in Part II.]

Sources: *Ashley*, pp. 117–118; *Baring-Gould*, Vol. 16, pp. 133 and 261–262; *Baring-Gould and Fisher*, Vol. 2, pp. 11–12; *Holweck*, pp. 176, 199, and 425 (under "Geraint"); *Stuart*, line 405, nos. 56 through 53

St. Canoc

Canoc was the son of St. Brychan of Brecknock. He was martyred at Merthyr-Cynog during a barbarian invasion. Several churches in Wales are dedicated to him.

Canoc is also known as Canog or Cynog.

His Line

Husband		Wife	
St. Brychan, ruler of Brecknock in South Wales (b. 480/490)	+	**N.N.**	
St. Gabran mac Domangart, King of Dalriada (b. ca. 500 – md. bef. 532 – d. ca. 559)	+	**St. Lleian** (md. bef. 532)	Lleian's brother: ***St. Canoc***
Aidan (or Aedan) mac Gabran (b. 532 – d. 606), crowned King of Dalriada by St. Columba of Iona	+	N.N.	

[For the later generations that connect this line to the kings of England, see the line of St. Brychan in Part II.]

Sources: *Ashley*, pp. 158 and 197; *Baring-Gould*, Vol. 16, pp. 279–280; *Benedictine Monks*, p. 147; *Bunson*, p. 188; *Delaney and Tobin*, p. 206; *Holweck*, pp. 188 and 250; *Stuart*, line 165, nos. 49 and 48; *Weis, AR*, line 170, nos. 4 and 5; *Wells*, p. 177

St. Christina

Christina was born around 1055 and was the daughter of Edward "the Exile," son of King Edmund "Ironside" of England, and his wife Agatha von Braunschweig. She was a sister of St. Margaret of Scotland.

Her family returned to Britain from their exile in Hungary while Christina was a child. By 1086 she was a nun at Romsey Abbey in Hampshire. At the abbey, she raised her niece Matilda of Scotland, who would marry Henry I of England.

Christina died before 1102.

Her Line

Husband		Wife	
Edward "the Exile" (or Edward "the Atheling") (b. 1016 – md. ca. 1043 – d. ca. 1057), son of Edmund "Ironside," King of England	+	**Agatha von Braunschweig** (b. ca. 1025 – md. ca. 1043 – d. aft. 1066)	
Malcolm III Canmore, King of Scotland (b. ca. 1031 – md. (2) 1068/1069 – d. in battle 13 Nov 1093 while besieging Alnwick Castle)	+	**St. Margaret of Scotland** (b. ca. 1045 – md. 1068/1069 – d. 16 Nov 1093)	Margaret's sister: ***St. Christina***
David I "the Saint," King of Scotland (b. ca. 1080 – md. 1113/1114 – d. 24 May 1153)	+	Matilda of Huntingdon (md. (2) 1113/1114 – d. 1130/1131)	

Sources: *Ashley*, p. 497; *Dunbar*, Vol. I, p. 176; *Holweck*, p. 209; *Parbury*, p. 25; *Ronay*, pp. 116, 165, and 169; *Stuart:* line 233, nos. 34 through 32 + line 72, nos. 31 and 30; *Weir*, p. 28; *Weis, AR*, line 1, nos. 20 through 22 + line 170, nos. 21 and 22; *Wells*, pp. 205 and 519–520; *WWH*, Vol. 10, p. 231

St. Cledwyn

Cledwyn was the son of St. Brychan, ruler of Brecknock. When Brychan died, Cledwyn succeeded him. He was a warrior prince who drove the Irish out of territories they had occupied in south Wales. Llangledwyn is named after him. He is also known as Clydwyn.

His Line

Husband		Wife	
St. Brychan, ruler of Brecknock in South Wales (b. 480/490)	+	**N.N.**	
St. Gabran mac Domangart, King of Dalriada (b. ca. 500 – md. bef. 532 – d. ca. 559)	+	**St. Lleian** (md. bef. 532)	Lleian's brother: ***St. Cledwyn***
Aidan (or Aedan) mac Gabran (b. 532 – d. 606), crowned King of Dalriada by St. Columba of Iona	+	N.N.	

[For the later generations that connect this line to the kings of England, see the line of St. Brychan in Part II.]

Sources: *Ashley*, pp. 158 and 197; *Baring-Gould*, Vol. 16, p. 287; *Benedictine Monks*, p. 168; *Bunson*, p. 211; *Delaney and Tobin*, pp. 183 (under "Brychan") and 255; *Holweck*, p. 221; *Stuart*, line 165, nos. 49 and 48; *Weis, AR*, line 170, nos. 4 and 5; *Wells*, p. 177

St. Conrad,
Bishop of Constance

Conrad was born around 905 and was the son of Henry, Count of Altdorf, and his wife Beata von Hohenwarth. Trained to be a priest, he was made bishop of Constance in 934. He restored several churches, built others, and gave his entire inheritance to be used for ecclesiastical purposes. He made three pilgrimages to Jerusalem and was a close friend of St. Ulric, Bishop of Augsburg.

Conrad died on 26 November 975. During the Reformation, all his relics except his head were thrown into Lake Constance. That relic was saved and is in the cathedral at Constance.

His Line

	Husband		Wife
	Henry, Count of Altdorf and in the Ammergau (b. ca. 883 – d. aft. 934)	+	**Beata (or Atha) von Hohenwarth** (d. aft. 975)
Rudolf I's Brother: ***St. Conrad, Bishop of Constance***	**Rudolph I**, Count of Altdorf (b. 905/910 – liv. 950)	+	(md. perhaps) Siburgis
	Rudolph II, Count of the Swabian Altdorf (b. ca. 927 – d. 985/990)	+	Itha (or Ida) von Oeningen
	Welf II, Count of Altdorf and in the Lechrain (b. ca. 965 – md. ca. 1015 – d. 10 March 1030)	+	Ermentrude of Luxemburg (b. ca. 1000 – md. ca. 1015 – d. 21 Aug 1057)
	Alberto Azzo II, Marchese d'Este (b. 997 – md. ca. 1035 – d. 20 Aug 1097)	+	**Kunigunde of Altdorf** (b. ca. 1020 – md. ca. 1035 – d. aft. 1055)
	Welf IV, Duke of Bavaria, Crusader (b. 1037 – md. (3) ca. 1071 – d. 9 Nov 1101 in Cyprus on a Crusade)	+	Judith of Flanders (b. 1033 – md. (2) ca. 1071 – d. 5 March 1094)
	Henry I "the Black," Duke of Bavaria (b. 1074 – md. 1095/1100 – d. 13 Dec 1126)	+	Ulfhild of Saxony (b. ca. 1071 – md. 1095/1100 – d. 29 Dec 1126)
	Frederick II von Hohenstaufen, Duke of Swabia (b. 1090 – md. 1121 – d. 4/6 April 1147)	+	**Judith of Bavaria** (b. ca. 1100 – md. 1121 – d. 22 Feb 1130/1135)

Frederick III Barbarosa, Duke of Swabia, Emperor of Germany and the West, Crusader (b. 1122 – md. 10/16 June 1156 – drowned 10 June 1190 while on the 3rd Crusade)	+	Beatrice of Burgundy (b. ca. 1145 – md. 10/16 June 1156 – d. 15 Nov 1184)
Philip von Hohenstaufen, Duke of Tuscany and Swabia and Emperor of Germany (b. 1176 – md. 25 May 1197 – murdered 21 June 1208)	+	Eirene (or Maria) Angelina (b. ca. 1181 – md. (2) 25 May 1197 – murdered 27 Aug 1208), daughter of Isaac II Angelos, Emperor of Byzantium

[For the later generations that connect this line to the kings of England, see the line of St. Boris I, Khan of the Bulgars in Part II.]

Sources: *Baring-Gould*, Vol. 14, pp. 547–548; *BBKL*, Vol. 4, cols. 416–417; *Benedictine Monks*, p. 177; *Butler*, Vol. IV, pp. 425–426; *Delaney*, p. 158; *Delaney and Tobin*, p. 277; *Guiley*, pp. 81–82; *Holweck*, p. 231; *NCE*, Vol. 4, p. 188; *Stuart:* line 29, nos. 37 through 33 + line 43, nos. 33 through 30 + line 40, nos. 30 and 29 + line 125, nos. 29 and 28; *Tucker*, Vol. I, pp. 56–57 and 341–342; *Warncke*, pp. 240–241; *Weis, AR:* line 166, nos. 23 through 25 + line 45, nos. 25[1], 26, and 27; *Wells*, pp. 57–58 and 271–272

Bl. Conrad of Bavaria

Conrad was born in 1105 and was the son of Henry I "the Black," Duke of Bavaria, and his wife Ulfhild of Saxony. Conrad studied for the priesthood, but after both his parents died in 1126, he decided to become a Cistercian monk at the abbey of Clairvaux, which was led by St. Bernard at the time.

Several years later in 1151 he received Bernard's permission to go live as a hermit in the Holy Land. His labors of charity and personal austerities there ruined him physically. Unsettled conditions in Palestine and his own failing strength caused him to quit the Holy Land in 1153 and begin making his way back to Europe. By the time he reached the Italian port city of Molfetta on the Adriatic, he could go no further. He spent his final days in Molfetta and died there on 17 March 1154.

Known in Italian as "San Corrado," he became the patron saint of Molfetta. His relics are in a silver shrine there in the cathedral of San Corrado.

His Line

Husband		Wife	
Henry I "the Black," Duke of Bavaria (b. 1074 – md. 1095/1100 – d. 13 Dec 1126)	+	**Ulfhild of Saxony** (b. ca. 1071 – md. 1095/1100 – d. 29 Dec 1126)	
Frederick II von Hohenstaufen, Duke of Swabia (b. 1090 – md. 1121 – d. 4/6 April 1147)	+	**Judith of Bavaria** (b. ca. 1100 – md. 1121– d. 22 Feb 1130/1135)	Judith's brother: ***Bl. Conrad of Bavaria***
Frederick III Barbarosa, Duke of Swabia, Emperor of Germany and the West, Crusader (b. 1122 – md. 10/16 June 1156 – drowned 10 June 1190 while on the 3rd Crusade)	+	Beatrice of Burgundy (b. ca. 1145 – md. 10/16 June 1156 – d. 15 Nov 1184)	
Philip von Hohenstaufen, Duke of Tuscany and Swabia and Emperor of Germany (b. 1176 – md. 25 May 1197 – murdered 27 Aug 1208)	+	Eirene (or Maria) Angelina (b. ca. 1181 – md. (2) 25 May 1197 – murdered 27 August 1208), daughter of Isaac II Angelos, Emperor of Byzantium	

[For the later generations that connect this line to the kings of England, see the line of St. Boris I, Khan of the Bulgars in Part II.]

Sources: *BBKL*, Vol. 4, cols. 384–385; *Benedictine Monks*, p. 176; *Butler*, Vol. I, pp. 337–338; *Delaney*, p. 158; *Delaney and Tobin*, p. 277; *Holweck*, p. 231; *NCE*, Vol. 4, pp. 187–188; *Stuart:* line 43, nos. 31 and 30 + line 40, nos. 30 and 29 + line 125, nos. 29 and 28; *Tucker*, Vol. I, pp. 56–57 and 341–342; *Weis, AR:* line 166, nos. 24 and 25 + line 45, nos. 25[1], 26, and 27; *Wells*, pp. 57–58 and 271–272

Bl. Constance

Constance was the daughter of Bela IV, King of Hungary, and his wife Maria Laskarina. Around 1251/1252, Constance married Leo I, Duke of Galicia.

Constance is also known as Konstanza. She was a sister of St. Cunegund, St. Margaret of Hungary, and Bl. Yolande of Hungary.

Her Line

	Husband		Wife
	Bela IV, King of Hungary (b. 1206 – md. 1218 – d. 3 May 1270)	+	**Maria Laskarina** (b. ca. 1206 – md. 1218 – d. 1270), daughter of Theodore I Lascaris, Emperor of Byzantium
Stephen's sister: ***Bl. Constance***	**Stephen V**, King of Hungary (b. Dec 1239 – md. 1253 – d. 1 Aug 1272)	+	Elizabeth (md. 1253 – d. aft. 1290), daughter of Kuthen, Khan of the Kumans
	Charles II "le Boiteux" ("the Lame"), King of Naples and Prince of Salerno (b. 1254 – md. 1270 – d. 5 June 1309)	+	**Maria** (b. ca. 1257 – md. 1270 – murdered 25 March 1323)

[For the later generations that connect this line to the kings of England, see the line of St. Adalbero, Bishop of Wuerzburg in Part III.]

Sources: *Butler*, Vol. II, p. 550 (under "Jolenta"); *Klaniczay*, p. 208 and Appendix B, Geneal. Table 8; *Stuart*, line 78, nos. 27 through 25; *Weis, AR*, line 103, nos. 29 through 31; *Wells*, pp. 309 and 421

St. Cunegund, Empress of the Holy Roman Empire

Cunegund was born around 978 and was the daughter of Siegfried, Count of Luxemburg, and his wife Hedwig. Around 998, she married Henry IV, Duke of Bavaria. In 1002, Henry became king of the Germans, and in 1014 as Henry II he became the next emperor of the Holy Roman Empire. On both occasions, Cunegund was also crowned, first as queen and then as empress.

Although Henry and Cunegund never had children, they were an extraordinarily close couple. Cunegund was Henry's closest adviser. She frequently helped Henry make decisions in affairs of state and also represented him during his absences. The one surviving letter written by Cunegund shows that she was an extraordinarily well-educated woman whose advice on many subjects would be very welcome.

Henry and Cunegund were also profoundly spiritual people who did much for the church. They created the new see of Bamberg and built the cathedral there, and Cunegund donated her dowry for its support. In addition, Cunegund founded a Benedictine convent in Kaufungen.

After Henry died in 1024, Cunegund became a nun and entered her own convent at Kaufungen. In her final years, she worked there as a nurse and died on 3 March 1039/1040. She was buried next to Henry in the cathedral they built in Bamberg.

Henry and Cunegund both became saints, with Cunegund becoming a patron saint of Luxemburg.

Her Line

	Husband		Wife
	Siegfried, Count of Luxemburg and in the Moselgau (b. ca. 922 – md. ca. 950 – d. 998)	+	**Hedwig** (md. ca. 950 – d. 13 Dec 992)
Frederick's sister: ***St. Cunegund, Empress of the Holy Roman Empire***	**Frederick I,** Count of Luxemburg and in the Moselgau (b. ca. 965 – md. aft. 985 – d. 6 Oct 1019)	+	Ermentrude von Gleiburg (md. aft. 985)
	Baldwin IV de Lille "the Bearded," Count of Flanders and Valenciennes (b. ca. 980 – md. (1) ca. 1012 – d. 30 May 1035)	+ +	**Ogive (or Otgiva) of Luxemburg** (b. ca. 995 – md. ca. 1012 – d. 21 Feb 1030)

Baldwin V de Lille, Count of Flanders (b. ca. 1013 – md. 1028 – d. 1 Sept 1067)	+	St. Adela (md. (2) 1028 – d. 8 Jan 1078/1079), daughter of Robert II, King of France
William I the Conqueror, Duke of Normandy and King of England (b. 1027/1028 – md. 1053 – d. 9 Sept 1087)	+	**Mathilde of Flanders** (b. 1032 – md. 1053 – d. 1083)

Sources: *Baring-Gould*, Vol. III, pp. 52–54; *BBKL*, Vol. 4, cols. 817–820; *Benedictine Monks*, p. 185; *Bentley*, p. 45; *Bunson*, p. 229; *Butler*, Vol. I, pp. 470–471; *Chervin*, p. 182–183; *Delaney*, pp. 164–165; *Delaney and Tobin*, p. 302; *Dunbar*, Vol. I, pp. 210–211; *Giorgi*, pp. 140–141; *Holboeck*, pp. 133–138; *Holweck*, p. 247; *Klaniczay*, Appendix B, Geneal. Table 3; *NCE*, Vol. 8, pp. 270–271; *O'Malley*, pp. 25–26; *Snodgrass*, p. 63; *Stuart:* line 353, nos. 36 through 34 + line 141, nos. 33 through 31; *Tucker:* Vol. II, pp. 490–491 + Vol. I, pp. 314–315; *Warncke*, pp. 84-85; *Weis, AR:* line 143, nos. 19 and 20 + line 162, nos. 21 through 23; *Wells*, pp. 360 and 248; *WWH*, Vol. 4, pp. 239-240

St. Cunegund,
Patron Saint of Poland and Lithuania

Cunegund was born around 1224 and was the daughter of Bela IV, King of Hungary, and his wife Maria Laskarina. In 1239, she married Boleslaus V, King of Poland. She and Boleslaus agreed to live in a perpetually unconsummated marriage, and for this reason her husband is also known as Boleslaus "the Chaste."

In 1241, Mongol invaders devastated Poland. Afterwards, Cunegund devoted herself to the care of the poor and the sick, to the rebuilding of churches and hospitals, and to the ransoming of Christian captives.

After Boleslaus died in 1279, Cunegund became a nun and entered a convent she had founded at Sandecz. She performed the most menial tasks there and was made abbess very much against her wishes.

When the Mongols invaded Poland again in 1287, Cunegund and her nuns left Sandecz and took refuge in the castle of Pyenin. The Mongols besieged the castle, but after Cunegund prayed for deliverance, they departed.

Cunegund died on 24 July 1292 and in 1715 was made the patron saint of Poland and Lithuania.

Cunegund is also known as Cunegundis or Kinga.

Her Line

<table>
<tr><td></td><td><u>Husband</u></td><td></td><td><u>Wife</u></td></tr>
<tr><td></td><td>Bela IV, King of Hungary (b. 1206 – md. 1218 – d. 3 May 1270)</td><td>+</td><td>Maria Laskarina (b. ca. 1206 – md. 1218 – d. 1270), daughter of Theodore I Lascaris, Emperor of Byzantium</td></tr>
<tr><td>Stephen's sister: St. Cunegund, Patron Saint of Poland and Lithuania</td><td>Stephen V, King of Hungary (b. Dec 1239 – md. 1253 – d. 1 Aug 1272)</td><td>+</td><td>Elizabeth (md. 1253 – d. aft. 1290), daughter of Kuthen, Khan of the Kumans</td></tr>
<tr><td></td><td>Charles II "le Boiteux" ("the Lame"), King of Naples and Prince of Salerno (b. 1254 – md. 1270 – d. 5 June 1309)</td><td>+</td><td>Maria (b. ca. 1257 – md. 1270 – murdered 25 March 1323)</td></tr>
</table>

[For the later generations that connect this line to the kings of England, see the line of St. Adalbero, Bishop of Wuerzburg in Part III.]

Sources: *Benedictine Monks*, p. 422; *Bunson*, p. 477; *Butler*, Vol. III, p. 178; *Delaney*, p. 165; *Delaney and Tobin*, p. 302; *Dunbar*, Vol. I, pp. 211–213; *Holboeck*, pp. 215–216; *Holweck*, p. 586; *Klaniczay*, Appendix B, Geneal. Table 8; *O'Malley*, p. 93; *Stuart*, line 78, nos. 27 through 25; *Weis, AR*, line 103, nos. 29 through 31; *Wells*, pp. 309 and 421; *WWH*, Vol. 4, p. 239

St. Cuthburga

Cuthburga was the daughter of Cenred, a war leader in Somerset. St. Ina, King of Wessex, was her brother, and St. Quenburga was her sister.

Around 695, Cuthburga married Aldfrith, the first scholar-king of Northumbria. Some scholars have suggested that he was the author of *Beowulf.* What is certain is that he encouraged art and scholarship and that he turned the monasteries of Northumbria into the greatest seats of learning in England.

A few years before Aldfrith died in 704, Cuthburga became a nun and entered the convent at Barking. Later she and her sister St. Quenburga founded the abbey of Wimborne in Dorset.

Cuthburga was hard on herself but kind to others and died in 725.

Her Line

	Husband		Wife
	Cenred, a war leader in Somerset (liv. 644–694)	+	**N.N.**
Ingild's sister: ***St. Cuthburga***	**Ingild** (b. ca. 680 – d. 718)	+	N.N.
	Eoppa	+	N.N.
	Eafa (b. ca. 732)	+	N.N.
	Eahlmund (or Edmund), King of Kent (b. ca. 758 – d. 786)	+	N.N., a daughter of Aethelbert II, King of Kent

[For the later generations that connect this line to the kings of England, see the line of St. Aethelbert I, King of Kent in Part II.]

Sources: *Ashley*, pp. 285–286 and 298; *Baring-Gould*, Vol. 9, p. 400; *BBKL*, Vol. 15, col. 452; *Benedictine Monks*, p. 186; *Bunson*, p. 231; *Butler*, Vol. III, pp. 481–482; *Delaney*, p. 166; *Delaney and Tobin*, p. 304; *Dunbar*, Vol. I, p. 214; *Holweck*, pp. 248–249; *Kirby*, pp. 101, 103, and 181; *NCE*, Vol. 4, p. 554; *O'Malley*, pp. 72 and 92–93; *Parbury*, pp. 28–29; *Snodgrass*, pp. 63–64; *Stuart*, line 233, nos. 46 through 42; *Weis, AR*, line 1, nos. 8 through 12; *Wells*, p. 203; *Williamson*, pp. 209 (under "Ine") and 360; *Yorke*, pp. 144–145

St. Cybi

Cybi was born around 490 and was the son of St. Salamon I, King of Brittany, and his wife St. Gwen. Since St. Gwen was a sister of St. Non, Cybi was a first cousin of St. David of Wales.

Around 542, Cybi went to Anglesey in Wales. Near Holyhead, he founded a monastery called in Welsh "Caer Gybi" or "Cybi's Fort." He became its abbot and died there on 8 November 554.

Cybi's shrine in his monastery became a place of pilgrimage. He became one of the most venerated saints in Wales and is the patron saint of several towns there. There are also holy wells dedicated to him.

His Line

	Husband		Wife
	St. Salamon I "the Handsome," King of Brittany (liv. in the 400's)	+	**St. Gwen**
Audren's brother: ***St. Cybi***	**Audren**, King of Brittany	+	N.N.
	Budic I, King of Brittany	+	N.N., a daughter of Corun

[For the later generations that connect this line to the kings of England, see the line of St. Cunedda Wledig in Part II.]

Sources: *Baring-Gould*, Vol. 16, p. 279; *Baring-Gould and Fisher*, Vol. 2, pp. 202–215; *Benedictine Monks*, p. 184; *Bunson*, p. 231; *Butler*, Vol. IV, pp. 295–296; *CS*, pp. 663–664; *Delaney*, p. 166; *Delaney and Tobin*, p. 304; *Holweck*, p. 249; *Parbury*, pp. 53–54 (under "St. Gwen"); *Stuart*, line 405, nos. 55 through 53

St. Cynfarch Gul

Cynfarch Gul was the son of Meirchion Gul, king of Rheged. He married St. Nefyn, daughter of St. Brychan, the ruler of Brecknock.

Cynfarch became a leader of the northern Britons. When his father Meirchion died around 535, the kingdom was divided between Cynfarch and his brother Elidir. Cynfarch was also the father of the famous Urien of Rheged.

Cynfarch devoted the last years of his life to religion. Churches in Wales are dedicated to him.

Cynfarch Gul is also known as Cynfarch Oer.

His Line

	Husband		Wife
	Meirchion Gul ap Gwrwst Ledlum, King of Rheged (b. ca. 470 – d. ca. 535)	+	**N.N.**
Elidir Lydanwyn's Brother: ***St. Cynfarch Gul***	**Elidir Lydanwyn ap Meirchion Gul** (b. ca. 500)	+	Gwawr, a daughter of St. Brychan of Brecknock
	Llywarch Hen ap Elidir Lydanwyn (b. ca. 530)	+	N.N.
	Dwg ap Llywarch Hen (b. ca. 570)	+	N.N.
	Gwair ap Dwg (b. ca. 600)	+	N.N.
	Tegid ap Gwair (b. ca. 630)	+	N.N.
	Alcwn ap Tegid (b. ca. 670)	+	N.N.
	Sandde ab Alcwin (b. ca. 700)	+	Celeinion ferch Tudwal
	Elidir ap Sandde (b. ca. 730)	+	N.N.
	Gwriad ab Elidir (b. ca. 770)	+	Nest ferch Cadell
	Merfyn Frych "the Freckled" (d. 844)	+	Esyllt ferch Cynan Dindaethwy
	Rhodri Mawr "the Great," King of Wales (d. 878)	+	md. (1) Angharad ferch Meurig

[For the later generations that connect this line to the kings of England, see the line of St. Arddun "Benasgell" in Part II.]

Sources: *Baring-Gould*, Vol. 16, p. 272; *Baring-Gould and Fisher*, Vol. 2, pp. 241–242; *Benedictine Monks*, pp. 187 and 422; *Boyer:* nos. 6, 8, 10, 12, 14, 16, 18, 20, 22, and 24 on pp. 64–66 + nos. 1 and 2 on pp. 281-282; *Holweck*, p. 249

St. Cynfran

Cynfran was the son of St. Brychan of Brecknock. In Wales, he is the patron saint of the village of Llysfaen in Conwy County. A church there was founded by him, and a holy well is dedicated to him.

His Line

Husband		Wife	
St. Brychan, ruler of Brecknock in South Wales (b. 480/490)	+	**N.N.**	
St. Gabran mac Domangart, King of Dalriada (b. ca. 500 – md. bef. 532 – d. ca. 559)	+	**St. Lleian** (md. bef. 532)	Lleian's brother: ***St. Cynfran***
Aidan (or Aedan) mac Gabran (b. 532 – d. 606), crowned King of Dalriada by St. Columba of Iona	+	N.N.	

[For the later generations that connect this line to the kings of England, see the line of St. Brychan in Part II.]

Sources: *Ashley*, pp. 158 and 197; *Baring-Gould*, Vol. 16, p. 303; *Benedictine Monks*, p. 187; *Bunson*, p. 231; *Delaney and Tobin*, p. 304; *Holweck*, p. 250; *Stuart*, line 165, nos. 49 and 48; *Weis, AR*, line 170, nos. 4 and 5; *Wells*, p. 177

St. Cyngar

Cyngar was born around 470 and was the son of St. Geraint, King of Brittany, and his wife Enid.

Cyngar travelled widely in Brittany, England, and Wales and founded several churches. In Llangefni on the Isle of Anglesey in Wales, the last church he founded is called St. Cyngar's Church.

Cyngar died around 530 and was the brother of St. Cado, St. Jestin, and St. Salamon I "the Handsome."

His Line

	Husband		Wife
	St. Geraint, King of Brittany	+	**Enid**
Salamon's brother: ***St. Cyngar***	**St. Salamon I "the Handsome,"** King of Brittany (liv. in the 400's)	+	St. Gwen
	Auden, King of Brittany	+	N.N.
	Budic I, King of Brittany	+	N.N., a daughter of Corun

[For the later generations that connect this line to the kings of England, see the line of St. Cunedda Wledig in Part II.]

Sources: *Ashley*, p. 117; *Baring-Gould*, Vol. 16, pp. 133 and 261; *Baring-Gould and Fisher*, Vol. 2, pp. 248–253; *Holweck*, pp. 250 and 425 (under "Geraint"); *Stuart*, line 405, nos. 56 through 53

St. Dunawd "Fawr"

Dunawd was the son of St. Pabo "Post Prydyn," a ruler of northern Britain. He married St. Dwywai ferch Lleenog.

Dunawd's nickname "Fawr" means "the Great." Fighting alongside his father, he defended Pabo's kingdom several times. Dunawd has also been identified as fighting alongside his cousins Gwrgi and Peredur.

Like his father, Dunawd became a monk after the family moved to north Wales. About four miles southeast of Wrexham, Dunawd founded the large monastery of Bangor-is-y-Coed and became its first abbot.

Dunawd died around 535. He is the father of Saints Cynwyl, Deinol (or Deiniol), and Gwarthan.

Dunawd is also known as Dunod or Dinooth.

His Line

Husband		Wife	
St. Pabo "Post Prydyn" (the Pillar of Northern Britain) (b. ca. 430 – d. ca. 510)	+	**N.N.**	
St. Brochwel Ysgithrog, King of Powys (b. ca. 502 – d. ca. 560)	+	**St. Arddun "Benasgell"**	Arddun's brother: ***St. Dunawd "Fawr"***
Cynan Garwyn	+	N.N.	

[For the later generations that connect this line to the kings of England, see the line of St. Arddun "Benasgell" in Part II.]

Sources: *Ashley*, pp. 96 and 106; *Baring-Gould*, Vol. 16, pp. 136, 217 (under "Cynwyl"), and 272; *Boyer*, no. 3 on p. 63; *CE*, Vol. IV, p. 798; *Holweck*, pp. 102 (under "Arddun Benasgell"), 262 (under "Daniel (Deinol)"), 298 (under "Dunawd"), and 299 (under "Dwywai"); *Rees*, pp. 101, 103

St. Dwynwen

Dwynwen was a daughter of St. Brychan of Brecknock. She became a nun and moved to an island in the Welsh county of Anglesey which is known today as Llanddwyn Island. Parts of the church she founded there are still standing today. Before the Reformation, this church was one of the most popular shrines in Wales. Other churches in Wales and Cornwall are also dedicated to her.

As the patron saint of true lovers, Dwynwen is still known and prayed to today by people having difficulties in love. She is also said to have healed the sick, both humans and animals. She is remembered as a model of cheer and kindness, and the saying "Nothing wins hearts like cheerfulness" is attributed to her.

Her Line

Husband		Wife	
St. Brychan, ruler of Brecknock in South Wales (b. 480/490)	+	**N.N.**	
St. Gabran mac Domangart, King of Dalriada (b. ca. 500 – md. bef. 532 – d. ca. 559)	+	**St. Lleian** (md. bef. 532)	Lleian's sister: ***St. Dwynwen***
Aidan (or Aedan) mac Gabran (b. 532 – d. 606), crowned King of Dalriada by St. Columba of Iona	+	N.N.	

[For the later generations that connect this line to the kings of England, see the line of St. Brychan in Part II.]

Sources: *Ashley*, pp. 158 and 197; *Baring-Gould and Fisher*, Vol. 2, pp. 387–392; *Benedictine Monks*, p. 217; *Bunson*, p. 264; *Delaney and Tobin*, p. 183*; *Holweck*, pp. 174* and 299; *Parbury*, p. 31; *Snodgrass*, p. 71; *Stuart*, line 165, nos. 49 and 48; *Weis, AR*, line 170, nos. 4 and 5; *Wells*, p. 177 (references marked with a * are alphabetized under "Brychan")

St. Eanswitha

Eanswitha was the daughter of Eadbald, King of Kent, and his wife St. Emma.

From infancy, Eanswitha enjoyed prayer. She refused to marry a pagan Northumbrian prince, became a nun, founded a convent in 630, and became its first abbess. She died there around 640. Many legends about her miraculous powers were current in England during the Middle Ages.

Her convent was destroyed by the Danes and refounded as a monastery in 1095. Part of it was later undermined and swallowed by the sea. The church of Saints Mary and Eanswitha in Folkestone, where her relics are located, is its successor.

Eanswitha is also known as Eanswida and Eanswythe.

Her Line

	Husband		Wife
	Eadbald, King of Kent (md. (2) ca. 618 – d. 640)	+	**St. Emma** (md. ca. 618), daughter of Clothaire II, King of Neustria and the Franks
Erconbert's sister: ***St. Eanswitha***	**Erconbert (or Eorconbeorht)**, King of Kent (b. ca. 624 – md. ca. 640 – d. 14 July 664)	+	St. Sexburga (md. ca. 640 – d. 6 July 699)
	Egbert, King of Kent (b. ca. 641 – d. 4 July 673)	+	N.N.
	Wihtread, King of Kent (d. 23 April 725)	+	N.N.
	Eadbert, King of Kent (d. 748)	+	N.N.

[For the later generations that connect this line to the kings of England, see the line of St. Aethelbert I, King of Kent in Part II.]

Sources: *Baring-Gould*, Vol. 9, pp. 389–390; *Benedictine Monks*, p. 219; *Bunson*, p. 265; *Butler*, Vol. III, pp. 545–546; *Delaney*, p. 189; *Delaney and Tobin*, p. 359; *Dunbar*, Vol. I, p. 248; *Holweck*, p. 299; *Parbury*, p. 36; *Stuart*, line 233A, nos. 47 through 43; *Williamson*, p. 359; *Yorke*, p. 36

St. Ebba "the Elder"

Ebba was born around 615 and was the daughter of Aethelfrith, King of Bernicea and Northumbria. She was the half-sister of Saints Oswy and Oswald.

After her father was deposed, Ebba and her brothers and sisters took refuge in Scotland. After refusing offers of marriage, Ebba decided to become a nun. She built two monasteries, the first at Ebchester and the second at Coldingham, where she became the abbess. She was a close friend of St. Cuthbert of Lindisfarne.

Ebba died on 25 August 683. In the eleventh century, her relics were moved to Durham.

		Her Line The three marriages of **Aethelfrith**, King of Bernicea and Northumbria	
md. (1) **Bebba**		md. (2) Acha, daughter of Aella, King of Northumbria	md. (3) N.N.
One of the children of Aethelfrith and (1):		Two of the children of Aethelfrith and (2):	One of the children of Aethelfrith and (3):
		St. Oswald, King of Northumbria and St. Oswy, King of Northumbria	***St. Ebba "the Elder"***
Eanfrith, King of Bernicea (killed in battle in April 635/636 after ruling for only 18 months)	+	N.N., daughter of Eochaid Buide, King of the Picts	
Beli, King of Strathclyde (d. by 641)	+	**N.N.**, a sister of Talorcam (I), King of the Picts	
Ainftech (or Entfidach) (d. 693)	+	**N.N.**, a daughter of Beli	
Eochaid II "Crooked Nose," King of Dalriada (killed in battle ca. 697 after ruling ca. 3 years)	+	**Spondana**, a Pictish princess	
Eochaid III, King of Dalriada (d. 733)	+	N.N.	
Aed Find "the White," King of Dalriada (liv. 778)	+	N.N.	

[For the later generations that connect this line to the kings of England, see the line of St. Brychan in Part II.]

Sources: *Ashley:* pp. 270 (which shows St. Ebba "the Elder" as the child of Aethelfrith's second wife) and 279 + pp. 166 and 175 + pp. 185 and 189 + pp. 166 and 202 + pp. 195 and 203–205; *Baring-Gould,* Vol. 9, pp. 280–284 and Vol. 16, p. 154; *BBKL,* Vol. 17, cols. 285-286; *Benedictine Monks*, p. 220; *Bunson*, p. 266; *Butler*, Vol. III, p. 402; *CS*, pp. 485–486; *Delaney*, p. 189; *Delaney and Tobin*, p. 359; *Dunbar*, Vol. I, pp. 248–250; *HBC*, pp. 4–5; *Holweck*, p. 300; *NCE*, Vol. 5, pp. 25–26; *O'Malley*, pp. 73 and 97; *Parbury*, pp. 31–33; *Snodgrass*, p. 72; *Stuart:* line 406, nos. 51 through 49 + line 341, nos. 49 through 47 + line 165, nos. 44 through 42; *Weis, AR*, line 170, nos. 9 and 10; *Wells*, pp. 435 (which also shows St. Ebba "the Elder" as the child of Aethelfrith's second wife), 469, 541, 469, and 177; *Williamson*, p. 364

St. Edburga of Winchester

Edburga was born around 920 and was the daughter of Edward "the Elder," King of England, and his 3rd wife Eadgifu. She was educated at Nunnaminster Abbey in Winchester, which had been founded by her grandmother St. Eahlswith. When she was old enough, Edburga became a nun there.

Edburga was famous for her charity, humility, and miracles. She was revered even while she was still alive and died at Nunnaminster on 15 June 960. Most of her relics were later moved to Pershore Abbey in Worcestershire. Although it was very popular with medieval pilgrims, her shrine at Pershore disappeared during the Reformation.

Her Line

	Husband		Wife
	Edward "the Elder," King of England (b. 875 – md. (3) 919 – d. 924)	+	**Eadgifu** (md. 919 – d. 961)
Edmund's sister: ***St. Edburga of Winchester***	**Edmund I "the Magnificent,"** King of England (b. ca. 920 – murdered 26 May 946)	+	md. (1) St. Elgiva (d. 944)
	St. Edgar "the Peaceful," King of England (b. 943 – md. (2) ca. 964/965 – d. 8 July 975)	+	Elfrida (b. ca. 945 – md. (2) ca. 964/965 – d. ca. 1000), daughter of Ordgar the Ealdorman

Sources: *Ashley*, pp. 473 and 791; *Baring-Gould*, Vol. 16, p. 235; *Benedictine Monks*, p. 221; *Bunson*, p. 267; *Butler*, Vol. II, pp. 548–549; *Delaney*, p. 190; *Delaney and Tobin*, p. 362; *Dunbar*, Vol. I, p. 251; *HBC*, p. 24; *Holweck*, p. 302; *Parbury*, p. 34; *Stuart*, line 233, nos. 38 through 36; *Tucker*, Vol. I, pp. 281–283; *Weir*, pp. 11–20; *Weis, AR*, line 1, nos. 16 through 18; *Wells*, p. 204; *WWH*, Vol. 5, p. 37

St. Edith of Polesworth

Edith was the daughter of Egbert, king of Wessex, and his wife Redburga. She became a nun and was made the first abbess of Polesworth Abbey in Warwickshire. She died on 15 March 871 and is buried at the abbey.

Her Line

	Husband		Wife
	Egbert, King of Wessex (b. 775 – d. 4 Feb 839)	+	**Redburga (or Raedburh)** (b. ca. 788)
Aethelwulf's sister: ***St. Edith of Polesworth***	**Aethelwulf**, King of Wessex and King of England (b. ca. 806 – d. 13 Jan 858)	+	md. (1) Osburh (b. ca. 810 – d. aft. 876)
	St. Alfred "the Great," King of Wessex (b. 849 – md. 868 – d. 26 Oct 899)	+	St. Eahlswith of Mercia (b. ca. 852 – md. 868 – d. 904)

Sources: *Ashley*, pp. 313–316; *HBC*, p. 23; *Dunbar*, Vol. I, p. 252; *Holweck*, p. 302; *Stuart*, line 233, nos. 41 through 39; *Tucker*, Vol. I, pp. 280–281; *Weir*, pp. 3–6 and 9–11; *Weis, AR*, line 1, nos. 13 through 15; *Williamson*, pp. 126–127; *WWH*, Vol. 13, p. 145 (under "Redburga")

St. Edith of Wilton

Edith was born in 962 and was the child of St. Edgar the Peaceful, King of England, and an Anglo-Saxon girl named Wulfthryth (or Wulfrida), whom he took as a mistress. After Edith was born, Wulfthryth became a nun, entered a convent at Wilton, and became St. Wulfthryth. Given Edgar's positive relationship with Edith as she grew up, the occasional allegation that Edith was conceived when Edgar raped a nun whom he had carried off from a convent at Wilton is unconvincing.

Wulfthryth raised Edith in her convent at Wilton. When Edgar died, Edith became a nun too and succeeded her mother as the abbess at Wilton.

Edith declined all larger responsibilities. She was offered the governance of three other abbeys and refused it. When her brother St. Edward the Martyr King of England was murdered, Edith was offered the throne but refused it too. She did build the Church of St. Denis in Wilton.

Edith had the gift of prophecy. It is said she foretold the murder of her brother St. Edward the Martyr. She is credited with other prophecies and also with healings.

After spending her entire life at Wilton, Edith died on 16 September 984 at the age of 22. Veneration of her extended well past her own time. Wilton was a place of pilgrimage until well into the 15th century.

<table>
<tr><td></td><td>Her Line
St. Edgar "the Peaceful,"
King of England (b. 943 – d. 8 July 975)</td><td></td><td></td></tr>
<tr><td>daughter of Edgar and his mistress St. Wulfthryth: ***St. Edith of Wilton***</td><td></td><td></td><td>Edgar md. (2) ca. 964/965 **Elfrida** (b. ca. 945 – md. (2) ca. 964/965 – d. ca. 1000), daughter of Ordgar the Ealdorman</td></tr>
<tr><td></td><td>son of Edgar and his second wife Elfrida:
Aethelred II "the Redeless," King of England (b. 968 – md. (1) 985 – d. 1016)</td><td>+</td><td>Aelfgifu (or Elgiva or Alfflaed) (b. ca. 968 – md. 985), daughter of Thored (or Thorod or Torin) of Northumbria</td></tr>
<tr><td></td><td>**Edmund "Ironside,"** King of England (b. 989 – md. (2) August 1015 – d. 30 Nov 1016)</td><td>+</td><td>Ealdgyth (md. (2) August 1015), daughter of Morcar, High Reeve of Northumbria</td></tr>
</table>

Sources: *Baring-Gould*, Vol. 10, pp. 269–271; *BBKL*, Vol. 17, col. 305; *Benedictine Monks*, p. 222; *Bunson*, p. 268; *Butler*, Vol. III, p. 571; *Chervin*, pp. 5–6; *Delaney*, p. 190; *Delaney and Tobin*, p. 363; *Dunbar*, Vol. I, pp. 252–253; *HBC*, p. 27; *Holweck*, p.

303; *Parbury*, pp. 38–39; *Snodgrass*, p. 73; *Stuart*, line 233, nos. 36 through 34; *Weir*, pp. 19–24 and 27–29; *Weis, AR*, line 1, nos. 18 through 20; *Wells*, pp. 204–205; *Williamson*, p. 107; *WWH*, Vol. 5, p. 55

St. Edmund, King of the Scottish Lowlands

Edmund was born around 1071 and was the son of Malcolm III Canmore, King of Scotland, and his wife St. Margaret.

Malcolm died in 1093, and Edmund became king of all of the Lowlands south of the Clyde in November 1094. His uncle Donald became the ruler of the Highlands.

This arrangement lasted until late in 1097, when Edmund and Donald were both deposed by Edmund's brother Edgar, who was supported by William II of England. Donald was imprisoned and mutilated. Edmund became a monk, was briefly imprisoned, and then was sent to Montague Abbey in Somerset.

Edmund never left the abbey. He practiced great austerities there, died at an unknown date, and is buried somewhere on its grounds.

His Line

Husband		Wife	
Malcolm III Canmore, King of Scotland (b. ca. 1031 – md. (2) 1068/1069 – d. in battle 13 Nov 1093 while besieging Alnwick Castle)	+	**St. Margaret of Scotland** (b. ca. 1045 – md. 1068/1069 – d. 16 Nov 1093)	
Henry I "Beauclerc," King of England (b. 1068 – md. (1) 11 Nov 1100 – d. 1 Dec 1135)	+	**Mathilda** (b. 1079 – md. 11 Nov 1100 – d. 1 May 1118)	Mathilda's brother: ***St. Edmund, King of the Scottish Lowlands***
Geoffrey V "Plantagenet," Duke of Normandy and Count of Anjou (b. 24 Aug 1113 – md. 3 April 1127 – d. 7 Sept 1151)	+	**Matilda** (b. 1102/ 1104 – md. (2) 3 April 1127– d. 10 Sept 1167)	
Henry II, King of England (b. 5 March 1133 – md. 18 May 1152 – d. 6 July 1189)	+	Eleanor of Aquitaine (b. 1122 – md. (2) 18 May 1152 – d. 31 March 1204)	

Sources: *Ashley*, pp. 401–402; *Baring-Gould*, Vol. 16, pp. 278–279; *HBC*, p. 57; *Holweck*, p. 303; *Stuart:* line 165, nos. 31 and 30 + line 89, nos. 29 and 28 + line 2, nos. 28 and 27; *Weir*, pp. 184–186, 46–50, and 57–59; *Weis, AR*, line 1, nos. 22 through 25

St. Edward the Confessor, King of England

Edward was born in 1004 and was the son of Aethelred II "the Redeless," King of England, and his second wife Emma of Normandy. During the Danish rule of most of England, Edward was taken to Normandy for his own safety and remained there from 1014 until 1043. He was tall, well-built, had a ruddy face, and never expected to become king.

After the death of the last Danish monarch, Edward was invited to return to England and crowned on 3 April 1043 to great popular acclaim. At the time, the large and well-connected family of Godwin, Earl of Wessex, was the strongest possible power base for Edward in England, and on 23 January 1045 Edward married Godwin's daughter Edith.

Edward ruled for twenty-three years, and his reign is remembered as the last golden age of the Saxon kings of England. Edward was a deeply religious man who prayed often. He was generous to the poor and would lay his hands on the sick in the hope of healing them. Edward's country was at peace and prospered. His most lasting spiritual achievement was the construction of Westminster Abbey.

Edward's marriage to Godwin's daughter Edith in 1045 may have seemed like a politically expedient idea at the time, but it would prove to be the undoing of his kingdom. Nine years earlier in 1036, Edward's brother Alfred had returned to England and was seized, blinded, and ultimately slain on the orders of Godwin. Whether because of Edward's dislike of his wife's family or his personal vows of chastity, his marriage to Edith remained childless and was rumored to be unconsummated. When new trouble arose between Edward and Godwin in 1051, Edward had finally had enough, sent Edith off to a convent, and never brought her back. Years later as Edward lay dying at the end of 1065, his empty throne called forth three claimants: Harold the son of Godwin, Harold Haadraada, and Duke William of Normandy. The consequences for England were profound.

Edward died on 4 January 1066 and was buried in Westminster Abbey, where he remains today. He became the patron saint of the British royal family, and Westminster Abbey became the place where all later English monarchs would be crowned.

His Line
Aethelred II "the Redeless,"
King of England (b. 968 – d. 1016)

md. (1) **Aelfgifu** (or Elgiva or Aethelfleda or Alfflaed) (b. ca. 968 – md. 985), daughter of Thored (or Thorod or Torin) of Northumbria

md. (2) Emma (b. 985/987 – md. 5 April 1002 – d. 14 March 1052), daughter of Richard I, Duke of Normandy

Aethelred and Aelfgifu's son: **Edmund "Ironside,"** King of England (b. 989 – md. (2) Aug 1015 – d. 30 Nov 1016)	+	Ealdgyth (md. (2) Aug 1015), daughter of Morcar, High Reeve of Northumbria	Aethelred and Emma's son: ***St. Edward the Confessor, King of England***
Edward "the Exile," (b. 1016 – md. ca. 1043 – d. 1057)	+	Agatha von Braunschweig (b. ca. 1025 – md. ca. 1043 – d. aft. 1066)	
Malcolm III Canmore, King of Scotland (b. ca. 1031 – md. (2) 1068/1069 – d. in battle 13 Nov 1093 while besieging Alnwick Castle)	+	**St. Margaret of Scotland** (b. ca. 1045 – md. 1068/1069 – d. 16 Nov 1093)	
Henry I, King of England (b. 1070 – md. (1) 11 Nov 1100 – d. Dec 1135)	+	**Matilda of Scotland** (b. 1079 – md. 11 Nov 1100 1 – d. 1 June 1118)	

Sources: *Ashley*, pp. 482 and 491–494; *Baring-Gould*, Vol. 11, pp. 327–346; *Benedictine Monks*, p. 223; *Bentley*, p. 202; *Bunson*, pp. 271–272; *Butler*, Vol. IV, pp. 100–103; *Castleden*, pp. 146–147; *Cruz*, pp. 196–203; *CS*, pp. 601–605; *Delaney*, p. 191; *Delaney and Tobin*, p. 365; *Englebert*, pp. 389–390; *Giorgi*, pp. 16–17; *HBC*, pp. 27 and 29; *Holweck*, p. 304; *Joeckle*, pp. 136–137; *NCE*, Vol. 5, pp. 180–181; *Snodgrass*, pp. 75–76; *Stuart:* line 233, nos. 35 through 32 + line 165, nos. 31 and 30; *Weir*, pp. 22–24, 33–34, 27–29, 184–186 and 46–47; *Weis, AR*, line 1, nos. 19 through 23

St. Edward the Martyr,
King of England

Edward was born in 962 and was the son of St. Edgar "the Peaceful," King of England, and his first wife St. Elgiva, who died soon after Edward was born. When King Edgar died on 8 July 975 at the age of 32, only two of his sons were still alive—Edward (age 13) and Aethelred (age 7), who was King Edgar's son by his second wife. In spite of his youth, Edward was crowned.

Even after Edward became king, the second wife Elfrida wanted her own son Aethelred on the throne and feigned friendship with Edward as she plotted how to kill him. On 18 March 978 King Edward was out with a hunting party but rode off on his own to visit Elfrida and Aethelred at Corfe Castle in Dorset. While he was still on his horse, Elfrida offered him a cup of mead, and as he drank it, one of her servants stabbed him. Wounded, Edward rode off and tried to rejoin his hunting party. He slipped from his horse, his foot caught in the stirrup, and he was dragged to death.

Edward was remembered as an admirable youth, upright in all his dealings and fearing God, who in his short reign had defended the interests of the Church. Because of his unjust death and because many of Elfrida's allies were anti-clerical, Edward was seen as a martyr.

Immediately after his death, many miracles were reported at his tomb. After spending almost a thousand years at Shaftesbury Abbey, his remains were moved in the 20th century to a church in Brookwood Cemetery in the town of Woking in Surrey.

His Line

St. Edgar "the Peaceful," King of England (b. 943 – d. 8 July 975)

md. (1) Ethelfleda "the Fair" (md. ca. 961 – d. 964), daughter of Ordof Ordmaer the Ealdorman

md. (2) **Elfrida** (b. ca. 945 – md. (2) ca. 964/965 – d. ca. 1000), daughter of Ordgar the Ealdorman

Edgar and Ethelfleda's son: ***St. Edward the Martyr, King of England***

Edgar and Elfrida's son: **Aethelred II "the Redeless,"** King of England (b. 968 – md. (1) 985 – d. 1016) + Aelfgifu (or Elgiva or Aethelfleda or Alfflaed) (b. ca. 968 – md. 985), daughter of Thored (or Thorod or Torin) of Northumbria

St. Edward the Martyr, King of England

<table>
<tr><td>Edmund "Ironside,"
King of England (b. 989 –
md. (2) Aug 1015 – d. 30
Nov 1016)</td><td>+</td><td>Ealdgyth (md. (2)
Aug 1015), daughter
of Morcar,
High Reeve of
Northumbria</td></tr>
</table>

Sources: *Ashley*, pp. 480–481; *Baring-Gould*, Vol. 3, pp. 324–326; *Benedictine Monks*, p. 223; *Bunson*, p. 272; *Butler*, Vol. I, pp. 627–628; *Castleden*, pp. 38–39; *CE*, Vol. V, p. 323; *Cruz*, pp. 190–193; *Delaney*, p. 191; *Delaney and Tobin*, p. 365; *HBC*, p. 27; *Holweck*, p. 304; *NCE*, Vol. 5, p. 181; *Stuart*, line 233, nos. 36 through 34; *Tucker*, Vol. I, pp. 283–285; *Weir*, p. 21; *Weis, AR*, line 1, nos. 18 through 20; *Wells*, pp. 204–205

St. Elizabeth of Hungary

Elizabeth was born on 7 June 1207 and was the daughter of Andrew II, King of Hungary, and his first wife Gertrude von Meran. When Elizabeth was four, she was betrothed to an eight-year-old boy who would grow up to be Ludwig (or Louis) IV, Landgrave of Thuringia. Shortly after her betrothal, Elizabeth was given to her future in-laws to be raised by them.

Elizabeth married Ludwig in 1221 when she was fourteen. They had three children, and their marriage was a very happy one. With her husband's approval, Elizabeth began to perform notable acts of charity. She began to personally renounce comfort and would often give her own food to the poor. To raise money for the poor, she also sold most of her personal jewels. She established a hospital for lepers. More ominously, she also agreed to take Pope Gregory IV's representative in Thuringia as her personal spiritual adviser. This representative was a Franciscan monk named Conrad of Marburg.

In the judgment of almost all historians of the period, Conrad was a demanding fanatic with a sadistic streak. He insisted on blind obedience and did not hesitate to punish weakness with beatings. His main ecclesiastical duties were to monitor the moral behavior of priests, monks, and nuns, and to find and punish heretics, and to these tasks he brought the zeal of a true inquisitor.

Elizabeth's acceptance of Conrad was only a foretaste of her future misfortunes. In 1227, her husband Ludwig left to join the Sixth Crusade but died of plague in Italy while his troops were waiting to sail. Back in Thuringia, Elizabeth's in-laws then decided that their own children would be better heirs to the titles and estates of the dead Ludwig than any of Ludwig's children by Elizabeth, and they turned Elizabeth and her children out into the cold.

The winter of 1227–1228 was a time of extreme hardship. To feed herself and her children, Elizabeth had to sell her last jewels. She and her children often had to sleep in parish churches. Her in-laws were ultimately pressured into giving Elizabeth a sum of money as a final settlement. Elizabeth then arranged for her children to be raised in monasteries and convents, opened a small hospital in Marburg, and became a Franciscan nun.

The final years of Elizabeth's life were a martyr's crown. She supported herself by spinning. She nursed the sick in her small hospital and would clean the houses of the poor. She continued to give away money and most of her own food. Conrad remained her spiritual director and the supervisor of her funds, and if he thought she was giving away too much, he would beat her.

On 19 November 1231, Elizabeth finally died of exhaustion and malnutrition at the age of twenty-four. She was buried in Marburg in the church of St. Elizabeth and promptly canonized. She became one of the most popular saints of the Middle Ages and the patron saint of the Teutonic Knights. She is also known as Elizabeth of Thuringia. One of her children grew up to be Bl. Gertrude of Altenberg.

During the Reformation, Elizabeth's bones were scattered. Her empty shrine is still in Marburg.

Her Line

	Husband		Wife
	Andrew II, King of Hungary (b. 1176 – md. (1) bef. 1203 – d. 21 Sept 1235)	+	**Gertrude von Meran** (md. bef. 1203 – d. 8 Sept 1213)
Bela's sister: ***St. Elizabeth of Hungary***	**Bela IV**, King of Hungary (b. 1206 – md. 1218 – d. 3 May 1270)	+	Maria Laskarina (b. ca. 1206 – md. 1218 – d. 1270), daughter of Theodore I Lascaris, Emperor of Byzantium
	Stephen V, King of Hungary (b. Dec 1239 – md. 1253 – d. 1 Aug 1272)	+	Elizabeth (md. 1253 – d. aft. 1290), daughter of Kuthen, Khan of the Kumans

[For the later generations that connect this line to the kings of England, see the line of St. Adalbero, Bishop of Wuerzburg in Part III.]

Sources: *Baring-Gould*, Vol. 14, pp. 415–457; *BBKL*, Vol. 1, cols. 1498–1500; *Benedictine Monks*, pp. 230–233; *Bentley*, p. 222; *Bunson*, p. 278; *Butler*, Vol. IV, pp. 386–391; *Castleden*, pp. 174–175; *CE*, Vol. V, pp. 389–391; *Chervin*, pp. 57–58; *Cruz*, pp. 209–225; *Delaney*, pp. 194–195; *Delaney and Tobin*, p. 371; *Dunbar*, Vol. I, pp. 259–264; *Englebert*, pp. 440–441; *Giorgi*, pp. 676–677; *Holboeck*, pp. 193–203; *Holweck*, p. 314; *Joeckle*, pp. 139–142; *Klaniczay*, pp. 202–203, 209–222, and Appendix B, Geneal. Table 7; *NCE*, Vol. 5, p. 282; *Snodgrass*, pp. 79–80; *Stuart*, line 78, nos. 28 through 26; *Warncke*, pp. 114–115; *Weis, AR*, line 103, nos. 28 through 30; *Wells*, p. 309; *WWH*, Vol. 5, pp. 162–166

St. Elizabeth Rose

Elizabeth was the daughter of Raoul III "the Great," Count of Crepy, Valois, and Vexin, and his wife Adele of Bar-sur-Aube.

Elizabeth founded the convent of St. Marie-du-Rozoy near Courtenay and became its first abbess. She was distinguished for miracles, both during her life and after her death on 13 December 1130.

Her convent was later destroyed during the wars with England.

Her Line

Husband		Wife	
Raoul III "the Great," Count of Crepy, Valois, and Vexin (b. 1025 – d. 8 Sept 1074)	+	**Adele of Bar-sur-Aube** (d. 1053) (Raoul was Adele's 4th husband)	
Herbert IV, Count of Vermandois (b. ca. 1032 – d. ca. 1080/ 96)	+	**Adele de Valois** (b. by 1043)	Adele's sister: ***St. Elizabeth Rose***
Hugh Magnus, Duke of France and Burgundy and a leader of the 1st Crusade (b. 1057 – md. aft. 1067 – d. 18 Oct 1101)	+	**Adelaide de Vermandois** (b. ca. 1062 – md. aft. 1067 – d. 1120/1124)	
William de Warenne, 2nd Earl of Surrey (md. ca. 1118 – d. prob. 11 May 1138)	+	**Isabel de Vermandois,** Countess of Leicester (b. 1081 – md. (2) ca. 1118 – d. prob. July 1147	
Henry of Huntingdon, Earl of Huntingdon and Northumberland (b. ca. 1115 – md. ca. 1139 – d. 12 June 1152), son of David I "the Saint," King of Scotland	+	**Adelaide (or Ada) de Warenne** (b. ca. 1120 – md. ca. 1139 – d. 1178)	
Florenz III, Count of Holland (France) and West Sealand, Crusader (b. ca. 1138 – md. 28 Aug 1161/1162 – d. 1 Aug 1190 at Antioch on the 3rd Crusade)	+	**Ada de Huntingdon** (b. ca. 1146 – md. 28 Aug 1161/1162 – d. 11 Jan 1216/1222)	
William I, Count of Holland (France) and East Friesland, Crusader (b. ca. 1174 – md. 1198 – d. 2 July 1222)	+	Adelaide of Guelders (b. ca. 1186 – md. 1198 – d. 4 Feb 1218)	

[For the later generations that connect this line to the kings of England, see the line of Bl. Adelheid von Odenkirchen in Part II.]

Sources: *Dunbar*, Vol. I, p. 257; *Holweck*, p. 314; *Stuart:* line 268, nos. 33 and 32 + line 239, nos. 31 and 30 + line 143, nos. 29 and 28 + line 135, nos. 29 and 28 + line 72, nos. 29 through 27; *Tucker:* Vol. II, pp. 872, 870, 910–911, and 762–763 + Vol. I, p. 414; *Weis, AR:* line 140, nos. 22 through 24 + line 89, nos. 24 and 25 + line 100, nos. 25 through 27; *Wells*, pp. 576, 586, 602, 520, and 305

St. Ercongota

Ercongota was the daughter of Erconbert, King of Kent, and his wife St. Sexburga.

Ercongota became a Benedictine nun and entered the monastery at Faremoûtier-en-Brie, where her aunt St. Ethelburga was abbess. According to Bede, Ercongota was a nun of outstanding virtue and also became the abbess there.

One day in the year 660, Ercongota had a vision which forewarned her of her own death. In her monastery, she went from person to person telling her nuns that she was about to die and asking for their prayers. She then died as she had foretold and was buried in the church of St. Stephen. Several miracles were reported shortly after her death.

Her Line

	Husband		Wife
	Erconbert (or Eorconbeorht), King of Kent (b. ca. 624 – md. ca. 640 – d. 14 July 664)	+	**St. Sexburga** (md. ca. 640 – d. 6 July 699)
Egbert's sister: ***St. Ercongota***	**Egbert**, King of Kent (b. ca. 641 – d. 4 July 673)	+	N.N.
	Wihtread, King of Kent (d. 23 April 725)	+	N.N.

[For the later generations that connect this line to the kings of England, see the line of St. Aethelbert I, King of Kent in Part II.]

Sources: *Baring-Gould*: Vol. 2, p. 382 + Vol. 7, pp. 158–159*; *BBKL*, Vol. 16, col. 463; *Benedictine Monks*, pp. 240 and 641*; *Bunson*, p. 287; *Butler*, Vol. III, pp. 25* and 34; *Delaney*, p. 200; *Delaney and Tobin*, pp. 381 and 1052*; *Dunbar*, Vol. I, p. 272; *HBC*, p. 13; *Holweck*, pp. 327 and 908*; *O'Malley*, pp. 42, 72, and 92; *Parbury*, pp. 41–42; *Stuart:* line 437, no. 46 + line 233A, nos. 46 through 44; *Wagner*, p. 188; *Williamson*, p. 359 (sources marked with a * are alphabetized under "Sexburga")

St. Erconwald,
Bishop of London

Erconwald was born around 630 and was the son of Anna, King of East Anglia, and his wife St. Hereswitha.

In a time when Christianity was first establishing itself in England, Erconwald was an important figure. On an island in the Thames, he founded the abbey of Chertsey and became its first abbot. In Essex, he also founded the convent of Barking. In 675, he was appointed bishop of London, and as bishop, he enlarged his flock, increased church revenues, and obtained special privileges from the king. Erconwald also helped St. Ina, King of Wessex, prepare his code of laws for the Saxons.

In his last years, Erconwald suffered from severe gout and had to be carried about in a litter. He died around 690 and is also known as Erkenwald.

His Line

Husband		Wife	
Anna, King of East Anglia (ruled ca. 641–653 – d. in battle with Penda of Mercia)	+	**St. Hereswitha** (b. sh. bef. 616 – d. 680/690)	
Erconbert (or Eorconbeorht), King of Kent (b. ca. 624 – md. ca. 640 – d. 14 July 664)	+	**St. Sexburga** (md. ca. 640 – d. 6 July 699)	St. Sexburga's brother: ***St. Erconwald, Bishop of London***
Egbert, King of Kent (b. ca. 641 – d. 4 July 673)	+	N.N.	

[For the later generations that connect this line to the kings of England, see the line of St. Aethelbert I, King of Kent in Part II.]

Sources: *Baring-Gould*, Vol. 4, p. 375; *Benedictine Monks*, p. 240; *Bunson*, p. 288; *Butler*, Vol. II, pp. 299–300; *CE*, Vol. 5, p. 517; *Delaney*, p. 200; *Delaney and Tobin*, p. 381; *Holweck*, p. 327; *Kirby*, p. 83; *NCE*, Vol. 5, p. 512; *O'Malley*, pp. 73 and 98; *Stuart:* line 437, nos. 47 and 46 + line 233A, nos. 46 and 45

St. Ermenburga

Ermenburga was the daughter of Ermenric, King of Kent. She married Merewal, King of the Magonsaete. Merewal's realm was on the Welsh borders and was a sub-kingdom of Mercia. Merewal converted to Christianity around the time of his marriage to Ermenburga, and three of their daughters became saints: Milburga, Mildgith, and Mildred.

Merewal and Ermenburga were very active in spreading the Christian religion. After Merewal died, Ermenburga founded the convent of Minster-in-Thanet and became its first abbess.

Ermenburga herself died around 590, and during the Middle Ages she became an object of extraordinary devotion. Her tomb in her convent became a place of pilgrimage.

Ermenburga has also been called "Eaba," "Eafa," "Eormenburga," and "Domneva."

Her Line

	Husband		Wife
	Ermenric, King of Kent (d. 560)	+	**N.N.**
Aethelbert's sister: ***St. Ermenburga***	**St. Aethelbert (or Ethelbert) I**, King of Kent (b. ca. 552 – md. (1) ca. 578 – d. 24 Feb 616)	+	St. Bertha (b. ca. 560 – md. ca. 578 – d. ca. 602)
	Eadbald, King of Kent (md. (2) ca. 618 – d. 640)	+	St. Emma (md. ca. 618)

[For the later generations that connect this line to the kings of England, see the line of St. Aethelbert I, King of Kent in Part II.]

Sources: *Ashley*, pp. 212 and 267; *Baring-Gould*, Vol. 16, pp. 257 and 309; *Benedictine Monks*, p. 241; *Butler*, Vol. III, p. 91 (under "St. Mildred"); *Delaney*, p. 201; *Dunbar*, Vol. I, p. 274; *HBC*, pp. 12–13; *Holweck*, p. 328; *NCE*, Vol. 5, pp. 516–517; *O'Malley*, p. 64; *Parbury*, pp. 30–31; *Stuart*, line 233A, nos. 48 through 46; *Wells*, p. 325; *WWH*, Vol. 5, p. 246

Bl. Ermengard,
Abbess of Buchan and Chiemsee

Ermengard was born in 832 and was the daughter of Louis II "the German," King of the East Franks, and his wife Bl. Emma of Bavaria.

Ermengard was a model of virtue, penance, and charitable care. After becoming a nun, she was first appointed abbess of the convent at Buchau and then made abbess of the royal abbey at Chiemsee. She died on 16 July 866, was buried at Chiemsee, and was venerated immediately after her death.

Ermengard is also known as Irmgard or Irmengard.

Her Line

	Husband		Wife
	Louis II "the German," King of the East Franks (b. 806 – md. 827 – d. 28 Aug 876)	+	**Bl. Emma of Bavaria** (b. ca. 808 – md. 827 – d. 31 Jan 876)
Carloman's sister: ***Bl. Ermengard, Abbess of Buchan and Chiemsee***	**Carloman**, King of Bavaria (liv. 820–880)	+	Litwinde of Carinthia
	Arnulf, King of the East Franks (i.e., Germany) (liv. 863–899)	+	Oda of Bavaria

[For the later generations that connect this line to the kings of England, see the line of Bl. Emma of Bavaria in Part II.]

Sources: *BBKL*, Vol. 2, cols. 1333–1334; *Benedictine Monks*, p. 361; *Butler*, Vol. III, p. 119; *Delaney*, p. 201; *Delaney and Tobin*, p. 381; *Holweck*, p. 509; *NCE*, Vol. 7, p. 657; *Stuart*, line 172, nos. 41 through 39; *Weis, AR*, line 141, no. 17; *Wells*, p. 138

Bl. Ermengarde of Anjou

Ermengarde was born shortly after 1068 and was the daughter of Fulk IV "Rechin," Count of Anjou, and his first wife Hildegarde de Beaugency. Ermengarde's first husband was William IX, Duke of Aquitaine (and as William VII Count of Poitou), whom she married in 1089. The two were extraordinarily ill-suited to each other, and their marriage was dissolved in 1090 on the ground of consanguinity. Ermengarde's second husband was Alain IV "Fergant," Duke of Brittany, whom she married in 1093.

Ermengarde was a woman of great ability who also had a deeply spiritual side. Soon after she married Alain, she began to take an active part in the government of Brittany. Alain had such confidence in her that, when he left in 1096 with Duke Robert III of Normandy to go fight in the First Crusade, he made her regent of Brittany. Alain did not return until 1101, and in the five years that he was away, Ermengarde ruled Brittany on her own. Her sense of justice and her attempts to improve the living conditions of the Bretons won the affection of many of her subjects.

After Alain's return, he was once again the ruler of his realm, but he depended on Ermengarde even more than when he left. In 1114, his ill health finally forced him to abdicate in favor of his son Conan, who would be known as Conan III "the Great," Duke of Brittany. Alain retired to the abbey of Redon and remained there until his death in 1119.

For several years after the accession of Conan, Ermengarde was deeply involved in the government of Brittany. Her name appears in many charters, and she was often present at political and religious assemblies. In her old age, she turned more and more of her attention to spiritual matters. Around 1129, she received her nun's veil from the hands of St. Bernard of Clairvaux. Around 1132, she went to the Holy Land when her younger half-brother Fulk became Fulk V, King of Jerusalem, and she lived there in the convent of St. Anne. After some years in Jerusalem, she returned to Brittany, founded a monastery, and made donations to other religious houses.

Ermengarde finally died in 1147 and is buried with her second husband Alain in the abbey of Redon.

Her Line

	Fulk IV "Rechin," Count of Anjou (b. 1043 – d. 14 April 1109)		
md. (1) ca. 1068 Hildegarde de Beaugency			md. (5) ca. 1090 Bertrade de Montfort (b. ca. 1060 – d. 14 Feb 1117)
Fulk and Hildegarde's daughter: ***Bl. Ermengarde of Anjou***	Fulk and Bertrade's son: **Fulk V "le Jeune,"** Count of Anjou, Crusader, and King of Jerusalem (b. 1092 – md. (1) ca. 1108 – d. 10 Nov 1143)	+	Erembourge, heiress of Maine (md. ca. 1108 – d. 1126)

Geoffrey V Plantagenet, Count of Anjou and Duke of Normandy (b. 24 Aug 1113 – md. 22 May 1127 – d. 7 Sept 1151)	+	Matilda, Princess of England and Empress of Germany (b. ca. Feb 1102 – md. (2) 22 May 1127 – d. 10 Sept 1167)
Henry II, King of England (b. 5 March 1133 – md. 18 May 1152 – d. 6 July 1189)	+	Eleanor of Aquitaine (b. 1122 – md. (2) 18 May 1152 – d. 31 March 1204)

Sources: *Benedictine Monks*, p. 241 (under "Ermengardis"), *Dunbar*, Vol. I, pp. 275–276; *Stuart*, line 2, nos. 30 through 27; *Weis, AR:* line 118, nos. 23 through 25 + line 1, nos. 24 and 25; *Wells*, pp. 17–18 and 208–209; *WWH*, Vol. 5, p. 247

St. Ermengytha

Ermengytha was the daughter of Ermenic, King of Kent.

Ermengytha became a nun and lived in the convent of Minster-in-Thanet, where her sister St. Ermenburga was abbess. She died ca. 580.

Her Line

	Husband		Wife
	Ermenric, King of Kent (d. 560)	+	**N.N.**
Aethelbert's sister: ***St. Ermengytha***	**St. Aethelbert (or Ethelbert) I,** King of Kent (b. ca. 552 – md. (1) ca. 578 – d. 24 Feb 616)	+	St. Bertha (b. ca. 560 – md. ca. 578 – d. ca. 602)
	Eadbald, King of Kent (md. (2) ca. 618 – d. 640)	+	St. Emma (md. ca. 618)

[For the later generations that connect this line to the kings of England, see the line of St. Aethelbert I, King of Kent in Part II.]

Sources: *Ashley*, pp. 212–215; *Baring-Gould*, Vol. 16, p. 257; *Benedictine Monks*, p. 241; *Holweck*, p. 328; *Parbury*, p. 42; *Stuart*, line 233A, nos. 48 through 46; *Wells*, p. 325

St. Ermenilda

Ermenilda was born around 630/640 and was the daughter of Erconbert, King of Kent, and his wife St. Sexburga. Around 660, she married Wulfhere, son of the pagan king Penda of Mercia, which was the last Anglo-Saxon kingdom that was still heathen. When Wulfhere married Ermenilda, he was still a pagan. By her own piety and good example, Ermenilda converted him, and together they turned Mercia into a Christian kingdom. One of their children was St. Werburga.

After Wulfhere died in 675, Ermenilda became a Benedictine nun and entered the monastery at Minster-in-Sheppey, where her mother St. Sexburga was abbess. In time, Ermenilda became the abbess there. She later followed Sexburga to the abbey at Ely and became abbess there too.

Ermenilda died in 703 and is buried at Ely next to her mother St. Sexburga and her aunt St. Etheldreda.

Ermenilda is also known as "Ermengild," "Eormengild," and "Eormenhild."

Her Line

	Husband		Wife
	Erconbert (or Eorconbeorht), King of Kent (b. ca. 624 – md. ca. 640 – d. 14 July 664)	+	St. Sexburga (md. ca. 640 – d. 6 July 699)
Egbert's sister: ***St. Ermenilda***	**Egbert**, King of Kent (b. ca. 641 – d. 4 July 673)	+	N.N.
	Wihtread, King of Kent (d. 23 April 725)	+	N.N.

[For the later generations that connect this line to the kings of England, see the line of St. Aethelbert I, King of Kent in Part II.]

Sources: *Ashley*, pp. 242 and 253; *Baring-Gould:* Vol. 2, pp. 292–293 + Vol. 7, pp. 158–159*; *Benedictine Monks*, pp. 241–242 and p. 641*; *Bunson*, p. 288; *Butler*: Vol. I, p. 323 + Vol. III, p. 25*; *Delaney*, p. 201; *Delaney and Tobin*, pp. 381 and 1052*; *Dunbar*, Vol. I, pp. 276–277; *Holweck*, pp. 328–329 and 908*; *O'Malley*, pp. 42, 72, and 92; *Parbury*, pp. 42–43; *Stuart*: line 437, no. 46 + line 233A, nos. 46 through 44; *Williamson*, p. 359; *WWH*, Vol. 5, p. 248 (sources marked with a * are alphabetized under "Sexburga")

St. Ethelburga, Queen of Northumbria

Ethelburga was the daughter of St. Aethelbert I, King of Kent, and his wife St. Bertha. Around 624, Ethelburga became the second wife of Edwin, King of Northumbria.

When their marriage began, Edwin was a pagan, but Ethelburga was a Christian. Edwin had agreed that Ethelburga could freely practice her religion, but Edwin himself seemed like an unlikely convert. A typical Dark Ages pagan monarch, he was a ruthless, cunning, and vengeful king who manipulated people and events to his own advantage. His ultimate conversion may have been due to any of several events: to Ethelburga's efforts, to narrowly surviving an assassination attempt, or to winning a battle after praying to Ethelburga's God. In any event, on Easter of 627, Edwin was finally baptized at York on the site of the present York Minster. He then burned the temples and altars of the old gods and encouraged the spread of Christianity.

Edwin was not allowed to practice his new faith for very long. On 12 October 633 in the battle of Hatfield Chase, he was slain by the men of Penda of Mercia and Cadwalon of Wales. After Edwin's death, his pagan adversaries overran his land.

Ethelburga had to flee Edwin's kingdom of Northumbria and return to her native Kent. She founded a convent at Lyming, became a nun, and entered her own convent. She became its abbess and died there around 647.

In the end, the deposed ruling family of Northumbria produced three saints: Edwin, Ethelburga, and their daughter Eanfleda.

Her Line

	Husband		Wife
	St. Aethelbert (or Ethelbert) I, King of Kent (b. ca. 552 – md. (1) ca. 578 – d. 24 Feb 616)	+	**St. Bertha** (b. ca. 560 – md. ca. 578 – d. ca. 602)
Eadbald's sister: ***St. Ethelburga, Queen of Northumbria***	**Eadbald**, King of Kent (md. ca. 618 – d. 640)	+	St. Emma (md. ca. 618)
	Erconbert (or Eorconbeorht), King of Kent (b. ca. 624 – md. ca. 640 – d. 14 July 664)	+	St. Sexburga (md. ca. 640 – d. 6 July 699)

[For the later generations that connect this line to the kings of England, see the line of St. Aethelbert I, King of Kent in Part II.]

Sources: *Ashley*, pp. 277–279; *BBKL*, Vol. 14, cols. 961–962; *Benedictine Monks*, p. 243; *Bunson*, p. 290; *Butler*, Vol. II, p. 35 and Vol. IV, pp. 94–95; *Delaney*, p. 202; *Delaney and Tobin*, p. 385; *Dunbar*, Vol. I, pp. 278–279; *HBC*, p. 12; *Holweck*, p. 331; *Klaniczay*, p. 82; *O'Malley*, p. 42; *NCE*, Vol. 5, pp. 566–567; *Parbury*, pp. 43–45; *Snodgrass*, p. 82; *Stuart*, line 233A, nos. 48 through 46; *Wells*, p. 325; *WWH*, Vol. 5, p. 287

St. Ethelburga, Princess of the East Angles

Ethelburga was the daughter of Anna, King of East Anglia, and his wife St. Hereswitha.

Ethelburga became a nun and went with her half-sister St. Sethrida to the convent at Faremoûtier-en-Brie. After the death of the convent's founder St. Burgundofara, Sethrida became abbess first and then Ethelburga.

As abbess, Ethelburga began to build a new church at the convent. She didn't live to see it completed, and when she died around 664 she was buried in the unfinished building. After seven years, the new church was still not finished, and it was decided to move her remains to the church of St. Stephen the Martyr. When her old tomb was opened, her body was found to be incorrupt.

Ethelburga is also known as Aethelburh.

Her Line

Husband		Wife	
Anna, King of East Anglia (ruled ca. 641–653 – d. in battle with Penda of Mercia)	+	**St. Hereswitha** (b. sh. bef. 616 – d. 680/690)	
Erconbert (or Eorconbeorht), King of Kent (b. ca. 624 – md. ca. 640 – d. 14 July 664)	+	**St. Sexburga** (md. ca. 640 – d. 6 July 699)	St. Sexburga's sister: ***St. Ethelburga, Princess of the East Angles***
Egbert, King of Kent (b. ca. 641 – d. 4 July 673)	+	N.N.	

[For the later generations that connect this line to the kings of England, see the line of St. Aethelbert I, King of Kent in Part II.]

Sources: *Ashley*, p. 239; *Baring-Gould*, Vol. 7, p. 169; *Benedictine Monks*, p. 243; *Bentley*, pp. 129 and 201; *Bunson*, p. 290; *Butler*, Vol. III, p. 34; *Delaney*, p. 202; *Delaney and Tobin*, p. 385; *Dunbar*, Vol. I, p. 280; *HBC*, p. 8; *Holweck*, p. 331; *O'Malley*, pp. 73 and 98; *Parbury*, p. 43; *Stuart:* line 437, nos. 47 and 46 + line 233A, nos. 46 and 45

St. Etheldreda

Etheldreda was born around 636 and was the daughter of Anna, King of East Anglia, and his wife St. Hereswitha.

From an early age, Etheldreda wanted to become a nun, but it would be many years before she reached her goal. Marriage to a prince who would strengthen the position of the East Anglian royal family was what Etheldreda's parents had in mind for her. Around 652, she entered into an arranged marriage with Tondberht of South Gwyrwas. She somehow persuaded him to leave the marriage unconsummated, and he died in 655. Etheldreda had received the isle of Ely as a dowry and withdrew there to spend five years in seclusion and prayer.

In 660, her family arranged a second marriage for her, this time with Egfrith, the younger son of St. Oswy, King of Northumbria. Egfrith was only fifteen years old at the time, Etheldreda was almost ten years older, and at first she was also able to persuade Egfrith to live in an unconsummated union. When Egfrith became king in 670 after the death of Oswy, he saw his situation differently and wanted Etheldreda to be a real wife. She refused, then fled, and in 672 they ended their marriage.

Around the age of 36 and finally free of all marital ties, Etheldreda founded a double monastery at Ely in 673, became a nun, entered her own monastery, and became its abbess.

Etheldreda's way of life was very austere. She normally ate only one meal a day. In all seasons, she washed only in cold water. Throughout the year, she wore only rough woolen clothing. She frequently prayed throughout the night while everyone else was asleep.

Besides running the monastery, Etheldreda also ministered to the poor and practiced medicine. After six years at Ely, she finally died on 23 June 679. Since in her final illness she had a large swelling on her neck, some writers say she died of throat cancer. Others say plague. She was succeeded as abbess by her sister St. Sexburga.

Etheldreda was much more famous in death than she had been in life. Sixteen years after her death, her tomb was opened so that her remains could be moved to a different site, and her body was found to be incorrupt. The many miracles at her old and new tombs made her final resting place a very popular center of devotion and ultimately one of the principal pilgrimage sites in England.

Of all the women who became Anglo-Saxon saints, Etheldreda was the most popular one for a very long time. There are many churches dedicated to her in England and elsewhere. Her shrine is still to be seen in Ely Cathedral.

Her Line

Anna, King of East Anglia (ruled ca. 641–653 – d. in battle with Penda of Mercia)	+	**St. Hereswitha** (b. sh. bef. 616 – d. 680/ 690)	
Erconbert (or Eorconbeorht), King of Kent (b. ca. 624 – md. ca. 640 – d. 14 July 664)	+	**St. Sexburga** (md. ca. 640 – d. 6 July 699)	St. Sexburga's sister: ***St. Etheldreda***

Egbert, King of Kent (b. ca. 641 – d. 4 July 673) + N.N.

[For the later generations that connect this line to the kings of England, see the line of St. Aethelbert I, King of Kent in Part II.]

Sources: *Ashley*, p. 242; *Baring-Gould*, Vol. 12, pp. 440–447; *BBKL*, Vol. 14, col. 962; *Benedictine Monks*, pp. 243–244; *Bentley*, p. 117; *Bunson*, p. 290; *Butler*, Vol. II, pp. 620–621; *Castleden*, pp. 148–149; *CE*, Vol. V, p. 554; *Chervin*, pp. 247–248; *CS*, pp. 340–341; *Delaney*, p. 202; *Dunbar*, Vol. I, pp. 281–284; *Englebert*, p. 241; *Holweck*, pp. 331–332; *Joeckle*, pp. 146–147; *Klaniczay*, pp. 80, 86–89, and 430; *O'Malley*, pp. 73 and 98; *Parbury*, pp. 46–49; *Snodgrass*, pp. 82–83; *Stuart:* line 437, nos. 47 and 46 + line 233A, nos. 46 and 45; *WWH*, Vol. 5, pp. 201–202

St. Ethelgiva

Ethelgiva was the daughter of St. Alfred the Great, King of England, and his wife St. Eahlswith.

Ethelgiva became a Benedictine nun, and Alfred appointed her abbess of the monastery he had built at Shaftesbury in Dorset. After a life of great sanctity, she died in 896, three years before Alfred.

Ethelgiva is also known as Aethelgifu.

Her Line

	Husband		Wife
	St. Alfred the Great, King of Wessex (b. 849 – md. 868 – d. 26 Oct 899)	+	St. Eahlswith of Mercia (b. ca. 852 – md. 868 – d. 904)
Edward's sister: ***St. Ethelgiva***	**Edward "the Elder,"** King of England (b. 875 – md. (3) 919 – d. 924)	+	Eadgifu (md. 919 – d. 961)
	Edmund I "the Magnificent," King of England (b. ca. 920 – murdered 26 May 946)	+	md. (1) St. Elgiva (d. 944)

Sources: *Baring-Gould*, Vol. 16, p. 321; *Benedictine Monks*, p. 244; *Bunson*, p. 290; *Delaney and Tobin*, p. 385; *HBC*, pp. 23–24; *Holweck*, p. 331; *Parbury*, p. 49; *Stuart*, line 233, nos. 39 through 37; *Weir*, p. 10; *Weis, AR*, line 1, nos. 15 through 17; *Wells*, p. 204

St. Eugenia

Eugenia was the daughter of Adalbert, Duke of Alsace, and his wife Gerlinde. She was the sister of St. Attalia and St. Gundelindis of Alsace.

Eugenia became a nun, entered the abbey of Hohenburg (now Odilienberg), and in 720 succeeded her aunt St. Odilia as abbess. She was revered for her holy life and wise government of the abbey.

Eugenia died in 735 and was buried in the chapel of St. John the Baptist at Hohenburg. Most of her relics were lost during the Thirty Years' War.

Her Line

	Husband		Wife
	Adalbert, Duke of Alsace (d. 722)	+	**Gerlinde**
Luitfride's sister: ***St. Eugenia***	**Luitfride I**, Duke of Alsace (d. 767)	+	Edith
	Luitfride II, Count of Upper Alsace (d. 802)	+	Hiltrude

[For the later generations that connect this line to the kings of England, see the line of St. Attalia in Part III.]

Sources: *Baring-Gould*, Vol. 16, p. 152; *Benedictine Monks*, p. 247; *Bunson*, p. 295; *Delaney and Tobin*, p. 388; *Dunbar*, Vol. I, p. 287; *Holweck*, p. 335; *NCE*, Vol. 5, p. 627; *Stuart*, line 224, nos. 41 through 39; *Weis, AR*, line 181, nos. 2 through 4; *Wells*, p. 9

Bl. Euphemia of Andechs

Euphemia was the daughter of Berthold IV, Count of Andechs and Diessen, and his first wife Sophia of Istria.

After becoming a nun, Euphemia entered the convent of Altomuenster and became its abbess. She died in 1180 and at her own request was buried next to her sister St. Mechtildis, Abbess of Diessen.

Her Line

	Husband		Wife
	Berthold IV, Count of Andechs and Diessen (b. 1096/1098 – d. 27 June 1151)	+	md. (1) **Sophia of Istria** (d. 6 Sept 1128)
Berthold V's sister: ***Bl. Euphemia of Andechs***	**Berthold V**, Count of Andechs and Margrave of Istria (b. 1122/1123 – md. 1152 – d. ca. 1188)	+	Hedwig von Formbach-Puttin (md. (1) 1152 – d. 16 July 1174)
	Berthold VI, Count of Andechs, Margrave of Istria, and Duke of Croatia; Crusader (b. ca. 1152 – md. 1170 – d. 12 Aug 1204)	+	Agnes von Groitzsch-Rochlitz (md. 1170 – d. 25 March 1195)

[For the later generations that connect this line to the kings of England, see the line of St. Adalbero, Bishop of Wuerzburg in Part III.]

Sources: *Benedictine Monks*, p. 249; *Dunbar*, Vol. I, p. 291; *Holweck*, p. 340; *Stuart*, line 7, nos. 31 through 29; *Wells*, p. 15

St. Euriella

Euriella was the daughter of Hoel III, King of Brittany, and his wife Pritelle. Saint Judicael and Saint Judoc were her brothers. There is a church dedicated to her at Tremeur near Dinan.

Her Line

	Husband		Wife
	Hoel III, King of Brittany (d. 612)	+	**Pritelle**
Judicael's sister:	**St. Judicael II**, King of Brittany (b. ca. 590 – d. 17 Dec 658)	+	N.N.
St. Euriella	**Alain II de Long**, King of Brittany (d. 690)	+	N.N.

[For the later generations that connect this line to the kings of England, see the line of St. Cunedda Wledig in Part II.]

Sources: *Ashley*, p. 728; *Dunbar*, Vol. I, pp. 296–297; *Holweck*, p. 343; *Stuart*, line 405, nos. 49 through 47

St. Feidhlimidh

Feidhlimidh was the son of Fergus Cennfada ("Long Head") and his wife Eirc. His wife was Eithne. They lived in Ireland in Gartan, which is in County Donegal.

Feidhlimidh and Eithne would probably have been forgotten long ago if their son had not become one of the greatest saints in the whole history of Britain. This was Columba, who was born around 7 December 521 in Ireland. Large and athletically built, he had a voice that could be heard at a very great distance. After becoming a monk, he spent fifteen years preaching and founding monasteries in Ireland. Following a disagreement with the High King Diarmaid in 563, Columba and twelve companions sailed away from Ireland and landed on the Isle of Iona. They spent the next two years building a monastery there, and Columba became its first abbot. The rule which Columba wrote for his monks was widely followed elsewhere in Europe.

Columba and his monks then spent the next 34 years making trips to the British mainland to begin the work of converting the Scots to Christianity. It was this work that earned Columba the name "the Apostle to the Picts." By the time he died on Iona on 9 June 597, his monastery had become the center of Celtic Christianity.

Feidhlimidh died around 560. Columba outlived him by almost forty years and became the most famous of all the Scottish saints.

His Line

	Husband		Wife
	Fergus Cennfada ("Long Head")	+	**Eirc**, daughter of Loarn Mor, a king of the Scots
Setna's brother: ***St. Feidhlimidh***	**Setna**, a prince in Ulster	+	Eithne (but not the same woman who married Feidhlimidh)
	Ainmere mac Setnai, High King of Ireland (d. 569)	+	N.N.
	Aed mac Ainmerech, High King of Ireland (d. 598)	+	N.N.
	Maelcobha (or Mael Cobo), King of Tir Conaill and High King of Ireland (d. 615)	+	N.N.
	Maelduin, King of Ailech (killed 681 at the battle of Leathairbhe)	+	**Cacht**

[For the later generations that connect this line to the kings of Scotland, see the line of St. Abban in Part III.]

Sources: *Burke's*, Vol. II, p. 2151; *Byrne*, p. 283; *CS*, pp. 441–442; *Jaski*, p. 306; *Williamson*, p. 387; *Woods*, p. 71

St. Florentina

Florentina was born around 554 and was the daughter of Severinus, Count of Cartagena, and his wife Theodora, daughter of Theodoric "the Great," the Ostrogoth King of Italy.

Losing her parents at an early age, Florentina was educated by her brother St. Leander. When she decided to become a nun, Leander founded a convent in Ecija for her called St. Maria de Valle. She later became its abbess and died there in 633.

Florentina was the first canonized nun in Spain. All of her brothers also won religious honors, and so did her sister. Besides her brother St. Leander, her other brothers were St. Fulgentius and St. Isidore of Seville. Her sister was Theodosia, who would become the mother of St. Hermenegild.

Florentina is buried at Berzoncana in the diocese of Plasencia in Spain. Some of her relics are also in Seville.

Her Line

Husband		Wife	
Severinus, Count of Cartagena	+	**Theodora**, daughter of Theodoric "the Great," the Ostrogoth King of Italy	
Leovigildo (or Leovigild), King of the Visigoths in Spain (d. 586)	+	md. (1) **Theodosia**	Theodosia's sister: ***St. Florentina***
Recaredo (or Recared) I, King of the Visigoths in Spain (d. 601)	+	Chlodesindis (or Clodoswindis)	
Suintila (or Suintilo), King of the Visigoths in Spain (deposed in 631)	+	Theodora, daughter of Sisebuto, King of the Visigoths in Spain	
Ervigio, King of the Visigoths in Spain (d. 687)	+	**Liubigotona**	
Pedro, Duke of Cantabria (d. 730)	+	N.N.	
Fruela of Bardalia, Count of Bartulio (d. ca. 765)	+	N.N.	
Vermudo I, King of the Asturias (d. 797)	+	Ursinda Munilona	
Ramiro I, King of the Asturias (b. ca. 790 – d. 1 Feb 850)	+	Paterna of Castile	
Ordogno I, King of the Asturias and Galicia (b. ca. 830 – d. 27 May 866)	+	Nuna	
Alfonso III "the Great," King of the Asturias (b. 848 – md. 869/870 – d. 20 Dec 910)	+	Jimena Garces (md. 869/870 – d. by 912)	

Ordogno II, King of Asturia, Galicia, and Leon (b. ca. 873 – d. 3 Jan 924) + md. (1) Nunja Elvira Menendez (d. Sept/Oct 921)

Ramiro II, King of Leon (b. ca. 900 – md. (1) 925 – d. 1 Jan 951) + Adosinda Gutierrez (md. 925)

Ordogno III, King of Leon (b. ca. 926 – md. (2) 952 – d. 955) + Aragonta (or Gontvoda) Pelaez (md. 952)

Vermudo II "the Gouty," King of Leon (b. ca. 953 – md. (2) 26/30 Nov 991 – d. Sept 999) + Elvira Garcia of Castile (b. ca. 970 – md. 26/30 Nov 991 – d. aft. 1 March 1028)

Alfonso V, King of Castile and Leon (b. 994 – md. (1) 1015 – slain 7 Aug 1028) + Elvira Menendez (b. ca. 996 – md. 1015 – d. Dec 1022)

Fernando I "the Great," King of Castile and Leon (b. 1016/1018 – md. Nov/Dec 1032 – d. 27 Dec 1065) + **Sancha** (b. 1013 – md. Nov/Dec 1032 – d. 7 Nov 1067)

Alfonso VI "the Brave," King of Castile, Leon, and Navarre (b. June 1040 – md. (2) 8 May 1081 – d. 29 June 1109) + Constance of Burgundy (b. ca. 1046 – md. 8 May 1081 – d. Jan/Feb 1093)

Raymond of Burgundy and Ivrea, Count of Castile, Coimbra, d'Amous, and Galicia, Crusader against the Moors in Spain (b. ca. 1070 – md. ca. 1095 – d. 13/20 Sept 1107) + **Urraca** (b. ca. 1082 – md. (1) ca. 1095 – d. 8 March 1126)

Alfonso VII "El Emperador," King of Castile, Leon, Galicia, Toledo, Zaragoza, and the Asturias (b. 1 March 1105 – md. (2) July 1152 – d. 21 Aug 1157) + Richilde (or Richenza) of Poland (b. 1130/1140 – md. July 1152 – d. 1166)

[For the later generations that connect this line to the kings of England, see the line of Bl. Agnes of Franconia in Part II.]

Sources: *Baring-Gould:* Vol. 2, pp. 445–447** + Vol. 4, pp. 64–68* + Vol. 6, p. 279; *BBKL*, Vol. 21, cols. 401–402; *Benedictine Monks*, pp. 278 and 364*; *Bunson*, pp. 327 and 415–416*; *Butler*, Vol. II, pp. 26–27; *CE*, Vol. VI, p. 114; *Dunbar*, Vol. I, p. 320 (under "Florence"); *Holweck*, pp. 388 and 513–514*; *NCE*, Vol. 8, p. 590**; *O'Malley*, pp. 77* and 78; *Stuart*: line 276 + line 248, nos. 32 through 30 + line 94, nos. 30 and 29; *Tucker*, Vol. II, pp. 638 and 469; *Wells*, pp. 593, 37; *WWH*, Vol. 5, pp. 637–638 (All the references marked with a * are alphabetized under "Isidore of Seville." All the references marked with a ** are alphabetized under "Leander.") Also see ***fmg.ac>Projects>Medieval Lands>Medieval Lands – data by region>Iberia>Vandals, Suevi & Visigoths>Recaredo I 586–601, Liuva II 601–603***. In addition, see ***fmg.ac>Projects>Medieval Lands>Medieval Lands – data by region>Iberia>Vandals, Suevi & Visigoths>Suintila 621–633***.

St. Fulgentius, Bishop of Ecija

Fulgentius was born in the late 500's and was the son of Severinus, Count of Cartagena, and his wife Theodora, a daughter of Theodoric "the Great," the Ostrogoth King of Italy.

Fulgentius became a priest and was later appointed bishop of Ecija in Andalusia. An active preacher, he became one of the leaders of the Spanish church.

In the spring of 585 following the death of St. Hermenegild at the hands of the Arian heretic King Leovigild, a violent persecution of the Trinitarian Christians by Arian heretics began. Property and revenues of Trinitarian churches were seized. Several nobles were put to death and their lands confiscated. Fulgentius and several other bishops were exiled.

A year later as he was about to die, Leovigild repented of his Arian heresy, the murder of his son Hermenegild, and his other cruelties. Fulgentius and the other bishops returned. Under Leovigild's son and successor Recared, the whole country converted to Trinitarian Christianity.

Fulgentius died around 633. His relics are at Berzoncana and Murcia. He is the patron saint of Cartagena.

Fulgentius' brothers were St. Isidore of Seville and St. Leander. His sisters were St. Florentina and Theodosia, who would become the mother of St. Hermenegild.

His Line

Husband		Wife	
Severinus, Count of Cartagena	+	**Theodora**, daughter of Theodoric "the Great," the Ostrogoth King of Italy	
Leovigildo (or Leovigild), King of the Visigoths in Spain (d. 586)	+	md. (1) **Theodosia**	Theodosia's brother: ***St. Fulgentius, Bishop of Ecija***
Recaredo (or Recared) I, King of the Visigoths in Spain (d. 601)	+	Chlodesindis (or Clodoswindis)	
Suintila (or Suintilo), King of the Visigoths in Spain (deposed in 631)	+	Theodora, daughter of Sisebuto, King of the Visigoths in Spain	
Ervigio, King of the Visigoths in Spain (d. 687)	+	**Liubigotona**	

[For the later generations that connect this line to the kings of England, see the line of St. Florentina in Part III.]

Sources: *Benedictine Monks*, p. 294; *Bunson*, p. 344; *CE*, Vol. VI, pp. 315–316; *Delaney and Tobin*, p. 451; *Holweck*, p. 407; *O'Malley*, pp. 77–78; *Stuart*, line 276, no. 44; *Tucker*, Vol. II, pp. 638 and 469; *Wells*, p. 593. Also see ***fmg.ac>Projects>Medieval Lands>Medieval Lands – data by region>Iberia>Vandals, Suevi & Visigoths> Recaredo I 586–601, Liuva II 601–603***. In addition, see ***fmg.ac>Projects>Medieval Lands> Medieval Lands – data by region>Iberia>Vandals, Suevi & Visigoths>Suintila 621–633***.

St. Galswintha

Galswintha was the daughter of Athanagildo, King of the Visigoths in Spain, and his wife Gosvinta. Her sister was Brunhilda, who married Sigebert I, King of Austrasia.

After Sigebert's marriage to Brunhilda, his half-brother Chilperic I, King of Neustria, became interested in Brunhilda's sister Galswintha. Chilperic was already married, but in negotiations with Athanagildo he agreed to end his first marriage and have Galswintha as his only wife. Athanagildo then sent Galswintha to Neustria to marry Chilperic and also paid a substantial dowry to Chilperic.

Chilperic and Galswintha were married, and for a time all was well. To honor her new husband, Galswintha converted from the Arian Christianity practiced in Visigothic Spain to the Trinitarian (or Catholic) Christianity of the Merovingians.

Trouble began when Chilperic once again began paying attention to his mistress Fredegunde. At first, Galswintha suffered the loss of Chilperic's affections in silence. Then she began to complain. She told Chilperic he could keep her dowry if he would just let her return to her Spanish homeland.

Assisted by Fredegunde, Chilperic chose a different solution for his family problems. One night around 568, Galswintha was strangled in her bed by an assassin sent by her husband and his mistress. After a few days of mourning, Chilperic made Fredegunde his third wife.

Galswintha's murder had serious consequences. Brunhilda's husband Sigebert declared war on Chilperic, and the two men fought each other in one battle after another for the rest of their lives. A terrible blood feud between Brunhilda and Fredegunde also erupted that would go on for decades and do much damage to both of their countries. All their acts of mutual cruelty gave both women an infamous reputation that survives to this day.

Galswintha was remembered differently. Because of her conversion to Catholicism, her patient suffering of Chilperic's bad treatment, her murder by him, and subsequent miracles at her tomb, she became a saint.

Her Line

Husband		Wife	
Athanagildo (or Athanagild), King of the Visigoths in Spain (d. 568)	+	**Gosvinta (or Goiswintha)**	
Sigebert I, King of Metz (Austrasia) (murdered 575)	+	**Brunhilda (or Brunechildis)**	Brunhilda's sister: ***St. Galswintha***
Recaredo (or Recared) I, King of the Visigoths in Spain (d. 601)	+	**Chlodesindis (or Clodoswindis)**	
Suintila (or Suintilo), King of the Visigoths in Spain (deposed in 631)	+	Theodora, daughter of Sisebuto, King of the Visigoths in Spain	

Ervigio, King of the Visigoths in Spain + **Liubigotona**
(d. 687)

[For the later generations that connect this line to the kings of England, see the line of St. Florentina in Part III.]

Sources: *Dunbar*, Vol. I, pp. 331–332; *Stuart*, line 276, no. 44; *Wells*, pp. 593, 37; *WWH*, Vol. 6, pp. 35–36. Also see ***fmg.ac>Projects>Medieval Lands>Medieval Lands – data by region>Iberia>Vandals, Suevi & Visigoths>Recaredo I 586–601, Liuva II 601–603***. In addition, see ***fmg.ac>Projects>Medieval Lands>Medieval Lands – data by region>Iberia>Vandals, Suevi & Visigoths>Suintila 621–633***.

Bl. Gerard

Gerard was born shortly before 1090 and was the son of Tescelin Sorrel, Lord of Les Fontaines, and his wife Bl. Aleth of Montbard. He was an older brother of St. Bernard of Clairvaux.

Well educated in childhood, Gerard trained in military exercises and feats of arms. He then became a knight and fought in the local wars. At first he had no interest in the monastic life, but then he was wounded at the siege of Grancey, taken prisoner, and miraculously escaped after a long captivity.

Gerard then decided to become a monk and follow Bernard into his abbey. He had always been Bernard's favorite brother and was appointed cellarer of the abbey and manager of its domestic affairs. He was so good in his position that craftsmen would come from great distances to see how things were made at Clairvaux.

At Clairvaux, Gerard became Bernard's close confidant. He died on 13 June 1138, and the sermon which Bernard preached at his funeral is still admired today.

His Line

Husband		Wife	
Tescelin Sorrel (or Sorus), Lord of Les Fontaines (md. ca. 1085)	+	**Bl. Aleth of Montbard** (b. ca. 1070 – md. ca. 1085 – d. 1105/1110)	
Anseric II, Sire de Chacenay (d. 1137)	+	md. (1) **Bl. Humbeline de Troyes** (b. 1092 – d. 21 Aug 1141)	Humbeline's brother: ***Bl. Gerard***
Gui, Count of Bar-sur-Seine (d. 1145)	+	**Petronille de Chacenay** (d. 1161)	

[For the later generations that connect this line to the kings of England, see the line of Bl. Aleth of Montbard in Part II.]

Sources: *Baring-Gould*, Vol. 6, pp. 179–180; *BBKL*, Vol. 2, col. 215; *Benedictine Monks*, p. 306; *Butler*, Vol. III, p. 360; *Delaney*, p. 251; *Holweck*, p. 427; *NCE*, Vol. 6, p. 377; *O'Malley*, pp. 73 and 99; *Stuart:* line 385 + line 384, nos. 29 and 28; *Wells*, p. 144

St. Gertrude of Nivelles

Gertrude was born in 626 and was the daughter of Bl. Pepin of Landen and his wife Bl. Itta. She was a sister of St. Begga.

After Pepin died in 640, Itta built a monastery at Nivelles near Brussels. She and Gertrude both became nuns and entered it, with Gertrude becoming the first abbess.

After her mother Itta died in 652, Gertrude used her inheritance to build churches, monasteries, and hospitals. She was also known for her hospitality to pilgrims. Gertrude's self-imposed penances were so severe that by the time she turned thirty in 656, she was worn out. She resigned her position as abbess that year and spent the rest of her life studying Scripture, doing additional penances, and receiving visions.

Gertrude died on 17 March 659. She was venerated as a saint immediately after her death, and many miracles were credited to her. She became one of the most popular saints of the Middle Ages.

In 1940, the reliquary at Nivelles containing Gertrude's remains was destroyed.

Her Line

Husband		Wife	
Bl. Pepin (or Pippin) of Landen "the Old," Mayor of the Palace in Austrasia (b. 580/585 – d. 640/646)	+	**Bl. Itta** (b. ca. 597 – d. 8 May 652)	
Ansgise (or Ansegisel), Mayor of the Palace in Austrasia (b. 602 – md. bef. 639 – murdered 685)	+	**St. Begga** (b. ca. 613 – md. bef. 639 – d. ca. 698)	Begga's sister: ***St. Gertrude of Nivelles***
Pepin (or Pippin) of Heristal, Mayor of the Palace in Austrasia (b. ca. 635 – d. 16 Dec 714)	+	Aupais, a concubine (b. ca. 654)	

[For the later generations that connect this line to the kings of England, see the line of St. Arnulf, Bishop of Metz in Part II.]

Sources: *Baring-Gould*, Vol. 3, pp. 306–309; *BBKL*, Vol. 2, cols. 232–233; *Benedictine Monks*, p. 311; *Bunson*, p. 363; *Butler*, Vol. I, pp. 620–621; *CE*, Vol. VI, pp. 533–534; *Delaney*, p. 255; *Delaney and Tobin*, p. 479; *Dunbar*, Vol. I, pp. 342–345; *Holweck*, p. 432; *Joeckle*, pp. 184–185; *NCE*, Vol. 6, p. 451; *O'Malley*, pp. 41, 72, and 92; *Snodgrass*, pp. 97–98; *Stuart:* line 260 + line 171, nos. 45 and 44; *Tucker*, Vol. I, pp. 182–183; *Weis, AR*, line 190, nos. 9 and 10; *Wells*, p. 135; *WWH*, Vol. 6, p. 180

St. Gisela, Abbess of Chelles

Gisela was born in 757 and was the daughter of Pepin III "the Short," Mayor of the Palace in Austrasia and King of the Franks, and his wife Bertha "Bigfoot." She was a sister of Bl. Charlemagne.

Gisela became a nun, entered the abbey at Chelles, and ultimately became abbess there. She died on 30 July 810. She is also known as Idaberga and Isberga.

Her Line

	Husband		Wife
	Pepin (or Pippin) III "the Short," Mayor of the Palace in Austrasia and King of the Franks (b. 715 – md. ca. 740 – d. 24 Sept 768)	+	**Bertha (or Bertrada) "Bigfoot"** (b. ca. 720 – md. ca. 740 – d. 12 July 783)
Charlemagne's sister: ***St. Gisela, Abbess of Chelles***	**Bl. Charlemagne**, King of France and First Emperor of the West (b. 2 April 747 – md. (2) 771 – d. 28 Jan 814)	+	Bl. Hildegarde, Countess of Vinzgau (b. 758 – md. 771 – d. 30 April 783)
	Louis I "the Fair," King of France and Emperor of the West (b. Aug 778 – md. (2) 819 – d. 20 June 840)	+	Judith of Altdorf (or Judith of Bavaria) (b. ca. 800 – md. 819 – d. 19 April 843)

[For the later generations that connect this line to the kings of England, see the line of St. Arnulf, Bishop of Metz in Part II.]

Sources: *Baring-Gould*, Vol. 5, 320–322; *Chamberlin*, pp. 65–70, 155, and 219; *Dunbar*, Vol. I, pp. 403–404 (under "Idaberg"); *Holweck*, p. 512 (under "Isberga"); *Riché, The Carolingians*, pp. 73 and 79; *Riché, Daily Life*, pp. 60–61; *Stuart*, line 171, nos. 42 through 40; *Weis, AR:* line 50, nos. 23 and 13 + line 148, nos. 13 and 14; *Wells*, pp. 136–137; *WWH*, Vol. 6, p. 262. Also see ***fmg.ac>Projects>Medieval Lands>Medieval Lands – data by region>France>Kings & early nobility>Carolingian Kings>Pepin 751–768, Carloman 768–771***.

St. Gistald

Gistald was the son of St. Sigismund, King of Burgundy, and his wife Theodogotho. He was martyred along with his father, mother, and brother St. Gundebald in 523/524. His relics are at the abbey of St. Maurice in Valais.

His Line

	Husband		Wife
	St. Sigismund, King of Burgundy (reigned 516–523)	+	**Theodogotho**, daughter of Theodoric I of the Ostrogoths
Wacho's brother: ***St. Gistald***	**Wacho**, King of the Lombards	+	Austigusa, princess of the Gepidae
	Garibald I, Duke of Bavaria (liv. 553–592)	+	**Waldrada**

[For the later generations that connect this line to the kings of England, see the line of St. Sigismund, King of Burgundy in Part II.]

Sources: *Holweck*, p. 437; *Stuart*, line 380, nos. 51 through 49

St. Gladys

Gladys was a daughter of St. Brychan of Brecknock. She married a son of Glywys, King of Glywysing. There are several forms of her husband's name: Gwynllyw, or Gwynllyw Filwr ("the Warrior") or Gwynllyw Farfog ("the Bearded"), or Gundleus, Woolo, or Woolos. The first child of Gwynllyw and Gladys was their son St. Cadoc.

Gwynllyw was a feared warlord who often attacked nearby kingdoms. In all his deeds of blood, he was supported by his wife Gladys.

It was not until St. Cadoc had grown to be a man that his example and preaching caused both of his parents to abandon their violent way of life and seek forgiveness for their sins. Their conversion seems to have been sincere. It is written that Gwynllyw gave up his throne and that he and his wife then spent their last years at Newport in Wales in religious contemplation. They both became saints.

The life span suggested for Gwynllyw begins around 466 and ends around 523. Gladys' dates are unknown but probably similar. They are buried in St. Woolo's Cathedral in Newport.

Her Line

Husband		Wife	
St. Brychan, ruler of Brecknock in South Wales (b. 480/490)	+	**N.N.**	
St. Gabran mac Domangart, King of Dalriada (b. ca. 500 – md. bef. 532 – d. ca. 559)	+	**St. Lleian** (md. bef. 532)	Lleian's sister: ***St. Gladys***
Aidan (or Aedan) mac Gabran (b. 532 – d. 606), crowned King of Dalriada by St. Columba of Iona	+	N.N.	

[For the later generations that connect this line to the kings of England, see the line of St. Brychan in Part II.]

Sources: *Ashley*, pp. 158 and 197; *Baring-Gould and Fisher:* Vol. 2, pp. 14–15 and 21 + Vol. 3, pp. 202–204; *Benedictine Monks*, pp. 315 and 328*; *Bunson*, p. 367; *Butler*, Vol. I, pp. 699–700; *CS*, pp. 167–169; *Delaney*, p. 273; *Delaney and Tobin*, pp. 489 and 522*; *Holweck*, pp. 437 and 462 (under "Gwynllw"); *Rees*, p. 69; *Stuart*, line 165, nos. 49 and 48; *Weis, AR*, line 170, nos. 4 and 5; *Wells*, p. 177 (references marked with a * are alphabetized under "Gundleus")

St. Gleb the Passion-Bearer, Prince of Kiev

Gleb was born around 995/1000. He was the youngest son of St. Vladimir I "the Great," Grand Prince of Kiev and ruler of Kievan Rus, and Anna, daughter of the Byzantine Emperor Romanos II.

Like his brother St. Boris, Gleb was devoutly Christian. His father Vladimir had made him ruler of the city of Murom, and he was still in his teens when his brother Sviatpolk "the Accursed" seized power after Vladimir's death in July 1015 and murdered St. Boris.

Believing that Vladimir was gravely ill but still alive, Gleb was returning to Kiev by boat on 5 September 1015 when his vessel was approached by another boat carrying Sviatpolk's henchmen. After they boarded, Gleb learned of the death of Vladimir, the murder of St. Boris, and Sviatpolk's plans to kill him too. At first Gleb begged to be spared, saying he was still only a boy. Then he grew calm, prayed for his murderers, and offered no further resistance. He was killed by his own cook who cut his throat.

After Sviatpolk was vanquished in the subsequent civil war by his brother St. Jaroslav I Vladimirovich "the Wise," Gleb's body was found and reburied next to his brother Boris. Many miracles were attributed to Gleb, who was made one of the first saints of the Russian Church along with his brother Boris and who was also given the title of Passion-Bearer. In later centuries he was esteemed equally with Boris and is often pictured together with him.

Gleb is sometimes called "David."

His Line

St. Vladimir I Sviatoslavich "the Great," Grand Prince of Kiev and Novgorod (b. ca. 955 – d. 15 July 1015)

md. (3) **Rognieda of Polotsk** (b. ca. 956 – d. 1102)
Son of Vladimir and Rognieda:

md. (7) Anna, daughter of Romanus II, Emperor of Byzantium
Son of Vladimir and Anna: ***St. Gleb the Passion-Bearer, Prince of Kiev***

St. Yaroslav I Vladimirovich "the Wise," Grand Prince of Kiev (b. 978 – md. (2) Feb 1019 – d. 20 Feb 1054) + St. Ingegerd, Princess of Sweden (b. ca. 1001 – md. Feb 1019 – d. 10 Feb 1050)

St. Izyaslav I Yaroslavich, Grand Prince of Kiev (b. 1024/1025 – md. ca. 1043 – slain 3 Oct 1078)	+	Gertrude (md. ca. 1043), daughter of Mieszko II, King of Poland

[For the later generations that connect this line to the kings of England, see the line of St. Izyaslav I Yaroslavich, Grand Prince of Kiev in Part II.]

Sources: *Baring-Gould*, Vol. 10, pp. 75–76; *Benedictine Monks*, p. 613; *Bunson*, pp. 174–175; *Butler*, Vol. III, pp. 175–176; *Cruz*, pp. 102–105; *Delaney and Tobin*, p. 161 (under "Boris"); *Fedotov*, p. 72; *Guilev*, p. 52; *Holweck*, pp. 168 (under "Boris") and 265 (under "David") and 437 (under "Gleb"); *Klaniczay*, pp. 109–115 and Appendix B, Geneal. Table 2; *O'Malley*, pp. 90–91; *One Hundred Saints*, pp. 178–179; *Snodgrass*, p. 46; *Tucker*, Vol. II, pp. 731–732; *Weis, AR*, line 241, nos. 4, 5², and 6²; *Wells*, pp. 328–330

St. Grigoris

Grigoris was born in the early 300's and was the son of St. Vardanes, Bishop of Armenia. He was the brother of St. Yusik.

Grigoris became a missionary to the lands between eastern Armenia and the Caspian Sea. As he traveled, he preached and built churches. When he reached the territory around the present-day city of Derbent in Dagestan in 348, he began to preach to a people called the Mazkuts. Their king Sanesan was not pleased with the message of Grigoris and thought it was part of an Armenian plot. On his order, Grigoris was tied to the tail of a wild horse and dragged to death.

Grigoris' body was taken to a church in Amaras which he himself had completed and buried beneath the altar. Today that church is called the church of St. Grigoris. It is part of the monastery of Amaras, which is near the town of Soss in Nagorno-Karabakh.

Grigoris is also known as Krikoris.

His Line

	Husband		Wife
	St. Vardanes (d. 339/341)	+	N.N.
Yusik's brother: ***St. Grigoris***	**St. Yusik I** (b. ca. 305 – martyred ca. 348)	+	N.N., a daughter of St. Tiridates "the Great," King of Armenia
	Athenagenes	+	Bambishu (b. 315)

[For the later generations that connect this line to the kings of England, see the line of St. Ashken in Part II.]

Sources: *Koushagian*, pp. 10, 19, and 21; *Stone*, Chart 80; *Stuart*, line 416, no. 56; *Wagner*, p. 195

St. Gundebald

Gundebald was the son of St. Sigismund, King of Burgundy, and his wife Theodogotho. He was martyred along with his father, mother, and brother St. Gistald in 523/524. His relics are at the abbey of St. Maurice in Valais.

His Line

	Husband		Wife
	St. Sigismund, King of Burgundy (reigned 516–523)	+	**Theodogotho**, daughter of Theodoric I of the Ostrogoths
Wacho's brother: ***St. Gundebald***	**Wacho**, King of the Lombards	+	Austigusa, princess of the Gepidae
	Garibald I, Duke of Bavaria (liv. 553–592)	+	**Waldrada**

[For the later generations that connect this line to the kings of England, see the line of St. Sigismund, King of Burgundy in Part II.]

Sources: *Holweck*, p. 457; *Stuart*, line 380, nos. 51 through 49

St. Gundelindis of Alsace

Gundelindis was the daughter of Adalbert, Duke of Alsace, and his wife Gerlinde. She was educated by her aunt St. Odilia and became a Benedictine nun.

Gundelindis ultimately became abbess of a convent at Niedermuenster founded by St. Odilia. She died there around 750.

Gundelindis was a sister of St. Attalia and St. Eugenia. She is also known as Gudelindis.

Her Line

	Husband		Wife
	Adalbert, Duke of Alsace (d. 722)	+	**Gerlinde**
Luitfride's sister: ***St. Gundelindis of Alsace***	**Luitfride I**, Duke of Alsace (d. 767)	+	Edith
	Luitfride II, Count of Upper Alsace (d. 802)	+	Hiltrude

[For the later generations that connect this line to the kings of England, see the line of St. Attalia in Part III.]

Sources: *BBKL*, Vol. 17, cols. 546–547; *Benedictine Monks*, p. 327; *Bunson*, p. 381; *Delaney and Tobin*, p. 522; *Holweck*, p. 454; *NCE*, Vol. 5, p. 627 (under "St. Eugenia"); *Stuart*, line 224, nos. 41 through 39; *Weis, AR*, line 181, nos. 2 through 4; *Wells*, p. 9

St. Guntram I, King of Burgundy

Guntram was born in 525 and was the son of Clothaire I, King of Soissons, and his third wife Inguda.

When Clothaire I died in 561, his realm was divided among his sons, and Guntram was given the kingdom of Burgundy.

In the Dark Ages, rulers were judged by two different measures. One was the domestic one: Is a ruler a fair monarch who cares about his subjects and who works hard to provide for their welfare? By this measure, Guntram was an outstanding and very saintly ruler. He prayed and fasted often. He endowed churches and monasteries, sponsored three synods, and was also very popular with the clergy. He would visit his people in their own homes and sit at their tables. He was a just ruler, accessible and clement. He was well known for his charity and deeply loved by his subjects. When plague reached the Burgundian city of Marseilles in 588, Guntram went out and walked among his suffering people, giving them food and leading them in prayers for relief from the scourge of disease.

The other measure of a Dark Ages ruler was the military one: Is a ruler an effective leader of his troops? Does he win his battles and destroy the armies of his enemies? By this measure, Guntram was an utter failure. He was afraid of war and wouldn't lead his own armies into battle. He was unable to even control his own troops as they marched, thus allowing them to degenerate into looters and brigands who plundered the surrounding countryside without limit. Fortunately for Guntram, he had the services of competent generals, and his nearest neighbors—Neustria ruled by his brother Chilperic and Austrasia ruled by his brother Sigebert—were so often at war with each other that Burgundy was left relatively unmolested.

Guntram had children by an unknown mistress, by his first wife Marcatrude, and by his second wife Austrechild. After a reign of 31 years, Guntram died in his bed in 592. He is also known as Gunthrammus and Gontran.

His Line

	Husband		Wife
	Clothaire I, King of Soissons, Orleans, and France (b. 500 – d. 561)	+	md. (4) **Arnegundis (or Aregonde or Aregund)**
Chilperic's brother: ***St. Guntram I, King of Burgundy***	**Chilperic I**, King of Neustria (b. 523 – d. 584)	+	md. (3) Fredegunde "one of the most bloodthirsty women in history" (b. 543 – d. 597)
	Clothaire II, King of Neustria and the Franks (b. 584 – d. 629), signed the "Perpetual Constitution" 614/615, an early Magna Charta	+	Haldetrude (d. 604)

[For the later generations that connect this line to the kings of England, see the line of St. Clothilde in Part II.]

Sources: *BBKL*, Vol. 22, cols. 484–485; *Benedictine Monks*, pp. 328–329; *Butler*, Vol. I, pp. 695–696; *Cruz*, pp. 281–283; *Delaney*, pp. 273–274; *Delaney and Tobin*, p. 523; *Holweck*, p. 459; *Klaniczay*, p. 69; *Scherman, Birth of France*, frontispiece and pp. 149, 169–171, 180–181, and 183; *Stuart*, line 303, nos. 51 through 49; *Wells*, pp. 384–385. N.B.: Stuart mistakenly claims that Rodegunda is the mother of Chilperic I. For confirmation that Arnegundis is Chilperic's mother, see ***fmg.ac>Projects>Medieval Lands>MedievalLands–data by region>France>Kings & early nobility>Merovingian Kings> Clotaire 511–561, Charibert 561–567, Gontran 561–592***.

Bl. Guy

Guy was born shortly before 1090 and was the son of Tescelin Sorrel, Lord of Les Fontaines, and his wife Bl. Aleth of Montbard. He was the oldest brother of St. Bernard of Clairvaux.

When Bernard first answered the call to the monastic life, Guy was already married and the father of two daughters. As all his other brothers began to follow Bernard into the life of the spirit, Guy held out the longest, but ultimately he and his wife agreed to separate. Guy then entered Bernard's abbey and spent the rest of his life there. His wife and daughters entered a convent at Laire near Dijon.

His Line

Husband		Wife	
Tescelin Sorrel (or Sorus), Lord of Les Fontaines (md. ca. 1085)	+	**Bl. Aleth of Montbard** (b. ca. 1070 – md. ca. 1085 – d. 1105/1110)	
Anseric II, Sire de Chacenay (d. 1137)	+	md. (1) **Bl. Humbeline de Troyes** (b. 1092 – d. 21 Aug 1141)	Humbeline's brother: ***Bl. Guy***
Gui, Count of Bar-sur-Seine (d. 1145)	+	**Petronille de Chacenay** (d. 1161)	

[For the later generations that connect this line to the kings of England, see the line of Bl. Aleth of Montbard in Part II.]

Sources: *Butler*, Vol. III, p. 360; *Holweck*, p. 456; *O'Malley*, pp. 73 and 99; *Stuart:* line 385 + line 384, nos. 29 and 28; *Wells*, p. 144

Bl. Hathumoda

Hathumoda was born around 839 and was one of the twelve children of Ludolph, Duke of Saxony, and his wife Oda.

Hathumoda was educated at the abbey at Herford and like four of her sisters became a nun. In 851 when she was twelve years old, she became abbess of a monastery which her parents had founded at Brunshausen for the daughters of princes. Five years later, it moved to Gandersheim, and Hathumoda spent the rest of her life there.

Hathumoda was well known for her knowledge of Scripture and for her charity. She was a mother to all and especially to the sick. Late in 874 when an epidemic visited her monastery and many fell ill, Hathumoda worked hard caring for all the sick until she caught the illness herself and died on 29 November 874.

Her Line

	Husband		Wife
	Ludolph, Duke of Saxony (b. 816 – d. 866)	+	**Oda** (b. 806 – d. 913), daughter of Billung, Count of Thuringia
Otto's sister: ***Bl. Hathumoda***	**Otto "the Illustrious,"** Duke of Saxony and Count in South Thuringia (b. ca. 836 – md. 869 – d. 30 Nov 912)	+	Hedwig (md. 869 – d. 906), daughter of Arnulf, King of the East Franks
	Henry I "the Fowler," Duke of Saxony and Emperor of the West (b. 876 – md. (2) 909 – d. 2 July 936)	+	St. Mathilda of Ringelheim (b. ca. 890/900 – md. 909 – d. 14 March 968)
	Giselbert, Duke of Lorraine and Count of Hainault (b. ca. 890 – md. 929 – d. 2 Oct 934)	+	**Gerberge of Saxony** (b. 913/914 – md. (1) 929 – d. 5 May 984)

[For the later generations that connect this line to the kings of England, see the line of St. Adela, Princess of Austrasia in Part II.]

Sources: *BBKL*, Vol. 15, cols. 692–693; *Dunbar*, Vol. I, p. 360; *Stuart*, line 92, nos. 38 through 35; *Weis, AR:* line 141, nos. 16 through 18 + line 142, nos. 17 and 18; *Wells*, pp. 138 and 269–270; *WWH*, Vol. 7, p. 61

St. Hedwig of Silesia

Hedwig was born in 1174 and was the daughter of Berthold IV, Count of Andechs, and his wife Agnes von Groitzsch-Rochlitz. She was one of eight children, many of whom became prominent in the Central European church. Two of her brothers became bishops. One sister became an abbess. Another sister became the mother of St. Elizabeth of Hungary.

Hedwig was educated in the monastery of Hitzingen. In 1186 at the age of twelve, she married Henry, Duke of Silesia, who was eighteen. In a very happy marriage, they had seven children. Henry was a pious man who let Hedwig use her dowry to found a large monastery for nuns at Trebnitz near Breslau. The two of them also founded other monasteries, convents, and hospitals.

Hedwig was a remarkable woman who was considered a saint even during her own lifetime. She lived like a penitent, with prayers, fasts, and mortifications. She was also famous for always walking to church barefoot, even in winter. She wore the same cloak in summer and winter, with a hair shirt next to her skin.

As she practiced her several austerities, Hedwig was a very visible figure in the public life of her realm. She taught religion to the poor and founded a home for women who were lepers. She performed several miraculous cures of the sick. She was also an adviser to her husband as he governed his domains. After he died in 1238, she acted as regent for their son Henry II, who succeeded his father. After Henry II died fighting the Mongols in 1240, she also acted as regent for her grandson Boleslas II.

Hedwig lived like a nun but never became one. She moved into her own monastery at Trebnitz after her husband died in 1238. Wanting to remain free to administer her own property in her own way for the relief of suffering, she never took vows. She died on 15 October 1243 and is buried at Trebnitz next to her husband.

Hedwig was deeply loved by her people and is the patron saint of Silesia.

Her Line

Husband		Wife	
Berthold VI, Count of Andechs, Margrave of Istria, and Duke of Croatia; Crusader (b. ca. 1152 – md. 1170 – d. 12 Aug 1204)	+	Agnes von Groitzsch-Rochlitz (md. 1170 – d. 25 March 1195)	
Andrew II, King of Hungary (b. 1176 – md. (1) bef. 1203 – d. 21 Sept 1235)	+	**Gertrude von Meran** (md. bef. 1203 – d. 8 Sept 1213)	Gertrude's sister: ***St. Hedwig of Silesia***
Bela IV, King of Hungary (b. 1206 – md. 1218 – d. 3 May 1270)	+	Maria Laskarina (b. ca. 1206 – md. 1218 – d. 1270), daughter of Theodore I Lascaris, Emperor of Byzantium	

[For the later generations that connect this line to the kings of England, see the line of St. Adalbero, Bishop of Wuerzburg in Part III.]

Sources: *Baring-Gould*, Vol. 12, pp. 456–464; *BBKL*, Vol. 2, cols. 636–638; *Benedictine Monks*, p. 333; *Bentley*, p. 204; *Bunson*, p. 385; *Butler*, Vol. IV, pp. 124–125; *CE*, Vol. VII, pp. 189–190; *Cruz*, pp. 293–295; *Delaney*, p. 277; *Delaney and Tobin*, p. 538; *Dunbar*, Vol. I, pp. 362–366; *Giorgi*, pp. 608–609; *Holboeck*, pp. 174–181; *Holweck*, p. 466; *Joeckle*, pp. 193–195; *Klaniczay*, pp. 203–204, 223, 251–257, and Appendix B, Geneal. Table 9; *NCE*, Vol. 6, pp. 984–985; *O'Malley*, p. 125; *Snodgrass*, p. 113; *Stuart:* line 7, nos. 29 and 28 + line 78, nos. 28 and 27; *Warncke*, pp. 116–117; *Weis, AR*, line 103, nos. 28 and 29; *Wells*, pp. 381 and 309; *WWH*, Vol. 7, p. 148

Bl. Henry Zdik, Bishop of Olmuetz

Henry was the son of Wratislav I, the Chief Duke of Bohemia, and his wife Drahomir of Stodar. He became a priest at an early age.

In the central European church. Henry received several responsible positions. In 1126, he became the bishop of Olomouc in the Czech Republic, where he rebuilt the cathedral. In 1138 he went on a pilgrimage to Jerusalem, and while he was in the Holy Land he became a monk and joined the Norbertine Order. After returning home, he founded several houses for the Norbertines and also worked to restore monastic discipline in Bohemia. When St. Bernard of Clairvaux went out to preach the 2nd Crusade (1147–1149), Henry took his message to Bohemia and Moravia.

Henry died on 25 June 1151 and is buried at the Mount Sion Abbey in Strahov, one of the monasteries he founded.

His Line

	Husband		Wife
	Wratislaw I, Chief Duke of Bohemia (md. bef. 910 – d. 13 Feb 921)	+	**Drahomir of Stodar**
Boleslaw's brother: ***Bl. Henry Zdik, Bishop of Olmuetz***	**Boleslaw I "the Cruel,"** Duke of Bohemia (d. 15 July 972)	+	Biagota of Stockow
	Boleslaw II "the Pious," Duke of Bohemia (d. 7 Feb 999)	+	Hemma (d. ca. 1005)

[For the later generations that connect this line to the kings of England, see the line of St. Ludmilla, Duchess of Bohemia in Part II.]

Sources: *Benedictine Monks*, p. 337; *Delaney*, p. 281; *Holweck*, p. 471; *Stuart*, line 362, nos. 38 through 36; *Wells*, pp. 78–79

St. Hermenegild

Hermenegild was born in the early 560's and was the son of Leovigild the Visigoth, King of Spain, and his first wife Theodosia.

Leovigild was a Christian but followed the Arian heresy. The greatest difference which Arians had with other Christians was their belief that Jesus was not one with God the Father but rather a being created by God the Father at a definite point in time. This belief led Arians to reject the concept of the Blessed Trinity, which is the central concept of the Nicene Creed as adopted by the Council of Nicea. Opponents of the Arians were called Trinitarians.

In his youth, Hermenegild was an Arian too. His beliefs began to change in 579 after he married Ingudis, who was a Trinitarian and the daughter of King Sigebert I of Austrasia. Under the influence of Ingudis and St. Leander, who was Hermenegild's uncle, in 580 Hermenegild became a Trinitarian Christian too.

Leovigild refused to accept his son's conversion. At first, he exiled Hermenegild. Then Hermenegild revolted against Leovigild. The revolt was poorly planned and did not have enough troops or equipment to prevail against Leovigild. After being besieged in Seville for over a year, Hermenegild was betrayed by his allies, captured, and imprisoned around March 584.

In an effort to make him return to Arianism, Hermenegild was tortured but remained steadfast. When he refused communion offered to him by an Arian priest on 13 April 585, he was beheaded.

After Leovigild died, Hermenegild's brother Recared assumed the throne, and the kingdom of Spain returned to Trinitarian Christianity. Seen as a victim of Arianism and a martyr, Hermenegild was canonized. His relics are in Seville.

His Line

	Husband		**Wife**
	Leovigildo (or Leovigild), King of the Visigoths in Spain (d. 586)	+	md. (1) **Theodosia**, sister of St. Leander, Archbishop of Seville
Recared's brother: ***St. Hermenegild***	**Recaredo (or Recared) I**, King of the Visigoths in Spain (d. 601)	+	Chlodesindis (or Clodoswindis)
	Suintila (or Suintilo), King of the Visigoths in Spain (deposed in 631)	+	Theodora, daughter of Sisebuto, King of the Visigoths in Spain
	Ervigio, King of the Visigoths in Spain (d. 687)	+	**Liubigotona**

[For the later generations that connect this line to the kings of England, see the line of St. Florentina in Part III.]

Sources: *Baring-Gould*, Vol. 4, pp. 184–185; *Benedictine Monks*, p. 340; *Bunson*, p. 391; *Butler*, Vol. II, pp. 82–83; *CE*, Vol. VII, p. 276; *Cruz*, pp. 318–321; *Delaney*, p. 282; *Delaney and Tobin*, p. 554; *Giorgi*, pp. 224–225; *Holweck*, p. 476; *Klaniczay*, p.

68; *NCE*, Vol. 6, pp. 1074–1075; *O'Callaghan*, p. 44; *Stuart*, line 276, no. 44; *Wells*, pp. 593 and 37. Also see ***fmg.ac>Projects>Medieval Lands>Medieval Lands – data by region>Iberia>Vandals, Suevi & Visigoths>Recaredo I 586–601, Liuva II 601–603***. In addition, see ***fmg.ac>Projects>Medieval Lands>Medieval Lands – data by region>Iberia>Vandals, Suevi & Visigoths>Suintila 621–633***.

St. Hilda of Whitby

Hilda was born in 614, and in her early life, contact with saints was not always a blessing. Hilda's father was Hereric, who was a nephew of St. Edwin, King of Northumbria. When Hilda was two, Edwin sent Hereric to spy on a rival monarch, who was less than glad to see his Northumbrian guest. Hereric was invited to dinner and promptly poisoned. When Hilda was nineteen, Edwin himself was killed at the battle of Hatfield Chase, and Northumbria was overrun by pagans. Luckily, Hilda's sister St. Hereswitha was married to Anna, the king of East Anglia, and Hilda, her mother Berguswida, and other family members fled to Anna's court.

In exile in East Anglia, Hilda continued to live like a typical Dark Ages royal until 647 when she was thirty-three. Although she had been baptized twenty years earlier, Hilda had given no outward signs of having a religious vocation. Nevertheless, she suddenly decided to become a nun. After taking vows, she was on the point of leaving England to enter a convent in France when St. Aidan persuaded her to return to Northumbria and to start organizing religious communities among her own people.

The work for which Hilda is remembered began once she was back in Northumbria. Her first community was a group of nuns on a small estate on the banks of the River Wear. She then moved to a small monastery at Hartepool and became its abbess. In 649, she moved again to begin her greatest creation, the double monastery at Whitby.

Situated on the spot where St. Edwin was buried, Whitby would become the preeminent center of learning in Anglo-Saxon England. Supported by a vast land grant from St. Oswy, King of Northumbria, the school at Whitby trained several people who would go onto play leading roles in English Christianity. As the abbess of Whitby, Hilda not only ran the school but also managed all the land, animals, and people that supported the abbey. At Whitby, this amounted to thousands of acres.

After just a few years, Whitby had become prominent enough to host the synod of Whitby in 664. Called to settle a dispute about the proper day to celebrate Easter, the synod became one of the defining events in the shaping of the early Christian church. Hilda was both the organizer of the synod and one of its leaders as it took up its work. Among other things, this synod was the first to number the years since the birth of Christ. The synod's decision that it was meeting in the year 664 was the beginning of the system of numbering years that is still used today.

Hilda was famous for her wisdom generally and was an adviser to princes and kings. She was also dearly loved by the members of her abbey. After suffering from some form of wasting disease for the last six years of her life, she died on 17 November 680 and was immediately recognized as a saint.

Her Line

Husband		Wife	
Hereric (d. 616), a nephew of St. Edwin, King of Northumbria	+	**Berguswida**	
Anna, King of East Anglia (ruled ca. 641–653, until he died in battle with Penda of Mercia)	+	**St. Hereswitha (or Saeware)** (b. sh. bef. 616 – d. 680/690)	Hereswitha's sister: ***St. Hilda of Whitby***
Erconbert (or Eorconbeorht), King of Kent (b. ca. 624 – md. ca. 640 – d. 14 July 664)	+	**St. Sexburga** (md. ca. 640 – d. 6 July 699)	
Egbert, King of Kent (b. ca. 641 – d. 4 July 673)	+	N.N.	

[For the later generations that connect this line to the kings of England, see the line of St. Aethelbert I, King of Kent in Part II.]

Sources: *Baring-Gould*, Vol. 7, p. 158 (under "St. Sexburga") and Vol. 14, pp. 390–394; *BBKL*, Vol. 2, cols. 842–843; *Benedictine Monks*, p. 345; *Bunson*, p. 397; *Butler*, Vol. IV, pp. 369–370; *Castleden*, pp. 170–171; *CE*, Vol. VII, p. 350; *Chervin*, pp. 244–245; *CS*, pp. 709–711; *Delaney*, p. 286; *Delaney and Tobin*, p. 561; *Dunbar*, Vol. I, pp. 381–383; *Guiley*, pp. 146–147; *Holweck*, p. 474 (under "Hereswitha") and pp. 484–485; *Jones*, pp. 100–102; *NCE*, Vol. 6, p. 1116; *O'Malley*, pp. 181–182; *Parbury*, pp. 55–58; *Snodgrass*, pp. 118–119; *Stuart:* line 437, nos. 47 and 46 + line 233A, nos. 46 and 45; *Wells*, pp. 197 and 325; *WWH*, Vol. 7, pp. 299–303; *Yorke*, p. 80

St. Hugh the Great, Abbot of Cluny

Hugh was born in 1024 and was the son of Dalmace, Count of Semur, and his wife Aremburga. At an early age, he showed a very strong interest in the religious life and became a Benedictine monk at age 15 and an ordained priest at 20.

Hugh was a tall man with a striking appearance. His intellectual and spiritual abilities made such a profound impression on everyone he met that in 1049 at the age of 25 he was made abbot of the monastery at Cluny. He spent the next 60 years turning Cluny into what was, next to the papacy, the most influential institution in Christendom. At its apogee, Cluny controlled about 200 other Benedictine monasteries throughout Europe. Several of these had been built by Hugh, who also recruited the monks for them.

Hugh was one of the most influential men of his era. Besides heading a network of 200 monasteries, he counseled the greatest men of his age. He was an adviser to 9 popes and outlived 8 of them: St. Leo IX (d. 1054), Victor II (d. 1057), Stephen X (d. 1058), Nicholas II (d. 1061), Alexander II (d. 1073), St. Gregory VII (d. 1085), Bl. Victor III (d. 1087), and Bl. Urban II (d. 1099). Only Paschal II, who died in 1118, survived him. Hugh was also consulted by all the monarchs of Western Europe. He was entrusted with important diplomatic missions to Hungary (in 1051) and Germany (1072). At the Council of Clermont in 1095, he argued for and helped to organize the First Crusade.

Besides being a great man, Hugh was also a good man. At a hospital for lepers which he founded at Marcigny, he would tend to the patients with his own hands. His years as abbot were prodigiously fruitful, and he died on 29 April 1109. He was buried at Cluny.

Hugh is also known as Hugh of Cluny and Hugh of Semur.

His Line

Husband		Wife	
Damas (or Dalmace), Count of Semur (d. aft. 1048)	+	**Aremburga**	
Robert III "the Old," Duke of Burgundy (b. ca. 1011 – md. (1) ca. 1033 – d. 21 March 1076), son of Robert II "the Pious," King of France	+	**Helie de Semur** (b. 1016 – md. ca. 1033 – d. 1109)	Helie's brother: ***St. Hugh the Great, Abbot of Cluny***
Henry, Duke of Burgundy (b. ca. 1035 – md. ca. 1056 – d. 27 Jan 1070/1074)	+	Sibylle (or Sybilla) of Barcelona (md. ca. 1056 – d. 6 July 1074)	
Henry I of Burgundy, Count of Portugal and Crusader in Spain (b. 1069/1070 – md. 1093 – d. 1 Nov 1112)	+	Teresa (md. 1093 – d. 1 Nov 1130), daughter of Alfonso VI, King of Castile and Leon	

Alfonso I Henriques, first King of Portugal (b. 25 July 1110 – md. 1146 – d. 6 Dec 1185)	+	Matilda (or Maud) of Savoy (md. 1146 – d. 4 Dec 1157)
Fernando II, King of Leon (b. 1137 – md. (1) 1164 – d. 22 Jan 1188)	+	**Urraca** (b. ca. 1150 – md. 1164 – d. 16 Oct 1188)
Alfonso IX "el Barboro," King of Leon (b. 15 Aug 1171 – md. Dec 1197 – d. 24 Sept 1230)	+	Berengaria (b. 1180 – md. (2) Dec 1197 – d. 8 Nov 1246), daughter of Alfonso IX "the Noble," King of Castile, Toledo, and Extramadura
St. Fernando III, King of Castile, Galicia, Leon, Toledo, and Extramadura (b. 24 June 1198 – md. (2) 1237 – d. 30 May 1252)	+	**Jeanne de Dammartin**, Countess of Ponthieu (b. ca. 1208 – md. 1237 – d. 16 March 1279)
Edward I "Longshanks," King of England (b. 17 June 1239 – md. (1) 18 Oct 1254 – d. 8 July 1307)	+	**Eleanor of Castile** (b. 1240 – md. 18 Oct 1254 – d. 28 Nov 1290)

Sources: *Baring-Gould*, Vol. 4, pp. 365—366; *BBKL*, Vol. 2, cols. 1136–1137; *Benedictine Monks*, p. 351; *Bunson*, p. 402; *Butler*, Vol. II, pp. 188–189; *CE*, Vol. VII, pp. 524–526; *CS*, pp. 240 and 242; *Delaney*, pp. 291–292; *Delaney and Tobin*, p. 578; *Holweck*, p. 493; *NCE*, Vol. 7, p. 189; *O'Malley*, pp. 149–150; *Snodgrass*, p. 122; *Stuart*: line 85, nos. 32 through 27 + line 52, nos. 27 through 24; *Weis, AR:* line 110, no. 22 + line 108, nos. 22 and 23 + line 112 + line 114, nos. 26 and 27 + line 110, nos. 28 through 30

St. Ina, King of Wessex

Ina (or Ine) was born around 660/664 and was the son of Cenred, one of the several war leaders or sub-kings who ruled different parts of a fragmented Wessex. After marrying Ethelburga, Ina succeeded his father around 688.

In a reign of about 38 years, Ina fought several wars with his neighbors, won most of them, and became the first king of a united Wessex. He created a strong administrative system and was the first to codify a set of laws for his subjects. These laws became the basis of the more famous law code of Alfred the Great.

Besides being one of most capable of all the Anglo-Saxon kings, Ina also promoted the Christian faith. He built Glastonbury Abbey, which became a great religious center, and six other monasteries. After abdicating in 726, he and his wife Ethelburga went to Rome as pilgrims. In Rome today, the Church of the Holy Spirit in Saxony ("Santo Spirito in Sassia") stands on the site where Ina built the Saxon School, which was a charitable institution for Saxon pilgrims.

In the last two years of his life, Ina performed many acts of piety and penance. He died in Rome in 728 and is buried there along with Ethelburga.

His Line

	Husband		Wife
	Cenred, a war leader in Somerset (liv. 644–694)	+	**N.N.**
Ingild's brother: ***St. Ina, King of Wessex***	**Ingild** (b. ca. 680 – d. 718)	+	N.N.
	Eoppa	+	N.N.

[For the later generations that connect this line to the kings of England, see the line of St. Ceolwald in Part II.]

Sources: *Ashley*, pp. 298 and 308–309; *Baring-Gould*, Vol. 2, pp. 186–188; *Benedictine Monks*, p. 359; *Bunson*, p. 410; *CE*, Vol. VII, pp. 789–790; *Holweck*, pp. 331 (under "Ethelburga") and 504; *Snodgrass*, p. 127; *Stuart*, line 233, nos. 46 through 44; *Weis, AR*, line 1, nos. 8 through 10

St. Irmina

Irmina was the daughter of St. Dagobert II, King of Austrasia, and his wife Mechtilde. She was the sister of St. Adela of Austrasia. According to a legend, on the day Irmina was to be married, her fiancé was thrown off a cliff by a rival suitor, who also leaped to his death.

It is beyond dispute that Irmina became a nun and entered a convent founded by her father. She was generous to monks and helped St. Willibrod as he worked to spread Christianity.

At the end of her life, Irmina was abbess at Weissenberg monastery in Alsace. She died in 708. Her relics are at Sponheim and Weissenberg.

Her Line

Husband		Wife	
St. Dagobert II, King of Austrasia (b. 652 – murdered 23 Dec 678)	+	Mechtilde	
Alberic	+	**St. Adela**, Princess of Austrasia (d. 734/ 735)	Adela's sister: ***St. Irmina***
Aubri I, Count of Blois	+	N.N.	

[For the later generations that connect this line to the kings of England, see the line of St. Adela, Princess of Austrasia in Part II.]

Sources: *Baring-Gould*, Vol. 15, pp. 224–225; *BBKL*, Vol. 2, col. 1336; *Benedictine Monks*, pp. 361–362; *Bunson*, p. 413; *Butler*, Vol. IV, pp. 605–606; *Delaney and Tobin*, p. 593; *Dunbar*, Vol. I, pp. 413–414; *Englebert*, p. 467; *Holweck*, p. 509; *Snodgrass*, p. 129; *Stuart*, line 303, nos. 45 through 43; *Wells*, p. 385; *WWH*, Vol. 1, p. 72.

Bl. Isabel

The only daughter of Louis VIII "the Lion," King of France, and Bl. Blanche of Castile, Isabel (or Isabella) was born in March 1225 and was a beautiful woman with an exceptional mind. She was an excellent student of Latin, Eastern languages, history, logic, biology, and medicine. While still a child, she also became extraordinarily devoted to prayer and pious exercises. At one point, she almost died from an overdone fast. She took a vow of virginity and refused offers of marriage from many European monarchs. Since she was the only sister of St. Louis IX, King of France, even the pope urged Isabel to marry for the good of her country and the Church. She politely declined his advice, too.

Isabel was a model of the virtues. She rose for prayer long before dawn and continued her devotions until midday. She would invite several poor people in for dinner and wait on them before she ate anything herself. Then she would go out to visit the sick and the poor. After her mother Blanche died, Isabel founded the famous Franciscan convent at Longchamps, whose site is within what is now the Bois de Boulogne in Paris. As her contribution to the Crusades, she also paid all the expenses of keeping ten knights in the Holy Land. Long before she died, many people already thought of Isabel as a saint.

Isabel's mortifications contributed to several long illnesses. Without taking vows, in 1263 at the age of 38 she entered her own convent and spent the rest of her life there. Keeping her fasts and disciplines, she observed almost constant silence. After spending several nights in ecstasies of prayer, she died on 23 February 1270 lying on a bed of straw.

Isabel was buried in her convent, which stood until the early 19th century when it was demolished.

Her Line

	Husband		Wife
	Louis VIII "the Lion," King of France (b. 5 Sept 1187 – md. 23 May 1200 – d. 8 Nov 1226)	+	**Bl. Blanche of Castile** (b. 4 March 1188 – md. 23 May 1200 – d. 27 Nov 1252), daughter of Alfonso IX "the Noble," King of Castile
Louis IX's sister: ***Bl. Isabel***	**St. Louis IX,** King of France and Crusader (known as "St. Louis") (b. 25 April 1214 – md. 27 May 1234 – d. 25 Aug 1270 during the Eighth Crusade)	+	Margaret of Provence (b. 1221 – md. 27 May 1234 – d. 20/21 Dec 1295)

Philip III "the Bold," King of France (b. 1 May 1245 – md. (1) 28 May 1262 – d. 5 Oct 1285)	+	Isabella of Aragon (b. 1243 or 1247 – md. 28 May 1262 – d. 28 Jan 1271), daughter of James I "the Conqueror," King of Aragon
Philip IV "the Fair," King of France (b. 1268 – md. 16 Aug 1284 – d. 29 Nov 1314)	+	Jeanne of Navarre (b. Jan 1272 – md. 16 Aug 1284 – d. 2 April 1305)
Edward II, King of England (b. 25 April 1284 – md. 25 Jan 1308 – murdered 21 Sept 1327)	+	**Isabella** (b. 1292 – md. 25 Jan 1308 – d. 27 Aug 1357)

Sources: *Benedictine Monks,* p. 362; *Butler*, Vol. I, pp. 427–428; *CE*, Vol. VIII, p. 179; *Chervin*, pp. 263–264; *Cruz*, pp. 332–334; *Delaney*, pp. 302–303; *Delaney and Tobin*, p. 594; *Dunbar*, Vol. I, pp. 414–415; *Englebert*, pp. 73–74; *Holweck*, p. 511; *Klaniczay*, p. 237 and Appendix B, Geneal. Table 10; *O'Malley*, p. 73; *NCE*, Vol. 2, p. 602 (under "Blanche of Castile") and Vol. 7, pp. 664–665; *Snodgrass*, p. 129; *Stuart:* line 88, no. 27 + line 70, nos. 27 through 25 + line 51, nos. 25 through 23; *Tucker*, Vol. I, pp. 191 and 175–177; *Weis, AR:* line 113, nos. 27 and 28 + line 101, nos. 27 through 31; *Wells*, pp. 141 and 256–256; *WWH*, Vol. 7, p. 736

St. Isidore of Seville, Doctor of the Church

Isidore was born around 560 and was the son of Severinus, Count of Cartagena, and his wife Theodora. Like his sister St. Florentina and his brothers St. Fulgentius and St. Leander, he chose a career in the Church.

Very little is known about Isidore's early roles in the Church. He doesn't fully step onto the pages of history until 600, when his older brother St. Leander the archbishop of Seville died. Isidore was chosen to succeed him and held the post for the next thirty-six years.

As a scholar, Isidore had no equal. He wrote prodigiously: seventeen major works, and many smaller ones that kept turning up for centuries after his death. His largest and most important work was the *Etymologiae*, which was conceived as an encyclopedia of all of mankind's knowledge. Its 448 chapters filled twenty volumes, and in all of the libraries that would be built in the Middle Ages, it was the most consulted reference work. New editions of it were still appearing when Columbus discovered America.

An indefatigable compiler of knowledge, Isidore was seen as the most learned man of his age. Among other things, he taught that the earth was round.

Leander had begun the conversion of Spain from the Arian heresy to Trinitarian Christianity, but Isidore completed it. By guiding the Second Synod of Seville in 619 and the Fourth Council of Toledo in 633, Isidore set Spain on a spiritual path that it would follow for centuries. For the Christian church in Spain, he also wrote the beautiful Mozarabic liturgy. He founded schools, and monasteries with good libraries. He promoted the study of art, medicine, and law.

After a long and extraordinarily fruitful life, Isidore died on 4 April 636. His remains are in Leon in the Basilica of San Isidoro. In 1722, he was declared a Doctor of the Church. He is the patron saint of Spain and the proposed patron saint of the Internet.

His Line

Husband		Wife	
Severinus, Count of Cartagena	+	**Theodora**, daughter of Theodoric "the Great," the Ostrogoth King of Italy	
Leovigildo (or Leovigild), King of the Visigoths in Spain (d. 586)	+	md. (1) **Theodosia**	Theodosia's brother: ***St. Isidore of Seville, Doctor of the Church***
Recaredo (or Recared) I, King of the Visigoths in Spain (d. 601)	+	Chlodesindis (or Clodoswindis)	

Suintila (or Suintilo), King of the Visigoths in Spain (deposed in 631)	+	Theodora, daughter of Sisebuto, King of the Visigoths in Spain
Ervigio, King of the Visigoths in Spain (d. 687)	+	**Liubigotona**

[For the later generations that connect this line to the kings of England, see the line of St. Florentina in Part III.]

Sources: *Baring-Gould*, Vol. 4, pp. 64–68; *BBKL*, Vol. 2, cols. 1374–1379; *Benedictine Monks*, p. 364; *Bentley*, p. 66; *Bunson*, pp. 415–416; *Butler*, Vol. II, pp. 26–27; *CE*, Vol. VIII, pp. 186–188; *Delaney*, p. 304; *Delaney and Tobin*, p. 595; *Englebert*, pp. 131–132; *Giorgi*, pp. 206–207; *Guiley*, p. 159; *Holweck*, pp. 513–514; *Joeckle*, pp. 223–225; *NCE*, Vol. 7, pp. 674–676; *O'Malley*, p. 77; *Snodgrass*, p. 130; *Stuart*, line 276, no. 44; *Tucker*, Vol. II, pp. 638 and 469; *Wells*, p. 593. Also see ***fmg.ac>Projects>Medieval Lands>Medieval Lands – data by region>Iberia>Vandals, Suevi & Visigoths> Recaredo I 586–601, Liuva II 601–603***. In addition, see ***fmg.ac>Projects>Medieval Lands>Medieval Lands – data by region>Iberia> Vandals, Suevi & Visigoths>Suintila 621–633***.

Bl. Jeanne of Flanders

Jeanne was born in 1200 and was the daughter of Baldwin IX, Count of Flanders and (as Baldwin VI) Count of Hainault, who also became Latin Emperor of Constantinople, and his wife Marie of Champagne. In 1202 Baldwin left on Crusade, in 1204 Marie left to join him, both died abroad, and by 1205 the little orphaned Jeanne was being raised by her uncle Philip of Namur.

Little Jeanne's vast inheritance made her an extraordinarily desirable little girl, and in January 1212, she married twenty-four-year-old Fernando, son of Sancho I, King of Portugal. While the newlyweds were on their way back to Flanders, the future Louis VIII of France took them prisoner, hoping to force them to hand over a large part of Flanders to him. The captives agreed to this extortion and were released. They then repudiated their promises, made an alliance with England and Germany, and went to war against France. At the battle of Bouvines in July 1214, the French won and took Fernando prisoner again.

During the next twelve years while Fernando was held captive, Jeanne ruled Flanders and Hainault alone. She is remembered as a wise and benevolent ruler, and she also built the convent of Marquette. In 1225, Jeanne put down a revolt incited by "the false Baldwin," a man who claimed to be her father returning after spending twenty years on Crusade!

After payment of a huge ransom, Fernando was finally released in 1226 but only survived until 27 July 1233. In 1237, Jeanne married Thomas II of Savoy but had no children with him. She ultimately separated from Thomas, become a nun, entered the convent she had founded at Marquette, and died there on 5 December 1244.

Her Line

Husband		Wife	
Baldwin VI (IX of Flanders), Count of Hainault, Latin Emperor of Constantinople, and a leader of the 4th Crusade (b. July 1171 – md. 6 June 1186 – d. 11 June 1205)	+	**Marie of Champagne** (b. 1174 – md. 6 June 1186 – d. 9 Aug 1204)	
Bouchard d'Avesnes (b. ca. 1180 – md. (1) bef. 23 July 1212 – d. 1244)	+	**Margaret**, heiress of Hainault and Flanders (b. 2 June 1202 – md. bef. 23 July 1212 – d. 10 Feb 1280)	Margaret's sister: ***Bl. Jeanne of Flanders***
Jean I d'Avesnes, Count of Hainault, Holland, and Flanders (b. 1 May 1218 – md. 9 Oct 1246 – d. 24 Dec 1257)	+	Adelaide of Holland (b. ca. 1225 – md. 9 Oct 1246 – d. 1284)	

[For the later generations that connect this line to the kings of England, see the line of Bl. Adelheid von Odenkirchen in Part II.]

Sources: *Dunbar*, Vol. I, p. 423; *Stuart:* line 73, nos. 27 and 26 + line 50, nos. 26 and 25; *Weis, AR*, line 168, nos. 28 through 30; *Wells*, pp. 125 and 43–44

St. Jestin

Jestin was the son of St. Geraint, King of Brittany, and his wife Enid. He was the brother of Saints Cado, Cyngar, and Salamon I.

After taking vows, Jestin went to Plestin in Brittany and lived a hermit's life. He also made a pilgrimage to Rome.

His Line

	Husband		Wife
	St. Geraint, King of Brittany	+	**Enid**
Salamon's brother: ***St. Jestin***	**St. Salamon I "the Handsome,"** King of Brittany (liv. in the 400's)	+	St. Gwen
	Audren, King of Brittany	+	N.N.
	Budic I, King of Brittany	+	N.N., a daughter of Corun

[For the later generations that connect this line to the kings of England, see the line of St. Cunedda Wledig in Part II.]

Sources: *Ashley*, p. 117; *Baring-Gould*, Vol. 16, pp. 133 and 261; *Baring-Gould and Fisher*, Vol. 3, pp. 293–295; *Holweck*, pp. 425 (under "Geraint"), 434 (under "Gestin"), and 529 (under "Jestin"); *Stuart*, line 405, nos. 56 through 53

St. Judoc

Judoc (also known as Josse) was born around 600 and was the son of Hoel III, King of Brittany, and his wife Pritelle. He was the brother of St. Judicael and was educated in the monastery of St. Maelmon. In 636, he renounced his wealth and position and became a priest.

When St. Judicael decided to give up the throne of Brittany around 642, he initially wanted to abdicate in favor of his brother Judoc. When asked to assume the throne, Judoc accepted the crown for a few months but then renounced it when some of his brothers began to want it for themselves. Judoc then went on several pilgrimages and finally moved into a forest to live alone. He then spent the rest of his life living as a hermit in several remote locations.

Near the end of his life, Judoc settled at what is now the abbey of St. Josse-sur-Mer. He died around 669.

After Judoc's death, veneration of him spread throughout Europe. In 902, his relics were taken from the abbey of St. Josse-sur-Mer and brought to the New Minster Monastery in Winchester.

When Chaucer's "Wife of Bath" swears by "God and by Seint Joce" and when British parents today name their sons or daughters "Joyce," they are unknowingly acknowledging St. Judoc.

His Line

	Husband		Wife
	Hoel III, King of Brittany (d. 612)	+	**Pritelle**
Judicael's brother: ***St. Judoc***	**St. Judicael II**, King of Brittany (b. ca. 590 – d. 17 Dec 658)	+	N.N.
	Alain II de Long, King of Brittany (d. 690)	+	N.N.

[For the later generations that connect this line to the kings of England, see the line of St. Cunedda Wledig in Part II.]

Sources: *Baring-Gould*, Vol. 15, pp. 173–174; *Benedictine Monks*, p. 410; *Bunson*, p. 464; *Butler*, Vol. IV, p. 550 (which mistakenly states that Judicael is both the father and brother of St. Judoc); *Holweck*, p. 532; *Joeckle*, pp. 258–259; *Stuart*, line 405, nos. 49 through 47

Bl. Jutta of Diessenberg

Jutta was born around 1090 and was the daughter of Stephen, Count of Sponheim, and his wife Sophia von Hamm. From her earliest years, Jutta received mystical visions and became a nun when she was very young.

Jutta's true vocation appeared as if by accident. On 1 November 1106 she moved into a small house next to the monastery of Diessenberg on the Rhine and began to live there as a kind of recluse. To support herself she began to teach local children. One of her students was a young girl named Hildegarde, who was physically weak but who was also experiencing mystical visions. Jutta taught her reading, hymns, psalms, Latin, and how to know whether she was truly called to be a mystic. Little Hildegarde grew up to be St. Hildegarde of Bingen, Jutta's greatest student and one of Germany's great mystics.

Besides growing numbers of students, Jutta also attracted many adult nuns who wanted to spend their lives learning from her. She finally founded a Benedictine convent for her disciples, became its first abbess, and continued as its spiritual leader for the next twenty years.

Jutta finally died in 1136. St. Hildegarde of Bingen became the next abbess of Jutta's convent, and regarding her old tutor, she wrote:

> "This woman overflowed with the grace of God like a river fed by many streams. Watching, fasting, and other works of penance gave no rest to her body till the day that a happy death set her free from this mortal life. God has given testimony to her holiness by many startling miracles."

Jutta's relics drew crowds of people to Diessenberg, and her tomb became a place of pilgrimage and miracles.

Her Line

	Husband		Wife
	Stephen, Count of Sponheim (d. ca. 25 Feb 1118)	+	**Sophia von Hamm** (liv. 1118)
Meginhard's sister: ***Bl. Jutta of Diessenberg***	**Meginhard I**, Count of Sponheim (md. bef. 1124 – d. 1136/1145)	+	Mechtilde von Morsberg (md. bef. 1124)
	Simon I, Count of Saarbrucken (b. ca. 1120 – d. 23 June 1181/1182)	+	**Mathilda von Sponheim** (b. ca. 1127)

[For the later generations that connect this line to the kings of England, see the line of Bl. Eberhard V in Part II.]

Sources: *BBKL*, Vol. 17, col. 742; *Benedictine Monks*, p. 419; *Bentley*, p. 244; *Butler*, Vol. IV, pp. 597–598; *Delaney*, p. 336; *Delaney and Tobin*, p. 641; *Dunbar*, Vol. I, p. 448; *Holweck*, p. 581; *NCE*, Vol. 8, p. 102; *Stuart*, line 365, nos. 30 through 28; *Wells*, pp. 538 and 503; *WWH*, Vol. 8, p. 401

St. Khosrowidukht

Khosrowidukht was the daughter of Chosroes (or Khosrow) II "the Valiant," King of Western Armenia. She was also the sister of St. Tiridates "the Great."

Following the martyrdom of Ripsime, Gaiana, and other nuns during a persecution of Christians in 301, Tiridates—who was still a pagan and who had ordered the persecution—went mad. After all measures to help him had failed, it was his sister Khosrowidukht who remembered that Tiridates had also thrown St. Gregory the Illuminator into prison. She ordered the palace guards to release Gregory and bring him to Tiridates. After Gregory laid his hands on the deranged king, said a few prayers, and miraculously restored him to his reason, Tiridates accepted Christianity.

Khosrowidukht was baptized along with her brother and became a nun. She died around 340.

Her Line

	Husband		Wife
	Chosroes (or Khosrow) II "the Valiant," King of Western Armenia (b. ca. 236 – d. 287)	+	**N.N.**
Sister of Tiridates "the Great": ***St. Khosro-widukht***	**St. Tiridates "the Great,"** King of Armenia (b. ca. 280 – assassinated 330)	+	St. Ashken, daughter of Ashkhadar, King of Alania
	Chosroes (or Khosrow) III, King of Armenia (d. 338)	+	N.N.
	Athenagenes	+	**Bambishu** (b. 315)

[For the later generations that connect this line to the kings of England, see the line of St. Ashken in Part II.]

Sources: *Holweck*, pp. 585 and 986 (under "Tiridat III"); *Hovannisian*, p. 81; *Kaloustian*, pp. 16–17; *Koushagian*, p. 5; *Stone*, Chapter 8, Chart 80; *Stuart*, line 416, nos. 59 through 56

St. Laurence O'Toole, Archbishop of Dublin

Laurence was born around 1128. Also known as Lorcan Ua Tuathail, he was the son of Muirchertach Ua Tuathail and his wife Cacht Ua Morda.

At age 10, Laurence was taken as a hostage by King Diarmait MacMurchada, who later became infamous for trying to win a power struggle with other Irish kings by bringing English troops to Ireland. After two years in very unpleasant conditions, Laurence was finally released and became a monk at the monastery at Glendalough. In 1153 at the age of twenty-five, he also became the abbot there.

At Glendalough, Laurence practiced great austerities. He ate little, wore a hair shirt under his clerical garb, and spent the forty days of Lent meditating in a cave near the monastery. To the poor, he was very generous. While he was at Glendalough, there was a famine in the surrounding country, and his boundless charity saved many.

In 1162, Laurence was made archbishop of Dublin, and he is primarily remembered for his efforts to protect the Irish during the English invasions that began in 1170 thanks to Diarmait MacMurchada, whose name was later anglicized to Dermot MacMurrough. After the first English army commanded by Richard de Clare "Strongbow" had arrived, Laurence tried to unite the Irish chiefs and rally a national army against the invaders. When the next English army arrived commanded by King Henry II, Laurence often acted as a peacemaker between Henry II and the Irish chiefs. His efforts to control English expansion following the invasions were so troublesome to Henry that an assassin almost killed Laurence while he was visiting the shrine of St. Thomas Becket in England in 1175.

Until the end of his life, Laurence continued to receive ecclesiastical honors. For example, he was made Papal Legate to Ireland by the Lateran Council in Rome in 1179.

After falling ill while he was trying to see Henry II in Normandy, Laurence died on 14 November 1180. English rule of Ireland—whose consequences Laurence had hoped to mitigate—would last for about 750 years.

Laurence was buried near Rouen in the crypt of the church of Our Lady at Eu.

His Line

Husband		Wife	
Muirchertach Ua Tuathail (or O'Toole)	+	**Cacht Ua Morda (or Ua Chaelluide),** daughter of Loigsech Ua Morda, King of Leix	
Diarmait MacMurchada, King of Leinster (b. 1100 – d. 1 Jan 1171)	+	**Mor** (d. 1164)	Mor's brother: ***St. Laurence O'Toole,***

Richard de Clare "Strongbow," 2nd Earl of Pembroke and Justiciar of Ireland (b. ca. 1130 – md. ca. 26 Aug 1171 – d. ca. 20 April 1176)	+	**Aoife (or Eve) of Leinster** (md. ca. 26 Aug 1171 – liv. 1186)	***Archbishop of Dublin***
William Marshal, 3rd Earl of Pembroke, Regent of England, and the greatest knight in English history (b. ca. 1146 – md. Aug 1189 – d. 14 May 1219)	+	**Isabel de Clare** (md. Aug 1189 – d. 1220)	

[For the later generations that connect this line to the kings of Scotland, see the line of St. Abban in Part III.]

Sources: *Baring-Gould*, Vol. 13, pp. 328–333; *Benedictine Monks*, p. 428; *Bunson*, p. 483; *Butler*, Vol. IV, pp. 341–344; *CE*, Vol. IX, pp. 91–92; *CS*, pp. 692–694; *Delaney*, p. 350; *Delaney and Tobin*, p. 677; *Holweck*, p. 595; *NCE*, Vol. 8, pp. 568–569; *Tucker*, Vol. I, p. 443; *Weis, AR:* line 175, nos. 6 and 7 + line 66, nos. 26 and 27; *Weis, MCS*, line 145, no. 1; *Wells*, pp. 457, 368, 153, and 374; *Woods*, pp. 99–100

St. Leander, Archbishop of Seville

Leander was born around 535 and was the son of Severinus, Count of Cartagena, and his wife Theodora, daughter of Theodoric "the Great," the Ostrogoth King of Italy. Leander was his parents' first child and became a monk while he was still quite young.

Around 577 Leander became the archbishop of Seville and began actively working to convert Spain from the Arian heresy to Trinitarian Christianity (later called "Catholicism"). He was instrumental in persuading King Leovigild's son Hermenegild to reject Arianism. After Leovigild was stricken by grief for ordering the execution of Hermenegild, Leander also converted the king's other son Recared. Leander later led the Third Council of Toledo in 589, where the Arian heresy in Spain was finally stamped out.

Leander was the first to add the Nicene Creed to the Mass. He was known for his eloquence, and several letters written to him by Pope St. Gregory the Great survive. In Spain, he is considered a Doctor of the Church.

Leander died on 13 March 600/601 and he was buried in the cathedral of Seville. His brother St. Isidore became the next archbishop of Seville.

His Line

Husband		Wife	
Severinus, Count of Cartagena	+	**Theodora**, daughter of Theodoric "the Great," the Ostrogoth King of Italy	
Leovigildo (or Leovigild), King of the Visigoths in Spain (d. 586)	+	md. (1) **Theodosia**	Theodosia's brother: ***St. Leander, Archbishop of Seville***
Recaredo (or Recared) I, King of the Visigoths in Spain (d. 601)	+	Chlodesindis (or Clodoswindis)	
Suintila (or Suintilo), King of the Visigoths in Spain	+	Theodora, daughter of Sisebuto, King of the Visigoths in Spain	
Ervigio, King of the Visigoths in Spain (d. 687)	+	**Liubigotona**	

[For the later generations that connect this line to the kings of England, see the line of St. Florentina in Part III.]

Sources: *Baring-Gould*, Vol. 2, pp. 445–447; *BBKL*, Vol. 4, cols. 1288–1291; *Benedictine Monks*, p. 430; *Bunson*, p. 484; *Delaney*, pp. 351–352; *Delaney and Tobin*, p. 682; *Englebert*, p. 80; *Giorgi*, pp. 130–131; *Holweck*, p. 597; *NCE*, Vol. 8, p. 590; *O'Malley*, p. 77; *Snodgrass*, p. 150; *Stuart*, line 276, no. 44; *Tucker*, Vol. II, pp. 638 and 469; *Wells*, p. 593. Also see ***fmg.ac>Projects>Medieval Lands>Medieval Lands – data by***

region>Iberia>Vandals, Suevi & Visigoths>Recaredo I 586–601, Liuva II 601–603. In addition, see ***fmg.ac>Projects>Medieval Lands>Medieval Lands – data by region>Iberia>Vandals, Suevi & Visigoths>Suintila 621–633***.

St. Leo IX,
Pope

Leo's given name was Bruno von Egisheim.

Bruno was born on 21 June 1002 and was the son of Hugh VI, Count of Egisheim, and his wife Heilwig von Dagsburg. He first became a priest and was sent to the court of the German emperor Conrad II. Besides being a cleric, he was also a very capable warrior. When Conrad took an army into Italy, Bruno led several units of Conrad's troops. After returning home, Bruno was made bishop of Toul in 1027. When a local rebellion against Conrad broke out, Bruno was once again at the head of the troops that put it down. He remained bishop of Toul until he became pope on 12 February 1049.

Bruno, now called Leo IX, was the first of several truly great reform popes. He immediately called a council in Rome in April 1049 where he declared his strong opposition to simony and clerical marriage. To visit his European flock, he began to travel widely, and he never really stopped. During his entire papacy, he spent less than six months in Rome. He moved through Italy, France, and Germany and went as far as Hungary. He held twelve synods outside of Rome. His tenure was a papacy of action.

Sadly, Leo's conduct of the Church's foreign relations was much less successful than his internal reforms. After receiving many complaints about the cruelties of the Norman conquerors of southern Italy, Leo decided to lead a papal army against them. At the battle of Civitate on 18 June 1053, the Normans routed the papal army. To avoid further bloodshed, Leo then surrendered himself to the Normans and spent the next nine months in captivity.

Released from captivity and back in Rome, Leo turned his attention to the extraordinarily low state of relations between the Eastern and Western churches. Developments before Leo's ill-fated Italian campaign gave him ample cause for concern. The Patriarch (i.e., Archbishop) of Constantinople had decided that he was the head of all the churches in the east, and he had begun to close Latin churches and to force Latin priests and monks to adopt the Greek rite. Leo had protested to the Byzantine emperor, who then ordered the patriarch to stop. Leo then sent a papal legate along with other churchmen to Constantinople to investigate and report back to him. Shortly after they had left Rome, Leo died unexpectedly on 9 April 1054.

Once Leo's men arrived in Constantinople, events there took the worst possible turn. After the patriarch defied the papal legate, the legate excommunicated the patriarch on 16 July 1054. The patriarch responded by excommunicating the legate. The Eastern and Western churches had now formally split up. What would be known as the Great Schism would be dated from 1054.

Leo was buried in St. Peter's, and with the passage of time he was seen as the most important German pope of the Middle Ages. What would have happened between the Eastern and Western churches if he had lived longer will always be one of history's great unanswered questions.

His Line

Husband		Wife	
Hugh VI, Count of Egisheim and in the Nordgau (md. 990/995 – d. 1049)	+	**Heilwig von Dagsburg** (b. 970/975 – md. 990/995 – d. 1046)	
Ludwig (or Ludolf) von Braunschweig, Margrave of West Friesland and Count in the Derlingau (md. bef. 1036 – d. 23 April 1038)	+	**Gertrude von Egisheim** (md. bef. 1036 – d. 21 July 1077)	Gertrude's brother: Bruno von Egisheim, who became ***St. Leo IX, Pope***
Edward "the Exile" (or Edward "the Atheling") (b. 1016 – md. ca. 1043 – d. ca. 1057), son of Edmund "Ironside," King of England	+	**Agatha von Braunschweig** (b. ca. 1025 – md. ca. 1043 – d. aft. 1066)	
Malcolm III Canmore, King of Scotland (b. ca. 1031 – md. (2) 1068/1069 – d. in battle 13 Nov 1093 while besieging Alnwick Castle)	+	**St. Margaret of Scotland** (b. ca. 1045 – md. 1068/1069 – d. 16 Nov 1093)	

Sources: *Baring-Gould*, Vol. 4, pp. 233–247; *BBKL*, Vol. 4, cols. 1443–1448; *Benedictine Monks*, p. 431; *Bentley*, p. 74; *Brusher*, pp. 300–301; *Bunson*, p. 487; *Butler*, Vol. II, pp. 126–128; *CE*, Vol. IX, pp. 160–162; *Delaney*, p. 355; *Delaney and Tobin*, p. 690; *Giorgi*, pp. 236–237; *Guiley*, pp. 208–209; *Holweck*, p. 599; *NCE*, Vol. 8, pp. 642–643; *Snodgrass*, p. 152; *Stuart:* line 33, nos. 33 and 32 + line 318 + line 233, nos. 33 and 32; *Tucker*, Vol. I, pp. 12–13 and 126; *Warncke*, pp. 96–97; *Weis, AR*, line 1, nos. 20 and 21; *Wells*, pp. 197, 92, and 205

St. Leodegar of Autun

Leodegar was born around 616 in the kingdom of Neustria and was the son of Bodilon of Treves and St. Sigrada. He became a priest, and shortly after 636 at the abbey of Saint-Maixent near Poitiers he was made the abbot.

Accounts of him describe an awe-inspiring person—very well educated, an excellent teacher of other clergy, and a strict judge in his treatment of sinners. After King Clothaire II died, Leodegar also became an adviser to the king's widow St. Bathildis and helped her govern during the minority of her son Clothaire III.

Acting as regent for her son, St. Bathildis appointed Leodegar bishop of Autun in 663. He managed to make peace among factions that had been at war prior to his arrival. He also adorned churches, instructed the clergy, preached to the people, gave to the poor, and fortified the town.

As bishop, Leodegar also continued to participate in the highest levels of Neustrian politics, perhaps unaware that he was choosing a martyr's path in doing so. When King Clothaire III died in 673, the infamous Ebroin was the mayor of the palace and began to scheme about how to enlarge his own power. Leodegar steadfastly resisted his designs, and the struggle between Ebroin and Leodegar would become one of the most famous chapters in Merovingian history.

Childeric II succeeded Clothaire III and after a short reign was himself succeeded by Theuderic III. The rule of all these monarchs had been so weak that in August of 676 Ebroin decided to get rid of his most formidable opponent and sent troops to Autun to capture Leodegar. After a siege that lasted a few days, Leodegar decided to avoid a massacre, told the men of Autun to cease resisting, and then turned himself over to the forces of Ebroin.

For the next two years, Leodegar would be treated very cruelly. As soon as he surrendered, Ebroin's men blinded him with hot irons and led him away to prison. Later his lips were cut off, and his tongue was torn out. He was also subjected to other tortures. One day he was brought out of his cell and made to stand by while his brother St. Guerin was stoned to death. After two years in confinement, he was tried on trumped-up charges and beheaded on 2 October 678.

At Saint-Maixent, France, the church dedicated to Leodegar stands over the spot where he was originally buried. Many other churches in France and Belgium are dedicated to him. A letter which he wrote to his mother St. Sigrada after his mutilation and Guerin's death survives.

Leodegar is also known as Leodegarius or Leger.

His Line

	Husband		Wife
	Bodilon of Treves	+	**St. Sigrada** (d. ca. 678)
Guerin's brother: ***St. Leodegar of Autun***	**St. Guerin (or Warinus)**, Count of Poitiers (d. 677)	+	Kunza (d. 690)
	Lambert of Hesbaye (liv. 725)	+	N.N.

[For the later generations that connect this line to the kings of England, see the line of St. Clodulf, Bishop of Metz in Part II.]

Sources: *Baring-Gould*, Vol. 11, pp. 19–31; *BBKL*, Vol. 4, cols. 1466–1468; *Benedictine Monks*, p. 433; *Bunson*, pp. 487–488; *Butler*, Vol. IV, pp. 9–11; *CE*, Vol. 9, p. 174; *Delaney*, p. 356; *Delaney and Tobin*, p. 693; *Englebert*, pp. 374–375; *Holweck*, pp. 601–602; *NCE*, Vol. 8, pp. 654–655; *Stuart:* line 236, no. 44 + line 2, nos. 46 through 44; *Tucker*, Vol. I, p. 331; *Wells*, p. 303

St. Leonorius

Leonorius was the son of Hoel I "the Great," King of Brittany, and his wife St. Pompeja. He was also the brother of St. Sève and St. Tugdual.

Leonorius was educated by St. Illtyd and made a bishop by St. Dyfrig. He then went to Brittany and founded the monastery of Pontual near St. Malo.

Leonorius died around 560/570. Also known as Lunaire, he was buried in St. Malo in the church called St. Lunaire today.

His Line

	Husband		Wife
	Hoel I "the Great," King of Brittany (b. ca. 491 – d. ca. 545)	+	**St. Pompeja**
Hoel II's brother: ***St. Leonorius***	**Hoel II**, King of Brittany (murdered 547)	+	Rimo
	Judicael I, King of Brittany (b. 535)	+	N.N.

[For the later generations that connect this line to the kings of England, see the line of St. Cunedda Wledig in Part II.]

Sources: *Baring-Gould*, Vol. 16, pp. 246–248; *Benedictine Monks*, p. 435; *Delaney*, p. 357; *Delaney and Tobin*, p. 695; *Holweck*, pp. 603–604; *Stuart*, line 405, nos. 52 through 50

St. Louis, Bishop of Toulouse

Louis was born in February 1274 and was the son of Charles II "the Lame," King of Naples, and his wife Maria.

In 1288, Louis' life took a fateful turn. While at war with Pedro III of Aragon, his father was captured. To secure his father's release, Louis and his two brothers became hostages and were held for the next seven years. While he was confined, Louis was educated by Franciscan friars, who were impressed by his holiness and learning. While he was still a hostage, Louis reached the age of majority and was made archbishop of Lyon by the pope on 9 October 1294.

The true depth of Louis' religious commitment was revealed in 1295 after he was finally released. When his older brother died later that year, Louis was the heir to his father's crown and all his other titles and estates. Louis immediately resigned all of them in favor of his brother Robert of Anjou and took Franciscan vows of poverty, chastity, and obedience.

On 5 February 1296 Louis became bishop of Toulouse. He rapidly gained a reputation for serving the poor, feeding the hungry, and ignoring his own needs.

The world will never know what Louis would have accomplished if he had been kinder to himself. Utterly exhausted after just six months as bishop of Toulouse, he resigned his post. A year later on 19 August 1297, he died.

Louis was originally buried at the Franciscan monastery at Marseilles. In 1433 his relics were moved to the cathedral in Valencia.

His Line

Husband		Wife	
Charles II "le Boiteux" ("the Lame"), King of Naples and Prince of Salerno (b. 1254 – md. 1270 – d. 5 June 1309)	+	**Maria** (b. ca. 1257 – md. 1270 – murdered 25 March 1323), daughter of Stephen V, King of Hungary	
Charles of Valois (b. 12 March 1270/1271 – md. 16 Aug 1290 – d. 16 Dec 1325), son of Philip III "the Bold," King of France	+	**Marguerite** (b. ca. 1273– md. 16 Aug 1290 – d. 31 Dec 1299)	Marguerite's brother: ***St. Louis, Bishop of Toulouse***
William III d'Avesnes, Count of Hainault and Holland (b. ca. 1286 – md. 19 May 1305 – d. 7 June 1337)	+	**Jeanne de Valois** (b. ca. 1294 – md. 19 May 1305 – d. 7 March 1342)	
Edward III, King of England (b. 13 Nov 1312 – md. 24 Jan 1328 – d. 21 June 1377)	+	**Philippa of Hainault** (b. 24 June 1311 – md. 24 Jan 1328 – d. 15 Aug 1369)	

Sources: *Baring-Gould*, Vol. 9, pp. 185–191; *BBKL*, Vol. 16, cols. 965–966; *Benedictine Monks*, p. 442; *Bunson*, p. 496; *Butler*, Vol. III, pp. 357–358; *CE*, Vol. IX, pp. 385–386; *Delaney*, p. 364; *Delaney and Tobin*, pp. 715–716; *Holweck*, p. 615; *Klaniczay*, pp. 304–310; *Stuart:* line 88, nos. 25 and 24 + line 70, nos. 24 and 23 + line 50, nos. 23 and 22; *Weis, AR*, line 103, nos. 31 through 34; *Wells*, pp. 421, 257, and 293

Bl. Ludwig III,
Count of Arnstein

Ludwig III was born in 1109 and was the son of Ludwig II, Count of Arnstein, and his wife Bl. Adelheid von Odenkirchen. He married Guda von Baumburg.

For the first 30 years of his life, Ludwig III seemed more destined for damnation than divinity. As a young man, he was wild, dissolute, and prone to violence, and this way of life continued even after he married. There is no record of exactly what changed him, but in 1139 he separated from his childless wife, turned his castle into a monastery, invited in a dozen Premonstrian monks, and became a lay brother. His wife Guda became a recluse and settled near Ludwig's monastery of Arnstein-on-the-Lahn.

Ludwig founded other monasteries in the next forty-six years, remained a monk for the rest of his life, and died on 25 October 1185.

His Line

Husband		Wife	
Ludwig II, Count of Arnstein and in the Einrichgau (b. ca. 1074 – d. aft. 1117)	+	**Bl. Adelheid von Odenkirchen** (d. 5 July 1158)	
Henry I, Count of Guelders and Zutphen (b. 1117 – md. 1135 – d. 1182)	+	**Agnes von Arnstein** (md. 1135 – d. 1179)	Agnes' brother: ***Bl. Ludwig III, Count of Arnstein***
Otto I, Count of Friesland, Guelders, Holland, Zealand, and Zutphen, Crusader (md. bef. 1188 – d. betw. 30 April and 24 Sept 1207)	+	Richardis von Wittlesbach (md. bef. 1188 – d. 7 Dec 1231)	

[For the later generations that connect this line to the kings of England, see the line of Bl. Haziga of Diessen in Part II.]

Sources: *Holweck*, p. 617; *Stuart:* line 304A, nos. 30 and 29 + line 304, nos. 29 and 28; *Wells*, pp. 284–285

St. Magnus of Orkney

Magnus was born in 1075 and was the son of Erlend II and his wife Thora.

Magnus and his family lived in the Orkney Islands, whose ultimate ruler at the time was the king of Norway. Erlend II and his brother Paul ruled the Orkneys as Norwegian vassals until 1098, when King Magnus III of Norway removed both of them and replaced them with his own son Sigurd. Magnus the son of Erlend then fled to Scotland and stayed there until after the Norwegian king Magnus III died in 1102.

After Magnus the son of Erlend returned to the Orkneys, the new king of Norway made him and his cousin Haakon, who was the son of Magnus' deposed uncle Paul, joint rulers like their fathers had been. From 1105 until 1114, they ruled the Orkneys together. After nine years, Haakon had become very unhappy with their arrangement and wanted to be sole ruler of the Orkneys. The followers of each ruler armed themselves and prepared for battle.

Magnus and Haakon agreed to meet on the island of Egilsay to try to negotiate a peace. Each of them was to come to the island with just two ships and a corresponding number of men. Magnus arrived first with his two ships and waited. Haakon arrived with eight ships and took Magnus prisoner.

Haakon's followers demanded that Magnus be put to death, and he was executed on 16 April 1115. On Egilsay, what remains of St. Magnus Kirk stands on the spot where he was killed.

In death, Magnus came to be regarded as a martyr, and miracles were reported at his grave. After Magnus's nephew St. Ragnald became earl of Orkney, he began the church that became the cathedral of St. Magnus. During restoration of the cathedral in 1919, the relics of St. Magnus were found there.

On the eve of the battle of Bannockburn, St. Magnus is said to have appeared to Robert the Bruce with a promise of victory. He is the patron saint of the Orkneys.

His Line

Husband		Wife	
Erlend II, Joint Earl of Orkney (d. 1098)	+	**Thora**, daughter of Somerled	
Kol Kalisson, a Norseman (d. 1098/1099)	+	**Gunnhilda**	Gunnhilda's brother: ***St. Magnus of Orkney***
St. Ragnald III, Earl of Orkney and Caithness (d. 20 Aug 1158)	+	N.N.	

[For the later generations that connect this line to Prince Henry Sinclair, see the line of St. Ragnald III, Earl of Orkney and Caithness in Part II.]

Sources: *Ashley*, pp. 448 and 452–454; *Baring-Gould*, Vol. 4, pp. 211–217; *Benedictine Monks*, p. 457; *Bunson*, p. 511; *Burke's*, Vol. I, p. 469; *Butler*, Vol. II, pp. 103–104; *CS*, pp. 192–195; *Delaney*, p. 373; *Delaney and Tobin*, pp. 734–735; *Holweck*, p. 640

St. Margaret of Hungary

Margaret was born in 1242 and was the daughter of Bela IV, King of Hungary, and his wife Maria Laskarina. She was born while her parents were fleeing the Mongol invasion of Hungary. In their prayers, Bela and Maria promised that if God would spare their land, they would offer their new daughter to the Church. The Mongols withdrew, and when Margaret was just a few years old, her parents gave her to nuns to be educated.

Margaret grew up to be a profoundly religious woman. She refused offers of marriage from several kings, became a Dominican nun herself, and entered a convent on an island in the Danube near Budapest.

In caring for the poor and the sick, Margaret was an example of heroic charity. Of all the work to be done, she always chose the most menial, repulsive, and exhausting. She experienced visions and was known for miracles.

Worn out by a life of penance, fasting, and very hard work, she died on 18 January 1270.

The process which resulted in Margaret's canonization began just seven years after her death. Many of the depositions given by witnesses who testified to her sanctity and miracles have survived to this day.

Her Line

	Husband		Wife
	Bela IV, King of Hungary (b. 1206 – md. 1218 – d. 3 May 1270)	+	**Maria Laskarina** (b. ca. 1206 – md. 1218 – d. 1270), daughter of Theodore I Lascaris, Emperor of Byzantium
Stephen's sister: ***St. Margaret of Hungary***	**Stephen V**, King of Hungary (b. Dec 1239 – md. 1253 – d. 1 Aug 1272)	+	Elizabeth (md. 1253 – d. aft. 1290), daughter of Kuthen, Khan of the Kumans
	Charles II "le Boiteux" ("the Lame"), King of Naples and Prince of Salerno (b. 1254 – md. 1270 – d. 5 June 1309)	+	**Maria** (b. ca. 1257 – md. 1270 – murdered 25 March 1323)

[For the later generations that connect this line to the kings of England, see the line of St. Adalbero, Bishop of Wuerzburg in Part III.]

Sources: *BBKL*, Vol. 14, cols. 1238–1240; *Benedictine Monks*, p. 467; *Bentley*, p. 18; *Bunson*, p. 522; *Butler*, Vol. I, pp. 176–178; *CE*, Vol. IX, pp. 654–655; *Delaney*, p. 382; *Delaney and Tobin*, p. 751; *Dunbar*, Vol. II, pp. 19–20; *Giorgi*, pp. 44–45; *Holweck*, p. 656; *Joeckle*, pp. 288–289; *Klaniczay*, pp. 205–206 and Appendix B: Geneal. Table 8; *NCE*, Vol. 9, p. 201; *Stuart*, line 78, nos. 27 through 25; *Weis, AR*, line 103, nos. 29 through 31; *Wells*, pp. 309 and 421; *WWH*, Vol. 10, p. 269

Bl. Margaret of Vau-le-Duc

Margaret was the daughter of Henry II "the Courageous," Duke of Brabant and Lorraine, and his first wife Maria von Hohenstaufen. She became a Cistercian nun and entered the convent of Vau-le-Duc in Brabant which her father had built. After becoming its abbess, she died on 4 June 1277.

Her Line

Husband		Wife	
Henry II "the Courageous," Duke of Brabant and Lorraine (b. 1207 – md. (1) by 22 Aug 1215 – d. 1 Feb 1248)	+	**Maria von Hohenstaufen** (b. 1201 – md. by 22 Aug 1215 – d. 1235), daughter of Philip von Hohenstaufen, Emperor of Germany	
Robert I, Count of Artois and Crusader (b. Sept 1216 – md. 14 June 1237 – slain 9 Feb 1250 while crusading in Egypt with his brother St. Louis IX)	+	**Matilda of Brabant** (md. 14 June 1237 – d. 29 Sept 1288)	Matilda's sister: ***Bl. Margaret of Vau-le-Duc***
Henry I, King of Navarre (b. ca. 1244 – md. (2) 1269 – d. 22 July 1274)	+	**Blanche of Artois** (b. ca. 1248 – md. (1) 1269 – d. 2 May 1302)	
Philip IV "the Fair," King of France (b. 1268 – md. 16 Aug 1284 – d. 29 Nov 1314)	+	**Jeanne of Navarre** (b. Jan 1272 – md. 16 Aug 1284 – d. 2 April 1305)	
Edward II, King of England (b. 25 April 1284 – md. 25 Jan 1308 – murdered 21 Sept 1327)	+	**Isabella** (b. 1292 – md. 25 Jan 1308 – d. 27 Aug 1357)	

Sources: *Benedictine Monks*, p. 468; *Dunbar*, Vol. II, p. 20; *Holweck*, p. 656; *Stuart:* line 125, nos. 27 and 26 + line 147, nos. 26 and 25 + line 81, nos. 25 and 24 + line 51, nos. 24 and 23; *Weis, AR:* line 45, nos. 28 through 31 + line 101, nos. 30 and 31; *Wells*, pp. 89, 36, 424, and 257

Bl. Marie of Brabant

Marie was born around 1226 and was the daughter of Henry II "the Courageous," Duke of Brabant and Lorraine, and his first wife Maria, daughter of Philip von Hohenstaufen, Duke of Tuscany and Swabia and Emperor of Germany.

It was Marie's destiny to be very unlucky in love. In 1247 she was betrothed to Edward, son of King Henry III of England and Eleanor of Provence. The engagement did not last long. Edward married Eleanor of Castile instead and was later crowned King Edward I of England.

Six years later in 1253, Marie finally married. Her husband was Ludwig II "der Strenge" ("the Stern"), Duke of Bavaria and Count Palatine of the Rhine. No one foresaw how the marriage would end.

Early in 1256, Marie was in the duke's castle at Donauworth and wrote two letters, one to her husband and one to his cousin Count Ruchon of Wittelsbach. She asked a servant who couldn't read to deliver the letters. The servant delivered the wrong letter to Ludwig, who jumped to the conclusion that his wife was having an affair with another man. With no investigation, he hurried back to Donauworth and had his wife arrested. Over her protests of innocence, she was beheaded on January 18, 1256. According to some accounts, Ludwig had already killed the servant who brought the letter, the governor of the castle, and one of Marie's maids with his own hands.

Afterwards Ludwig was seized with great remorse. Although he was only 27, it is said that his hair and beard turned white in one night. He buried Marie with great honor in the Monastery of the Holy Cross in Donauworth. He also made a pilgrimage to Rome to seek absolution from the Pope, who told him to build a new monastery in Germany as penance, which Ludwig did.

Ludwig's bloody deed horrified medieval Europe and ended his own ambitions of becoming the next Holy Roman Emperor. Marie's story was retold by many poets and became the basis for the legend of Geneviève of Brabant, which Jacques Offenbach turned into an opera in 1859.

Her Line

Husband		Wife	
Henry II "the Courageous," Duke of Brabant and Lorraine (b. 1207 – md. (1) by 22 Aug 1215 – d. 1 Feb 1248)	+	**Maria von Hohenstaufen** (b. 1201 – md. by 22 Aug 1215 – d. 1235)	
Robert I, Count of Artois and Crusader (b. Sept 1216 – md. 14 June 1237 – slain 9 Feb 1250 while crusading in Egypt with his brother St. Louis IX)	+	**Matilda of Brabant** (md. 14 June 1237 – d. 29 Sept 1288)	Matilda's sister: ***Bl. Marie of Brabant***
Henry I, King of Navarre (b. ca. 1244 – md. (2) 1269 – d. 22 July 1274)	+	**Blanche of Artois** (b. ca. 1248 – md. (1) 1269 – d. 2 May 1302)	

Philip IV "the Fair," King of France (b. 1268 – md. 16 Aug 1284 – d. 29 Nov 1314)	+	**Jeanne of Navarre** (b. Jan 1272 – md. 16 Aug 1284 – d. 2 April 1305)
Edward II, King of England (b. 25 April 1284 – md. 25 Jan 1308 – murdered 21 Sept 1327)	+	**Isabella** (b. 1292 –md. 25 Jan 1308 – d. 27 Aug 1357)

Sources: *Dunbar*, Vol. II, p. 55; *Stuart:* line 68, no. 27 + line 125, nos. 27 and 26 + line 147, nos. 26 and 25 + line 81, nos. 25 and 24 + line 51, nos. 24 and 23; *Warncke*, pp. 194–195; *Weis, AR:* line 45, nos. 28 through 31 + line 101, nos. 30 and 31; *Wells*, pp. 89, 36, 424, and 257; *WWH*, Vol. 10, p. 396

Bl. Mary,
Princess of Bohemia

Mary (or Mlada) was the daughter of Boleslaw I "the Cruel," Duke of Bohemia, and his wife Bigota of Stockow. She founded the convent of St. George in Prague, became a nun there, and ultimately the abbess. She died in 994.

Her Line

	Husband		Wife
	Boleslaw I "the Cruel," Duke of Bohemia (d. 15 July 972)	+	**Biagota of Stockow**
Boleslaw II's sister: ***Bl. Mary, Princess of Bohemia***	**Boleslaw II "the Pious,"** Duke of Bohemia (d. 7 Feb 999)	+	Hemma (d. ca. 1005)
	Udalrich, Duke of Bohemia (d. 9 Nov 1034)	+	Bozena (d. 1055)

[For the later generations that connect this line to the kings of England, see the line of St. Ludmilla, Duchess of Bohemia in Part II.]

Sources: *Benedictine Monks*, p. 478; *Dunbar*, Vol. II, p. 94 (under "Mlada"); *Stuart*, line 362, nos. 37 through 35; *Wells*, pp. 78–79

Bl. Mathilde of Quedlinburg

Mathilde was born in 955 and was the firstborn child of Otto I "the Great," Emperor of the West, and his second wife St. Adelaide of Burgundy.

In 966 at the age of eleven, Mathilde became the first abbess of a secular abbey founded for women by her father. The abbey's population consisted of the unmarried daughters of royalty and the nobility, who did not take vows or become nuns. The abbey was called Quedlinburg. Constant prayer for the souls of King Henry the Fowler and all the German rulers who came after him was its purpose.

As an adult, Mathilde's activities vastly exceeded the normal duties of an abbess, and she became one of the most powerful women in the empire. She accompanied her brother Otto II on his Italian campaigns. After her nephew Otto III ascended the throne, she became regent of the empire for him while he was away in Italy.

Mathilde died on 7 February 999 and is buried in the church at Quedlinburg next to her grandparents Henry the Fowler and his wife St. Matilda.

Her Line

	Husband		Wife
	Otto I "the Great," Emperor of the West (b. 23 Nov 912 – md. (2) 25 Dec 951 – d. 7 May 973)	+	**St. Adelaide of Burgundy** (b. 932 – md. (2) 25 Dec 951 – d. 16/17 Dec 999)
Otto II's sister: ***Bl. Mathilde of Quedlinburg***	**Otto II**, Emperor of the West (b. 955 – md. (2) 14 April 972 – d. 7 Dec 983)	+	St. Theophano Skleros (b. 956 – md. 14 April 972 – d. 15 Sept 991)
	Ezzo, Count Palatine of Lorraine, Lord of Duisburg and Kaiserwerth (b. ca. 955 – md. 991 – d. 21 May 1034)	+	**Bl. Matilda of Saxony** (b. 981 – md. 991 – d. 4 Nov 1025)

[For the later generations that connect this line to the kings of England, see the line of St. Adelaide of Burgundy in Part II.]

Sources: *Dunbar*, Vol. II, p. 71; *Stuart*, line 237, nos. 37 through 35; *Weis, AR*, line 147, nos. 19 through 21; *Wells*, pp. 270 and 356

St. Mechtildis of Diessen

Mechtildis was born in 1125 and was the daughter of Berthold IV, Count of Andechs and Diessen, and his first wife Sophia of Istria. She was the sister of Bl. Euphemia of Andechs.

When Mechtildis was five, her parents put her in a convent they had founded in Diessen, where Mechtildis grew up to be a Benedictine nun and the abbess of the convent. Her real fame rested on her ability to perform miracles. She healed the sick and restored sight to the blind and speech to the dumb. She also experienced intense religious ecstasies.

In 1153, her bishop sent Mechtildis to reform a convent at Edelstetten. After finishing her work there, she had a premonition of her own death and returned to Diessen, where she died on 31 May 1160. Her grave there became a place of pilgrimage.

Her Line

	Husband		Wife
	Berthold IV, Count of Andechs and Diessen (b. 1096/1098 – d. 27 June 1151)	+	**Sophia of Istria** (d. 6 Sept 1128)
Berthold V's sister: ***St. Mechtildis of Diessen***	**Berthold V**, Count of Andechs and Margrave of Istria (b. 1122/1123 – md. 1152 – d. ca. 1188)	+	Hedwig von Formbach-Puttin (md. (1) 1152 – d. 16 July 1174)
	Berthold VI, Count of Andechs, Margrave of Istria, and Duke of Croatia; Crusader (b. ca. 1152 – md. 1170 – d. 12 Aug 1204)	+	Agnes von Groitzsch-Rochlitz (md. 1170 – d. 25 March 1195)

[For the later generations that connect this line to the kings of England, see the line of St. Adalbero, Bishop of Wuerzburg in Part III.]

Sources: *BBKL*, Vol. 21, col. 974; *Benedictine Monks*, p. 496; *Bunson*, p. 576; *Butler, Vol. II*, pp. 435–436; *Delaney*, pp. 401–402; *Delaney and Tobin*, p. 790; *Dunbar*, Vol. II, pp. 73–74 (under "Matilda"); *Holweck*, p. 683 (under "Mathildis"); *Snodgrass*, p. 168; *Stuart*, line 7, nos. 31–29; *Warncke*, pp. 106–107; *WWH*, Vol. 10, p. 823

St. Modoald

Modoald was the son of St. Arnulf of Metz and his wife Doda. He was also the brother of Bl. Itta and St. Severa.

Modoald became a priest, and during his frequent appearances at court he also became a counselor and spiritual adviser to Dagobert I, King of Austrasia, whose Christian faith was shallow at best. He was so vocal in his complaints about the immorality of the Austrasian court that instead of executing Modoald, Dagobert confessed his sins and changed his ways. In 622 Dagobert even appointed Modoald bishop of Treves (also known as Trier).

Modoald took part in the synod of Rheims in 623 and also founded several religious houses. He was a close friend of St. Cunibert of Cologne.

Modoald died around 646/647. He is also known as Modoaldus, Modowald, and Romoald.

His Line

Husband		Wife	
St. Arnulf (or Arnoul), Mayor of the Palace in Austrasia and Bishop of Metz (b. 13 Aug 582 – md. ca. 596 – d. 16 Aug 641)	+	**Dode (or Clothilde)** (b. ca. 586 – md. ca. 596)	
Bl. Pepin of Landen "the Old," Mayor of the Palace in Austrasia (b. 580/585 – d. 640)	+	**Bl. Itta** (b. ca. 597 – d, 8 May 652)	Itta's brother: ***St. Modoald***
Ansgise (or Ansegisel), Mayor of the Palace in Austrasia (b. 602 – md. bef. 639 – murdered 685)	+	**St. Begga** (b. ca. 613 – md. bef. 639 – d. ca. 698)	

[For the later generations that connect this line to the kings of England, see the line of St. Arnulf, Bishop of Metz in Part II.]

Sources: *BBKL*, Vol. 21, cols. 1011–1012; *Benedictine Monks*, p. 509; *Bunson*, p. 592; *Butler*, Vol. II, p. 287; *Delaney*, p. 411; *Delaney and Tobin*, p. 812; *Holweck*, p. 718; *Stuart*, line 260; *Wells*, p. 135

St. Nefyn

Nefyn was a daughter of St. Brychan, the ruler of Brecknock. She married St. Cynfarch Gul (also known as Cynfarch Oer), a war leader in northern Britain. One of their sons was Urien, King of Rheged.

Her Line

Husband		Wife	
St. Brychan, ruler of Brecknock in South Wales (b. 480/490)	+	**N.N.**	
St. Gabran mac Domangart, King of Dalriada (b. ca. 500 – md. bef. 532 – d. ca. 559)	+	**St. Lleian** (md. bef. 532)	Lleian's sister: ***St. Nefyn***
Aidan (or Aedan) mac Gabran (b. 532 – d. 606), crowned King of Dalriada by St. Columba of Iona	+	N.N.	

[For the later generations that connect this line to the kings of England, see the line of St. Brychan in Part II.]

Sources: *Ashley*, pp. 158 and 197; *Baring-Gould*, Vol. 16, p. 272*; *Baring-Gould and Fisher*, Vol. 4, pp. 26–27; *Boyer*, p. 64; *Holweck*, p. 249*; *Stuart*, line 165, nos. 49 and 48; *Weis, AR*, line 170, nos. 4 and 5; *Wells*, p. 177 (references marked with a * are alphabetized under "Cynfarch")

Bl. Nivard

Nivard was born around 1100 and was the son of Tescelin Sorrel, Lord of Les Fontaines, and his wife Bl. Aleth of Montbard. Nivard was the youngest brother of St. Bernard of Clairvaux.

After becoming a monk and joining his brother Bernard at the abbey of Clairvaux for several years, Nivard left Clairvaux to found other abbeys. He died in 1150.

His Line

Husband		Wife	
Tescelin Sorrel (or Sorus), Lord of Les Fontaines (md. ca. 1085)	+	**Bl. Aleth of Montbard** (b. ca. 1070 – md. ca. 1085 – d. 1105/1110)	
Anseric II, Sire de Chacenay (d. 1137)	+	md. (1) **Bl. Humbeline de Troyes** (b. 1092 – d. 21 Aug 1141)	Humbeline's brother: ***Bl. Nivard***
Gui, Count of Bar-sur-Seine (d. 1145)	+	**Petronille de Chacenay** (d. 1161)	

[For the later generations that connect this line to the kings of England, see the line of Bl. Aleth of Montbard in Part II.]

Sources: *Benedictine Monks*, p. 527; *Butler*, Vol. III, p. 360; *Delaney and Tobin*, p. 856; *Holweck*, p. 746; *NCE*, Vol. 10, p. 475; *O'Malley*, pp. 73 and 99; *Stuart:* line 385 + line 384, nos. 29 and 28; *Wells*, p. 144

St. Non

Non was the daughter of Gwynr Ceinfarfog (Gwynr "the Fair Bearded"), Lord of Caer Gawch, and his second wife Anna. Non married a Welsh chieftain named Sant (or Sandde). Non's sister St. Gwen married St. Salamon I, King of Brittany.

But for her extraordinary son, Non might be completely forgotten today. Her child David grew up to be a tall and eloquent speaker, well known for his kindness and compassion. He made the conversion of the Welsh to Christianity his life's work. After building several monasteries in Wales, he became its bishop. Made the patron saint of the Welsh after his death, St. David of Wales is remembered today as one of the greatest of all the British saints. His relics are in St. David's Cathedral today.

At the end of her own life, Non was a nun in a convent in Brittany. She is buried in a church at Divinon, ten miles east of Brest.

There has been considerable devotion to Non in both Wales and Brittany. For many centuries pilgrims and the sick visited healing wells named after her, and many miraculous cures were attributed to her.

Non is also known as Nonna or Nonnita.

Her Line

Husband		Wife	
Gwynr (or Gynyr or Cynyr) Ceinfarfog ("the Fair Bearded"), Lord of Caer Gawch (or Caer Goch) in Pembrokeshire, Wales	+	md. (2) **Anna**, daughter of Gwerthefyr (or Vortimer) Fendigaid ("the Blessed")	
St. Salamon I "the Handsome," King of Brittany (liv. in the 400's)	+	**St. Gwen**	Gwen's sister: ***St. Non***
Audren, King of Brittany	+	N.N.	
Budic I, King of Brittany	+	N.N., a daughter of Corun	

[For the later generations that connect this line to the kings of England, see the line of St. Cunedda Wledig in Part II.]

Sources: *Baring-Gould*, Vol. 3, p. 10* and Vol. 16, pp. 134 and 189–190; *Baring-Gould and Fisher*, Vol. 2, pp. 285–322 and Vol. 4, pp. 22–25 and 172–173; *Benedictine Monks*, p. 528; *Bentley*, p. 44; *Boyer*, p. 67; *Bunson*, p. 610; *Butler*, Vol. I, pp. 468–469; *Castleden*, pp. 30–31*; *CS*, pp. 125–126; *Delaney and Tobin*, p. 857; *Dunbar*, Vol. II, p. 109; *Holweck*, pp. 265*, 460 (under "St. Gwen"), and 747; *Jones*, pp. 58–59; *One Hundred Saints*, p. 154; *Parbury*, pp. 53–54 (under "St. Gwen") and 73–74; *Rees*, p. 60; *Snodgrass*, pp. 66–67; *Stuart*, line 405, nos. 55 through 53; *Wolf*, p. 185; *Woods*, pp. 122 and 124 (sources marked with a * are accounts of the life of St. David)

St. Octavian

Octavian was born around 1060 and was the son of William II "the Great," Count of Burgundy, and his wife Stephanie of Longwy. He was the brother of Pope Callistus (or Callixtus) II (whose given name was Guy of Burgundy) and of Bl. Ayrald. During the First Crusade, three of his other brothers died in the Holy Land.

Octavian became a Benedictine monk and entered the abbey at Cluny. In 1123 he was made bishop of Savona. He died on 6 August 1128.

His Line

	Husband		Wife
	William II "the Great," Count of Burgundy and Macon (b. ca. 1024 – md. 1049/1057 – d. 12 Nov 1087)	+	**Stephanie of Longwy** (b. ca. 1035 – md. 1049/ 1057 – d. aft. 1088)
Raymond's brother: ***St. Octavian***	**Raymond of Burgundy and Ivrea,** Count of Castile, Galicia, Coimbra, and d'Amous, went to Spain on a Crusade against the Moors (b. ca. 1070 – md. ca. 1095 – d. 13/20 Sept 1107)	+	Urraca (b. ca. 1082 – md. ca. 1095 – d. 8 March 1126), daughter of Alfonso VI, King of Castile and Leon
	Alfonso VII, King of Castile, Leon, Galicia, Toledo, Zaragoza, and the Asturias (b. 1 March 1105 – md. (2) July 1152 – d. 21 Aug 1157)	+	Richilde (b. 1130/ 1140 – md. July 1152 – d. 1166), daughter of Wladislaw II, King of Poland

[For the later generations that connect this line to the kings of England, see the line of Bl. Ayrald in Part III.]

Sources: *Delaney and Tobin*, p. 865; *Holweck*, p. 751; *Stuart*, line 94, nos. 31 through 29; *Weis, AR:* line 132, nos. 24 and 25 + line 113, nos. 24 and 25

St. Odilia

Odilia was born around 660 and was the daughter of Eticho I, Duke of Alsace, and his wife Berswinde.

When Eticho learned that Odilia had been born blind, he decided that his new daughter was a shame and a dishonor to his family. He was about to kill his child by exposing her to the elements. Odilia's mother persuaded him not to do this, but only by agreeing that Odilia would be sent away and that no one would ever be told whose child Odilia really was.

Odilia was given to a peasant woman who raised her. At twelve, she was taken to a convent, where it was discovered that she had never been baptized. The ceremony was performed by St. Erhard, bishop of Regensburg, and at the moment when he touched her eyes with chrism, her sight was restored.

Odilia became a nun, and her father ultimately repented of his earlier cruelty. With his help, she founded an abbey at Hohenburg (now Odilienberg) in Alsace and became its first abbess. Nearby, she also founded a convent at Niedermuenster.

Odilia died on 13 December 720 and was buried in the Chapel of St. John the Baptist in Odilienberg. In the Middle Ages, Odilia was a very popular saint and was favored by monarchs and also by common people. Her tomb was a place of pilgrimage but was destroyed during the French Revolution.

Odilia is the patron saint of the blind and of people afflicted with eye diseases. She is also the patron saint of Alsace.

Her Line

	Husband		Wife
	Eticho (or Adalric) I, Duke of Alsace (d. 20 Feb 690)	+	**Berswinde**, daughter of St. Sigebert III, King of Austrasia
Adalbert's sister: ***St. Odilia***	**Adalbert**, Duke of Alsace (d. 722)	+	Gerlinde
	Luitfride I, Duke of Alsace (d. 767)	+	Edith

[For the later generations that connect this line to the kings of England, see the line of St. Attalia in Part III.]

Sources: *Baring-Gould*, Vol. 15, pp. 174–175 and Vol. 16, p. 152; *BBKL*, Vol. 6, cols. 1108–1109; *Benedictine Monks*, p. 538; *Bunson*, p. 614; *Butler*, Vol. IV, pp. 551–552; *CE*, Vol. XI, p. 207; *Delaney*, p. 433; *Dunbar*, Vol. II, pp. 114–116; *Holweck*, p. 752; *Joeckle*, pp. 343–345; *Snodgrass*, p. 175; *Stuart*, line 224, nos. 42 through 40; *Warncke*, pp. 264–265; *Weis, AR*, line 181, nos. 1 through 3; *Wells*, p. 9; *WWH*, Vol. 12, p. 53

St. Oswald,
King of Northumbria

Oswald was born around 604/605 and was the son of Aethelfrith, King of Bernicea and Deira, and his second wife Acha.

Oswald's early years were turbulent. Around 616, Aethelfrith was killed in a battle with Redwald, King of East Anglia. Acha's brother Edwin returned from exile to claim the empty throne of Bernicea and Deira. Acha fled with her children to the court of the king of Dalriada, Eochaid Buide. In Dalriada Acha and her children were converted to Christianity, and Oswald was sent to the monastery on the isle of Iona to be educated. When he was old enough to fight, Oswald began to accompany the Dalriadan soldiers on their campaigns and built a reputation as a very capable warrior.

Oswald's opportunity to reclaim his inheritance came when King Edwin was killed at the battle of Hatfield Chase on 12 October 633. After leading a small army south from Dalriada in 634, Oswald met a much larger enemy army led by Cadwallon ap Cadfan. The night before the battle, Oswald erected a wooden cross and asked his men—who were mostly pagans—to kneel before it and join him in a prayer for victory for their righteous cause. The next day in the battle of Heavenfield, Cadwallon ap Cadfan was killed, Oswald's army triumphed, and his men were baptized.

Combining Bernicea and Deira into the kingdom of Northumbria, King Oswald knew that among his subjects there were many people who were only nominally Christian or outright pagans. He resolved to complete their conversion. St. Aidan arrived from Dalriada to help him. Oswald donated the island of Lindisfarne for the construction of a monastery and built many other churches. Until St. Aidan had mastered the Northumbrian language, Oswald translated many of his sermons for him.

Historians of Oswald's reign regarded him as a model Christian ruler. He prayed often and was generous to the poor. At an unknown date, he married Cyneburga, daughter of King Cynegils of Wessex.

After reigning for about eight years, Oswald died a warrior's death. On 5 August 642, he was slain in the battle of Maserfield by Penda of Mercia. Even as he died, his last words were a prayer for the souls of his men.

In the Middle Ages, Oswald was a very well known saint. Outside of England, he was venerated in Ireland, Scotland, southern Germany, Switzerland, and northern Italy. In England, he became a national hero and an early model of the royal soldier saint.

His Line

The three marriages of **Aethelfrith**, King of Bernicea and Deira

md. (1) **Bebba**	md. (2) Acha, daughter of Aella, King of Deira	md. (3) N.N.
One of the children of Aethelfrith and (1):	Two of the children of Aethelfrith and (2):	One of the children of Aethelfrith and (3):

		St. Oswald, King of Northumbria and St. Oswy, King of Northumbria	St. Ebba "the Elder"
Eanfrith, King of Bernicea (killed in battle in April 635/ 636 after ruling for only 18 months)	+	N.N., daughter of Eochaid Buide, King of the Picts	
Beli, King of Strathclyde (d. by 641)	+	**N.N.**, a sister of Talorcam (I), King of the Picts	

[For the later generations that connect this line to the kings of England, see the line of St. Ebba "the Elder" in Part III.]

Sources: *Ashley:* pp. 270 (which shows St. Ebba "the Elder" as the child of Aethelfrith's second wife) and 279 + pp. 166 and 175 + pp. 185 and 189 + pp. 166 and 202 + pp. 195 and 203–205; *Baring-Gould*, Vol. 9, pp. 63–74 and Vol. 16, p. 154; *BBKL*, Vol. 6, cols. 1325–1327; *Benedictine Monks*, p. 537; *Bentley*, p. 151; *Bunson*, p. 621; *Butler*, Vol. III, pp. 293–295; *Castleden*, pp. 104–105; *CE*, Vol. XI, pp. 348–349; *CS*, pp. 430–431; *Delaney*, pp. 439–440; *Delaney and Tobin*, p. 883; *Guiley*, pp. 263–264; *HBC*, pp. 4–5; *Holweck*, p. 761; *Joeckle*, pp. 346–347; *Jones*, pp. 95–97; *Klaniczay*, pp. 82–86 and Appendix 2, Geneal. Table 1; *NCE*, Vol. 10, pp. 810–811; *O'Malley*, p. 97; *Rees*, pp. 177–181; *Stuart:* line 406, nos. 51 through 49 + line 341, no. 49; *Wells*, pp. 435 (which also shows St. Ebba "the Elder" as the child of Aethelfrith's second wife) and 469; *Williams*, pp. 287, 363, and 364; *Yorke*, p. 78

St. Oswy, King of Northumbria

Oswy (or Oswin) was born around 612. His father was Aethelfrith, King of Bernicea and Deira, and his mother was Acha, Aethelfrith's second wife. St. Oswald (b. ca. 604/605), who would become king of Bernicia and Deira and unite them into the new kingdom of Northumbria, was his older brother.

When their father was killed in battle around 616, the two brothers followed their mother into exile in Dalriada. Like Oswald, Oswy was educated by the monks on Iona and grew to manhood there. The brothers' life in exile would continue until King Edwin, who had become the ruler of their homeland, was killed in battle in October 633. The victor in that battle, Cadwallon ap Cadfan, spent the next two years trying to establish himself as the ruler of Bernicia and Deira by a campaign of slaughter and destruction.

Oswy's first deeds as an adult were to fight beside his brother Oswald in the reconquest of their homeland. After Oswald triumphed in October 633 at the battle of Heavenfield, he was crowned king, and Oswy became a prince of Bernicea and Deira. For the next several years, Oswy assisted Oswald in his military campaigns and in the other tasks of government.

As Oswy's fortunes had risen following his brother's victory at Heavenfield in 635, they also sank after Oswald's defeat and death at Maserfield in 642. With the pagan Penda as the new ruler of all the lands of Oswald, Northumbria once again split up into the separate kingdoms of Bernicia and Deira. Oswy became king of the first, while his cousin Oswin became the ruler of the second. Both were vassal lords of Penda.

Whatever goodwill there was between Oswy and Oswin at the beginning of their reigns did not last long. Their relationship became severely strained, and by 651 each of them was preparing to go to war with the other. On the eve of battle and vastly outnumbered, Oswin changed his mind, refused to fight, and took refuge with one of his own noblemen, who promptly handed him over to the soldiers of Oswy. On Oswy's orders, Oswin was executed on 20 August 651.

With Oswin dead, Oswy became both the sole ruler of Bernicea and Deira and a serious rival to Penda of Mercia, who immediately began preparing for war. As Penda led a large army against Oswy in 654, his ferocity and record of victory in battle were unrivaled. He was also the same man who had slain Oswy's brother Oswald at Maserfield in 642. At the battle of Winwaed, Oswy's numerically inferior force nevertheless triumphed. Penda was killed, his army was destroyed, and Oswy became the leading ruler in England. His victory made him the king of most of England between Scotland and the Thames.

Oswy used his new power to continue the conversion of England to Christianity. As penance for the death of Oswin, he built the monastery at Gilling. After defeating Penda at Winwaed, he also made good on his promise to found a dozen more monasteries and to give his daughter Elfleda to the Church if he was victorious in battle. As the new ruler of Mercia, Oswy also sent many missionaries to begin converting the pagan subjects of Penda's pagan kingdom.

In practical terms, Oswy's influence on history was as great as that of the Apostles, and it began when he summoned English Churchmen to a synod at Whitby in 664. Until then, two different sets of Christian customs were followed in different parts of England. One was the customs of the church which was headquartered in Rome. The other was the customs of the Celtic church which was centered in Ireland. Among other things, the two churches disagreed over the date when Easter should be celebrated. After hearing the arguments of both sides at the synod, Oswy decided that henceforth the churches in his realm would follow the Roman customs generally, including the Roman method of setting the date of Easter. By unifying Christian practice in most of England and by placing it under the leadership of Rome, Oswy's decision profoundly affected English history for the rest of the Middle Ages in ways that he could scarcely have imagined.

The system of recording the passage of time according to the number of years since the birth of Christ was also adopted at Whitby. The universal acknowledgment today that a particular year was or will be 1900, 2000, or 2100 goes back to the determination of the synod of Whitby that its delegates were meeting in the year 664. By thus establishing how years would be counted, Oswy indirectly became the ruler of us all, right down to the present day.

Like his father, Oswy was married three times. While he was still in exile in Dalriada, he married Rhiainmelt, the daughter of Rhoeth, Prince of Rheged. Rhiainmelt died shortly after the first reconquest of Bernicea and Deira in 635, and Oswy's second wife was the Irish princess Fin of the Cenél Eógain. After the pagan Penda slew King Oswald in 642 at the battle of Maserfield, Fin also died. Oswy's third wife would be St. Eanfleda. Oswy and Eanfleda's daughter Elfleda would also become a saint.

Oswy was one of the few kings of Northumbria who was neither killed nor deposed. After dying of natural causes on 15 February 670, he was buried in the abbey at Whitby.

His Line
The three marriages of
Aethelfrith, King of
Bernicea and Northumbria

md. (1) **Bebba**	md. (2) Acha, daughter of Aella, King of Deira	md. (3) N.N.
One of the children of Aethelfrith and (1):	Two of the children of Aethelfrith and (2):	One of the children of Aethelfrith and (3):
Eanfrith, King of Bernicea	St. Oswald, King of Northumbria and ***St. Oswy, King of Northumbria***	St. Ebba "the Elder"

[For the later generations that connect this line to the kings of England, see the line of St. Ebba "the Elder" in Part III.]

Sources: *Ashley*, pp. 270 and 281–283; *Baring-Gould*, Vol. 9, pp. 192–196 (under "St. Oswin"); *Bunson*, p. 266 (under "Ebba"); *CE*, Vol. 9, p. 269; *de Vere*, p. 142; *HBC*, pp. 4–5; *Stuart*, line 406, nos. 51 and 50; *Webb*, p. 13; *Wells*, pp. 435 and 469; *Williamson*, pp. 288 and 364; *Yorke*, pp. 76 and 78–79

St. Owain

Owain was the son of Morgan Mawr, King of the Welsh realm of Morgannwg, and his wife Lleucu ferch Enflew. He succeeded his father as king of Morgannwg.

Owain died around 1001. The church of Ystra Owen in Glamorgan is dedicated to him.

His Line

Husband		Wife	
Morgan Mawr ap Owain, (also known as Morgan Hen), King of Morgannwg (d. 974)	+	**Lleucu ferch Enflew**	
Seferws ap Cadwr, Lord of Buallt and Maes Yfed	+	**Lucy ferch Morgan Hen**	Lucy's brother: ***St. Owain***
Ifor ap Seferws, Lord of Buallt and Maes Yfed	+	Isabell ferch Tryffin	

[For the later generations that connect this line to the kings of Scotland, see the line of St. Meurig ap Tewdrig, King of Gwent and Glywysing in Part II.]

Sources: *Boyer:* no. 15 on p. 161 + no. "1–14" on p. 137; *Holweck*, p. 762

St. Podius

Podius was born in 930 and was the son of Humbert, Margrave of Tuscany, and his wife Willa of Camerino. He was educated in Pavia and became an Augustinian monk.

Podius was made the bishop of Florence in 990 and died in 1002. He is buried in the Basilica di Santa Maria del Fiore, also known as the Cathedral of Florence, near St. Zenobius, who was the first bishop there (337–417).

His Line

Husband		Wife	
Humbert, Margrave of Tuscany (md. ca. 945 – d. 967/970)	+	**Willa of Camerino** (md. ca. 945 – d. aft. 978)	
Ardoino, Marquis of Ivrea and King of Italy (b. ca. 960 – d. 1015)	+	**Berta**, Princess of Lorraine	Berta's brother: ***St. Podius***
Ardicino, Prince of Italy (b. ca. 980 – md. bef. 1019 – liv. 1029)	+	Willa of Tuscany (md. bef. 1019)	
Ardoino II of Ivrea	+	N.N.	
William Bertrand, Count of Provence (b. ca. 1025 – d. aft. May 1065/1067)	+	**Adelaide of Ivrea** (d. aft. 12 Oct 1113)	
Armengol IV, Count of Urgel (b. ca. 1056 – md. (2) 1076/1080 – d. 28 March 1092)	+	**Adelaide**, heiress of Avignon, Forcalquier, and Provence (md. 1076/1080 – d. 1129)	
William III, Count of Forcalquier and Marquis of Provence (d. Oct 1129)	+	Gersende of Albon (liv. 1158/1160)	
Bertrand II, Count of Forcalquier (b. ca. 1110 – d. 1149/1150)	+	Josserande de la Flotte	
William IV, Count of Forcalquier (b. 1130 – d. Nov 1208)	+	Adelaide de Beziers	
Raimon de Sabran, Seigneur de Castellar (b. ca. 1155 – md. ca. 1178 – d. 1224)	+	**Gersinde** (md. ca. 1178 – d. aft. 1193)	
Alfonso of Aragon (b. 1180 – md. 1193 – d. Feb 1209), son of Alfonso II, King of Aragon	+	**Gersinde of Sabran** (i.e., Gersinde II), heiress of Provence and Forcalquier (md. 1193 – was a nun in 1222 – d. aft. 1222)	
Raymond Berenger V, Count of Forcalquier and Provence (b. 1198 – md. Dec 1220 – d. 19 Aug 1245)	+	Beatrice of Savoy (b. 1198 – md. Dec 1220 – d. Dec 1266)	

Henry III, King of England (b. 1 Oct 1207 – md. 14 Jan 1236 – d. 16 Nov 1272)	+	**Bl. Eleanor of Provence** (b. ca. 1223 – md. 14 Jan 1236 – d. 25 June 1291)

Sources: *Benedictine Monks*, p. 582; *Bunson*, p. 679; *Delaney and Tobin*, p. 948; *Holweck*, p. 821; *Stuart:* line 186, nos. 37 and 36 + line 198, nos. 36 through 33 + line 197, nos. 33 and 32 + line 195, nos. 32 through 28 + line 116, nos. 28 and 27 + line 54, nos. 27 through 25; *Weis, AR:* line 111, nos. 28 through 30 + line 1, no. 27; *Wells*, pp. 568, 317, 482, 572, 253, 508, and 482

St. Quenburga

Quenburga was the daughter of Cenred, a war leader in Wessex. She was also the sister of St. Cuthburga.

After Cuthburga became a nun, so did Quenburga. Around 705, she helped Cuthburga found a new abbey at Wimborne and then joined the convent there. She died around 735.

Wimborne produced many of the nuns who brought Christianity to Germany.

Her Line

	Husband		Wife
	Cenred, a war leader in Wessex (liv. 644–694)	+	**N.N.**
Ingild's sister: ***St. Quenburga***	**Ingild** (b. ca. 680 – d. 718)	+	N.N.
	Eoppa	+	N.N.
	Eafa (b. ca. 732)	+	N.N.
	Eahlmund (or Edmund), King of Kent (b. ca. 758 – d. 786)	+	N.N., a daughter of Aethelbert II, King of Kent

[For the later generations that connect this line to the kings of England, see the line of St. Aethelbert I, King of Kent in Part II.]

Sources: *Ashley*, p. 298; *Baring-Gould*, Vol. 9, p. 400*; *Benedictine Monks*, p. 186*; *Butler*, Vol. III, pp. 481–482*; *Delaney and Tobin*, p. 304*; *Holweck*, p. 840; *Kirby*, pp. 101, 103, and 181; *O'Malley*, pp. 72 and 92–93; *Parbury*, p. 29; *Snodgrass*, p. 197; *Stuart*, line 233, nos. 46 through 42; *Weis, AR*, line 1, nos. 8 through 12; *Wells*, p. 203; *Williamson*, pp. 209 and 360; *Yorke*, pp. 144–145 (references marked with a * are alphabetized under St. Cuthburga)

St. Remigius of Rouen

Remigius was the son of Charles Martel by an unknown mistress. He was also a half-brother of Pepin III "the Short" and therefore an uncle of Charlemagne. He entered the church and became bishop of Rouen in 755.

In 760, Remigius accompanied Pepin on a diplomatic mission to Italy and was so impressed by the liturgy and Gregorian chant which he heard there that he spent the rest of his life introducing them throughout France.

Remigius died around 772.

His Line

	Husband		Wife
	Charles Martel, Mayor of the Palace in Austrasia, and the victor at the battle of Poitiers (732) (b. ca. 688 – d. 22 Oct 741)	+	Chrotrude of Allemania (d. 724)
Pepin's half-brother: ***St. Remigius of Rouen***	**Pepin (or Pippin) III "the Short,"** Mayor of the Palace in Austrasia and King of the Franks (b. 715 – md. ca. 740 – d. 24 Sept 768)	+	Bertha (or Bertrada) "Bigfoot" (b. ca. 720 – md. ca. 740 – d. 12 July 783)
	Bl. Charlemagne, King of the Franks and First Emperor of the West (b. 2 April 747 – md. (2) 771 – d. 28 Jan 814)	+	Bl. Hildegarde, Countess of Vinzgau (b. 758 – md. 771 – d. 30 April 783)

[For the later generations that connect this line to the kings of England, see the line of St. Arnulf, Bishop of Metz in Part II.]

Sources: *Benedictine Monks*, p. 603; *Bunson*, p. 708; *Delaney and Tobin*, p. 982; *Holweck*, p. 852; *NCE*, Vol. 12, p. 342; *Stuart*, line 171, nos. 43 through 41; *Weis, AR*, line 190, nos. 11 through 13

St. Richardis

Richardis was born in 840 and was the daughter of Erchanger, Count of Alsace. In 862, she married Charles "the Fat," who became king of Alemannia in 876 and who was crowned Holy Roman Emperor in 881.

As a man, Charles was lethargic and inept. He also had repeated illnesses and is believed to have suffered from epilepsy.

Deaths among his relatives caused vast territories to pass to Charles, which increased his responsibilities as a ruler. At one point, the entire Carolingian empire was reunited under him. As this occurred, Charles' shortcomings as a ruler were more and more apparent. Many important people in the empire began to see him as spineless and incompetent.

By 887, Charles wanted to remove his own chancellor Liutward, whose vast powers were making Charles quite uneasy. The way Charles decided to do this was by accusing his own wife Richardis of infidelity with Liutward. Before an imperial assembly, Richardis underwent the ordeal of fire—specifically, she walked with bare feet across burning embers. When she was found to be unharmed, she was declared innocent.

It was the government of Charles that did not survive the ordeal. Liutward was removed from his office anyway, but later in 887 Charles himself was turned out of power by his own nobles. Richardis separated from Charles after the ordeal, became a nun, entered her own monastery at Andlau in Alsace, died there around 895, and was honored as a saint.

Richardis is buried in the abbey church at Andlau. Her grave became a place of pilgrimage.

Her Line

Husband		Wife	
Erchanger I, Count of Alsace (liv. 811–841)	+	**N.N.**	
Louis II (b. ca. 823 – md. bef. 5 Oct 851 – d. 12 Aug 875), Emperor of the West and son of Lothair I, King of Italy and Emperor of the West	+	**Engelberge** (md. bef. 5 Oct 851 – d. 896/901)	Engelberge's sister: ***St. Richardis***
Boso II, King of Lower Burgundy and Count of Vienne (md. 876 – d. 897)	+	**Ermengard** (b. 852/855 – md. 876 – d. 896)	
Rudolph I, King of Upper Burgundy (md. 888 – d. 25 Oct 912)	+	**Willa of Vienne** (md. 888 – d. 14 June 929)	
Rudolph II, King of Burgundy and Italy (md. 922 – d. 11 July 937)	+	Bertha of Swabia (md. (1) 922 – d. 2 Jan 966)	

[For the later generations that connect this line to the kings of England, see the line of St. Adelaide of Burgundy in Part II.]

Sources: *BBKL*, Vol. 17, cols. 1141–1142; *Benedictine Monks*, p. 607; *Bunson*, p. 714; *Butler*, Vol. III, pp. 592–593; *Delaney*, p. 492; *Delaney and Tobin*, p. 990; *Englebert*, p. 356; *Holweck*, p. 857; *Roesch*, p. 96; *Stuart:* line 25, nos. 41 and 40 + line 343, nos. 39 and 38 + line 175, nos. 36 and 35 + line 323; *Tucker:* Vol. II, pp. 481 and 847 + Vol. I, p. 146; *Wells*, pp. 138, 589, and 110; *WWH*, Vol. 13, p. 283

St. Rosendo

Rosendo was born on 26 November 907 and was the son of Gutierre Menendez, who governed six counties in Galicia granted to him by Alfonso IV, King of Leon. Gutierre's wife was St. Ilduara Eriz.

Rosendo is remembered as both a churchman and a war leader. At the age of 18, he was appointed bishop of Mondonedo. He founded the monastery of Cellanueva (or Celanova) in Galicia and supported reforms in his Benedictine order.

In 955 King Ordono III made him governor of the lands around Cellanueva. During the king's absence, Rosendo led armies that defeated invading Norsemen in Galicia and invading Moors in Portugal.

Rosendo was later made abbot of the monastery at Cellanueva. He became one of the leading Spanish religious figures of his time and acquired a reputation for performing miracles.

Rosendo died on 1 March 977. His relics are at Cellanueva. He is also known as Rudesind.

His Line

<table>
<tr><th>Husband</th><th></th><th>Wife</th><th></th></tr>
<tr><td>Gutierre Menendez, Count in Galicia</td><td>+</td><td>St. Ilduara Eriz
(d. 958)</td><td></td></tr>
<tr><td>Pelayo Gonzalez, Count of Galicia
(d. ca. 959)</td><td>+</td><td>Hermesenda Gutierrez</td><td>Hermesenda's brother:
St. Rosendo</td></tr>
<tr><td>Gonzalo Menendez, Count of Galicia
(d. ca. 985)</td><td>+</td><td>Ilduara Pelaez
(d. by 985)</td><td></td></tr>
<tr><td>Menendo Gonzalez, Count of Galicia</td><td>+</td><td>md. (1) Totadomna
(d. ca. 1022)</td><td></td></tr>
<tr><td>Alfonso V, King of Castile and Leon
(b. 994 – md. (1) 1015 – slain 7 Aug 1028)</td><td>+</td><td>Elvira Menendez
(b. ca. 996 – md. 1015 – d. Dec 1022)</td><td></td></tr>
</table>

[For the later generations that connect this line to the kings of England, see the line of St. Florentina in Part III.]

Sources: *Benedictine Monks*, p. 617; *Bunson*, p. 725; *Delaney*, p. 501; *Delaney and Tobin*, p. 1101; *Dunbar*, Vol. I, p. 404 (under "Ilduarda"); *Holweck*, pp. 503 (under "Ilduara") and 870; *Stuart*, line 277, nos. 36 through 33; *Tucker*, Vol. I, pp. 79–80; *Wells*, p. 263

St. Rostislav I Mstislavich, Grand Prince of Kiev

Rostislav was born around 1110. He was the son of St. Mstislav I Vladimirovich "the Great," Grand Prince of Kiev, and his first wife Christina. By a wife whose name is unknown, he had eight children.

In 1125 Rostislav was made prince of Smolensk, which he would rule for the next forty-three years. His city grew substantially and became influential in national affairs. Thanks to Rostislav, several new churches and monasteries were also built.

Rather than being a ruler, Rostislav would have preferred to be a monk. He surrounded himself with monks as advisers and had a firm sense of justice. In 1154 and again from 1159 to 1167, he received additional responsibilities when he was made Grand Prince of Kiev. He worked particularly hard to keep peace among all the factions that were grasping for power.

While returning from a campaign against Novgorod, Rostislav was stricken with plague. He hoped to live long enough to take monastic vows once he reached Kiev, but he died on the way there on 14 March 1167. His relics are in Kiev at the Theodosiev monastery.

His Line

	St. Mstislav Vladimirovich (a.k.a. Mstislav I Harold), Grand Prince of Kiev (b. 1076 – d. 15 April 1132)		
md. (1) 1095 Christina, daughter of Inge I, King of Sweden			md. (2) 1122 Lyubawa (d. 1168), daughter of Dmitri Zaviditsch, Possadnik of Novgorod Daughter of Mstislav and Lyubawa:
Son of Mstislav and Christina: ***St. Rostislav I Mstislavich, Grand Prince of Kiev***	Geza II, King of Hungary (b. ca. 1130 – md. 1146 – d. 3 May 1162)	+	**Euphrosyne Mstislavna** (b. 1130 – md. 1146 – d. 1175/1176)
	Bela III, King of Hungary (b. ca. 1148 – md. (1) 1172 – d. 23 April 1196)	+	Agnes (or Anne) de Chatillon-sur-Loing (b. 1153 – md. 1172 – d. 1184)

[For the later generations that connect this line to the kings of England, see the line of St. Harold III "Bluetooth," King of Denmark, in Part II.]

Sources: *Hist. Rus. Ch.*, Vol. 2, p. 689; *Holweck*, p. 869; *Klaniczay*, pp. 436 and 438; *Stuart:* line 240, nos. 29 and 28 + line 51, nos. 29 and 28; *Walsh*, pp. 522–523; *Weis, AR*, line 242, nos. 8 through 10; *Wells*, pp. 329 and 309

Bl. Sancia

Sancia was born around 1180 and was the daughter of Alfonso IX "el Barboro," King of Leon, and his first wife Bl. Teresa of Portugal. She was the half-sister of St. Fernando III, King of Castile.

Sancia became a nun in the Order of Santiago. She died on 13 March 1229, and her relics are in the monastery of Santa Fe in Toledo.

She is also known as Sancha.

Her Line

<table>
<tr><td></td><td>Alfonso IX "el Barboro," King of Leon (b. 15 Aug 1171 – d. 24 Sept 1230)</td><td></td><td></td></tr>
<tr><td>md. (1) in 1191 Bl. Teresa of Portugal (b. 1181 – d. 18 June 1250), daughter of Sancho I, King of Portugal</td><td></td><td></td><td>md. (2) in Dec. 1197 Bergaria (b. 1180 – d. 8 Nov 1246), daughter of Alfonso IX "the Noble," King of Castile, Toledo, and Extramadura</td></tr>
<tr><td>Daughter of Alfonso IX "el Barboro" and Teresa: Bl. Sancia</td><td>Son of Alfonso IX "el Barboro" and Berengaria:</td><td></td><td></td></tr>
<tr><td></td><td>St. Fernando III, King of Castile, Galicia, Leon, Toledo, and Extramadura (b. 24 June 1198 – md. (2) 1237 – d. 30 May 1252)</td><td>+</td><td>Jeanne de Dammartin, Countess of Ponthieu (b. ca. 1208– md. 1237 – d. 16 March 1279)</td></tr>
<tr><td></td><td>Edward I "Longshanks," King of England (b. 17 June 1239 – md. (1) 18 Oct 1254 – d. 8 July 1307)</td><td>+</td><td>Eleanor of Castile (b. 1240 – md. 18 Oct 1254 – d. 28 Nov 1290)</td></tr>
</table>

Sources: *Dunbar*, Vol. II, p. 215; *Holweck*, p. 883; *Stuart:* line 83, nos. 27 and 26 + line 52, nos. 26 through 24; *Weis, AR*, line 110, nos. 27 through 30

St. Sawyl "Benisel"

Sawyl was the son of St. Pabo "Post Prydyn," a ruler of northern Britain. Sawyl's nickname "Benisel" means "of the low head." Sawyl's first wife was Deichter, daughter of Muiredach, King of Ulster. His second wife was St. Gwenaseth.

In his youth, Sawyl was a warrior in northern Britain. Like his father and brother, Sawyl became a monk after the family moved to north Wales. It is said that he served under his brother St. Dunawd.

Sawyl and St. Gwenaseth were the parents of Asaph, the great Welsh saint.

His Line

Husband		Wife	
St. Pabo "Post Prydyn" (the Pillar of Northern Britain) (b. ca. 430 – d. ca. 510)	+	**N.N.**	
St. Brochwel Ysgithrog, King of Powys (b. ca. 502 – d. ca. 560)	+	**St. Arddun "Benasgell"**	Arddun's brother: ***St. Sawyl "Benisel"***
Cynan Garwyn	+	N.N.	

[For the later generations that connect this line to the kings of Scotland, see the line of St. Arddun "Benasgell" in Part II.]

Sources: *Baring-Gould*, Vol. 16, pp. 172–173; *Baring-Gould and Fisher*, Vol. 4, pp. 175–176; *Benedictine Monks*, p. 629; *Boyer*: no. 3 on p. 63, no. 21 on p. 70; *Bunson*, p. 737; *Holweck*, pp. 102 (under "Arddun Benasgell") and 888; *Maund*, p. 35; *Rees*, p. 101

St. Sethryda

Sethryda was the daughter of Aethelhere, King of East Anglia, and his wife St. Hereswitha.

Before marrying Aethelhere, St. Hereswitha had several children by her first husband Anna, who had also been king of East Anglia. These children included St. Erconwald, St. Ethelburga of the East Angles, St. Etheldreda, St. Sexburga, and St. Withburga. Sethryda thus became the half-sister of all of them.

Sethryda became a Benedictine nun and entered the abbey of Faremoutier-en-Brie in France, where she was made the abbess. She died around 660.

Sethryda is also known as Sethrida or Saethryth.

Her Line

St. Hereswitha (or Saeware)
(b. sh. bef. 616 – d. 680/690)

md. (1) Anna, King of East Anglia (ruled ca. 641–653)			md. (2) Aethelhere, King of East Anglia (d. on 15 Nov 655 at the battle of Winwaed)
Daughter of Hereswitha and (1):			Daughter of Hereswitha and (2): ***St. Sethryda***
Erconbert (or Eorconbeorht), King of Kent (b. ca. 624 – md. ca. 640 – d. 14 July 664)	+	**St. Sexburga** (md. ca. 640 – d. 6 July 699)	
Egbert, King of Kent (b. ca. 642 – d. 4 July 673)	+	N.N.	

[For the later generations that connect this line to the kings of England, see the line of St. Aethelbert I, King of Kent in Part II.]

Sources: *Ashley*, pp. 242 and 218–219; *Baring-Gould*, Vol. I, p. 138; *Benedictine Monks*, p. 641*; *Browne*, pp. 85 and 87; *Bunson*, pp. 731 and 749*; *Butler*, Vol. III, p. 25*; *Delaney and Tobin*, p. 1050; *HBC*, p. 8; *Holweck*, p. 903; *Stuart*: line 437, nos. 47 and 46 + line 233A, nos. 46 and 45; *Wells*, pp. 197 and 325; *Williamson*, pp. 144–145 and 127 (references marked with a * are alphabetized under "Sexburga")

St. Sève

Sève was born around 539 and was the daughter of Hoel I "the Great," King of Brittany, and his wife St. Pompeja.

After Hoel died around 545, Sève entered a convent in Brittany along with her mother.

Sève is the sister of St. Leonorius and St. Tugdual.

Her Line

	Husband		Wife
	Hoel I "the Great," King of Brittany (b. ca. 491 – d. ca. 545)	+	**St. Pompeja**
Hoel II's sister: ***St. Sève***	**Hoel II**, King of Brittany (murdered 547)	+	Rimo
	Judicael I, King of Brittany (b. 535)	+	N.N.

[For the later generations that connect this line to the kings of England, see the line of St. Cunedda Wledig in Part II.]

Sources: *Ashley*, p. 728; *Baring-Gould*, Vol. 16, pp. 246–247; *Dunbar*, Vol. II, p. 222; *Holweck*, p. 903; *Stuart*, line 405, nos. 52 through 50

St. Severa,
Abbess of St. Sevère

Severa was the daughter of St. Arnulf of Metz and his wife Doda. She was the sister of Bl. Itta and St. Modoald.

Severa became a nun and was made abbess of the convent of St. Symphorian at Trèves, which had been founded by her brother St. Modoald. She later founded the convent of St. Gemma (later Ste. Sevère) at Villeneuve near Bourges and was the abbess there until her death.

Severa died around 660.

Her Line

Husband		Wife	
St. Arnulf (or Arnoul), Mayor of the Palace in Austrasia and Bishop of Metz (b. 13 Aug 582 – md. ca. 596 – d. 16 Aug 641)	+	**Dode (or Clothilde)** (b. ca. 586 – md. ca. 596)	
Bl. Pepin of Landen "the Old," Mayor of the Palace in Austrasia (b. 580/585 – d. 640/646)	+	**Bl. Itta** (b. ca. 597 – d. 8 May 652)	Bl. Itta's sister: ***St. Severa, Abbess of St. Sevère***
Ansgise (or Ansegisel), Mayor of the Palace in Austrasia (b. 602 – md. bef. 639 – murdered 685)	+	**St. Begga** (b. ca. 613 – md. bef. 639 – d. ca. 698)	

[For the later generations that connect this line to the kings of England, see the line of St. Arnulf, Bishop of Metz in Part II.]

Sources: *Benedictine Monks*, p. 638; *Bunson*, p. 747; *Butler*, Vol. II, p. 287 (under "St. Modoaldus"); *Delaney and Tobin*, p. 1051; *Holweck*, p. 904; *Stuart*, line 260; *Wells*, p. 135

St. Simon,
Count of Crepy

Simon was born around 1047 and was the son of Raoul III "the Great," Count of Crepy, and his wife Adele of Bar-sur-Aube. He grew up at the court of William, Duke of Normandy (known to history as William the Conqueror) and fought for William against Philip I of France.

Simon changed profoundly after his father died in 1074. He and his wife, who was the daughter of the count of Auvergne, both took religious vows. She went to a convent, and he became a Benedictine monk at the abbey of St. Claude in Condat. Time passed, and after deciding that life at the abbey was too comfortable, Simon and a few companions walked off into a nearby forest and built a few huts there, intending to live as hermits.

Simon was not allowed to remain in the forest for long. Pope St. Gregory VII sent him as a mediator on several diplomatic missions to resolve quarrels between various rulers in France. Later in life Simon also went on two pilgrimages, one to the Holy Land and another to Rome, where he died in 1081 after receiving the last rites from Pope St. Gregory, who was at his bedside when he died.

Simon was buried in St. Peter's. Today his relics are in France at Mouthe, not far from the place where he and his companions built their huts.

His Line

Husband		Wife	
Raoul III "the Great," Count of Crepy, Valois, and Vexin (b. 1025 – d. 8 Sept 1074)	+	md. (her 4th) **Adele of Bar-sur-Aube** (d. 1053)	
Herbert IV, Count of Vermandois (b. ca. 1032 – d. ca. 1080/1096)	+	**Adele de Valois** (b. by 1043)	Adele's brother: ***St. Simon, Count of Crepy***
Hugh Magnus, Duke of France and Burgundy and a leader of the 1st Crusade (b. 1057 – md. aft. 1067 – d. 18 Oct 1101)	+	**Adelaide de Vermandois** (b. ca. 1062 – md. aft. 1067 – d. 1120/24)	

[For the later generations that connect this line to the kings of England, see the line of St. Elizabeth Rose in Part III.]

Sources: *BBKL*, Vol. 10, cols. 390–391; *Benedictine Monks*, p. 648; *Bunson*, p. 757; *Butler*, Vol. III, pp. 695–696; *Delaney*, p. 524; *Delaney and Tobin*, p. 1062; *Stuart:* line 268, nos. 33 and 32 + line 239, nos. 31 and 30 + line 143, no. 29; *Tucker*, Vol. II, pp. 872 and 870; *Weis, AR*, line 140, nos. 22 and 23; *Wells*, pp. 576 and 586

St. Stephen I, King of Hungary

Stephen was born in 969 and was the son of Geza, Duke of the Magyars, and his wife Sarolta. Geza was a pagan, but Sarolta was a Christian, and she ultimately managed to convert both her husband and her son. Both were baptized on 26 December 986 by St. Adalbert of Prague. In 995, Stephen married Bl. Gisela, the ten-year-old daughter of St. Henry II, King of Germany and Holy Roman Emperor.

The deeds for which Stephen is remembered began after he became the Duke of the Magyars in 997. At the time, Hungary was not yet a unified nation. In spite of the baptism of Geza, Stephen, and some of the other nobles, it was also still a very pagan land. Throughout his 42-year reign, Stephen had one goal, and it was to make his country one Christian nation. Stephen was a short man, but his extraordinary energy, courage, and leadership made him a giant.

In spreading Christianity in his country, Stephen moved quickly and boldly. On the map of his lands, Stephen drew the dioceses that would be the foundation of the new religion. Every tenth town had to build a church and support a priest. Abbeys and monasteries were built, and prominent foreign monks were invited into the country. The great cathedral at Szekesfehervar was begun, which would become the place where later kings of Hungary were crowned and buried.

Not everyone in Hungary was pleased with Stephen's plans. A rebellion in 997–998 led by the pagan noble Koppány was crushed, and Koppány's body parts were nailed above the gates of various towns. A rebellion in 1002–1003 led by the pagan Vászoly was also smashed. Vászoly himself died in some discomfort. His eyes were gouged out, and hot lead was poured into his ears. Stephen also successfully defended his realm against invasions by the Germans, the Poles, the Bulgarians, and the Pechenegs.

Tragedy in Stephen's own family became the greatest threat to his achievement. In 1031, his son and heir Bl. Emeric was killed in a hunting accident, and Stephen's final years were embittered by the resulting squabbles over the succession. Stephen himself died on 15 August 1038 and was originally buried next to Bl. Emeric in the cathedral of Szekesfehervar. His remains were later moved to the Church of our Lady in Budapest.

Stephen is considered to be the real founder of the state of Hungary and one of the most important rulers in the history of central Europe. Statues of him are everywhere, and he has been a popular theme in art. "The Baptism of Vajk" [Stephen's name in Hungarian] by Gyula Benczur and Beethoven's "King Stephen Overture" are just two examples. He became the patron saint of Hungary, and his crown, his regalia, and his incorrupt right hand are treasured as sacred relics.

His Line

Husband		Wife
Geza, Duke of the Magyars (b. ca. 945 – d. 997)	+	**Sarolta**, daughter of Gayula (or Gyula), Duke of Transylvania

Ottone Orseolo, Doge of Venice (b. bef. 980 – md. aft. 1005 – d. 1032)	+	**Grimelda (or Maria)** (b. 989 – md. aft. 1005 – d. 1026)	Grimelda's brother: ***St. Stephen I, King of Hungary***
Adalbert I "the Victorious," Margrave of Austria (md. (2) bef. 1027 – d. 26 May 1053)	+	**Frowila Orseolo (also known as Adela of Austria)**, b. ca. 1012 – md. bef. 1027 – d. 17 Feb 1071)	

[For the later generations that connect this line to the kings of England, see the line of St. Peter Orseolo, Doge of Venice in Part II.]

Sources: *ABD*, Vol. 1, pp. 65–66; *Baring-Gould*, Vol. 10, pp. 19–33; *BBKL*, Vol. 10, cols. 1258–1261; *Benedictine Monks*, pp. 657–658; *Bunson*, p. 767; *Butler*, Vol. III, pp. 466–469; *CE*, Vol. XIV, pp. 287–288; *Cruz*, pp. 681–686; *Delaney*, p. 532; *Delaney and Tobin*, p. 1081; *Giorgi*, p. 484; *Guiley*, pp. 312–314; *Hantsch*, p. 52; *Holboeck*, pp. 463–467; *Holweck*, p. 934; *Joeckle*, p. 426; *Klaniczay*, p. 435; *NCE*, Vol. 13, pp. 697–698; *NDB*, Vol. I, p. 45; *O'Malley*, pp. 33–34; *Snodgrass*, pp. 100–101 and 219; *Wells*, p. 582; *Wolf*, pp. 100–101; *WWH*, Vol. 10, p. 299 (under "Maria") and Vol. 13, p. 806 (under "Sarolta"); *Zoellner*, Tafel I at pp. 676–677

St. Stephen,
Patriarch of Constantinople

Stephen was a younger son of the Byzantine Emperor Basil I and his second wife Eudokia Ingarina. He was born around 870 and was a weak, sickly child.

His rise to ecclesiastical prominence was both unexpected and swift. While hunting near his country palace of Apamea on 29 August 886, his father Basil died violently. The official story was that he died of injuries sustained while being dragged through the forest by a wild stag. In fact he may have been murdered by Stylian Zautses, who was the father of the mistress of Stephen's half-brother, who would succeed Basil as Emperor Leo VI.

One of Leo VI's first priorities as emperor was to end 40 years of squabbling between previous patriarchs and emperors over church-state relations. In the fall of 886, Leo removed the old patriarch Photios and exiled him to a remote monastery. On Christmas Day 886 the Christian Church in the East received a new leader when Leo appointed his own half-brother Stephen to be the new Patriarch of Constantinople.

At 16, Stephen was the youngest patriarch in the whole history of the Eastern Church. As Leo tried to repair imperial relations with the church, Stephen faithfully supported him but died in 893, just six years and a few months after his appointment.

His Line

Eudokia Ingarina (b. ca. 840 – d. 882/883): As Michael's mistress, she was the mother of St. Leo VI—as Basil's wife, she was the mother of St. Stephen the Patriarch. For a summary of the reasons supporting the conclusion that Michael III and not Basil I was the father of St. Leo VI, see the chapter on Leo earlier in this book.

Was first the mistress of **Michael III "the Drunkard,"** Emperor of Byzantium (b. 840 – d. 24 Sept 867)

Son of Michael and Eudokia:

Then wife of Basil I "the Macedonian," Emperor of Byzantium (b. ca. 811 – md. (2) 865 – d. 29 Aug 886)

Son of Basil and Eudokia: ***St. Stephen, Patriarch of Constantinople***

St. Leo VI "the Philosopher," Emperor of Byzantium (b. 1 Sept 866 – md. (2) 898 – d. 12 May 912)	+	Zoe Tzautzina (md. 898 – d. Dec 899)
Louis III "Beronides" (the Blind), King of Provence and Italy and Emperor of the West (b. ca. 883 – md. (1) ca. 900 – d. 5 June 928)	+	**Anna of Byzantium** (b. 899– md. ca. 900 – d. 962)

[For the later generations that connect this line to the kings of England, see the line of St. Irene, Empress of Byzantium in Part II.]

Sources: *Holweck*, p. 933; *Norwich*, Vol. 2, pp. 81 and 104–105; *Stuart:* line 322A, no. 40 + line 253, nos. 40 through 38; *Weis, AR*, line 141A, nos. 15 through 17; *Wells*, pp. 119 and 589

St. Sviatoslav II Yaroslavich, Grand Prince of Kiev

Sviatoslav was born in 1027. He was the son of St. Yaroslav I Vladimirovich "the Wise," Grand Prince of Kiev and ruler of Kievan Rus, and his wife St. Ingegerd of Sweden. Sviatoslav's wife was Kilikia von Dithmarschen, with whom he had six children.

Beginning with part of Kievan Rus, Sviatoslav in the end would rule it all. When Yaroslav "the Wise" divided his kingdom shortly before he died, he made Sviatoslav prince of Chernigov. At the time, Chernigov was a principality straddling parts of present-day Belarus, the Russian Federation, and the Ukraine. Sviatoslav ruled Chernigov from 1054 to 1073.

At the same time, Sviatoslav and his brothers Izyaslav and Vsevolod formed a princely triumvirate that watched over the affairs of Kievan Rus as a whole. As time passed, the power of Sviatoslav grew, and the power of Izyaslav shrank. After combining with Vsevolod to remove the ineffective Izyaslav from power, in 1073 Sviatoslav finally became Grand Prince of Kiev.

In Chernigov and in Kievan Rus as a whole, Sviatoslav was an avid patron of ecclesiastical building projects. He also founded schools and sponsored work on two very important books. One is the *Izborniki Svyatoslava*, which is a collection of writings on religion and other subjects and one of the very oldest examples of the written language of Kievan Rus. The other is a portion of the *Russkaya Pravda*, which is a compilation of the laws of Kievan Rus.

After ruling for three years, Sviatoslav sought medical help for a sore on one of his shoulders that had been troubling him for a long time. An attempt to heal it by cutting into it went badly wrong, and Sviatoslav died on 27 December 1076. He was buried in Chernigov in the cathedral of the Transfiguration of Our Saviour.

Sviatoslav is also known as Sviatoslav of Chernigov.

His Line

	Husband		Wife
	St. Yaroslav I Vladimirovich "the Wise," Grand Prince of Kiev (b. 978 – md. (2) Feb 1019 – d. 20 Feb 1054)	+	**St. Ingegerd**, Princess of Sweden (b. ca. 1001 – md. Feb 1019 – d. 10 Feb 1050)
Izyaslav's brother: ***St. Sviatoslav II Yaroslavich, Grand Prince of Kiev***	**St. Izyaslav I Yaroslavich**, Grand Prince of Kiev (b. 1025 – md. ca. 1043 – slain 3 Oct 1078)	+	Gertrude (md. ca. 1043), daughter of Mieszko II, King of Poland
	Sviatopolk II Izyaslavich, Grand Prince of Kiev, Novgorod, and Turow (b. 1050 – d. 16 April 1113)	+	N.N. (d. bef. 1094)

[For the later generations that connect this line to the kings of England, see the line of St. Izyaslav I Yaroslavich, Grand Prince of Kiev in Part II.]

Sources: *Hist. Rus. Ch.*, Vol. 2, p. 689; *Stuart*, line 363, nos. 34 through 32; *Weis, AR*, line 241, nos. 5, 6^2, and 7

St. Theobald, Archbishop of Vienne

Theobald was born around 927 and was the son of Hugh, Count of Vienne, and Willa of Burgundy. After his parents died, Theobald gave all of his possessions to the poor and became a priest.

In 970, Theobald was made the 58th archbishop of Vienne. He opposed royal interference and supported monastic reform. He died on 21 May 1001.

It is worth noting that the town of Vienne is a few miles south of Lyon and that for 900 years—from the arrival of St. Crescens who was martyred under the Roman emperor Trajan through the lifetime of St. Burchard who died in 1030—all the archbishops of Vienne became saints.

His Line

	Husband		Wife
	Hugh, Count of Vienne and Count Palatine of Burgundy (b. ca. 900 – md. bef. April 927 – d. ca. 948)	+	**Willa of Burgundy** (md. bef. April 927)
Humbert's brother: ***St. Theobald, Archbishop of Vienne***	**Humbert** (b. 926/930 – d. ca. 976)	+	N.N. (b. 930/945 – liv. May 976 – d. bef. Oct 993)
	Humbert I "Bianca Mano," Count of Aosta and of Maurienne (b. ca. 975 – md. bef. 1020 – d. 1048/1050)	+	Auxilia (md. bef. 1020)
	Odo (or Otto) I, Count of Maurienne (b. ca. 1020 – md. ca. 1036 – d. 19 Jan 1057/1058)	+	Bl. Adelaide of Susa (b. ca. 1015 – md. (3) ca. 1036 – d. 19 Dec 1091)
	Amadeus II, Count of Savoy and Margrave of Susa (b. ca. 1046 – md. 1065/1070 – d. 26 Jan 1080)	+	Johanna of Geneva (md. 1065/1070 – d. ca. 1095)
	Humbert II "il Gross," Count of Maurienne and Savoy and Marquis of Turin (b. ca. 1070 – md. (1) 1090 – d . 14 Oct 1103)	+	Gisela of Burgundy (b. ca. 1070 – md. 1090 – d. aft. 1133)
	Amadeus III, Count of Savoy Marquis of Maurienne, and Crusader (b. 1080/ 1092 – md. 1133/1134 – d. 30 March 1148 on the 2nd Crusade)	+	Matilda d'Albon (md. 1133/1134 – d. aft. Jan 1145)

[For the later generations that connect this line to the kings of England, see the line of Bl. Humbert III in Part II.]

Sources: *BBKL*, Vol. 11, cols. 818–819; *Benedictine Monks*, p. 670; *Bunson*, p. 785; *Holweck*, p. 955; *Stuart:* line 173, nos. 36 through 33 + line 93, nos. 32 through 29; *Tucker*, Vol. II, pp. 750–751; *Wells*, pp. 511–512

St. Theodehilda

Theodehilda was the daughter of Clovis I "the Great," King of the Salic Franks, and his wife St. Clothilde. Theodehilda became a nun and entered the convent of St. Pierre-le-Vif which she had founded at Sens. She later became its abbess.

Her Line

	Husband		Wife
	Clovis I "the Great," King of the Salic Franks (b. 466 – md. 492 – d. 27 Nov 511)	+	**St. Clothilde** (b. 470/475 – md. 492 – d. 3 June 545)
Clothaire's sister: ***St. Theodehilda***	**Clothaire I**, King of Soissons, Orleans, and France (b. 500 – d. 561)	+	md. (4) Arnegundis (or Aregonde or Aregund)
	Chilperic I, King of Neustria (b. 523 – d. 584)	+	md. (3) Fredegunde "one of the most bloodthirsty women in history" (b. 543 – d. 597)

[For the later generations that connect this line to the kings of England, see the line of St. Clothilde in Part II.]

Sources: *Baring-Gould*, Vol. 6, p. 413; *Holweck*, p. 948 (under "Tendechildis"); *Scherman, Birth of France*, frontispiece and p. 149; *Stuart*, line 303, nos. 51 through 49; *Wells*, pp. 384–385. N.B.: Stuart mistakenly claims that Rodegunda is the mother of Chilperic I. For confirmation that Arnegundis is Chilperic's mother, see ***fmg.ac>Projects>Medieval Lands>Medieval Lands – data by region>France>Kings & early nobility>Merovingian Kings> Clotaire 511–561, Charibert 561–567, Gontran 561–592***

St. Thomas,
2nd Earl of Lancaster

Thomas was born around 1277 and was the son of Edmund Plantagenet ("Crouchback"), 1st Earl of Lancaster, and his wife Blanche of Artois. On 28 October 1294, Thomas married Alice de Lacy, daughter of Henry de Lacy, 3rd Earl of Lincoln.

It is highly unlikely that anyone who actually met Thomas would describe him as saintly or holy. In life, Thomas was a coarse and violent man. The fact that he was also one of the wealthiest and most powerful men in England gave him several other qualities that were less than endearing. What redeemed him in the eyes of many was that for the last 15 years of his life he was usually the leader of the national opposition to a man who seemed to be even worse, and that man was the English king Edward II.

Of all of Edward's flaws, the ones mentioned most frequently by the chroniclers paint a picture of a man wholly unsuited to be king. It is said that he utterly lacked royal dignity and had almost no ambition, drive, or self-confidence. As a military leader, he was completely inept, and in peacetime he preferred light entertainment and simple pleasures to the duties of governing. When he did turn his attention to matters of state, he usually ignored any advice offered by his own barons and instead sought counsel from men who were outsiders. Any outsider that became one of the king's personal favorites could also expect to be showered with so much money, rewards, and personal attention from Edward that almost everyone became convinced that the king was a homosexual.

Baronial discontent with Edward began almost immediately after his accession to the throne in 1307. It was Edward's cousin Thomas, the 2nd Earl of Lancaster, who quickly became the leader of this opposition.

The first person that the barons took action against was Piers Gaveston, the king's special friend that Thomas absolutely despised. In 1308, Thomas was one of the lords who got Gaveston banished from England. Thomas was also one of the lords who took up arms upon his return in 1312. Serving as one of the "judges" who convicted Gaveston of capital offenses, Thomas was also present at his execution in June 1312.

Thomas also did not hesitate to lead revolts against Edward himself. The first such revolt had been sparked by Gaveston's return in 1312. After losing the battle of Bannockburn in 1314, Edward's standing in England fell so low that he submitted to Thomas, who effectively became the ruler of England for the next four years. Thomas was only deposed in 1318 after he began a private war with the king's ally John de Warenne, the 8th earl of Surrey, and a new faction of barons rose up to oppose Thomas and defend John. In 1321, Thomas started his last rebellion against Edward. During a battle with the king's allies at Boroughbridge, Thomas was taken prisoner, brought to his own castle of Pontefract, and beheaded on 22 March 1322 after being found guilty of treason.

With Thomas dead, the barons once again united against their real nemesis, the king. Edward's misrule continued for five more years until he was finally removed from the throne and imprisoned in Berkeley Castle. Since Edward was never seen alive again, the verdict of history is that he was murdered there. In time, his mortal remains were interred in a tomb in Gloucester Cathedral, where they rest to this day.

In time, the view that Thomas the 2nd Earl was a patriot and a martyr who died in defense of English liberties grew very rapidly. For over a hundred years after his death, miracles were reported at his tomb, crowds of people visited his statue in Old St. Paul's Cathedral, and he was venerated as a saint.

His Line

	Husband		Wife
	Edmund Plantagenet "Crouchback," 1st Earl of Lancaster and High Steward of England (b. 16 Jan 1245 – md. (2) ca. 1276 – d. 5 June 1296), son of Henry III, King of England	+	**Blanche of Artois** (b. ca. 1248 – md. (2) ca. 1276 – d. 2 May 1302)
Henry's brother: ***St. Thomas, 2nd Earl of Lancaster***	**Henry Plantagenet**, 3rd Earl of Lancaster (b. 1281 – md. bef. 2 March 1296/1297 – d. 22 Sept 1345)	+	Maud de Chaworth (b. 1282 – md. bef. 2 March 1296/1297 – liv. 1345)
	Richard Fitz Alan, Earl of Arundel and Warenne (b. ca. 1313 – md. (2) 6 Feb 1344/45 – d. 24 Jan 1375/76)	+	**Eleanor Plantagenet** (md. (2) 6 Feb 1344/45 – d. 11 Jan 1372)
	Sir Thomas de Holand, K.G., 2nd Earl of Kent (md. aft. 10 April 1364 – d. 25 April 1397)	+	**Alice Fitz Alan**, (md. aft. 10 April 1364 – d. 17 March 1415/16)

[For the later generations, see the line of Bl. Ela, Countess of Salisbury in Part II.]

Sources: *Ashley*, pp. 596–697; *Baring-Gould*, Vol. 3, pp. 414–421; *Holweck*, p. 978; *Joeckle*, p. 438; *Weis, AR:* line 45, no. 30 + line 17, nos. 27 through 30 + line 72, no. 32 + line 60, no. 32 + line 78, nos. 32 and 33 + line 47, no. 32; *Wells*, pp. 471, 230, and 306

St. Trigidia

Trigidia was the daughter of Sancho Garcia, Count of Castile, and his wife Urraca Gomez.

In 1002, Trigidia's parents bought an estate in Ona near Burgos. There they built the monastery of San Salvador de Ona. Trigidia became its first abbess.

Besides leading the monastery, Trigidia spent all of her own wealth on works of charity.

Both Trigidia and her parents are buried at Ona. She is also known as Tigridia.

Her Line

Husband		Wife	
Sancho Garcia, Count of Castile (b. ca. 965 – md. 994 – d. 5 Feb 1017)	+	**Urraca Salvadores (also called Urraca Gomez)** (md. 994 – d. 20 May 1025)	
Sancho Garcia III "the Great," King of Navarre (b. 990/992 – murdered 18 Oct 1035)	+	**Munia Mayor** (b. 995 – d. aft. 13 July 1066)	Munia's sister: ***St. Trigidia***
Garcia IV, King of Navarre (b. ca. 1020 – md. 1038 – died in battle 1 Sept 1054)	+	Stephanie de Foix (md. 1038 – d. aft. 1066)	
Sancho Garcia (md. (1) 1057 – d. aft. Dec 1073)	+	Constanza of Moranon (md. 1057)	
Ramiro II Sanchez, Count of Moncon, Lord of Urroz, and Crusader (b. ca. 1070 – md. aft. 1098 – d. Jan/Feb 1116)	+	Christina (also called Elvira) Diaz (b. 1077 – md. aft. 1098), daughter of Rodrigo Diaz de Castro, known to history as "el Cid"	
Garcia Ramirez V, King of Navarre (b. aft. 1110 – md. (1) 1130 – d. 21 Nov 1150)	+	Margaret de l'Aigle (b. ca. 1104 – md. 1130 – d. 25 May 1141)	
Sancho III, King of Castile (b. 1134 – md. 30 Jan 1151 – d. 31 Aug 1158)	+	**Blanca, Princess of Navarre** (b. ca. 1134 – md. 30 Jan 1151 – d. 12 Aug 1156)	
Alfonso IX "the Noble," King of Castile, Toledo, and Extramadura, the victor at the battle of Los Navas de Tolosa (b. 11 Nov 1155 – md. 1170 – d. 5 Oct 1214)	+	Eleanor (b. 13 Oct 1162 – md. 1170 – d. 25 Oct 1214), daughter of Henry II, King of England	
Alfonso IX "el Barboro," King of Leon (b. 15 Aug 1171 – md. Dec 1197 – d. 24 Sept 1230)	+	**Berengaria of Castile** (b. 1180 – md. (2) Dec 1197 – d. 8 Nov 1246)	

St. Fernando III, King of Castile, Galicia, Leon, Toledo, and Extramadura (b. 24 June 1198 – md. (2) 1237 – d. 30 May 1252)	+	Jeanne de Dammartin, Countess of Ponthieu (b. ca. 1208 – md. 1237 – d. 16 March 1279)
Edward I "Longshanks," King of England (b. 17 June 1239 – md. (1) 18 Oct 1254 – d. 8 July 1307)	+	**Eleanor of Castile** (b. 1240 – md. 18 Oct 1254 – d. 28 Nov 1290)

Sources: *Delaney and Tobin*, p. 1133; *Dunbar*, Vol. II, p. 271; *Stuart:* line 55, no. 34 + line 285, nos. 34 and 33 + line 151 + line 83, nos. 28 through 26 + line 52, nos. 26 through 24; *Weis, AR*, line 113A + line 113, nos. 26 through 28 + line 110, nos. 27 through 30 + line 1, no. 28

St. Tugdual,
Bishop of Tréguier

Tugdual was born in 509 and was the son of Hoel I "the Great," King of Brittany, and his wife St. Pompeja.

Tugdual became a monk, and around 545 he and several companions began a great campaign to convert all the Bretons who were still pagans. He founded the monastery of Tréguier. In 552, he also became the bishop of Tréguier. He died around 559/564, and his relics are at Laval and Chartres.

Tugdual is known as one of the seven Founder Saints of Brittany. Several villages in Brittany and Wales are named after him.

Tugdual is also known as Tudwal. He is the brother of St. Leonorius and St. Sève.

His Line

	Husband		Wife
	Hoel I "the Great," King of Brittany (b. ca. 491 – d. ca. 545)	+	**St. Pompeja**
Hoel II's brother: ***St. Tugdual, Bishop of Tréguier***	**Hoel II**, King of Brittany (murdered 547)	+	Rimo
	Judicael I, King of Brittany (b. 535)	+	N.N.

[For the later generations that connect this line to the kings of England, see the line of St. Cunedda Wledig in Part II.]

Sources: *Baring-Gould*, Vol. 16, p. 138; *BBKL*, Vol. 19, col. 1454; *Benedictine Monks*, p. 694; *Bunson*, p. 814; *Delaney*, pp. 560–561; *Holweck*, pp. 991–992; *Stuart*, line 405, nos. 52 through 50

St. Tysilio

Tysilio was the son of St. Brochwel Ysgithrog, King of Powys, and his wife St. Arddun "Benasgell."

Brochwel wanted his son to be a warrior, but Tysilio was determined to become a monk. He ran away to the monastery of Meifod in central Wales, and when his father's men arrived to take him home, he had already been tonsured and taken his vows.

After finishing his education at Meifod, Tysilio remained there for several years before he received permission to go live as a hermit on a tiny island in the Menai Strait which is today called Llandysilio Island after him. After several months of absolute seclusion, he returned to Meifod and was elected abbot.

Back in Powys, difficulties in the succession threatened to drag Tysilio back into the real world. His brother Iago had ascended to the throne after their father died around 560, only to die himself in 562. Ruling as regent for Iago's son, Iago's widow Haiarnwed knew that she couldn't hang on to the throne unassisted. Her problems would be solved, so she thought, by bringing Tysilio back from his monastery, marrying him, and making him the new king of Powys, and she wouldn't take no for an answer.

Equally determined to remain a monk, Tysilio along with some other monks sailed away from Wales and headed for Brittany. Once there, he started a new monastery at a place now known as St. Suliac, where he spent the rest of his life.

Tysilio is buried at St. Suliac. There are several churches dedicated to him in both Wales and Brittany.

His Line

	Husband		Wife
	St. Brochwel Ysgithrog, King of Powys (b. ca. 502 – d. ca. 560)	+	**St. Arddun "Benasgell,"** daughter of St. Pabo "Post Prydyn"
Cynan's brother:	**Cynan Garwyn**	+	N.N.
St. Tysilio	**Eiludd**	+	N.N.

[For the later generations that connect this line to the kings of Scotland, see the line of St. Arddun "Benasgell" in Part II.]

Sources: *Baring-Gould and Fisher*, Vol. 4, pp. 296–305; *Benedictine Monks*, p. 696; *Boyer*, no. 3 on p. 63; *Bunson*, p. 815; *Butler*, Vol. IV, pp. 296–297; *CS*, p. 686; *Delaney*, pp. 561–562; *Maund*, p. 35; *Rees*, pp. 103–107; *Tucker*, Vol. II, p. 898

St. Ulric, Bishop of Augsburg

Ulric was born in 890 and was the son of Ubald, Count of Dillingen-Kyburg, and his wife Ditperga.

Early in life, Ulric hardly seemed to be the stuff that saints are made of. As a child he was sent to the monastery school at Sankt Gallen in Switzerland but returned home in 908 without taking vows. He became chamberlain to his uncle Bishop Adalbert of Augsburg, but when Adalbert died in 909 Ulric again returned to his family's estates.

For the next fourteen years, the historical record is utterly silent as to where Ulric was and what he was doing. The deeds of his later life suggest that he was somehow acquiring considerable military experience, but the truth will never be known.

Ulric returned to public life on 28 December 923 when he was made bishop of Augsburg. As bishop, he founded the abbeys of Kempten and Ottobeuren and the women's monastery of St. Stephen. He rebuilt the cathedral at Augsburg after it was destroyed by fire. He also encouraged liturgical reform.

Besides his work in the church, Ulric also played a significant role in secular affairs. He became an adviser to Emperor Otto I, strongly supported Otto in his disputes with his relatives, and negotiated some of the truces that ended the fighting that periodically broke out. In an act of great foresight, when the walls of Augsburg were destroyed in 951 during one such revolt, Ulric personally supervised their rebuilding.

The fateful hour for Ulric and his country came in the summer of 955. Hoping to achieve a final victory, one of Otto's relatives who was leading a revolt against him turned the murderous Magyars into his allies. In mid-summer, a huge Magyar army left Hungary and crossed the border into Bavaria, hoping to lure Otto into battle and destroy him and his army. Upon receiving this news, Otto immediately led his army out to find them.

The Magyars devastated all the Bavarian country that they passed through, and in early August 955, their army appeared before Augsburg and demanded its surrender. Bishop Ulric mobilized his own troops, closed the city gates, and prepared for battle.

Around the end of the first week in August, the Magyars attacked. They tried to overwhelm the defenders by attacking the town's east gate. Ulric led his men out to meet them, and the three days of events known as the battle of Lechfeld began. The hard-fought struggle for the east gate continued all day until the leader of the Magyar attack was killed. The Magyars then returned to their own lines, and Ulric and his men returned to Augsburg and spent the night reinforcing the city walls and building blockhouses.

At dawn on the next day, the Magyars brought up siege engines and the bulk of their infantry and resumed their attack on Augsburg on a broad front. With Ulric leading the resistance, the second day's fighting continued until the Magyars learned that an army led by Otto had won two earlier battles with Magyar troops and was now closing in on Augsburg. The Magyars broke off their siege and retreated. That same evening Otto and his army reached Augsburg. After resting in the city for a night and after being reinforced by Ulric's troops, they set off in pursuit of the Magyars the next morning, and when they caught them on the Lechfeld plain later that day, they annihilated them.

Ulric's courage, leadership, and tenacious defense of Augsburg had bought the time that was the key to Otto's victory. The victory at Lechfeld was regarded as Otto's major achievement during his long reign. Following their defeat, the Magyars ultimately converted to Christianity and became fully integrated into European civilization.

The victory at Lechfeld was also seen as Ulric's greatest achievement. After the war he busied himself providing comfort and relief to everyone around Augsburg who had suffered at the hands of the Magyars.

Ulric died on 4 July 973 and was ultimately laid to rest in the crypt of St. Ulric's Church in Augsburg. Many miracles were reported at his tomb. In 993 he made history one last time by becoming the first person in the history of Christianity to be canonized in Rome in a formal ceremony led by the Pope (John XV).

Ulric is the patron saint of Augsburg.

His Line

Husband		Wife	
Ubald (or Huchbald or Hupald), Count of Dillingen-Kyburg (d. ca. 909)	+	**Ditperga (or Thetbirga)**	
Peiere (d. 973)	+	**Liutgard**	Liutgard's brother: ***St. Ulric, Bishop of Augsburg***
Manegold (liv. 973)	+	N.N.	
Wolfrad (d. 4 March 1010)	+	**Bertha** (d. 22 Dec 1032)	
Wolfrad of Altshausen (md. 1009 – d. ca. 8 April 1065)	+	Hiltrud (b. 991/996 – md. 1009 – d. 9 Jan 1052)	
Eberhard V "the Blessed," Count of Nellenburg and Count in the Zurichgau (b. ca. 1010 – d. 25 March 1075)	+	**Ida von Altshausen**	

[For the later generations that connect this line to the kings of England, see the line of Bl. Eberhard V in Part II.]

Sources: *Baring-Gould*, Vol. 7, pp. 116–123; *BBKL*, Vol. 14, cols. 1560–1562; *Benedictine Monks*, p. 698; *Bunson*, pp. 816–817; *Butler*, Vol. III, pp. 16–17; *CE*, Vol. XV, p. 123; *Delaney*, p. 563; *Delaney and Tobin*, p. 1141; *Englebert*, p. 258; *Guiley*, p. 335; *Holweck*, p. 996; *Joeckle*, pp. 443–445; *NCE*, Vol. 14, p. 379; *Stuart:* line 18A + line 18, no. 32; *Warncke*, pp. 76–77

Bl. Urban II,
Pope

Urban's given name was Odo de Châtillon. He was also known as Eudes de Châtillon and Odo of Lagery.

Odo was born around 1035/1042 and was the son of Gautier, Seigneur de Châtillon, and his wife Mahaud. He studied for the priesthood under St. Bruno, founder of the Carthusian Order. His first important post came when he was appointed archdeacon of Rheims. He then decided to become a monk, entered Cluny, and became the prior there. He was next made cardinal-bishop of Ostia in 1078 and also became one of the chief advisers of Pope St. Gregory VII. In 1082 he became papal legate to France and Germany, and on 12 March 1088, he was elected pope by acclamation.

The papacy of Urban II is primarily remembered for two historic events: the escalation of the conflict between the papacy and the Holy Roman Empire into war, and Urban's sermon at the Council of Clermont in November 1095.

The conflict between the papacy and the Holy Roman Empire was actually a battle for supremacy between the Roman popes and the rulers of Germany. The best way to understand the struggle is to understand what preceded it. Since the fall of the Roman Empire, church officials in most European countries had been appointed by the rulers of the lands where the officials' ecclesiastical territories were located and not by anyone in the Church bureaucracy in Rome. It was not uncommon for the offices of bishops or abbots to be sold, or at least traded for something of value that the local ruler badly needed. In the days since Charlemagne became the first Holy Roman Emperor, the successors of Charlemagne who ruled Germany and who were also called Holy Roman Emperors had the additional authority to appoint the pope in Rome. This filling of church offices with persons appointed by secular rulers was called secular investiture.

This practice was universal in Europe until several years past the end of the first millennium. The first serious challenge to it occurred in the young Urban's own lifetime and was mounted by churchmen who wanted to end the Holy Roman Emperor's power to appoint a pope.

In 1056 when the six-year-old Henry IV became the new ruler of the Germans, the rebels decided it was time to make their move. A call was issued for a church council which met in 1059 and declared that from that moment on the popes would only be chosen by the Church itself and specifically by the newly created College of Cardinals. The child emperor Henry IV did not challenge what the church had done, and from that moment on popes were elected by cardinals and no longer appointed by the German emperors.

Did a pope chosen by the church have the authority to appoint the bishops and archbishops who served in Germany? The drawn-out, bloody struggle over the answer to this question was the next battle in the long conflict over secular investiture. After becoming pope in 1088, Urban II said yes. Henry IV—who was now an adult—said no and thought he could prevail in the dispute by turning one of his own men into a more agreeable rival pope, technically called an "antipope." So it was that Henry raised archbishop Guibert of Ravenna to be the antipope Clement III.

Henry's deed led to war. German troops were on one side. Papal troops loyal to Urban II were on the other. The first eight months of fighting occurred between March and November of 1088. It was not until after a three-day battle in November that Clement fled and Urban was able to enter Rome and excommunicate Henry IV and Clement III. In 1089, Henry invaded Italy, and it was Urban who had to flee as Clement was reinstalled on the papal throne. During an itinerant papacy-in-exile that lasted four years, Urban gradually achieved diplomatic victories over his opponents and regained the papal throne at the end of 1093.

The other defining moment of Urban's papacy was his sermon at the Council of Clermont in 1095. In all of history, it is hard to find many other occasions when mere words unleashed such mighty deeds.

Urban's sermon at Clermont was his answer to a request he had received from the Byzantine emperor in March 1095. The emperor had asked for help in repulsing the Turks. Urban responded in November by calling on all European nations to rise up and liberate the Holy Land from the infidels who controlled it. He offered plenary indulgences to all who might perish in the effort. After Clermont, Urban spent the next nine months traveling all over France and preaching a holy war of liberation.

Urban's call was received with tremendous enthusiasm. In the spring of 1097, four European armies assembled in Constantinople and began their march to the Holy Land. The First Crusade had begun.

The Crusaders captured Jerusalem on 15 July 1099. Urban died in Rome on 29 July 1099 before the news of their victory arrived. He was buried in the crypt of St. Peter. The era of Crusades which he had started would go on for the next two hundred years.

His Line

	Husband		Wife
	Gautier, Seigneur de Châtillon-sur-Marne and Percy-sur-Marne (d. 1097 on the First Crusade)	+	**Mahaud (or Melende)** (b. ca. 1046 – d. ca. 1112)
Henry's brother: Odo (or Eudes) de Châtillon, who became ***Bl. Urban II, Pope***	**Henry I de Châtillon**, Crusader and Seigneur de Châtillon-sur-Marne and Montjoy (b. ca. 1063 – md. 1089/1094 – d. aft. 1135)	+	Ermengarde de Montjoy (md. 1089/ 1094 – d. 1139)
	Renaud de Châtillon, Prince of Antioch (md. (1) 1152 – executed by Saladin himself after the battle of Hattin in 1187)	+	Constance of Antioch (b. 1127 – md. (2) 1152 – d. 1163)
	Bela III, King of Hungary (b. ca. 1148 – md. 1172 – d. 23 April 1196)	+	**Agnes de Châtillon-sur-Loing** (b. 1153 – md. 1172 – d. 1184)

[For the later generations that connect this line to the kings of England, see the line of St. Harold III "Bluetooth," King of Denmark in Part II.]

Sources: *BBKL*, Vol. 15, cols. 1391–1394; *Benedictine Monks*, p. 699; *Brusher*, pp. 314–315; *Bunson*, p. 818; *Butler*, Vol. III, pp. 209–212; *CE*, Vol. XV, pp. 210–211; *Delaney*, p. 564; *Delaney and Tobin*, p. 1142; *Guiley*, pp. 336–337; *Holweck*, p. 998; *NCE*, Vol. 14, pp. 477–478; *Snodgrass*, p. 231; *Stuart:* line 99, nos. 31 through 29 + line 80, nos. 29 and 28 + line 51, no. 28; *Weis, AR*, line 103, nos. 26 and 27; *Wells*, p. 148

St. Vardan II,
Prince of the Mamikonids

Vardan was the son of Hamazasp I, Prince of the Mamikonids, and his wife Sahakanoysh. The name of Vardan's wife is unknown, but they were the parents of St. Shushaniki.

Vardan was the leader of the Armenian army, and in the late 440's Persia wanted to extend its influence over Armenia. Among other things, the Persians planned to abolish Armenian Christianity and replace it with Persian Zoroastrianism or sun-worship. Vardan and several other leading men of Armenia were brought before the Persian king Yazdagerd (or Yazdgird) II, who said he would attack Armenia and put all of their families to the sword if they did not apostasize and accept the sun god as their supreme being. The Armenians declared that the sun god was the only true god, and they were released.

Back in Armenia, Vardan renounced the sun god, reaffirmed his Christian faith and became the leader of the rebellion against Persia known as the Vardanite War.

When the first Persian army arrived in Armenia in 450 to put down the rebellion, Vardan met this army in battle and routed it.

The struggle quickly reached a climax in 451 when a much larger Persian army entered Armenia. The clash with Vardan's army occurred on 2 June 451 in a battle that went on all day. It has been called the battle of Avarair, Avarayr, Awarayr, and Vartanantz. In fierce fighting that surged back and forth throughout the day, both sides took heavy casualties. By sunset, Vardan and most of the other Armenian commanders were dead, and what was left of their army withdrew.

Although the battle was a Persian victory, Yazdagerd's losses forced him to withdraw his army for the time being. The surviving Armenians immediately began a guerilla war against Persia that went on for more than thirty years. In the end, the Persians finally had enough, and the Armenian victory which had eluded Vardan at the battle of Avarair was achieved.

In death, Vardan became the national hero of Armenia and is also known as Vardan the Brave. His slain warriors are known as the Vardanite martyrs. All of the Armenians who fell in the battle of Avarair were canonized.

His Line

	Husband		Wife
	Hamazasp I, Prince of the Mamikonids and High Constable of Armenia (b. 345 – d. ca. 416)	+	**Sahakanoysh**, daughter of St. Isaac I "the Great"
Hmayeak's brother: ***St. Vardan II, Prince of the Mamikonids***	**St. Hmayeak Mamikonian**, General and Mamikonian ambassador to Constantinople (b. 410 – d. in the battle of Avarayr 2 June 451)	+	Dzoyk, daughter of Vram, Prince of Rshtuni
	Vard, Mamikonian Viceroy of Armenia (b. 450 – d. aft. 509)	+	N.N.

[For the later generations that connect this line to the kings of England, see the line of St. Ashken in Part II.]

Sources: *Holweck*, pp. 908 (under "Shushaniki") and 1006; *Hovannisian*, pp. 99–100; *Kaloustian*, pp. 23–25; *Koushagian*, pp. 16 (under "Shooshan") and 18–19; *NCE*, Vol. 14, p. 539; *Stone*, Chap. 8, Chart 80; *Stuart:* line 416, no. 53 + line 322, nos. 53 through 51; *Wagner*, p. 196; *Wells*, p. 34

St. Verona

Verona was the daughter of Louis II "the German," King of the East Franks, and his wife Bl. Emma of Bavaria. After Louis died in 876, Verona became a nun and spent her life at a convent in Mayence. A chapel near Louvain is dedicated to her.

Her Line

	Husband		Wife
	Louis II "the German," King of the East Franks (b. 806 – d. 28 Aug 876)	+	**Bl. Emma of Bavaria** (d. 31 Jan 876)
Carloman's sister: ***St. Verona***	**Carloman**, King of Bavaria (liv. 820–880)	+	Litwinde of Carinthia
	Arnulf, King of the East Franks (i.e., Germany) (liv. 863–899)	+	Oda of Bavaria

[For the later generations that connect this line to the kings of England, see the line of Bl. Emma of Bavaria in Part II.]

Sources: *Holweck*, p. 1010; *Stuart*, line 172, nos. 41 through 39; *Weis, AR*, line 141, no. 17

St. Vladimir II Yaroslavich, Prince of Novgorod

Vladimir was born in 1020. He was the son of St. Yaroslav I Vladimirovich "the Wise," Grand Prince of Kiev and ruler of Kievan Rus, and his wife St. Ingegerd. He married Oda von Stade.

In 1043, Vladimir was made prince of Novgorod, and in 1045 he led a naval raid on Constantinople. The raid was unsuccessful, and it was also the last war between Kievan Rus and Byzantium.

Personally, Vladimir was a devout Christian who carefully studied Scripture and who built the cathedral of the Divine Wisdom in Novgorod.

Unfortunately Vladimir died in 1052 before his father Yaroslav, who lived on until 1054. As a result, Vladimir's descendants were passed over in Yaroslav's will and considered ineligible to be rulers of Kievan Rus.

Vladimir is buried in Novgorod in the cathedral of St. Sophia.

His Line

	Husband		Wife
	St. Yaroslav I Vladimirovich "the Wise," Grand Prince of Kiev (b. 978 – md. (2) Feb 1019 – d. 20 Feb 1054)	+	**St. Ingegerd**, Princess of Sweden (b. ca. 1001 – md. Feb 1019 – d. 10 Feb 1050)
Vsevolod's brother: ***St. Vladimir II Yaroslavich, Prince of Novgorod***	**Vsevolod I Yaroslavich**, Grand Prince of Kiev and Prince of Perejaslaw (b. ca. 1030 – md. (1) 1046 – d. 13 April 1093)	+	Maria Monomacha (md. 1046), daughter of Konstantinos Monomachos (Constantine IX), Emperor of Byzantium
	St. Vladimir Vsevolodovich Monomach (a.k.a. Vladimir II "Monomachos"), Grand Prince of Kiev (b. 1053 – md. (1) ca. 1070 – d. 19 May 1125)	+	Gytha of Wessex (md. ca. 1070), daughter of Harold II Godwinsson, King of England

[For the later generations that connect this line to the kings of England, see the line of St. Harold III "Bluetooth," King of Denmark in Part II.]

Sources: *Hist. Rus. Ch.*, Vol. 2, p. 120; *Orth. Encyc.*, Vol. 9, pp. 86–89; *Stuart*, line 240, nos. 33 through 30; *Walsh*, p. 620; *Weis, AR*, line 242, nos. 5 through 7; *Wells*, p. 549

St. Vsevolod Mstislavich, Prince of Novgorod and Pskov

Vsevolod was born in 1092. He was the son of Mstislav Vladimirovich, Grand Prince of Kiev and ruler of Kievan Rus, and his second wife Lyubawa. In 1123 Vsevolod married Sviatoslavna, daughter of Sviatoslav Davidovich, Prince of Lutsk, and had three children with her.

In 1117, Mstislav made Vsevolod the ruler of Novgorod, and Vsevolod began with the best of intentions. He worked hard to stamp out the remnants of the old pagan religion. He built schools, churches, and monasteries. During a terrible famine in 1127, he spent the entire treasury to feed his people. He was also a competent military leader who led his troops against the Chuds, the Estonians, and the Finns.

After twenty years of his rule, however, and a discouraging defeat on the battlefield, the people of Novgorod revolted against their lords in Kiev and their local representative Vsevolod.

Vsevolod and his family fled to Pskov, where the people made him their ruler. After reigning for only one year, however, Vsevolod died on 11 February 1138. His remains are in the cathedral of the Trinity in the Pskov Kremlin.

His Line

Husband		Wife	
St. Mstislav Vladimirovich (a.k.a., Mstislav I Harold), Grand Prince of Kiev (b. 1076 – md. (2) 1122 – d. 15 April 1132)	+	**Lyubawa** (md. 1122 – d. 1168), daughter of Dmitri Zaviditsch, Possadnik of Novgorod	
Geza II, King of Hungary (b. ca. 1130 – md. 1146 – d. 3 May 1162)	+	**Euphrosyne Mstislavna** (b. 1130 – md. 1146 – d. 1175/1176)	Euphrosyne's brother: ***St. Vsevolod Mstislavich, Prince of Novgorod and Pskov***
Bela III, King of Hungary (b. ca. 1148 – md. 1172 – d. 25 April 1196)	+	Agnes (or Anne) de Chatillon-sur-Loing (b. 1153 – md. 1172 – d. 1184)	

[For the later generations that connect this line to the kings of England, see the line of St. Harold III "Bluetooth," King of Denmark in Part II.]

Sources: *Holweck*, p. 1042 (under "Wsevolod"); *Stuart:* line 240, nos. 29 and 28 + line 51, nos. 29 and 28; *Tucker:* Vol. II, p. 733 + Vol. I, pp. 425–426; *Walsh*, pp. 620–621; *Weis, AR*, line 242, nos. 8 through 10

St. Wala

Wala was born around 755 and was the son of Duke Bernard and his second wife, "a Saxon woman." He was a half-brother of St. Adalard. Wala was educated at the court of Pepin "the Short," and around 792, he married a daughter of William, Count of Toulouse.

Charlemagne made Wala steward of the Carolingian household, a leader of the army in battle, and one of his personal advisers. Wala fought in Saxony, and in 812 he was ordered to Italy to assist the very young Bernard, King of Italy and Charlemagne's grandson, in a campaign against Moslem raiders from North Africa and Spain.

After Charlemagne died, Wala became a monk and entered the monastery at Corvey, where his brother St. Adalard was abbot. Together, they founded the monastery known as New Corvey.

Wala returned to the secular world in 822, when Louis the Pious asked Wala to help his son Lothair govern Italy. Wala's opposition to all those who wanted to divide up the Carolingian empire after the death of Charlemagne was a great virtue in the eyes of Louis the Pious.

By 833, Wala had had enough of court life. He entered the monastery of St. Columban in Bobbio, where he later became abbot. On 21 August 836 he died there. His relics are at a convent at Herford.

His Line

Husband		Wife	
Duke Bernard (d. ca. 784), a natural son of Charles Martel	+	md. (2) **"a Saxon woman"**	
N.N.	+	**Theoderada (or Theodrada)**	Theoderada's brother: ***St. Wala***
Pepin (or Pippin) I, King of Italy (b. 776 – d. 8 July 810)	+	**Chrothais**	
Bernard, King of Italy (b. 797 – d. 17 April 818)	+	Cunegunde (d. ca. 835)	

[For the later generations that connect this line to the kings of England, see the line of St. Adalard in Part III.]

Sources: *BBKL*, Vol. 13, cols. 164–165; *Bibliotheca Sanctorum*: Vol. 1, cols. 170–171 (under "Adalardo") + Vol. 12, cols. 1381–1382; *Cabaniss*, pp. 3–4; *Holweck*, p. 1030; *McKitterick*, p. 134; *Settipani*, pp. 170–172, 211–227, 355–358, "Tableau 4: Les Pippinides," and "Tableau 8: Les Descendants de Pippin d'Italie"; *Stuart:* line 231, no. 40 through 36 + line 169, nos. 36 and 35 + line 141, nos. 36 and 35; *Weis, AR:* line 50, nos. 14 through 18 + line 48, nos. 19 and 20 + line 162, nos. 18 and 19 (According to Weis, Pepin I King of Italy married a daughter of Duke Bernard. Settipani persuasively argues that Pepin I's wife Chrothais was actually a granddaughter of Duke Bernard and that her mother was Duke Bernard's daughter Theoderada.) Also see ***fmg.ac>Projects>Medieval Lands> Medieval Lands—data by region>France>Kings &***

early nobility>Carolingian nobility>Family of Adalhard & Wala. In addition, see ***fmg.ac>Projects>MedievalLands>MedievalLands—databyregion>Italy>Emperors & Kings>Kings of Italy 774–887 (Carolingians)***.

St. Waltheof, Abbot of Melrose

Waltheof was born around 1100 and was the son of Simon de St. Liz, Earl of Huntingdon, and his wife Maud. After Simon died in 1111, Maud's next husband would be St. David I, King of Scotland.

Growing up at the Scottish court, Waltheof became keenly interested in religion and was a close friend of St. Aelred. After becoming a monk, Waltheof was first made an Augustinian canon and then was appointed abbot of Kirkham. As time passed, Waltheof decided that the Augustinian rules were too lax, and he became a Cistercian. St. David I founded Melrose Abbey in 1136, and when it was ready to receive monks, Waltheof became the first abbot there.

Waltheof was very well known for his cheerfulness, his personal austerities, and his generosity to the poor. He also performed several miracles where he multiplied food and healed the sick.

Waltheof died around 1160 and is buried in the chapter house at Melrose. Miraculous cures occurred at his tomb.

His Line

Husband		Wife	
Simon de St. Liz, Earl of Huntingdon and Northampton, Crusader (md. ca. 1190 – d. 1111)	+	**Maud of Huntingdon** (b. 1072 – md. ca. 1090 – d. 1130/1131). Maud md. (2) in 1113 David I "the Saint," King of Scotland.	
Saher de Quincy of Buckley and Daventry	+	**Maud St. Liz** (d. 1140),who md. (1) Robert Fitz Richard and (2) Saher de Quincy	Maud's brother: ***St. Waltheof, Abbot of Melrose***
Robert de Quincy, Lord of Buckley and Fawside, Crusader (d. ca. 1198)	+	Orabel (or Orabella), daughter of Ness Fitz William	
Saher de Quincy, 1st Earl of Winchester, Magna Charta Surety, and Crusader (b. 1155 – md. bef. 1173 – d. 3 Nov 1219)	+	Margaret de Beaumont (md. bef. 1173 – d. shortly bef. 12 Feb 1234/1235)	

Sources: *Baring-Gould*, Vol. 9, pp. 29–33; *Benedictine Monks*, p. 722; *Bunson*, p. 848; *Butler*, Vol. III, pp. 254–255; *Delaney*, pp. 581–582; *Delaney and Tobin*, p. 1185; *Holweck*, p. 1031; *NCE*, Vol. 14, p. 792; *Stuart*, line 221, no. 31; *Weir*, p. 192; *Weis, AR:* line 148, nos. 24 and 25 + line 53, no. 27; *Wells*, pp. 504–505 and 482

Bl. Warin,
Abbot of Corvie

Warin was the son of Ecbert "the Loyal," Count in the Ittergau, and his wife St. Ida of Herzfeld. Warin was raised at the court of Louis the Pious and was an excellent warrior before he decided to enter the monastic life.

In 826 Warin was made abbot of the monastery at Corvey, which for the next 200 years would be one of northern Europe's major centers of culture. As abbot, Warin strongly supported Louis the Pious, who granted Corvey several additional estates in return.

Warin helped to convert northwestern Germany to Christianity by founding several new monasteries there. He died on 20/21 September 856.

His Line

Husband		Wife	
Ecbert "the Loyal," Count in the Ittergau (d. aft. 834)	+	**St. Ida of Herzfeld** (d. aft. 21 Nov 838)	
Reginhart, son of Walbert, Count of Ringelheim and of the Threkwitigau	+	**Mathilda** (alive in 909)	Mathilda's brother: ***Bl. Warin, Abbot of Corvie***
Dietrich, Count of Ringelheim, Saxony, and the Saxon Hamalant (b. ca. 872 – md. (1) 882 – d. 8 Dec 917)	+	Gisela of Lorraine (b. 860/865 – md. 882 – d. bef. 26 Oct 907)	
Henry I "the Fowler," Duke of Saxony and Emperor of the West (b. 876 – md. (2) 909 – d. 2 July 936)	+	**St. Mathilda of Ringelheim** (b. ca. 890/900 – md. 909 – d. 14 March 968)	
Giselbert, Duke of Lorraine and Count of Hainault (b. ca. 890 – md. 929 – d. 2 Oct 934)	+	**Gerberge of Saxony** (b. 913/914 – md. (1) 929 – d. 5 May 984)	

[For the later generations that connect this line to the kings of England, see the line of St. Adela, Princess of Austrasia in Part II.]

Sources: *BBKL*, Vol. 13, cols. 358–359; *Holboeck*, p. 115; *Holweck*, pp. 500 (under "Ida of Herzfeld") and 1031; *NCE*, Vol. 14, pp. 811–812; *Stuart:* line 338 + line 92, nos. 36 and 35; *Weis, AR*, line 142, nos. 17 and 18; *Wells*, pp. 515 and 270

St. Wenceslaus I, Duke of Bohemia

Wenceslaus (in Czech: Vaclav) was born around 903 and was the son of Ratislav, the Duke of Bohemia, and his wife Drahomir of Stodar. Wenceslaus married young, but his wife's name has been lost.

Christianity had been introduced into Bohemia in the time of Wenceslaus' grandparents, but two generations later it was still not deeply rooted. Most of Wenceslaus' family—such as his grandparents Borivoy I and Ludmilla and his father Ratislav—were sincere converts. So was Wenceslaus, who had been devoutly Christian since he was very young. His mother Drahómir was not, and in the whole country many nobles and common people were still actively pagan.

Ratislav died fighting the Magyars before Wenceslaus was old enough to succeed him, which made Drahomir regent of the kingdom for a time. As ruler, she repudiated Christianity and tried to wipe it out by murdering Ludmilla, expelling priests, and persecuting Christians. She also tried and failed to re-convert Wenceslaus.

All these measures forced Wenceslaus to take action. He claimed his throne early and then proceeded to exile Drahomir, recall the priests, invite missionaries into Bohemia, restore support to the churches, and work to strengthen Christianity generally.

Wenceslaus' efforts weakened the pagan revolt which Drahomir had led but did not kill it completely. The new leader of the pagan reaction was Wenceslaus' brother Boleslaw, who had grown up a pagan and who would succeed to the throne if anything should happen to Wenceslaus. To prevent a German invasion of Bohemia, in 929 Wenceslaus made an act of submission to the German ruler Henry "the Fowler." This plus the spread of Christianity under Wenceslaus convinced Boleslaw that it was time to take further action.

Boleslaw invited his brother to come and celebrate a Christian feastday with him. Wenceslaus came, and on 28 September 929 the two of them were walking to the church of Alt Bunzlau. At the doorway of the church, Boleslaw and his men turned on Wenceslaus, drew their swords, and murdered him. Wenceslaus' last words were, "Brother, may God forgive you." Boleslaw assumed the throne and is remembered as Boleslaw "the Cruel."

Wenceslaus was immediately considered a saint. He became the patron saint of the Czech Republic, and in the English-speaking world he is the subject of the Christmas carol "Good King Wenceslaus."

His Line

	Husband		Wife
	Wratislaw (or Vratislav) I, Duke of Bohemia (md. bef. 910 – d. 13 Feb 921)	+	**Drahomir of Stodar** (md. bef. 910)
Boleslaw's brother: ***St. Wenceslaus I, Duke of Bohemia***	**Boleslaw I "the Cruel,"** Duke of Bohemia (d. 15 July 972)	+	Biagota of Stockow
	Boleslaw II "the Pious," Duke of Bohemia (d. 7 Feb 999)	+	Hemma (d. ca. 1005)

Udalrich, Duke of Bohemia (d. 9 Nov 1034)	+	Bozena (d. 1055)
Bretislaw I "the Warrior," Duke of Bohemia, Moravia, and Silesia (b. ca. 1021 – d. 10 Jan 1055)	+	Judith von Schweinfurt (md. 1005 – md. ca. ca. 1021 – d. 2 Aug 1058)
Wratislaw II, King of Bohemia and Hungary and Lord of Olmutz (b. ca. 1035 – md. (2) ca. 1056/1058 – d. 14 Jan 1092)	+	Adelaide (b. ca. 1038/1040 – md. ca. 1056/1058 – d. 27 Jan 1062), daughter of Andrew I, King of Hungary
Ladislas I (or Wladislaw I Hermann), King of Poland (b. ca. 1040 – md. ca. 1080 – d. 4 June 1102)	+	**Judith of Bohemia** (b. ca. 1058 – md. ca. 1080 – d. 25 Dec 1086)

[For the later generations that connect this line to the kings of England, see the line of St. Adelaide of Burgundy in Part II.]

Sources: *Baring-Gould*, Vol. 10, pp. 421–427; *Benedictine Monks*, p. 723; *Bunson*, p. 849; *Butler*, Vol. III, pp. 663–664; *CE*, Vol. XV, p. 587; *Cruz*, pp. 731–732; *Delaney*, p. 584; *Delaney and Tobin*, p. 1193; *Englebert*, pp. 368–369; *Giorgi*, pp. 570–571; *Guiley*, pp. 349–350; *Holweck*, p. 1032; *Joeckle*, pp. 469–470; *NCE*, Vol. 14, p. 873; *O'Malley*, pp. 108–110; *Snodgrass*, p. 240; *Stuart*, line 362, nos. 38 through 32; *Tucker*, Vol. I, p. 91; *Weis, AR*, line 244, nos. 7 and 8; *Wolf*, pp. 118–119

St. William,
Archbishop of York

William was born around 1085/1090 and was the son of Herbert of Winchester and his first wife Emma of Blois. Also known as William Fitzherbert, William became a priest and was made prebendary of Weighton in the archdiocese of Yorkshire in 1109.

Other men might have remained in this post a long time, but William's excellent family connections created much higher opportunities for him. His father Herbert served as Chamberlain and Treasurer to Kings William II and Henry I of England. Not surprisingly, William was himself appointed to be treasurer of the Cathedral at York (known as York Minster) sometime between 1109 and 1114. When King Henry I died in 1135, William's prospects seemed even brighter. The next king of England might be Stephen of Blois, who was Emma's brother and William's uncle.

To understand what happened next in William's life, one must first know a little about the political situation in England as a whole. For several years before King Henry died, his last living legitimate child and acknowledged heir apparent was his daughter Matilda. Stephen was just a nephew of Henry, but as soon as Henry died Stephen hurried to England. He was first acclaimed king by the people of London. He then won the backing of most of the English barons, who were not willing to be ruled by a woman. Stephen was then crowned on 26 December 1135. Matilda was outraged and refused to accept Stephen's usurpation of her inheritance. For the next eighteen years, England was so unsettled that the period became known to history simply as "the Anarchy." As Stephen and Matilda wrestled for supremacy by fighting a civil war with each other, the common people suffered so grievously that the era was remembered as a time "when Christ and his saints slept."

The office of the archbishop of York became one of the battlegrounds in the nationwide struggle between Stephen and Matilda. When the old archbishop died in 1140, William was elected to replace him. Clerics allied with Matilda protested that Stephen had unduly influenced the election and took their complaints to Rome. After Pope Anastasius IV decided that the election was fair, William was consecrated on 26 September 1143 and quickly became very popular with the people of York.

Matilda's friends among the clergy of York did not give up, however, and looked for new ways to dispute William's authority. In 1147, William had to defend himself in Rome again, and this time Eugenius III, who had succeeded Anastasius IV as pope, decided against William, removed him as archbishop, and replaced him with a churchman named Henry Murdac.

The pope's decision settled nothing. William left the archbishop's residence and entered a monastery. King Stephen refused to accept the removal of William and the appointment of Henry Murdac and prevented the new archbishop from entering his residence and performing his duties. For the next seven years, the faithful of York were without a shepherd.

The endgame in this struggle began in 1153. Eugenius III and Murdac both died that year. In November, Matilda's son Henry had signed the treaty of Wallingford with Stephen. It provided that Henry would succeed Stephen as king.

With Murdac gone, early in 1154 William went to Rome again, this time to meet with the new pope Anastasius IV. Anastasius reversed the decision of Eugenius and reappointed William as archbishop of York. Back in York by May 1154, William was warmly welcomed by the people and took his old duties once again.

All was well for about one month. While saying Mass in early June, William was suddenly seized with violent pain. He died a few days later on 8 June 1154.

There were those who thought that the wine in William's chalice at his last mass had been poisoned. About five months later on 25 October 1154, William's patron King Stephen also died, and on 19 December Matilda's son Henry was crowned King Henry II of England. Whether William's death was an early exercise in spring cleaning engineered by the clerical friends of Matilda and Henry will never be known.

William was buried in York Minster, and many miracles were reported at his tomb. He was canonized by Pope Honorius III in 1226.

The greatest memorial to William is still visible in York Minster. Sixty-two scenes from his life and the miracles attributed to him are depicted in separate panels of the masterpiece of medieval stained glass known as the "Saint William Window." It is one of the very largest medieval windows anywhere in Europe. Its survival intact down to the present day may be William's greatest miracle.

His Line

	Husband		Wife
	Herbert of Winchester (b. ca. 1052 – md. (1) ca. 1074 – d. in or sh. bef. 1130), Chamberlain and Treasurer under William II and Henry I of England	+	**Emma of Blois** (md. ca. 1074), half-sister of King Stephen of England
Herbert's brother: ***St. William, Archbishop of York***	**Herbert Fitz Herbert** (succeeded to his father's lands in 1130 – d. by 1155)	+	Sibyl Corbet (liv. 1157)
	Herbert Fitz Herbert (adult by 1165 – md. by 1196 – d. sh. bef. June 1204)	+	Lucy of Hereford (md. by 1196 – liv. 1219/1220)
	Piers Fitz Herbert (md. (1) with settlement dated 28 Nov 1203– d. sh. bef. 6 June 1235)	+	Alice de Warkworth (md. with settlement dated 28 Nov 1203 – d. by 1225)
	Sir William de Ros of Helmsley (md. ca. 1226 – d. prob. 1264), son of Robert de Ros, Magna Charta Surety	+	**Lucy Fitz Piers** (b. ca. 1212 – md. ca. 1226 – liv. 1266)
	Sir William de Ros of Ingmanthorpe (md. ca. 1268 – d. sh. bef. 28 May 1310)	+	Eustache (md. ca. 1268), daughter of Ralph Fitz Hugh
	Sir Robert de Plumpton, Knt. (d. 1325)	+	**Lucy de Ros**
	Sir William de Plumpton, Knt. and High Sheriff of Yorkshire (md. (2) ca. 1338 – d. 1362)	+	Christian de Mowbray (md. ca. 1338 – d. 1365)

Sources: *Baring-Gould*, Vol. 6, pp. 82–86; *Benedictine Monks*, pp. 727–728; *Bentley*, p. 108; *Bunson*, p. 857; *Butler*, Vol. II, pp. 503–505; *Delaney*, p. 590; *Delaney and Tobin*, p. 1202; *Holweck*, p. 1036; *Tucker*, Vol. I, p. 402; *Weis, AR*, line 262, nos. 26 through 29; *Weis, MCS*, line 116, nos. 2 through 5

St. Wistan

Wiglaf, king of Mercia, had a son named Wigmund. Wigmund and his wife Elfleda had a son named Wistan. Wigmund died of dysentery before he could succeed his father and was survived by Elfleda and the very young Wistan.

In 840, Wiglaf finally died. The throne of Mercia was claimed by Wiglaf's brother Berhtwulf (or Beorhtwulf), who became king.

For an ambitious man, the most eligible woman in the kingdom was Elfleda, who had never remarried. Hoping to consolidate his power, Berhtwulf began what would become a long-term effort to marry her. Wistan—still in his minority and immersed in religious studies—steadfastly refused to consent to such a union.

On 1 June 849, Berhtwulf had finally had enough. He lured Wistan to a meeting and murdered him when he arrived.

Wistan was considered a martyr and buried in Evesham Abbey. His remains were later removed to Evesham Cathedral. Berhtwulf died in 851 in a battle with Viking invaders. Whether he ever succeeded in marrying Elfleda is not recorded.

His Line

Husband		Wife	
Wigmund (liv. 840), son of Wiglaf, King of Mercia	+	**Elfleda (or Aelflaed)**, (b. ca. 805), daughter of Ceolwulf, King of Mercia	
Aethelred, Earl of Mercia	+	**Eadburh of Mercia** (b. ca. 830)	Eadburh's brother: ***St. Wistan***
St. Alfred "the Great," King of Wessex (b. 849 – md. 868 – d. 26 Oct 899)	+	**St. Ealhswith** (b. ca. 852 – md. 868 – d. 904)	

Sources: *Ashley*, p. 321; *Baring-Gould*, Vol. 6, p. 5; *BBKL*, Vol. 15, cols. 1523–1524; *Benedictine Monks*, p. 732; *Bunson*, p. 860; *Butler*, Vol. II, pp. 440–441; *Delaney*, p. 592; *Holweck*, p. 1040; *Kirby*, p. 157; *Stuart:* line 238 + line 367, no. 41; *Weis, AR*, line 1, no. 15; *Wells*, pp. 204 and 382; *Yorke*, pp. 119–120

St. Withburga, Abbess of Dereham

Withburga was the youngest daughter of Anna, King of East Anglia, and his wife St. Hereswitha.

Withburga became a nun when she was very young. After her father Anna died in battle with Penda of Mercia in 654, Withburga and a few companions fled to Dereham in Norfolk. They lived in great poverty but laid the foundation for a convent and a church. The nuns were revered by the people in the surrounding area. By the time Withburga died, the church was still unfinished, but she was already regarded as a saint.

The correctness of the people's judgment was confirmed several times after Withburga's death. In the late 700's and also in 974 and 1106, it was decided to move her remains to a new resting place. She was first reburied in a more splendid grave in Dereham, then moved from Dereham to Ely, and finally laid to rest next to the high altar of the new cathedral in Ely so that she might await the Second Coming next to her sisters Saints Ermenilda, Ethelburga, and Sexburga. On each occasion her body was found to be incorrupt. After she was moved from her original resting place in Dereham, a fresh spring also appeared at her empty grave, which flows to this day. It is called Withburga's Well and is on the west side of St. Nicholas Church.

Her Line

Husband		Wife	
Anna, King of East Anglia (ruled ca. 641–653, until he died in battle with Penda of Mercia)	+	**St. Hereswitha** (b. sh. bef. 616 – d. 680/690)	
Erconbert (or Eorconbeorht), King of Kent (b. ca. 624 – md. ca. 640 – d. 14 July 664)	+	**St. Sexburga** (md. ca. 640 – d. 6 July 699)	St. Sexburga's sister: ***St. Withburga, Abbess of Dereham***
Egbert, King of Kent (b. ca. 641 – d. 4 July 673)	+	N.N.	

[For the later generations that connect this line to the kings of England, see the line of St. Aethelbert I, King of Kent in Part II.]

Sources: *Ashley*, pp. 239 and 242; *Baring-Gould*, Vol. 3, pp. 309–310 and Vol. 16, p. 251; *Benedictine Monks*, p. 732; *Browne*, p. 87; *Bunson*, p. 860; *Butler*, Vol. III, p. 41; *Delaney*, p. 592; *Delaney and Tobin*, p. 1210; *Dunbar*, Vol. II, p. 304; *Holweck*, p. 1041; *Klaniczay*, p. 88; *NCE*, Vol. 14, p. 980; *O'Malley*, pp. 64, 73, and 98; *Parbury*, pp. 90–91; *Stuart:* line 437, nos. 47 and 46 + line 233A, nos. 46 and 45; *Wells*, pp. 197 and 325

St. Wulfhilda

Wulfhilda was born around 1117 and was the daughter of Henry I "the Black," Duke of Bavaria, and his wife Wulfhilda of Saxony. She married Rudolph, Count of Bregenz and had several children with him.

After her husband Rudolph died in April 1160, Wulfhilda became a nun and entered the convent at Wessobrunn in Bavaria. She cared for the sick and performed the most menial work with genuine humility. She was so amiable that the other nuns in her convent called her "angelic." She was also sent several times as a mediator to resolve disputes among her royal relatives. She died sometime after 1180.

Her Line

Husband		Wife	
Henry I "the Black," Duke of Bavaria (b. 1074 – md. 1095/1100 – d. 13 Dec 1126)	+	**Wulfhilda of Saxony** (b. ca. 1071 – md. 1095/1100 – d. 29 Dec 1126)	
Frederick II von Hohenstaufen, Duke of Swabia (b. 1090 – md. 1121 – d. 4/6 April 1147)	+	**Judith of Bavaria** (b. ca. 1100 – md. 1121 – d. 22 Feb 1130/1135)	Judith's sister: ***St. Wulfhilda***
Frederick III Barbarosa, Duke of Swabia, Emperor of Germany and the West, Crusader (b. 1122 – md. 10/16 June 1156 – drowned 10 June 1190 while on the 3rd Crusade)	+	Beatrice of Burgundy (b. ca. 1145 – md. 10/16 June 1156 – d. 15 Nov 1184)	
Philip von Hohenstaufen, Duke of Tuscany and Swabia and Emperor of Germany (b. 1176 – md. 25 May 1197 – murdered 21 June 1208)	+	Eirene (or Maria) Angelina (b. ca. 1181 – md. (2) 25 May 1197 – murdered 27 Aug 1208), daughter of Isaac II Angelos, Emperor of Byzantium	

[For the later generations that connect this line to the kings of England, see the line of St. Boris I, Khan of the Bulgars in Part II.]

Sources: *Dunbar*, Vol. II, p. 305; *Holboeck*, pp. 166–167; *Holweck*, p. 1042; *Stuart:* line 43, nos. 31 and 30 + line 40, nos. 30 and 39 + line 125, nos. 29 and 38; *Weis, AR:* line 166, nos. 24 and 25 + line 45, nos. 26 and 27; *Wells*, pp. 57–58 and 271–272

St. Yaropolk Izyaslavich, Prince of Turov and Vladimir-in-Volynia

Yaropolk was the son of St. Izyaslav I Yaroslavich, Grand Prince of Kiev and ruler of Kievan Rus, and his wife Gertrude. He married Cunigunde of Weimar in 1073 and had four children.

Yaropolk's early life was one of service to his father as Izyaslav tried to hang on to the throne of Kiev in the face of a popular revolt in 1068, attacks by the troops of his brothers in 1073, and finally a civil war in 1078. Seeking help for his father, Yaropolk went on diplomatic missions to the king of Poland, the emperor of Germany, and the pope. He also fought beside his father in some of his battles. After Izyaslav was slain on 3 October 1078, Yaropolk's victorious relatives were magnanimous enough to make him prince of Turov and of Vladimir-in-Volynia.

Personally, Yaropolk was a devout Christian who was generous to the poor and a benefactor of the Kievan Caves monastery. His life was cut short on 22 November 1087, however, when he was slain by an assassin.

Yaropolk was buried in Kiev in the church of St. Peter.

His Line

	Husband		Wife
	St. Izyaslav I Yaroslavich, Grand Prince of Kiev (b. 1025 – md. ca. 1043 – slain 3 Oct 1078)	+	**Gertrude** (md. ca. 1043), daughter of Mieszko II, King of Poland
Sviatpolk's brother: ***St. Yaropolk Izyaslavich, Prince of Turov and Vladimir-in-Volynia***	**Sviatpolk II Izyaslavich**, Grand Prince of Kiev, Novgorod, and Turov (b. 1050 – d. 16 April 1113)	+	N.N. (d. bef. 1094)
	Boleslas III, King of Poland (b. 20 Aug 1086 – md. (1) 1103 – d. 28 Oct 1138)	+	**Zbyslava of Kiev** (md. 1103 – d. 1110/1111)

[For the later generations that connect this line to the kings of England, see the line of St. Adelaide of Burgundy in Part II.]

Sources: *Holweck*, p. 526; *Stuart*, line 363; *Walsh*, p. 295; *Weis, AR*, line 241, nos. 6 through 8; *Wells*, p. 330

Bl. Yolande of Hungary

Yolande was born around 1235 and was the daughter of Bela IV, King of Hungary, and his wife Maria Laskarina. In 1256, she married Boleslaus "the Pious," Duke of Greater Poland (i.e., the provinces of Gniezno, Kalisz, and Poznan).

Yolande was deeply loved by her husband and by her people, especially the poor. She and Boleslaus founded several religious institutions and performed many works of charity.

After Boleslaus died in 1279, Yolande became a nun and entered the convent at Sandecz. Later in life, she moved to a convent she had founded in Gniezno and became the abbess there. She died on 6 March 1298.

Yolande is sometimes called Yolanda or Jolenta. She is also known as Helen of Poland.

Her Line

	Husband		Wife
	Bela IV, King of Hungary (b. 1206 – md. 1218 – d. 3 May 1270)	+	**Maria Laskarina** (b. ca. 1206 – md. 1218 – d. 1270), daughter of Theodore I Lascaris, Emperor of Byzantium
Stephen's sister: ***Bl. Yolande of Hungary***	**Stephen V**, King of Hungary (b. Dec 1239 – md. 1253 – d. 1 Aug 1272)	+	Elizabeth (md. 1253 – d. aft. 1290), daughter of Kuthen, Khan of the Kumans
	Charles II "le Boiteux" ("the Lame"), King of Naples and Prince of Salerno (b. 1254 – md. 1270 – d. 5 June 1309)	+	**Maria** (b. ca. 1257 – md. 1270 – murdered 25 March 1323)

[For the later generations that connect this line to the kings of England, see the line of St. Adalbero, Bishop of Wuerzburg in Part III.]

Sources: *Benedictine Monks*, pp. 333 (under "Helen") and 736 (under "Yolanda"); *Butler*, Vol. II, p. 550 (under "Jolenta"); *Delaney*, pp. 327–328 (under "Jolenta"); *Delaney and Tobin*, p. 627 (under "Jolenta"); *Dunbar*, Vol. I, p. 436 (under "Jolenta"); *Holweck*, pp. 467 (under "Helen") and 559 (under "Jolenta"); *Klaniczay*, pp. 207, 277, and Appendix B, Geneal. Table 8; *NCE*, Vol. 7, p. 1091; *O'Malley*, p. 93; *Stuart*, line 78, nos. 27 through 25; *Weis, AR*, line 103, nos. 29 through 31; *Wells*, pp. 309 and 421

St. Zwentibold, King of Lorraine

Zwentibold was born in 870 and was an illegitimate son of Arnulf of Carinthia, King of the East Franks (i.e., Germany), and an unknown concubine. Zwentibold married, but the name of his wife is also unknown.

With his wife Oda, Arnulf also had a legitimate son known to history as "Louis the Child." Although Zwentibold was born first, Louis the Child would one day inherit all of Arnulf's lands, and Zwentibold would be left with nothing. Hoping to prevent a very foreseeable war over the succession between his offspring, Arnulf made Zwentibold king of Lotharingia (also known as Lorraine) in May 895.

In his realm, Zwentibold tried to reconstruct everything that had been destroyed in earlier Norman incursions. He also built churches, monasteries, and the convent at Susteren. He was generous to the church overall and initially enjoyed the support of the nobility.

After Arnulf died in 899, however, the nobles of Lotharingia began to switch their allegiance from Zwentibold to his half-brother Louis the Child. In 900 under the leadership of Reginar I of Hainault, some of the nobles revolted. On 13 August 900 during a battle with the rebels at the River Meuse, Zwentibold was slain.

Zwentibold was buried in the convent at Susteren that he had built for his daughters St. Benedicta and St. Cecilia, who later became abbesses there.

His Line

Husband		Wife	
Arnulf, King of the East Franks (liv. 863–899)	+	**Oda of Bavaria**	
Otto "the Illustrious," Duke of Saxony and Count in South Thuringia (b. ca. 836 – md. 869 – d. 30 Nov 912)	+	**Hedwig** (md. 869 – d. 906)	Hedwig's half-brother: ***St. Zwentibold, King of Lorraine***
Henry I "the Fowler," Duke of Saxony and Emperor of the West (b. 876 – md. (2) 909 – d. 2 July 936)	+	St. Mathilda of Ringelheim (b. ca. 890/900 – md. 909 – d. 14 March 968)	
Giselbert, Duke of Lorraine and Count of Hainault (b. ca. 890 – md. 929 – d. 2 Oct 934)	+	**Gerberge of Saxony** (b. 913/914 – md. (1) 929 – d. 5 May 984)	

[For the later generations that connect this line to the kings of England, see the line of St. Adela, Princess of Austrasia in Part II.]

Sources: *BBKL*, Vol. 14, cols. 652–668; *Delaney and Tobin*, p. 73 (under "Arnulf"); *Holweck*, pp. 1052–1053; *Roesch*, p. 136; *Stuart:* line 172, nos. 39 and 38 + line 92, nos. 37 through 35; *Weis, AR*: line 141, nos. 17 and 18 + line 142, nos. 17 and 28; *Wells*, pp. 138 and 269–270

LIST OF ABBREVIATIONS

aft. – after
b. – born
bef. – before
betw. – between
Bl. – Blessed
ca. – about (circa)
cf. – compare
col. – column
cols. – columns
d. – died
liv. – living
md. – married
md. (1), md. (2), md. (3) – married first, married second, married third, etc.
N.N. – name not known
no. – number
p. – page
perh. – perhaps
prob. – probably
sh. – shortly
St. – Saint
vol. – volume

LIST OF ABBREVIATED SOURCES

ADB, Vol. ___:	*Allegemeine Deutsche Biographie.* In 56 volumes. In German. Leipzig, Germany: Verlag von Duncker & Humblot, 1875.
Allen:	Allen, W. E. D. *The Ukraine: A History.* Cambridge, England: Cambridge University Press, 1940.
Ashley:	Ashley, Mike. *The Mammoth Book of British Kings & Queens.* New York: Avalon Publishing Group, 1999.
Baring-Gould, Vol. ___:	Baring-Gould, Rev. S. *The Lives of the Saints.* New and revised edition in 16 volumes. Edinburgh, Scotland: John Grant, 1914.
Baring-Gould and Fisher, Vol. ___:	Baring-Gould, Rev. S. and Fisher, John. *The Lives of the British Saints.* London: The Honourable Society of Cymmrodorion. 1907 (reprinted in four volumes in 2008 by Kessinger Publishing, LLC).
BBKL, Vol. ___:	Bautz, Friedrich Wilhelm (continued by Traugott Bautz). *Biographisch-Bibliographisches Kirchenlexikon.* Complete edition in 27 volumes. In German. Herzberg, Germany: Verlag Traugott Bautz, 1970–2005.
Becher:	Becher, Matthias. *Charlemagne.* Translated by David S. Bachrach. New Haven, Connecticut: Yale University Press, 2003.
Benedictine Monks:	The Benedictine Monks of St. Augustine's Abbey, Ramsgate. *The Book of Saints: A Dictionary of Persons Canonized or Beatified by the Catholic Church.* 5th ed. New York: Thomas Y. Crowell Co., 1966.
Bentley:	Bentley, James. *A Calendar of Saints: The Lives of the Principal Saints of the Christian Year.* London: Time Warner Book Group UK, 2005.
Bibliotheca Sanctorum:	*Bibliotheca Sanctorum.* In twelve volumes. In Italian. Rome, Italy: Instituto Giovanni XXIII nella Pontificia Universita Lateranense, 1961–1969.
Boyer:	Boyer, Carl, 3rd. *Medieval Welsh Ancestors of Certain Americans.* Santa Clarita, California: Published by the author, 2004.
Bradbury:	Bradbury, Jim. *The Capetians.* New York: Continuum Books, 2007.
Browne:	Browne, G. F. *The Conversion of the Heptarchy.* London: Society for Promoting Christian Knowledge, 1896.
Brusher:	Brusher, Joseph S. *Popes through the Ages.* Revised edition. Princeton, New Jersey: D. Van Nostrand Company, Inc., 1964.
Bunson:	Bunson, Matthew and Bunson, Margaret and Bunson, Stephen. Our Sunday Visitor's *Encyclopedia of Saints.* Huntington, Indiana: Our Sunday Visitor, Inc., 2003.
Burke's:	*Burke's Peerage & Baronetage.* 106th edition. Crans, Switzerland: Burke's Peerage (Genealogical Books) Ltd., 1999.

Butler, Vol. ___:	Thurston, Herbert J., S.J. and Attwater, Donald, eds. *Butler's Lives of the Saints*. Complete edition in four volumes. Vol. I—*January, February, March*; Vol. II—*April, May, June*; Vol. III—*July, August, September*; and Vol. IV—*October, November, December*. Westminster, Maryland: Christian Classics, Inc., 1988 (originally published 1756–59).
Byrne:	Byrne, Francis John. *Irish Kings and High-Kings*. 2nd ed. Dublin, Ireland: Four Courts Press, 2001.
Cabaniss:	Cabaniss, Allen. *Charlemagne's Cousins: Contemporary Lives of Adalard and Wala*. Translated, with an Introduction and Notes, by Allen Cabaniss. Syracuse, New York: Syracuse University Press, 1967.
Castleden:	Castleden, Rodney. *The Book of Saints*. London: Quercus Publishing plc, 2006.
Catechism:	*Catechism of the Catholic Church*. Second edition. Washington, D.C.: United States Catholic Conference, 2000.
CE, Vol. ___:	*The Catholic Encyclopedia*. In 16 volumes. New York: Encyclopedia Press, Inc., 1913–14.
Chamberlin:	Chamberlin, Russell. *The Emperor Charlemagne*. New York: Franklin Watts, Inc., 1986.
Chervin:	Chervin, Ronda De Sola. *Treasury of Women Saints*. Ann Arbor, Michigan: Servant Publications, 1991.
Cruz:	Cruz, Jean Carroll. *Secular Saints*. Rockford, Illinois: TAN Books and Publishers, Inc., 1989.
CS:	Atwell, Robert (comp.). *Celebrating the Saints*. Enlarged edition. Norwich, Norfolk, England: Hymns Ancient & Modern Ltd., 2004.
Cunningham:	Cunningham, Lawrence S. *A Brief History of Saints*. Malden, Massachusetts: Blackwell Publishing, 2005.
Delaney:	Delaney, John J. *Dictionary of Saints*. Garden City, New York: Doubleday & Co., Inc., 1980.
Delaney and Tobin:	Delaney, John J. and Tobin, James Edward. *Dictionary of Catholic Biography*. Garden City, New York: Doubleday & Co., Inc., 1961.
de Vere:	de Vere, Aubrey. *Legends of the Saxon Saints*. London: C. Kegan Paul & Co., 1879.
Dowling:	Dowling, Archdeacon. *The Armenian Church*. New York: AMS Press, Inc., 1970.
Dunbar:	Dunbar, Agnes B. C. *A Dictionary of Saintly Women*. In two volumes. London: George Bell & Sons, 1904 (Vol. I) and 1905 (Vol. II).
Dunn:	Dunn-Mascetti, Manuela. *Saints: The Chosen Few*. New York: Ballantine Books, 1994.
Edberg:	Edberg, Rune. *Viking Princess, Christian Saint: Ingegerd, a Woman in the 11th Century*. Translated by Theodosia Tomkinson. Sigtuna, Sweden: Sigtuna Museum, 2005.
Englebert:	Englebert, Omer. *The Lives of the Saints*. Translated by Christopher and Anne Fremantle. New York: David McKay Co., Inc., 1951.

Fedotov: Fedotov, G. P. *Sviatie Drevney Rusi [Saints of Ancient Rus]*. 4th edition. In Russian. Paris: YMCA-Press, 1989.

fmg.ac/Projects/MedLands/Contents.htm
The Foundation for Medieval Genealogy (or fmg) is a research organization in Britain that has posted the first edition of Charles Cawley's *Medieval Lands* on its Web site. *Medieval Lands* is an astounding on-line encyclopedia of genealogical information about the royal and noble families which ruled the lands of the medieval Western world. The above URL leads to an overview of its contents. *Medieval Lands* can be consulted at no charge.

Giorgi: Giorgi, Rosa. *Saints: A Year in Faith and Art*. Translated by Jay Hyams. New York: Harry N. Abrams, Inc., 2006.

Golubinskii: Golubinskii, E. E. *Istoriya Kanonizatsii Sviatykh v Russkoy Tserkvi [History of the Canonization of Saints in the Russian Church]*. In Russian. Farnborough, Hampshire, England: Gregg International Publishers Ltd., 1969 (first published in 1903).

Goodich: Goodich, Michael. *Vita Perfecta: The Ideal of Sainthood in the Thirteenth Century*. Stuttgart, Germany: Anton Hiersemann, 1982.

Guiley: Guiley, Rosemary Ellen. *The Encyclopedia of Saints*. New York: Facts On File, Inc., 2001.

Gurney: Gurney, Gene. *Kingdoms of Europe: An Illustrated Encyclopedia of Ruling Monarchs from Ancient Times to the Present*. New York: Crown Publishers, Inc., 1982.

Hantsch, Vol. ___: Hantsch, Dr. Hugo. *Die Geschichte Oesterreichs*. 3rd edition. In 2 volumes. In German. Graz-Wien, Austria: Styria Steirische Verlagsanstalt, 1951.

HBC: Fryde, E. B. and Greenway, D. E. and Porter, S. and Roy, I. (eds.) *Handbook of British Chronology*. 3rd edition. London: The Royal Historical Society, 1986.

Hist. Rus. Ch., Vol. 2: *Istoriya Russkoy Tserkvi [History of the Russian Church]*. Volume 2. In Russian. Moscow: The Publishing House of the Monastery of the Saviour's Transfiguration in Vladimir, 1995.

Holboeck: Holboeck, Ferdinand. *Married Saints and Blesseds through the Centuries*. Translated by Michael J. Miller. San Francisco, California: Ignatius Press, 2002.

Holweck: Holweck, Rt. Rev. F. G. *A Biographical Dictionary of the Saints*. St. Louis, Missouri: B. Herder Book Co., 1924.

Hovannisian: Hovannisian, Richard G. (ed.). *The Armenian People from Ancient to Modern Times*. Volume I. New York: St. Martin's Press, 2004.

Hrushevsky: Hrushevsky, Michael. *A History of Ukraine*. New Haven, Connecticut: Yale University Press, 1941.

Jaski: Jaski, Bart. *Early Irish Kingship and Succession*. Dublin, Ireland: Four Courts Press, Ltd., 2000.

Joeckle: Joeckle, Clemens. *Encyclopedia of Saints*. Translated by the German Translation Center. London: Alpine Fine Arts Collection (UK) Ltd., 1995.

"John Paul II: Beatification and Canonization Ceremonies"
Statistics provided by the Holy See Press Office. For details, go to <www.vatican.va>, and click on "The Holy See—English". In the search box, type "Statistics on the Pontificate of John Paul II". and then scroll down to "Beatification and Canonization Ceremonies". Last updated Dec. 28, 2005.

Jones: Jones, Andrew. *Every Pilgrim's Guide to Celtic Britain and Ireland.* Liguori, Missouri: Liguori Publications, 2002.

Jones, *Celtic Saints*: Jones, Kathleen. *Who Are the Celtic Saints?* Norwich, Norfolk, England: Hymns Ancient & Modern Ltd., 2002.

Kaloustian: Kaloustian, S. *Saints and Sacraments of the Armenian Church.* Fresno, California: A-1 Printers, 1959.

Kelley: Kelley, David H. January 1978. "Descents from the High Kings of Ireland." *The American Genealogist* Vol. 54, No. 1: 1–5.

Kemp: Kemp, Eric Waldram. *Canonization and Authority in the Western Church.* London: Oxford University Press, 1948.

King: King, Richard John. *Handbook to the Cathedrals of England.* Ely, England: John Murray, 1862.

Kirby: Kirby, D. P. *The Earliest English Kings.* New York: Routledge, 2000.

Klaniczay: Klaniczay, Gabor. *Holy Rulers and Blessed Princesses: Dynastic Cults in Medieval Central Europe.* Translated by Eva Palmai. Cambridge, England: Cambridge University Press, 2002.

Koushagian: Koushagian, Torkom. *Saints & Feasts of the Armenian Church.* Translated by Haigazoun Melkonian. New York: Diocese of the Armenian Church of America (Eastern), 2005.

Lambertini: Lambertini, Prospero Cardinal de (who became Pope Benedict XIV). *De Servorum Dei Beatificatione et Beatorum Canonizatione.* In latin. Editio Secunda locupletior. Liber Primus [Book One]. Padova, Italy: Giovanni Manfré, 1743.

Langmuir: Langmuir, Erika. *Pocket Guides: Saints.* London: National Gallery Co., 2001.

"Making Saints": A "Backgrounder" prepared by the U.S. Conference of Catholic Bishops. For the full text go to <www.usccb.org/ comm/SaintsFinal.pdf>, and under "Backgrounders" click on "Making Saints". Visited ______ ______.

Maund: Maund, Kari. *The Welsh Kings.* Charleston, South Carolina: Tempus Publishing Inc., 2000.

McKitterick: McKitterick, Rosamond. *The Frankish Kingdoms under the Carolingians, 751–987.* New York: Longman Inc., 1983.

MI: Kleinhenz, Christopher (ed.). *Medieval Italy: An Encyclopedia.* In two volumes. New York: Routledge, 2004.

Moncrieffe: Moncrieffe of That Ilk, Sir Iain, BT. *Royal Highness: Ancestry of the Royal Child.* London: Hamish Hamilton Ltd., 1982.

NCE, Vol. ___: *New Catholic Encyclopedia.* In 15 volumes. Washington, D.C.: The Catholic University of America, 1967.

NDB, Vol. ___: *Neue Deutsche Biographie.* In 22 volumes. In German. Berlin, Germany: Duncker & Humblot, 1953.

Norwich, Vol. ___: Norwich, John Julius. *Byzantium.* In three volumes. Vol. 1—*The Early Centuries*; Vol. 2—*The Apogee*; and Vol. 3—*The Decline and Fall.* New York: Alfred A. Knopf, Inc., 1988–1995.

O'Callaghan: O'Callaghan, Joseph F. *A History of Medieval Spain.* Ithaca, New York: Cornell University Press, 1975.

Olson: Olson, Steve. May 2002. "The Royal We." *The Atlantic Monthly.* Vol. 289 No. 5: 62–64.

O'Malley: O'Malley, Vincent J., CM. *Saintly Companions: A Cross-Reference of Sainted Relationships.* Staten Island, New York: The Society of St. Paul, 1995.

One Hundred Saints: *One Hundred Saints: Their Lives and Likenesses Drawn from Butler's "Lives of the Saints" and Great Works of Western Art.* Boston, Massachusetts: Little, Brown and Co., Inc., 1993.

Orth. Encyc., Vol. 8: *Pravoslavnaya Entsiklopediya [Orthodox Encyclopedia].* Volume 8. In Russian. Moscow: Center for Religious Research of the Russian Orthodox Church. 2004.

Orth. Encyc., Vol. 9: *Pravoslavnaya Entsiklopediya [Orthodox Encyclopedia].* Volume 9. In Russian. Moscow: Center for Religious Research of the Russian Orthodox Church. 2005.

Oxford Dict. Byz.: *The Oxford Dictionary of Byzantium.* Complete edition in three volumes. New York: Oxford University Press, Inc., 1991.

Parbury: Parbury, Kathleen. *Women of Grace: A Biographical Dictionary of British Women Saints, Martyrs and Reformers.* Stocksfield, Northumberland, England: Oriel Press Ltd., 1984.

Parish: Parish, G. *The Canonization of a Saint.* Issued with *Butler's Lives of the Saints.* London: Virtue & Co. Ltd., 1956.

Pernoud: Pernoud, Régine. *Blanche of Castile.* Translated by Henry Noel. New York: Coward, McCann & Geoghegan, Inc., 1975.

Poulos, Vol. ___: Poulos, George. *Orthodox Saints: Spiritual Profiles for Modern Man.* In four volumes. Vol. 1—*January 1 to March 31*; Vol. 2—*April 1 to June 30*; Vol. 3—*July 1 to September 30*; and Vol. 4—*October 1 to December 31.* Brookline, Massachusetts: Holy Cross Orthodox Press, 1990–1992.

Rees: Rees, Elizabeth. *Celtic Saints in Their Landscape.* Stroud, Gloucestershire, England: Sutton Publishing Ltd., 2001.

Reilly: Reilly, Robert T. *Irish Saints.* New York: Random House Value Publishing, Inc., 2002.

Riché, *The Carolingians*: Riché, Pierre. *The Carolingians: A Family Who Forged Europe.* Translated by Michael Idomir Allen. Philadelphia, Pennsylvania: University of Pennsylvania Press, 1993.

Riché, *Daily Life:*	Riché, Pierre. *Daily Life in the World of Charlemagne*. Translated by Jo Ann McNamara. Philadelphia, Pennsylvania: University of Pennsylvania Press, 1978.
Roberts:	Roberts, Gary Boyd. November/December 2000. "Comments on Royal Descent." *Ancestry* Vol. 18 No. 6: 18.
Roesch:	Roesch, Siegfried. *Caroli Magni Progenies. Pars 1*. In German. Neustadt an der Aisch, Germany: Verlag Degener & Co., 1977.
Ronay:	Ronay, Gabriel. *The Lost King of England*. Woodbridge, Suffolk, England: Boydell & Brewer Ltd., 1989.
Salter:	Salter, Rev. A. T. John. September 1970. "Descent from the Saints." *The Genealogists' Magazine*. Vol. 16, No. 7: pp. 338–341.
Scherman, *Birth of France*:	Scherman, Katharine. *The Birth of France*. New York: Random House Inc., 1987.
Scherman, *Flowering of Ireland*:	Scherman, Katharine. *The Flowering of Ireland*. New York: Barnes & Noble, Inc., 1996.
Settipani:	Settipani, Christian with Kerrebrouck, Patrick Van. *La Préhistoire des Capétiens 481–987. Première Partie: Mérovingiens, Carolingiens et Robertiens*. In French. Villeneuve d'Ascq, France: Self-published, 1993.
Skene:	Skene, W. F. "Notes on the Earldom of Caithness," in Proceedings of the Society of Antiquaries of Scotland (Edinburgh: By the Society, 1898), pp. 571–576 (presented March 11, 1878).
Snodgrass:	Snodgrass, Mary Ellen. *Who's Who in the Middle Ages*. Jefferson, North Carolina: McFarland & Co., Inc., 2001.
Stone:	Stone, Don Charles. *Some Ancient and Medieval Descents of Edward I of England*. Philadelphia, Pennsylvania: By the author, 2000.
Stratton:	Stratton, Eugene A. November/December 2000. "Give Your Pedigree the Royal Treatment." *Ancestry* Vol. 18 No. 6: 15–17 and 19–20.
Stuart:	Stuart, Roderick W. *Royalty for Commoners: The Complete Known Lineage of John of Gaunt, Son of Edward III, King of England, and Queen Philippa*. 4th ed. Baltimore, Maryland: Genealogical Publishing Co., Inc., 2002.
Sweeney:	Sweeney, Jon M. *The Lure of Saints: A Protestant Experience of Catholic Tradition*. Brewster, Massachusetts: Paraclete Press, 2005.
Tucker:	Tucker, Leslie Ray. *Aristocratic and Royal Ancestors of Jane Harry*. 2 vols. Miami, Oklahoma: Timbercreek Ltd., 1991.
Vauchez:	Vauchez, André. *Sainthood in the Later Middle Ages*. Translated by Jean Birrell. Cambridge, England: Cambridge University Press, 1997.
Wagner:	Wagner, Anthony. *Pedigree and Progress: Essays in the Genealogical Interpretation of History*. London: Phillimore & Co. Ltd., 1975.
Walsh:	Walsh, Michael. *A New Dictionary of Saints: East and West*. Collegeville, Minnesota: Liturgical Press, 2007.
Warncke:	Warncke, Carsten Peter. *Bavaria Sancta-Heiliges Bayern*. In German. Dortmund, Germany: Harenberg Kommunikation, 1981.

Webb: Webb, Diana. *Pilgrimage in Medieval England.* London: Hambledon and London, 2000.

Weinstein and Bell: Weinstein, Donald and Bell, Rudolph M. *Saints & Society*. Chicago, Illinois: The University of Chicago Press, 1982.

Weir: Weir, Alison. *Britain's Royal Families: The Complete Genealogy*. London: Random House UK, 1996.

Weis, *AR* (1st ed.): Weis, Frederick Lewis. *Ancestral Roots of Sixty Colonists Who Came to New England between 1623 and 1650: The Lineage of Alfred the Great, Charlemagne, Malcolm of Scotland, Robert the Strong, and Some of Their Descendants*. First edition. Lancaster, Massachusetts: Self-published, 1950.

Weis, *AR*: Weis, Frederick Lewis. *Ancestral Roots of Certain American Colonists Who Came to America before 1700: The Lineage of Alfred the Great, Charlemagne, Malcolm of Scotland, Robert the Strong, and Some of Their Descendants*. 7th ed. Baltimore, Maryland: Genealogical Publishing Co., Inc., 1992.

Weis, *MCS*: Weis, Frederick Lewis. *The Magna Charta Sureties, 1215*. 5th edition. Baltimore, Maryland: Genealogical Publishing Co., Inc., 1999.

Wells: Wells, Ronald. *Ancient Ancestors with Modern Descendants*. 4th ed. Mawson, A.C.T., Australia: Riverlea Publishing, 2002.

Williams: Williams, George L. *Papal Genealogy: The Families and Descendants of the Popes*. Jefferson, North Carolina: McFarland & Co., Inc., 1998.

Williamson: Williamson, David. *Brewer's British Royalty*. London, Cassell, 1996.

Wolf: Wolf, Norbert. *The World of the Saints*. Translated by Julian Wheatley. New York: Prestel Publishing, 2005.

Wood: Wood, Ian. *The Merovingian Kingdoms 450–751*. New York: Addison Wesley Longman, 1994.

Woodruff: Woodruff, Douglas. *The Life and Times of Alfred the Great*. London: George Weidenfeld and Nicolson, 1974.

Woods: Woods, Richard J. *The Spirituality of the Celtic Saints*. Maryknoll, New York: Orbis Books, 2000.

Woodward: Woodward, Kenneth L. *Making Saints: How the Catholic Church Determines Who Becomes a Saint, Who Doesn't, and Why*. New York: Simon & Schuster, Inc., 1990.

WWH: *Women in World History: A Biographical Encyclopedia*. In 17 volumes. Farmington Hills, Michigan: Gale Group, Inc., 1999–2002.

www.stirnet.com/main/index

The Stirnet Project (or stirnet.com) is a research organization in Britain that has posted its Families Database on its Web site. The Families Database is a collection of outlines which offer an encyclopedic amount of genealogical information about the royal and noble families of medieval Europe. To access this database, a researcher must first become a member of the Stirnet Project and pay an annual membership fee.

Yerke: Yerke, Barbara. *Kings and Kingdoms of Early Anglo-Saxon England.* London: Routledge, 1997.

Zoellner: Zoellner, Erich. *Geschichte Oesterreichs.* 7th edition. In German. Vienna, Austria: Verlag fuer Geschichte und Politik, 1984.

ABOUT THE AUTHOR

A lawyer and an educator, Alan J. Koman graduated *summa cum laude* and *magna cum laude* from Cornell University in 1972. After obtaining a J.D. from Duke University and an L.L.B. from the University of Munich, he entered the private practice of law in Atlanta, Georgia in 1981. He has been involved in many kinds of business transactions and hundreds of litigations.

Alan has guest lectured at Harvard and other law schools. Closer to home, he has been an instructor in national security issues and military history at Emory University. His scholarly articles in the areas of law and national security have appeared in academic and professional journals.

Through his mother, Alan is a child of both the New World and the Old World. His earliest known American ancestors arrived in Virginia in 1619. By the 1770's, Alan's family was in Georgia. Alan is a life member of the Order of the Crown of Charlemagne in the United States of America, the National Society Americans of Royal Descent, the Baronial Order of Magna Charta, the Descendants of the Knights of the Garter, and several other hereditary societies. This book is his first work in the field of hagiography.

Happily struggling to accommodate a library and an LP record collection that have grown rather unwieldy, Alan is also a marksman with several weapons, a frequent concertgoer, and an enthusiastic ballroom dancer.